INDEX TO LAWS

RELATING TO THE

TREASURY DEPARTMENT,

COMPILED FROM THE

REVISED STATUTES,

APPROVED JUNE 22, 1874.

WASHINGTON:
GOVERNMENT PRINTING OFFICE.
1876.

INDEX.

A.

Section.

Abandoned Property,
(see *Captured and Abandoned Property.*)
Abandonment,
of goods in bonded warehouse, what constitutes; sale, &c., of 2971
Abatement of Duties,
on goods destroyed, &c., by accident 2984
Abatement of Taxes,
power of Commissioner of Internal Revenue to make 3220
on spirits destroyed by accident 3221
Abortion,
importation of articles to procure, prohibited. 2491
Abrasion of Coins,
not to exceed one-half of one per centum, &c. 3505
Abraided Coins,
certain, in Treasury to be recoined 3512
Absconding Debtor,
priority of claims of United States against .. 3466
Absence,
deductions for, from pay of Senators, Representatives, and Delegates 4041
in Army—
pay of Army officers on leave of 1265
forfeiture of pay, when dropped for 1266
leave of, to officers, &c., at Military Academy 1330
Absence of Proper Stamp,
on tobacco and snuff, to be notice and evidence of non-payment of tax 3373
on cigars 3398
Absent Debtor,
priority of claims of United States against .. 3466
Abstract,
from tobacco or snuff manufacturers' book to be furnished, &c., monthly, &c 3358
from cigar manufacturers' book 3390
Acapulco,
consul at, salary of 1690
Accident,
suspension of work at distilleries, caused by unavoidable 3310
stamps for spirits lost or destroyed by 3315
at brewery 3350
"Accompanying Documents,"
editing of, for distribution by Congress 75
number of, to be printed 3798
abridgment of, number to be printed 3798
Account,
by retail dealers in leaf-tobacco 3244
by internal-revenue store-keepers at warehouse 3301
by store-keepers, of distillery operations 3302
by distillers 3307
by collectors of internal revenue, of stamps for distilled spirits 3314
by rectifyers and wholesale liquor-dealers .. 3318
by brewers 3337, 3338
by collectors of internal revenue, of stamps sold and permits delivered for fermented liquors 3341
by tobacco and snuff manufacturers 3358
by dealers in leaf-tobacco 3359, 3360
by collectors of internal revenue, of sales of tobacco and snuff-stamps 3369

Section.

Account—Continued.
by cigar manufacturers 3390
by collectors of internal revenue, of sales of cigar-stamps 3395
of goods in bond, &c., to be rendered monthly 3444
Accounting Officers,
opinion of President as to absence of Territorial officers, to be filed with 1884
proof to be required by, in settlement of accounts for Territorial expenses 1886
when to allow, &c., expenses of commissions, &c 3681
shall be furnished copy of appointment of inspector of fuel 3712
when to allow account for fuel 3713
judgments against property of United States 3754
Accounts,
for travelling expenses of Members and Delegates, how certified 47
certified balances in public, conclusive on executive branch, revisable only by Congress or courts 191
by or against United States, where to be settled 236
of public expenditures, to be settled within fiscal year 250
reference of, to Court of Claims, by Secretary of Treasury, on certificate of Auditor or Comptroller 1063
proceedings on, same as in other cases 1064
judgment on, how paid 1065
of disbursements for Government, in Territories, how settled 1886
for expenses incurred in relief of refugees and freedmen, how settled 2034
of freedmen's hospital, supervision of 2038
annual settlement of, by officers disbursing to Indians 2091
copy of, to be laid before Congress 2091
delinquents to be reported to Congress .. 2091
of clerks, &c., employed in customs revenue, to be verified 2693
of collectors of internal revenue for pay, expenses, &c 3145
adjustment of, of collectors and assessors of internal revenue 3146, 3147
collectors of internal revenue may require production of books of 3173
of collectors of internal revenue, to be rendered as often as required 3212
collectors of internal revenue failing to render 3217
making or using false, by persons not in military or naval service, civil action for. 3490
of mints and assay offices 3405, 3562
public, shall be rendered monthly 3622
of naval paymasters, on foreign stations, consular certificates as to prices to accompany 3723
quarterly, to be rendered to Secretary of Treasury by Congressional Printer .. 3815
of Congressional Printer, for receipts and disbursements, how to be settled 3817

Section.

Accounts—Continued.
of receipts and expenditures of consular courts 4120
for rent of prisons, &c., in foreign countries 4121, 4123
making or using false, by any person, to obtaid approval, &c., of claim against United States 5438
officer or agent of United States, failing to render, as provided by law, of public moneys received by him 5491

Accounts and Revenues, Postal Service,
provisions relating to 4049

Accoutrements,
furnished to soldier, not to be sold, bartered, &c.; seizure of, in hands of person not a soldier 1242, 3748
punishment for loss, &c., of 1342
of persons enrolled in militia, and exemptions of, from execution, &c 1628
returns of actual condition of, by officers in militia 1635
inspection and returns of, by brigade-inspector of militia 1640
lost in military service, to be paid for 3482, 3486, 3487
of minor, lost in military service, how paid for 3486

Accrued Pensions,
(see *Pensions.*)

Accrued Rights,
not affected by Revised Statutes 5597

Acids, Chemical,
restrictions on carriage of, by steam-passenger vessels 4472
how packed and marked for shipment 4475
penalty for shipping contrary to law 4476

Acknowledgments,
of transfer, assignment, or power to receive claim on United States, how made 3477
authority of notaries public and commissioners of circuit courts to take 1778

Acting Midshipman,
rations or commutation therefor, to 1577

Acting Assistant Surgeons,
in Navy, appointment of 1411
in Army, when to have pension 4693
rate of total disability pension to 4695
pension to dependent relative of, when to begin 4710

Acting Assistant Treasurers,
duties as to public money 3639

Actions,
removal of personal, from State court, brought by alien against non-resident in State 644
for recovery of office when right of voting denied to any citizen 2010
for recovery of penalties under Title "Indians" 2124
in bankruptcy, upon assignee's bond, how prosecuted 5036
limitation of, by and against assignee 5057

Acts of Congress,
passed subsequent to Dec. 1, 1873, effect of 5601

Acts of Territorial Legislatures,
transmission of, to President and Congress 1844
copy of, to be furnished to Public Printer 1844
not to be deemed authority for certain disbursements 1886

Additional Compensation,
to collectors of internal revenue 3145

Additional Mail Service,
compensation for 3960

Additional Paymasters,
(see *Paymaster's Department of Army.*)

Section.

Adhesive Stamps,
cancellation of 3423, 3424
how supplied 3425
commissions on 3425
to be furnished to certain officers for sale 3427
forging, counterfeiting, &c., or fraudulently using or selling, &c 3429

Adjourned Terms,
of supreme court of Arizona, when and where held 1934
order for, how signed and entered 1934
what business may be done at 1934
mileage of clerk for attendance at 1934

Adjustment of Accounts,
of assessors and collectors of internal revenue 3146, 3147

Adjutant-General,
appointment and duties of, in militia 1634
annual return by, in each State to President, instruction by Secretary of War as to 1636
of Army, duty as to evidence in pension cases 4717

Adjutant-General's Department,
authorized 1094
organization of, and rank in 1128

Adjutants,
number, for artillery regiment 1099
for cavalry regiment 1102
for infantry regiment 1106
in Army, pay of 1261
forage allowed to, of regiments 1271
in regiments of militia, when called into United States service, rank of 1646

Administrators,
when to make oath to invoices in customs cases 2846
when liable for debts due United States 3467
holding national-bank stock not to be individually liable 5152

Admiral,
grade of, to cease 1362
number on active list 1363
secretary to 1367
pay of 1556
pay of secretary to 1556

Admiralty,
jurisdiction in, of district courts 563
courts of, for what purpose always open 574
in Florida 575
in Wisconsin 576
circuit courts, no jurisdiction in causes of, arising under revenue laws 629
writ of prohibition issued by Supreme Court to district courts, as courts of 688
exclusive jurisdiction of courts of United States 711
power of marshal to stay or release arrest of property, in causes of, except seizures for forfeiture 941
condemnations in, of property taken as prize on account of use, &c., in aid of rebellion 5309, 5311

Adulteration,
of distilled spirits 3252

Ad Valorem Duty,
goods subject to, currency to be used in making invoice of 2838
oath of purchaser 2843
oath of manufacturer to invoices of 2845
when legal representative may make oath to 2846
when goods subject to, may be admitted without invoice 2847
when bond given to produce invoice 2848
oath when owner resides abroad 2849
what to be collected in additions to entries. 2900
to be levied on true market value at time of exportation 2904

Section.

Ad Valorem Duty—Continued.
true market value for, to be price in markets of country producing 2905
appraisal of value of goods at time of exportation 2906
merchandise subject to, transported for exportation 3034
equipments of certain vessels liable to payment of 3114
when to be refunded by Secretary of Treasury 3115
Advances of Money,
to persons in naval service 1563
to disbursing-officers 3648
to Congressional Printer by Secretary of Treasury 3816
to certain postal agents 4055
Advances of Wages,
to seamen, shall be made in presence of shipping-commissioner 4531
Adverse Claim,
for mineral land, fee for filing application, &c 2238
when to be made 2325
proceedings on 2326
Advertising,
allowance for, to collectors of internal revenue 3145
postal accounts to show expenditures for 4049
Advertising Letters,
how to be done 3930
to foreigners 3931
compensation for 3934
extra postage charge for 3925
Advertisements,
for stationery for Congress 65–68
of public-land sales 2359
of notice of sale on distraint for internal-revenue taxes 3190
of real estate 3197
of notice of seizure 3460
for proposals, to be made before contract for supplies, &c 3709
for quartermaster's supplies, what to contain and where published 3716
for naval supplies, provisions concerning, 3718, 3721
to be delivered abroad, where and how made 3723
for proposals to furnish paper for Government Printing Office 3767
for new proposals for paper, &c., in case of default of contractor 3775
for engraving of maps, &c., to illustrate documents ordered by Congress 3780
in papers selected in certain States by Clerk of House of Representatives 3823
to be published in States enumerated, only in papers selected 3824
in papers of District of Columbia 3826
of what mail-routes to be made in papers of District of Columbia 3827
for Executive Departments, to be published and paid for only on written authority of head of Department 3828
for proposals for carrying mail 3941
by railways, not required 3942
by steamboats, not required 3943
through foreign countries 4006
to foreign countries 4007
of notice of seizure of vessel, what to specify 4379
of prize sales by United States marshal 4628
for contract for erection of light-house 4667
in likeness of national-bank notes prohibited, penalty 5188

Section.

Affidavits,
of two persons to be filed by applicant for patent to mining claim, of notice having been posted 2325
to be filed by claimant of mineral land, after publication of notice 2325
making or using, by persons not in military or naval service, of false, in claim against United States; civil liability for 3490
penalty for procuring, &c., false, in pension cases 4746
making or using by any person of false, in claim against United States; criminal punishment 5438
Affirmation,
included in oath 1
Affixing Stamps,
for distilled spirits 3322
contrary to law 3316
on fermented liquors 3342
for tobacco and snuff 3369
instruments for, to be prescribed by Commissioner and Secretary 3445
Africa,
transportation of colored emigrants to west coast of 4271
Agent,
no officer or agent of corporation or firm to act as officer or agent for United States, in transactions with same 1783
for entry of goods to give bond for account by owner 2787
residing abroad, of firm in trade in United States, vessel owned by, may be registered 4133
of owner of vessel may obtain certificate of registry, how 4161
oath to be taken by 4161
surrender of old certificate by 4162
penalty for failure 4162
forfeiture of vessel for false swearing by 4163
for owner of recorded vessel to countersign certificate of measurement 4181
of vessels to furnish collectors copy of consular receipts 4213
(see *Special Agents.*)
Agents for Sale of Postage-Stamps,
may buy stamps and envelopes at discount. 3919
Agent and Consul-General,
at Alexandria, salary of 1675
Agents, Diplomatic,
shall be deemed diplomatic officers 1674
salaries of 1675
Agents of United States,
abroad, vessel owned by, may be registered. 4134
Agents, Internal-Revenue,
(see *Special Agents, Treasury Department.*)
Agents, Treasury,
(see *Special Agents, Treasury Department.*)
Aggregate Circulation,
(see *National Banks.*)
Agreement,
with crew of fishing-vessel for shares of fish, &c 4391
penalty for violating, by fishermen 4392
recovery of shares of fish under 4393
vessel liable for, &c 4393
discharge of vessel on giving bond for judgment 4394
Agreements with Seamen,
(see *Shipping Articles.*)
Agricultural College Scrip,
(see *Lands, Public.*)
Agricultural Department,
(see *Department of Agriculture.*)

Section.

Aides-de-Camp,
to General 1096
to Lieutenant-General 1097
to major and brigadier generals 1098
to major and brigadier generals, pay of 1261
number of, to each division of militia 1631
to each brigade 1631
when called into United States service 1647
in each brigade 1648

Ailantus Trees,
purchasing, and planting in public grounds, prohibited 1830

Aix-la-Chapelle,
consul at, salary of 1690

Alabama,
district judge in, appointment and residence of 552
district attorney of northern, to perform duty in middle district 767
marshal of southern district of, to perform duty in middle 776
clearance from ports in, of vessels laden with live-oak timber 2463
collection district, port of entry and delivery in 2564
officers in 2565
restrictions on clearance of vessels laden with live-oak from ports of 4205
tolls on Tennessee, Coosa, Cahawba, and Black Warrior Rivers, in 5244
on canal at Muscle and Colbert's Shoals, Tennessee River 5245

Alaska,
United States laws extended over 1954
regulation of trade in arms, ammunition, and spirits 1955
forfeiture and penalty for violations 1955
bonds for exportation to, of arms, ammunition, and spirits 1955
bonds from consignee in 1955
killing of fur-bearing animals prohibited 1956
penalty for offense 1956
Secretary of Treasury may authorize killing of certain animals 1956
to prevent killing of fur-seal 1956
not to grant special privileges 1956
offenses committed in, where prosecuted 1957
arrest of persons and seizure of vessels 1957
jurisdiction and procedure of courts 1957
remission of fines, penalties, and forfeitures 1958
islands of Saint Paul and Saint George, made a special reservation 1959
landing or remaining on islands without authority prohibited 1959
removal of persons so found 1959
Secretary of War to carry provisions into effect 1959
when fur-seal may be killed 1960
use of fire-arms prohibited 1960
natives may kill, for food, &c 1960
regulations, how prescribed 1960
killing of female seal, &c., prohibited 1961
penalty for violations 1961
limit to number of seal which may be killed 1962
further limit, proportionate reduction of rents 1962
penalty for violations 1962
lease of islands to take fur-seal 1963
rental to be reserved and secured 1963
bond of lessees 1964
American citizens only may lease, &c 1965
foreign vessels not to be engaged in taking skins 1965
forfeiture of lease for violation of provisions 1965
covenant of lease against traffic in spirits 1966

Section.

Alaska—Continued.
revenue officers to seize and destroy spirits found upon islands 1966
to make reports of such seizures 1966
penalty and forfeiture for killing seal without permission 1967
for molesting lessees 1967
for killing greater number of seal than prescribed by law 1968
revenue tax upon fur-seal skins 1969
Secretary of Treasury to make regulations 1969
may terminate lease, when 1970
certified copies of lease to be furnished masters of vessels 1971
right reserved to alter or repeal laws relating to lease 1972
appointment of agents to manage seal-fisheries 1973
compensation and expenses of agents 1974
agents not to be interested in lease 1975
power of agents to administer oaths and take testimony 1976
collection-district and port of entry in 2591
collector in, residence of 2592
nationalization of vessels owned by residents of 4140
regulation of coasting trade with 4358
power of Secretary of Treasury to remit fines, penalties, &c., incurred in collection-district of 5294

Alaska Commercial Company,
(see *Alaska.*)

Albany, N. Y.
port of delivery 2535
surveyor in, to act as collector and reside at 2536
entry of goods for 2816
warehouse privileges, &c., extended to 2968
inspectors of hulls and boilers for 4414
salaries 4414
reserve of national banks in 5191
balances with banks in, may be part of reserve 5192
redemption agencies 5195

Albemarle, N. C.
collection-district 2555
collector in, residence of 2556

Alcohol,
definition of 3248
quantity of, in proof-spirits 3249
may be withdrawn from bond for scientific purposes without tax 3297

Ale,
(see *Fermented Liquors.*)

Alexandria, Egypt,
salary of agent and consul-general at 1675

Alexandria, Va.
collection-district and port of entry 2552
collector and surveyor to reside at 2553

Algiers,
consul at, salary of 1690

Aliens,
jurisdiction of district courts of suits by, for torts in violation of laws of nations or treaty 563
when allowed to prosecute claim in Court of Claims 1068

Alien Seamen,
how, may be admitted United States citizens 2174

Allotment of Wages,
(see *Seamen.*)

Allowances,
to officers of Army 1269
for fuel, quarters, and forage 1270
to officers of Navy 1558
for travel 1566

Section.
Allowances—Continued.
to surveyors-general for inspection of surveys in the field ... 2223
for clerk-hire ... 2226
for office-rent, fuel, books, stationery, &c. 2227
further, to collectors of internal revenue ... 3145
of deduction to brewers, of 7½ per cent. on sales of stamps ... 3341
of commission on sale of internal-revenue stamps ... 3425
for stamps spoiled ... 3426
Allowances and Drawbacks,
internal revenue, appropriation for ... 3689
Alloy,
for gold and silver coins ... 3514
Almanac, Nautical,
supervision and preparation of ... 436
Alna, Me.,
port of delivery ... 2517
Alphabetical List,
of special tax-payers to be kept in office of collector of internal revenue ... 3240
Altering,
(see *Forging*.)
Alton, Ill.
port of delivery in district of New Orleans, La ... 2568
surveyor to reside at, duties of ... 2569
Ambassador,
(see *Diplomatic Officers*.)
Amendments to Constitution of U. S.
when adopted, to be promulgated by Secretary of State ... 205
American Citizens,
(see *Citizens of United States*.)
American Colonization Society,
vessels of, subject to laws relating to carriage of passengers ... 4271
American Ephemeris,
supervision and preparation of ... 436
Amesbury, Mass.,
port of delivery ... 2527
Ammunition,
in militia, provided by men, exemption of, from execution ... 1628
returns of actual condition of, by officers .. 1635
inspection and returns of, by brigade inspector ... 1640
importation, &c., of, into Alaska ... 1955
Amoor River,
commercial agent at, salary of ... 1690
Amoy,
consul at, salary of ... 1690
Amsterdam,
consul at, salary of ... 1690
Analysis,
of imported drugs and medicines reported by examiner to be of inferior quality ... 2936
when examiner's return sustained by, duty of collector ... 2937
Annapolis, Md.,
collection-district and port of entry ... 2548
customs officers in, residence of ... 2549
Annual Reports,
time for submitting, to Congress, general rule ... 195
when to be furnished to Congressional Printer ... 196
Annual Trial of Coins,
(see *Coins*.)
Annuity,
false personation of person entitled to, in receiving money, &c ... 5435
endeavoring to obtain, &c., by means of forged power of attorney ... 5436

Section.
Anti-Scorbutics,
shall be served on merchant-vessels ... 4569
penalty for neglect to serve ... 4570
Antwerp,
consul at, salary of ... 1690
Apalachicola, Fla.,
collection-district ... 2562
President may designate port of entry in. 2562
collector in, residence of ... 2563
inspectors of hulls and boilers for ... 4414
salaries of ... 4414
Apia,
commercial agent at, salary of ... 1690
Apothecaries,
when special tax imposed upon ... 3246
Apparatus for Resection,
how, and to whom furnished, &c ... 4787–4791
Appeal,
proceedings of district court in prize causes, after ... 565, 4637
from decrees of circuit court, in equity or admiralty ... 692
final decrees of circuit court, reviewed by Supreme Court upon ... 693
in what cases allowed to Supreme Court ... 699
when and how taken from judgments of Court of Claims ... 707, 708
no bond required, when appeal taken by United States, or by Department ... 1001
to Supreme Court, in equity causes, when to be taken ... 1008
in bankruptcy proceedings,
regulations of practice and procedure ... 4990
customs,
from appraisement of wrecked and damaged imports ... 2928
from appraisement of imports, notice of, to whom given, proceedings ... 2930
from decision of collector as to rate, &c., of duties on imports and tonnage ... 2931
as to fees, &c ... 2932
from examiner's return of imported drugs, medicines, &c ... 2936
refund of duties and moneys paid under protest and appeal ... 3012½
refund in case of failure to comply with requirements relating to ... 3013
internal-revenue,
to Commissioner before suit in case of alleged illegal taxes ... 3226
inspection of steam-vessels,
to supervising inspectors on refusal or suspension, &c., of license ... 4452
Apples,
brandy made from ... 3255
Applications in Bankruptcy,
(see *Bankruptcy*.)
Appointments,
of commissioner to swear appraisers in cases of seizures under United States laws. 570
of appraisers, by judges in vacation ... 940
certain appointees during recess of Senate to receive no salary until confirmed ... 1761
penalty for accepting, contrary to law ... 1771
for making, contrary to law ... 1772
made without advice, &c., of Senate ... 1774
of examiners at New York ... 2939
original, of persons specially appointed under revenue laws ... 3060
Apportionment of Circulation,
(see *National Banks*.)
Appraisal,
customs; of imports,
power of Secretary of Treasury to prescribe regulations to secure just, &c ... 252, 2949
collector to appoint merchants to make ... 2609

Section.

Appraisal—Continued.
penalty for not assisting at 2610
of goods suspected to be undervalued 2840
provisions relating to 2899–2953
no delivery of imported goods without 2899
how made, in additions to entries 2900
designation of packages for, number, examination, forfeiture, remission 2901
mode of; of manufactures of wool, unfinished 2902
when duties to be levied on market value 2904
of goods subject to ad valorem duty, and of parcels not manufactured in country of exportation 2905
according to value of goods at time of exportation 2906
additions to market value to obtain dutiable value 2907
when value exceeds 10 per cent. of invoice value 2909
of different values invoiced at average price 2910
of different qualities in same package 2911
of wool of different qualities in same bale 2912
of kid and other gloves 2913
deficiency in package found on 2921
when final 2923
of goods damaged and taken from wrecks, appeals 2928
revision of report of 2929
when owner is dissatisfied with 2930
of drugs, medicines, &c 2933
at New York 2939
when Secretary of the Treasury may make special regulations for 2939
officers, &c., employed in department of, at New York, not to engage in mercantile business 2941
of damaged merchandise, to be made by assistant appraiser at New York 2943
when increase of importation, extra hours to be devoted to at New York 2944
at ports where no appraiser 2946
what customs-officers may lease or hire buildings for purpose of 2953
goods for immediate transportation, not subject to, at port of arrival 2991
of property seized under customs laws 3074
internal revenue, prize, &c.
of property exempt from distraint for internal-revenue taxes 3187
of value of seized distillery, &c., in case of bond for release before judgment 3331
of goods seized 3459, 3460
in prize cases, where property cannot be sent into port for adjudication 4615
report of appraisers to be sent into court 4615
of property taken for use of United Statss 4624
of property delivered on stipulation 4626
of real estate taken for national cemeteries 4871
Appraisers,
appointment of commissioners to swear, in cases of seizures 570
of vessel, goods, &c., delivered to claimant, in seizures under revenue laws 938
may be appointed by judge, in vacation 940
Appraisers of Customs,
for Alabama 2565
at Baltimore, Md 2549
at Boston, Mass 2529
clerks, &c., in office of 2530
at Charleston, S. C 2558
for Indiana and Illinois 2602
for Louisiana 2569
for Maine 2518
for Michigan 2600
for New York 2536

Section.

Appraisers of Customs—Continued.
officers and employés in office of 2538, 2539
for Ohio 2604
at Portland, On 2587
at Philadelphia, Pa 2544
clerks and employés in office of 2545
for Rhode Island 2532
at San Francisco, Cal 2583
at Savannah, Ga 2560
for Virginia 2553
for Wisconsin 2598
appointment by President, of four general, with certain duties 2608
salary of, at New York 2729
at Providence, Norfolk, Portland, Maine; Buffalo, Chicago, Detroit, Cincinnati, Saint Louis, Evansville, Milwaukee, Louisville, Cleveland, San Francisco, Portland, On.; Memphis, and Mobile 2730
at Savannah and Charleston 2724
of general, at New York 2726
of four general; traveling expenses 2727
of local and general, at Boston, Philadelphia, Baltimore, and New Orleans 2728
merchant, compensation of 2725
oath of, and of merchant appraisers 2614
at New York 2614
revision of assistant appraiser's report by, at New York 2615
additional compensation of, at San Francisco 2746
duties of, when imported articles omitted in entry 2901
duty of, in estimating value and quantity of imports, and manufactures of wool unfinished 2902
when, to adopt best article in package as fixing value 2911
wool of different qualities in same bale, &c., how appraised by 2912
how to certify deficiency in package, &c., to collector 2921
to examine upon oath owners, &c., as to value, and require production of papers 2922
to certify rate of damage 2927
to revise report of assistants, &c., reappraisement by, how ordered 2929
at New York not to engage in mercantile business 2941
what provisions to apply to 2942
to revise, &c., report of assistant appraiser to inspect damaged goods 2943
when, to direct extra labor of officers 2944
when, to attend in other districts 2947
what deemed to be certificate of 2950
powers of, to lease or hire buildings, &c 2953
buildings to be leased for use of 2955
to appraise goods remaining in public store beyond one year, preparatory to sale 2973
goods entitled to drawback, when to be inspected by 3034
duties of, in case of property seized, &c., per diem compensation of 3074
when, to certify deterioration, &c., of articles seized 3080
Apprentices to Sea-Service,
shipping commissioners shall procure 4509
indentures of, shall be produced, to commissioners 4510
shipping-articles of vessels in coasting-trade, not to be signed by 4520
wages not to depend on freight earnings 4525
not subject to attachment 4536
disposal of effects of deceased 4538
rules of procedure 4539

Section.

Apprentices to Sea-Service—Continued.
penalty for neglect 4540
duty of consuls, &c 4541
payment of wages, &c., on death of, in United States 4542
of deceased, delivery of wages, &c., to circuit court 4543
distribution of, by court 4544
disposal of, when unclaimed 4545
fees for shipping 5592
who shall pay, &c 4593
penalty for taking illegal 4595
offenses and punishment of 4596
arrest of, for desertion 4599
penalty for drunkenness and neglect of duty 4602
enforcement of forfeitures of 4603
part of wages to pay for expense of conviction of 4605
form of account of 4612

Appropriations,
style and title of acts for 11
for members, officers, and contingent expenses of Senate 56
statements of, by Secretary of Senate and Clerk of House 64
annual, for arms and equipments in militia 1661
for compensation of ministers and secretaries of legation not applicable if incumbent not United States citizen 1744
for public buildings and grounds in District of Columbia 1798
for Washington aqueduct and public works in District of Columbia 1802
for support of government in Territories, how disbursed and accounted for 1886
for legislative expenses in Territories, not to be exceeded 1888
for contingent expenses in Territories 1935, 1938
for legislative 1939, 1940
for Indian service, supervision of expenditure of, by commissioners 2041
for moneys required under Indian treaties 2094
to execute Indian treaties not to be transferred 2097
for Indian service not to be used to pay depredation claims 2098
restrictions on, for education of Indians 2099
not to apply to certain appropriations 2099
to fulfill treaties, not to be paid to tribes at war 2100
to refund payments for land sold erroneously 2362, 3689
money deposited by settlers for surveys to be deemed appropriated for that purpose 2402, 3689
for collecting revenue, when incidental expenses of collectors of customs to be paid out of 2692
accounts of disbursements shall be rendered according to 3623
Title XLI, "Appropriations" 3660–3692
manner of communicating estimates of 3660, 3672
to be annexed to estimates 3670
accounts shall be kept by Register, Comptroller, and Secretary 3675
shall only be expended for objects for which made 3678
expenditure shall not exceed 3679
for contingent expenses, &c., not to be used for compensation of clerks, &c 3682
for public buildings, available immediately 3684
for light-houses, how long available 3685
for publishing foreign hydrographic surveys, restrictions on 3686
permanent, for payment of public debt 3688
list of permanent 3687–3689

Section.

Appropriations—Continued.
customs 3689
for debentures and other charges 3048, 3689
debentures and drawbacks 3689
for distributive shares of fines, &c 3689
repayment of excess of deposits 3689
refunding duties on goods destroyed 3689
marine hospitals 3689
refunding duties under act July 14, 1870 3689
proceeds of goods seized, &c 3689
proceeds of unclaimed goods 3689
duty on tea and coffee 3689
drawback on building materials for burnt district of Chicago 3689
refunding certain discriminating duties 3689
for decisions of Supreme Court 3689
limit as to use of balances of annual 3690
disposal of balances after two years 3691
to pay judgment against certain property of United States 3754
of moneys received from sales of extra copies of documents, and of paper-shavings and imperfections 3818
for postal service shall be out of postal revenues 4054
permanent, for salaries of steamboat-inspection officers 4461
of fund for sick and disabled and destitute seamen 4545
authority of Light-House Board to purchase sites for light-houses 4660
expense of substituting light-houses on pile foundations 4668
for coast survey, how to be expended 4683
expenses of annual examination and destruction of plates, dies, &c., of national-bank notes 5174
expenditure for water-gauges, &c., on Lower Mississippi and tributaries 5252
for Departments, when not payable to telegraph companies 5266
officer paying to clerk, &c., less than lawful sum, &c., and requiring receipt for amount greater than paid 5483
contracting to pay on public building, &c., amount larger than sum appropriated 5503
not repealed by incorporation in Revised Statutes of parts of acts making 5596

Aransas, Tex.,
port of delivery 2578

Architect of Capitol,
to direct and supervise improvements and repairs 1816
to control electrical apparatus jointly with Chief of Engineers 1817
power of, and Sergeant-at-Arms to appoint police 1821

Architect of Treasury Department,
(see *Supervising Architect.*)

Argentine Republic,
salary of minister to 1675

Arizona Territory,
adjourned terms of supreme court in 1934
number of members of council and house of representatives of 1922
contingent expenses of executive department, appropriation for 1935
legislative expenses of, provisions for 1939
mileage of members of assembly of 1942
appointment of Indian superintendent for tribes in 2046
appointment of surveyor-general for, authorized 2207
salary of 2210

Section.

Arizona Territory—Continued.
50 per cent. addition to fees of registers and receivers in 2238
(see *Territories.*)

Arkansas,
clerks of district court for western district of. 556

Armed Vessels,
owners to give bond before clearing, not to commit hostilities 5289

Armorers,
enlistment of, for Ordnance Department 1162

Armories,
one at each arsenal, officers and workmen in. 1662
pay of ordnance officer, master-armorers, inspectors, and clerks at 1663, 1664
bond of storekeepers and paymasters at 1664

Arms,
sale of, in territory occupied by uncivilized Indians, prohibited 467
not to be bartered away by soldiers, &c. 1242, 3748
persons improperly in possession of 1242, 3748
payment of damage to, by persons in Army. 1303
of militia, and exemption of, from execution, &c 1628
returns of condition of, by officers of 1635
inspections and returns of, by brigade-inspector of 1640
appropriations for 1661
importation of, into Alaska 1955
for personal use, not distrainable 3187
of soldiers not to be sold, &c 3748

Army,
composition of 1094
officers on retired list, a part of 1094
General, title of 1095
staff of 1096
Lieutenant-General, aids and secretary 1097
aids of major and brigadier generals 1098
artillery regiments and batteries 1099–1101
cavalry regiments, &c 1102, 1103
infantry regiments, &c 1106, 1107
bands 1111
Indian scouts 1112
number of enlisted men in 1115
term of enlistment in 1119
premium for bringing recruit, &c 1120
corps of adjutants-general, organization 1128
of inspectors-general 1131
Quartermaster's Department, organization, &c., duties of officers, &c 1132–1137
Subsistence Department 1140–1150
Corps of Engineers 1151–1153
battalion of engineers, composition of, duties, &c 1154, 1155
Ordnance Department, organization, supplies, depots, &c 1159–1165
Medical Department, organization 1168
sick-diet in hospitals 1175
trusses, to whom furnished, &c 1176, 1178
hospital stewards 1179–1181
Paymaster General, rank of 1182
Pay Department, organization, duties .. 1182–1185
paymasters' clerks 1190
bonds of disbursing officers in 1191, 1192
signal-service, rank of chief 1195
men detailed for, may be mounted 1197
Bureau of Military Justice, organization, duties, powers 1198–1203
reporter for courts-martial 1203
certificates of merit in 1216
officers in, accepting, &c., civil office 1222
diplomatic or consular office 1223
privileges on account of volunteer service .. 1226
labor detail 1235
female nurses, how employed 1238
matrons, how employed 1239

Army—Continued.
laundresses 1240
sales of military stores 1241
arms and accoutrements in possession of persons not soldiers 1242, 3748
pay and allowances, provisions concerning, (see *Pay of Army*) 1261–1308
Military Academy, provisions concerning, (see *Military Academy*) 1309–1341
articles of war 1342
military prison, provisions concerning, (see *Military Prison*) 1344–1357
persons in, not to hold civil office in Territory 1860
employment of, in execution of judicial process 1984
officers, soldiers, &c., of, entitled to bounty-land, when, (see *Bounty-Lands*) .. 2418–2424
appointments from Engineer Corps of, on Light-House Board 4653
preliminary surveys on lakes for light-house purposes by Engineer Corps of 4663
details from Engineer Corps of, to superintend construction of light-houses 4664
plans, drawings, &c., by detailed officers . 4665
construction to be superintended by detailed officer 4666
officers of, assigned to light-house districts, as inspectors, &c 4671
employment of officers of, on coast-survey service 4684, 4687
of men of 4685
subsistence of such officers and men of ... 4688
persons in, not to draw both pay and pension 4724
officers, &c., disabled in Mexican war, to have pensions 4730
widows, &c., of soldiers in war of 1812, and Indian wars, to have pensions 4732
officers, &c., of, in war of 1812, to have pensions 4736
officers of, for government of Soldiers' Home. 4816
insane persons in, how received in Government hospital 4843
President may employ, in enforcement of neutrality laws 5287
to compel departure of foreign vessels, when forbidden by laws of nations or treaty to remain, &c 5288
in aid of collection of duties 5316

Army Officers,
when to have pension 4693
rate of total-disability pension to 4695
pension according to rank at time of disability, &c 4696

Army Pensions,
(see *Pensions.*)

Army Subsistence,
provisions of contracts for 3715

Aroostook, Me.,
collection-district 2517
collector in, residence of 2518

Arrears,
no money to be paid to person in arrears to the United States 1766

Arrears of Pension,
when and how paid; no fees to agents 4711

Arrest,
for violation of revenue laws, &c., in Alaska. 1957
customs officers, when to board vessels and make, &c 3059
when to demand assistance in making; penalty for refusal 3071
of vessels arriving and departing from port before making report or entry 2773
of wages of seamen, not legal 4536

Section.

Arrival of Vessels,
report by masters after 2774, 2775
in district other than that of first arrival. 2781
Arsenals,
assent of State legislatures to purchase of land for 1838
Articles for government of Navy,
provisions of 1624
Articles of Association,
for national banks, contents of, copy to Comptroller 5133
Articles of War,
provisions of 1342
United States armies to be governed by 1342
when militia subject to 1644
Artificers,
for battery of artillery 1100
enlistment of, for Ordnance Department 1162
detail of working-parties of soldiers as 1235
extra pay to such soldiers 1287
pensions to relatives of 4710
Artificial Limbs,
pension to those who cannot use 4698
who shall have 4787
commutation for 4788
how paid 4789
compensation to those who cannot use 4790
transportation to obtain 4791
Artillery,
regiments, number of 1094
composition of 1099
batteries, number of 1099
composition of 1100
light batteries of 1101
in militia, companies of, how formed, armed, and provided 1632
corps of, in States, not incorporated with, privileges 1641
organization by President 1646
Asia,
goods transported in bond through United States from or to 2997
Aspinwall,
consul at, salary of 1690
resident mail-agent at, authorized 4021
Assault,
upon officers, punishment of seamen for 4596
upon customs officer, &c., in execution of duty 5447
Assay Commission,
appointment, meetings, duties of 3547
test of standard weights, in presence of 3549
Assayer,
office created 3496
salaries 3498
oath of 3500
bond of 3501
power to nominate subordinates 3504
to verify and countersign bullion deposit-certificates 3506
duties of 3507
to determine fitness of bullion deposits 3521
to report quality of bullion 3523
to verify calculations 3525
duty as to ingots 3531
as to bars for payment of deposits 3534
as to trial pieces 3539
as to testing weights 3549
as to working dies 3550
at New York assay office, appointment 3554
duties, &c., of 3555
salary of 3556
at certain assay offices, appointment of 3559
powers and duties of 3560
oath and bonds of 3561
at certain assay offices, to have charge 3560

Section.

Assay Offices,
(see *Mints and Assay Offices.*)
Assessment, (Internal Revenue,)
of penalties to be made by Commissioner in case of false return or neglect 3176
collection of amount assessed 3176
of taxes, additional, for fifteen months' period 3182
to be made by Commissioner 3182
second, in case of supposed false return ... 3220
no suit to be maintained for restraining .. 3224
on spirits removed without deposit in warehouse 3253
on distillers for deficiency 3309
on tobacco, snuff, cigars, and other articles, sold or removed, not properly stamped 3371
Assets and Liabilities of Banks,
national banks to make, &c., reports of 5211
how reported by banks about to consolidate. 5223
United States to have paramount lien on ... 5230
Assets, Bankrupt,
(see *Bankruptcy.*)
Assignee,
when to make oath to invoices in customs cases 2846
when liable for debts due United States 3467
of debenture, (see *Debenture.*)
Assignee in Bankruptcy,
(see *Bankruptcy.*)
Assignment,
of pay by persons in Army 1291
in Navy 1576
of Indian contracts, restrictions upon 2106
internal revenue, of agents 3152
of storekeepers 3154
of supervisors 3159
of claims against United States 3477
of disloyal contractors 3480
of mail contracts prohibited 3963
of indentures of apprentices to sea-service .. 4510
of wages, not to prevent payment to seamen. 4536
of prize or bounty-money by persons in naval service 4643
Assimilated Rank,
to warrant officers of Navy 1491
Assistant Adjutant-General,
number and rank in militia called into United States service 1647
Assistant Appraisers of Customs,
in Boston, Mass 2529
in Maine 2518
in New York 2536
in Philadelphia, Pa 2544
at San Francisco, Cal 2583
oaths of, at New York, Boston, Philadelphia, and San Francisco 2615
reports of, at New York 2615
salary of, at New York 2731
at Boston, Philadelphia, Baltimore, New Orleans, Portland, and San Francisco. 2732
at New York, one to examine drugs, &c 2938
not to engage in mercantile business 2941
one to inspect and appraise damaged goods, report of 2943
labor beyond usual hours 2944
Assistant Attorneys-General,
appointment, duties, and salaries of 348
appointment and salary of, for Post Office Department 390
Assistant Cashier,
in office of Treasurer, salary of 235
Assistant Clerk,
of Court of Claims, appointment, removal, and oath of 1053
salary of 1054

Section.

Assistant Collectors of Customs,
at New York 2536
at Jersey City 2535, 2536
powers and duties of 2536
at Camden, N. J., powers of 2544
at New York, salary and duties of 2694
at Jersey City, N. J., salary of 2695
at Camden, N. J 2696
Assistant Commissaries-General of Subsistence,
number and rank of 1140
Assistant Commissioner of Patents,
appointment of 476
salary of 477
Assistant District Attorneys,
(see *District Attorneys.*)
Assistant Door-Keepers,
of Senate, salary 52
of House of Representatives, salary 53
Assistant Engineer in Treasury Department,
salary of 235
Assistant Inspectors of Steam-Vessels,
appointment of certain, authorized 4414
salary of, at New York 4414
in other districts 4414
permanent appropriations for salaries of 4461
Assistant Judge-Advocate-General,
rank of 1198
Assistant Librarians,
in Library of Congress 91
Assistant Marshals,
compensation of 2198–2200
(see *Census.*)
Assistant Medical Purveyors of the Army,
number and rank of 1168
to give bonds 1191
Assistant Naval Constructors,
relative rank of, on active list 1477
pay of 1556
Assistant Paymasters-General,
number and rank of 1182
Assistant Paymasters of Navy,
number of, on active list 1376
bonds of 1383
clerks to 1388
relative rank of, on active list 1475
pay of 1556
Assistant Photographers in Treasury Department,
salary of 235
Assistant Postmaster,
of Senate, salary 52
to House of Representatives, salary 53
Assistant Postmasters-General,
number, appointment, removal, and salary of 389
may be employed as special agents 4019
Assistant Quartermaster,
for each brigade of militia called into United States service 1647
Assistant Register of Treasury,
appointment and salary of 314
duties of 315
Assistant Secretary of Interior,
appointment and salary of 438
duties of 439
Assistant Secretary,
to President, salary of 155
of legation, salaries of, term for which payable 1740
of State, appointment and salaries of 200
of Treasury, appointment and salaries of 234
general duties of 245
delegation of, to sign warrants 246
validity of warrants signed by 247
Assistant Solicitor of Treasury,
appointment and salary of 349
Assistant Surgeon-General,
of Army, rank of 1168

Section.

Assistant Surgeons,
in Army, allowance to regiments of cavalry. 1102
number and rank of 1168
in militia, when called into United States service 1646
in Navy number of, on active list 1368
relative rank of, on active list 1474
pay of 1556
entitled to promotion 1556
Assistant Supervising Architect,
of Department of Treasury, salary of 235
Assistant Tellers,
in office of Treasurer, salary of 235
Assistant Treasurers,
in Treasury Department 303
may act as Treasurer, when 304
to report "outstanding liabilities" to Secretary of Treasury, when 310
how silver coins shall be sent to 3527
how, may redeem copper, &c., coins 3529
shall exchange United States notes for fractional currency 3574
superintendents of Carson and Denver mints to be 3594
at what places 3595
rooms, &c., of 3598
salaries of 3596
shall be in full for services 3597
shall have charge of rooms, &c 3599
shall give bond 3600
clerks, &c., in offices of 3601–3612
at New York may appoint deputy 3602
additional clerks 3604
may appoint deputies in case of sickness 3613
duties respecting public money 3639
bonds may be increased by President 3639
shall keep account of Post Office Department money separate 3642
to render accounts of receipts and payments 3644
shall pay duplicate checks 3646
examination of money, &c., in hands of. 3649, 3650
naval officer and surveyor shall examine books, &c., of 3650
to keep special account of money-order funds 4045
when to pay duplicate pension-checks 4770
failing safely to keep moneys deposited 5489
Associate Justices,
of Supreme Court, number of 673
salaries of 676
Associations,
definition of word 5
limit to right of religious, &c., in Territories, to hold real estate 1890
provisions in Title "National Banks" respecting, extended to all banking organizations under United States laws. 5157
Assorters of Money Orders,
in Treasury Department, salary of 235
Astoria, On.,
port of entry 2586
collector to reside at 2587
duties of collector at, in cases of vessels bound for Portland 2588
vessels arriving at 2590
Athens,
consul at, salary of 1690
Attached Property,
claims of United States, in case of, to have priority 3466
Attachment,
against marshals failing to pay into Treasury, fines assessed against militia 1660
against person disobeying summons of collector of internal revenue 3175
priority of debts due United States in cases of 3466

Section.

Attachment—Continued.
of property in which United States claim interest; stipulation for release; proceedings ... 3753, 3754
of wages of seamen, not legal ... 4536
pensions not liable to ... 4747
against national banks ... 5242
(see *Contempts.*)

Attorney-General,
to furnish professional service to Departments, when ... 187
to be head of Department of Justice ... 346
in case of vacancy in office of, or disability, by whom duties performed ... 347
to have control of solicitors, &c ... 350
to advise President on questions of law ... 354
land for public buildings, &c., not to be purchased without approval of ... 355
opinion of, may be required by heads of Departments ... 356
questions in administration of War and Navy Departments to be sent to ... 357
what questions of law submitted to, may be referred to subordinates ... 358
argument of cases ... 359
power of, to require general services from solicitors, &c., of Department ... 360
superintendence by, of district attorneys and marshals ... 362
to retain counsel to aid district attorneys ... 363
to provide counsel upon application of head of Department or Bureau ... 364
counsel-fees, to other than district attorneys, &c ... 365
commissions to be issued by, to special counsel ... 366
power to send officers to State, &c., to attend to suits, &c ... 367
supervisory power over accounts of marshals, district attorneys, clerks, &c ... 368
requisitions for payment of moneys to be signed by ... 369
designation of disbursing clerk by ... 371
publication, &c., of opinions by ... 383
annual reports to Congress by ... 384, 385
to prescribe rules for government of Territorial penitentiaries ... 1893
to fix pay of marshal and deputies ... 1893
with Secretary of Treasury and Commissioner of General Land-Office to form rules for settling suspended entry-cases, &c ... 2450
to approve adjudication of suspended entries, &c., by Commissioner ... 2450
recommendation of, in case of compromise of internal-revenue suit or proceeding ... 3229
discontinuance of prosecution for defrauding United States of tax on spirits ... 3230
proceedings of condemnation in cases of prize and capture of insurrectionary property ... 5311
(see *Department of Justice.*)

Attorneys of United States,
(see *District Attorneys.*)

Attorneys,
not to be employed by heads of Departments 189
not prohibited from charging clients reasonable compensation ... 823
fees of, in United States courts ... 824
prosecuting claims before Departments to take oath ... 3478, 3479
of pensioner to take oath that he has no interest, &c ... 4745
agreement with, to be sent to pension agent; fees of ... 4768
pension agent to forward fee to ... 4769

Section.

Attorneys—Continued.
fees of, limited, &c ... 4785
shall file with Commissioner duplicate articles of agreement, &c ... 4786

Auction at Mast,
when effects of deceased seamen may be sold at 4538

Auctioneer,
in prize sales, to be appointed by Secretary of Navy ... 4628
to collect and deposit proceeds ... 4628
commissions allowed to ... 4650

Auction, Public,
(see *Sales.*)

Auditors,
number, appointment, and salaries of ... 276
duties of ... 277–300
method of keeping accounts by, of War and Navy Departments ... 283
to report to Secretaries of War and Navy ... 283
empowered to administer oaths, when ... 297
reference of certain accounts to Court of Claims, upon certificate of ... 1063
proceedings in case of such accounts ... 1064
duties of, as to balances of appropriations .. 3691

Auditor for Post-Office Department,
(see *Sixth Auditor.*)

Augusta, Ga.,
port of delivery ... 2559
surveyor to reside at ... 2560
goods for, where entered ... 2817

Austria,
salary of minister and secretary to ... 1675

Aux Cayes,
consul at, salary of ... 1690

Awards,
of foreign consuls, &c., in differences between captain and crews, enforcement of ... 728

Axes,
what to be carried by river passenger-steamers ... 4483

B.

Baggage,
allowance in Navy for transporting ... 1566
entry of imported ... 2799
when not by owner, bond required ... 2800
examination and search of, dutiable articles in, permit to land, &c ... 2801
concealing dutiable articles in, penalty ... 2802
in transit to foreign country to be delivered to collector ... 2803
search of ... 3064
of passengers from contiguous foreign countries, inspection of ... 3100
when customs officer to retain, &c., forfeiture of ... 3101

Bahia,
consul at, salary of ... 1690

Bail,
officers of revenue-cutter service, when admitted to ... 2765
in certain suits for making false claims against United States ... 3492
of seamen committed on refusal to sail, &c. 4558

Bailiff,
of Court of Claims, appointment and term of office of ... 1053
salary of ... 1054

Balances,
certified by Comptrollers, &c., subject to revision only by Congress or courts ... 191
of appropriations, limit as to use of ... 3690
disposal of ... 3691
to foreign countries, Postmaster-General may provide against loss in paying ... 3912
postal accounts to show expenditures for. 4049

Section.

Baltimore, Md.,
collection-district and port of entry 2548
customs-officers in, residence of............ 2549
transportation in bond extended to........ 2997
assistant treasurer at, appointment, &c., of 3595–3597
clerks, &c , of 3606
collectors, &c., shall pay public money to. 3615
inspectors of hulls and boilers for.......... 4414
salaries of.............................. 4414
reserve of national banks in 5191
balances with banks in, may be part of reserve 5192
redemption-agencies........................ 5195

Banca Tin,
plug of, to be inserted in boiler............ 4436

Band,
at Military Academy 1094
composition and station of............... 1111
pay of leader of 1278
for militia called into United States service. 1647

Bangkok,
consul at, salary of 1690
interpreter at consulate of, salary of, marshal of, no salary........................ 1693

Bangor, Me.,
collection-district, port of entry............ 2517
collector and deputy collector in, residence of 2518

Bank-Bills,
shipper of, to notify carrier, &c 4281

Bank-Check,
tax on 3418

Bankers and Brokers,
not to use word "national" in title of firm.. 5243

Bank-Examiners,
appointment, powers, duty, and pay of..... 5240

Banking Associations,
(see *National Banks.*)

Banking Business,
(see *National Banks.*)

Bank-Notes,
not redeemable in compound-interest notes. 3590

Bank Officers,
(see *National Banks.*)

Bank or Banker,
definition of............................... 3407
internal-revenue taxes payable by.......... 3408
exemption as to savings-banks........... 3408
certain borrowed money not included in "capital employed" 3408
when internal-revenue taxes are payable ... 3409
tax on circulation and capital of State, &c 3410, 3411
tax payable by, on notes paid out 3412, 3413
returns by, of internal-revenue taxes....... 3414
penalties and proceedings in case of neglect or refusal to make returns 3415

Bankruptcy,
original jurisdiction of district courts in.... 563
jurisdiction of United States courts in...... 711
claims of United States in case of, to have priority 3466
general orders,
what may be followed...................... 4990
justices of Supreme Court may rescind, or vary, how 4990
may frame, rescind, or vary other, for what purposes 4990
commencement of proceedings,
what to be deemed 4991
registers in bankruptcy,
appointment of............................ 4993
bond and oath of.......................... 4995
attendance of, by direction of judge....... 5001
fees of, by whom paid 5008

Section.

Bankruptcy—Continued.
assignees,
bond of, how required 5036
to be approved and filed 5036
to inure to benefit of what creditors...... 5036
may be prosecuted, how.................. 5036
removal of, failing to give bond 5036
resignation or removal of, effect of......... 5040
limitation of suits between, and adverse claimants 5057
retention of funds for compensation and expenses 5099
commissions allowed 5100
when not obliged to proceed............... 5100
priority,
what claims and debts entitled to, in order for dividend 5101
discharge,
certain debts not released by.............. 5117
liability of other persons not released 5118
fees and costs,
of register 5124
to have priority of payment............. 5124
petitioner to deposit security for.......... 5124
to pay, when assets insufficient.......... 5124
execution against, for.................. 5124
traveling and incidental expenses of...... 5125
of marshal, as messenger.................. 5126
further allowance by court, when 5126
for other services, how prescribed......... 5127
justices of Supreme Court may change tariff of 5127

Bank Tax,
basis of; how and when paid................ 5214
statement to U. S. Treasurer, as basis of.... 5215
how assessed in default of return 5216
how collected in default of payment........ 5217
when and how refunded 5218
by State authority 5219

Barcelona, N. Y.,
port of delivery 2535
deputy collector at 2536

Barcelona, Spain,
consul at, salary of 1690

Barges, Passenger,
in tow of steamers; provision for security of life on 4492
penalty for violating provisions............ 4492

Barmen,
consul at, salary of 1690

Barnstable, Mass.,
collection-district and port of entry 2527
collector to reside at 2529

Barracks,
permanent, for Army, not to be constructed till estimates submitted, &c.......... 1136

Barrels,
of fermented liquors, measure of contents... 3339
fractional parts of...................... 3339
marks on 3349

Barrington, R. I.,
port of delivery 2531

Bars,
delivery of, to depositors of bullion 3544

Base Bullion,
deposits of, may be refused.................. 3519

Basle,
consul at, salary of........................ 1690

Batavia,
consul at, salary of........................ 1690

Bath, Me.,
collection-district and port of entry 2517
collector in, to reside at 2518

Battalion of Engineers,
in Army, authorized........................ 1094
composition of 1154
companies and enlisted men of............. 1155

Section.

Battalions,
in State militia, companies of ... 1630
commander of ... 1631
companies of grenadiers, light-infantry or riflemen in ... 1632
Batteries,
of artillery, number to regiment ... 1099
composition of ... 1100
of light artillery, to a regiment ... 1101
Bay of Islands,
consul at, salary of ... 1690
Bayou Saint John, La.,
port of delivery in district of New Orleans ... 2568
surveyor to reside at, duties of ... 2569
vessels bound for, what to do ... 2570
to unlade at, after making report, &c ... 2571
departing from, for foreign ports, how cleared. 2575
Bayport, Fla.,
port of delivery ... 2562
surveyor to reside at ... 2563
merchandise for, where entered ... 2819
Beaufort, N. C.,
collection-district and port of entry; when port of entry may be changed ... 2555
collector in, to reside at port of entry ... 2556
Beaufort, S. C.,
collection-district and port of entry ... 2557
collector in ... 2558
Beacons,
none to be erected until jurisdiction of site ceded to United States ... 4661
when cession deemed sufficient ... 4662
preliminary surveys for ... 4663
materials for construction or repair of ... 4666
Beer,
(see *Fermented Liquors.*)
Beer-Stamps,
(see *Stamps, Internal Revenue.*)
Beet-Sugar,
machinery for manufacture of, exempt from customs duties ... 2510
Beirut,
consul-general at, salary of ... 1690
Belfast, England,
consul at, salary of ... 1690
Belfast, Me.,
collection-district and port of entry ... 2517
collector to reside at ... 2518
Belgium,
salary of minister to ... 1675
Benedict, Md.,
port of delivery ... 2548
Benicia, Cal.,
inspector of customs to reside at ... 2583
Benzine and Benzole,
not to be carried on steam passenger-vessels. 4472
how packed and marked for shipment ... 4475
penalty for shipping contrary to law ... 4476
Berkley, Mass.,
port of delivery ... 2527
Bermuda Hundred, Va.,
port of entry to extend from Richmond and Manchester, Va., to ... 2552
surveyor to reside at ... 2553
Berries,
grown in United States, wines, &c., made from, exempt from tax ... 3328
Berths,
for vessels carrying passengers ... 4255
penalty for violating regulations ... 4255
Berwick, Me.,
port of delivery ... 2522
goods for, may be entered, &c., at Portsmouth, N. H., or York, Me ... 2524

Section.

Bidders,
for carrying mail, additional cost to be charged to defaulting ... 3951
for supplies, may be present at opening of bids. 3710
Bids,
for supplies to be advertised for ... 3709
notice of opening, who may be present ... 3710
record of all, to be kept ... 3710
for naval supplies, who to be present at opening ... 3722
for contracts for illuminating apparatus, or buildings for light-house service ... 4665
altering, forging, &c.; uttering false, as true, &c ... 5418, 5479
Biennial Examinations, (Pensions,)
medical evidence, to receive unclaimed pension ... 4719
of invalid pensioners, certificates of, to accompany vouchers ... 4771
Commissioner of Pensions may require more than ... 4772
certificate of unappointed surgeons ... 4773
Biennial Lists,
of officers and employés to be filed in Interior Department by heads of Departments. 198
Biennial Register,
by whom to be compiled ... 508
contents of ... 510
distribution of ... 511
number of, to be printed and bound ... 3800
Bill in Chancery,
may be filed to enforce lien of United States for tax on real estate ... 3207
Bill of Fees,
of clerk, marshal, attorney, witnesses, &c ... 983
Bill of Particulars,
in customs cases ... 3012
Bills,
drawn by or on authorized United States officers, included in words "obligation or other security of the United States". 5413
Bills, Congressional,
what number of, to be printed ... 3791
motions to print extra copies of ... 3793
Bills of Exchange,
national banks not limited as to certain ... 5200
may be liable for, in excess of capital ... 5202
may take at current discount and interest. 5197
Bills of Lading,
when to be produced to collectors of customs, &c ... 2785
when entry of goods imperfect for want of ... 2789
of spirits exported for drawback ... 3329
Bills of Sale,
by marshal, of personal property of delinquent collector of internal revenue ... 3217
of vessel to recite certificate of registry at length ... 4170
not valid unless recorded ... 4192
to be recorded by collectors of customs ... 4193
certificates discharging, to be recorded ... 4193
what record of, to be kept in books ... 4193
what to be certified on ... 4193
fee for recording ... 4193
not to be recorded unless acknowledged ... 4193
collectors to keep index of records ... 4194
index and record open to inspection ... 4194
collectors to furnish certificate relating to ... 4194
fee for such certificate ... 4194
fee for furnishing certified copy of record. 4195
interest of each owner to be named ... 4196
fees for recording, &c ... 4382
Binding,
foreman of, appointment and salary ... 3761
to make estimates of material and file requisitions, &c ... 3783

Section.

Binding—Continued.
what, not to be done at Government Printing-Office ... 3785
what, to be done ... 3786
what, may be done at Treasury Department. 3787
on whose order done for either House ... 3789
form of, for Departments ... 3790
Birmingham,
consul at, salary of ... 1690
Births,
happening on vessel, to be recorded in log-book ... 4290
Blacksmiths,
enlistment of, for Ordnance Department ... 1162
Black Warrior River,
in Alabama, tolls ... 5244
Bladders,
of snuff, maximum weight of ... 3362
Blank-Agency, Post-Office Department,
establishment of, at Washington, D. C ... 400
Blank-Books,
allowance for, to collectors of internal revenue ... 3145
Blanks,
to be kept for sale by collectors, &c., in certain districts, price of ... 2648
third-class mail-matter ... 3878
for money-orders, shall be furnished ... 4034
Blasting-Oil,
not to be shipped on passenger-vessel or vehicle ... 4278
how packed and marked for shipment ... 4279
State regulation of transportation of ... 4280
Blind Children,
appropriation for instructing ... 3689
Blind Persons,
education of indigent, provision for cost of, limited ... 4869
Block Island,
appointment of keepers of life-saving stations on coast of ... 4247
employment of crews of surf-men on ... 4247
supervision of life-saving stations on ... 4248
Blue Hill, Me.,
port of delivery ... 2517
Boarding-Officers,
shall report violations of provisions respecting crew-lists, &c ... 4575
crew-list and crew to be produced to, and examined, &c., by ... 4576
Boarding Vessels,
by unauthorized persons prohibited; penalty ... 4606
Board of Commissioners,
for Soldiers' Home, to recommend appointment and removal of officers ... 4816
to procure sites and buildings, when ... 4817
to repay unclaimed moneys to heirs of deceased soldiers ... 4818
may receive donations for use of Home ... 4819
Board of Directors, (see *Directors*,)
national banks to have; powers, &c., of ... 5136
Board of Examiners,
to be appointed for examination of clerks ... 164
Board of Examining Surgeons,
certificate of, shall be subject to approval of Commissioner of Pensions ... 4698½
may be organized; duties, fees, &c ... 4774
Board of Indian Commissioners,
(see *Indians*.)
Board of Managers,
of National Home for Disabled Volunteers ... 4825
corporate powers of ... 4825
managers, number and election of ... 4826
members to have no compensation ... 4828
actual expenses may be paid ... 4828

Section.

Board of Managers—Continued.
appointment and removal of officers by ... 4829
to procure sites and erect buildings ... 4830
may receive donations for Home ... 4831
persons admitted to Home, how ... 4832
assignment of pensions to Home ... 4832
out-door relief ... 4833
to make annual report to Congress ... 4834
to audit accounts of treasurer ... 4834
to visit Home quarterly ... 4834
Board of Supervising Inspectors of Steam-Vessels,
how constituted ... 4405
yearly meeting of, at Washington ... 4405
other meetings of, when to be held ... 4405
to establish regulations ... 4405, 4411
regulations to have force of law, when ... 4405
to assign supervising inspectors to districts. 4405
to establish regulations for steam-vessels passing each other ... 4412
penalty on pilot, engineer, master, &c., not observing ... 4413
for security of life on yachts, ferry, and canal-boats ... 4426
for carrying petroleum ... 4472
may require fire-extinguishers ... 4479
to prescribe life-boats for river passenger-steamers ... 4481
to decide what life-boats, rafts, preservers, &c., shall be used ... 4488
penalty for violating such regulations ... 4489
instruments for security of life to be approved by ... 4491
to prescribe regulations for security of life on passenger-barges, &c. ... 4492
Board of Visitors,
at Military Academy, appointment of ... 1327
compensation of ... 1329
for Government Hospital for Insane ... 4840
duty as to insane persons having insufficient property to defray expenses ... 4849
to determine rate of board of patients ... 4853
Boats,
small open, when to be employed by collectors of customs ... 2763
of revenue-cutters, how distinguished ... 2764
not employed in revenue-service, carrying ensign, &c., penalty for ... 2765
or lighters not masted, or, if masted, not decked, employed in harbor ... 4385
for river passenger-steamers ... 4481
for lake, ocean, &c., steamers ... 4488
penalty for not carrying ... 4489
Boatswains in Navy,
number and appointment of ... 1405
assimilated rank to ... 1491
pay of ... 1556
Boiler-Plates,
(see *Inspection of Steam-Vessels*.)
Boilers, Distillery,
forfeited, to be sold at auction ... 3450
maker of, to give notice before removing from place of manufacture ... 3265
not to be set up without permit of collector of internal revenue ... 3265
where not to be used for distilling ... 3266
for generating steam or heating water for distillery, where to be located ... 3266
Boilers of Steam-Vessels,
(see *Inspection of Steam-Vessels*.)
Boise City Assay Office,
legal designation of ... 3495
business of ... 3558
officers of ... 3559
to be place of deposit of public money ... 3592
superintendent of, to be assistant treasurer ... 3594

Section.

Bolivia,
salary of minister to 1675
Bond and Warehouse System,
provisions concerning 2954–3008
Bonded Account,
to be rendered monthly by collector of internal revenue 3444
Bonded Goods,
(see *Transportation of Merchandise.*)
Bonded Warehouse, (*Internal Revenue,*)
medicines, preparations, &c., may be manufactured in, for exportation, without stamps 3433
removal from, to Pacific Coast 3434
(see *Warehouse; Distillery Warehouse.*)
Bonds,
duty of Secretary of Treasury to prescribe forms of, required by revenue laws, &c. 251
form of, taken by Post-Office Department... 403
delivery upon, to claimant, of vessel, goods, &c., seized under customs-revenue laws, &c 938
may be ordered by judge, in vacation 940
property released from arrest upon, by marshal, in admiralty causes other than seizures for forfeiture 941
to United States, when paid by surety, &c., of insolvent debtor, priority of surety. 3468
custom-house,
when masters of vessels to give re-exportation; nature of 2776, 2777
when and by whom to be put in suit 2778
destroyed or lost,
called, how paid 3702, 3703
indemnity required........................3703, 3705
error or appeal,
none required when writ sued out or appeal taken by United States or by direction of Department 1001
navigation,
for registry of vessel........................ 4145
conditions of........................ 4146
cancellation of, on surrender of certificate. 4175
for passport for vessel in foreign commerce.. 4306
by alien owner, resident in United States, to secure enrollment and license of river, &c., steamboat 4317
by husband or master to secure license for coasting or fishing vessel 4320
for enrollment, or license, or renewal of vessel in another district................ 4328
to secure judgment against steam-vessel carrying more than lawful number of passengers 4469
official,
suits upon, by whom may be brought 784
when original to be produced............ 886
by whom to be given in Army................ 1191
renewal of, by disbursing officers of Army.. 1192
of officers of pay-corps of Navy 1383
when new bond to be given by........... 1384
new commissions not to affect............ 1385
of naval store-keepers on foreign stations... 1439
commencement of pay of officers in Navy who are required to give 1560
of collectors of customs, and others disbursing public moneys, may be increased by President 3639
provisions as to, of postmasters.........3834–3838
of marshals of consular courts 4113
suit on, how brought.................. 4114
original to be produced in suit, when..... 4115
forging, altering with fraudulent intent.... 5418
Bonds of States,
(see *State Bonds.*)

Section.

Bonds of United States,
(see *United States Bonds.*)
Book, Newspaper, and Pamphlet Postage,
accounts to show amounts derived from 4049
Book-Keepers,
in office of Treasurer, salary of.............. 235
Book-Manuscripts,
third-class mail-matter........................ 3878
Book of Estimates,
information required in.................3660–3672
Books,
deductions for, received by members and delegates in Congress 42
power of courts of United States to require production of, and of writings, in actions at law 724
(see *Copies; Transcripts.*)
blank, and stationery, furnished to customs officers, expense of.................. 2646
of a trade, and school, exempt from distraint for internal-revenue taxes 3187
to be kept by retail dealer in leaf tobacco... 3244
warehouse, to be kept by internal-revenue store-keeper........................ 3301
store-keeper's record of distillery operations. 3302
to be kept by distiller....................3303, 3304
of stamps for distilled spirits................ 3312
to be kept by rectifiers and wholesale liquor dealers 3318
of brewer 3337
to be kept by tobacco and snuff manufacturers 3358
of dealer in leaf-tobacco 3360
of cigar manufacturer 3390
to be third-class mail-matter................ 3878
published, &c., by Congress, weight of, in mail 3879
Books and Papers,
seizure of, in customs cases.............3091–3093
Booth Bay, Me.,
port of delivery 2517
Bordeaux,
consul at, salary of 1690
Boston, Mass.,
port of entry........................ 2527
customs officers to reside at.................. 2529
clerks and employés in office of appraiser of customs, how appointed, number and compensation of........................ 2530
transportation in bond extended to......... 2997
assistant treasurer at, appointment, &c.3595–3597
clerks, &c., in office of assistant treasurer... 3601
collectors, &c., in, shall pay public money to assistant treasurer 3615
inspectors of hulls and boilers for collection-district of........................ 4414
their salaries........................ 4414
reserve of national banks in.................. 5191
balances with banks in, may be part of reserve 5192
redemption agencies........................ 5195
Boston and Charlestown, Mass.,
collection-district 2527
officers, residence of 2529
additional inspectors for..................... 2605
Botanical Garden,
supervision over, by Capitol-police.......... 1826
superintendents and laborers in............ 1827
Bottling,
fermented liquors from unstamped packages, or on brewery premises 3354
Boulogne,
consul at, salary of........................ 1690
Bounty,
detail of clerk by Second Auditor to sign certificates relating to 279

Section.

Bounty—Continued.
allowance in settlements with paymaster, of payments of advance bounty 280
upon enlistment in the Navy 1569
to marines for re-enlisting 1612
due colored soldiers and sailors, laws for collection, &c., of, continued 2032
to soldiers, appropriation to pay 3689
to be paid for persons on board vessels of enemy destroyed 4635
to be divided in same manner as prize-money 4635
when number on board cannot be ascertained, how to be estimated 4635
sum to be paid in other cases of vessels destroyed 4635
awarded to vessels, how distributed 4642
assignments of naval, void unless attested .. 4643
shall be paid to colored soldiers enrolled as slaves 4723
for negroes taken from slave-ships, by commissioned vessels, &c 5562

Bounty-Certificates,
power of Second Comptroller to detail clerk to sign 275

Bounty-Fund,
retained, of colored soldiers, custody of 2035
for whose benefit to be holden 2035
investment of, &c 2036
payment of claims from 2036

Bounty-Lands,
warrants and patents for, for military service 457
appointment by Commissioner of Pensions of person to sign warrants 473
military warrants, fee for locating 2238
receivable in payment for pre-emption rights 2277
warrants for, may be located, where 2415
payment of difference in cash, when 2415
claims for, by virtue of certain acts, how located 2416, 2417
for soldiers of certain wars, or their widows, &c 2418
forty acres for certain soldiers 2419
for militia and volunteers serving between 1812 and 1852 2420
exceptions from foregoing 2421
time of prisoners of war counted 2422
warrant and patent for, to issue, when 2423
warrant to issue to widow, when 2424
marriage of widow subsequent to application not to impair her right 2424, 2429
instructions to claimants, &c., furnished; notice of issue of warrant 4748
limit of fee for prosecuting claim for 4785
filing of agreement for prosecuting claim 4786
fee for prosecuting claim for, when no agreement filed 4786
warrants, falsely making, altering, &c., uttering false as true 5420

Bounty-Land Warrants,
(see *Bounty-Lands*.)

Bowdoinham, Me.,
port of delivery 2517

Box-Rents,
quarterly account of, by postmasters 3843
neglect to render 3845
shall be part of basis for fixing salaries of postmasters 3855
at post-offices to be accounted for as revenues 4051

Box-Rents and Branch Offices,
accounts to show amounts derived from 4049

Branch Banks,
how taxed 3408

Section.

Branch Post-Offices,
account of receipts from, to be rendered 3843
Postmaster-General may establish 3871
expenses of, how limited 3874
provisions relating to 3865, 3874
money-order business at 4029

Brands,
on new packages of distilled spirits containing not less than ten gallons 3323
to be effaced, &c., at time of emptying casks for distilled spirits 3324
changing, &c., on cask of spirits 3326
on packages of fermented liquor 3349
on cigar-boxes 3397
on articles sold under distraint and forfeiture, &c 3458

Brandy,
distillers of, made from apples, peaches, or grapes, exemption of 3255

Branford, Conn.,
port of delivery 2533

Brashear, La.,
port of entry 2568
collector to reside at 2569

Brazil,
salary of minister and secretary to 1675

Brazilian Mail-Steamships,
exempted from port-charges, &c 4232
duration of such exemption 4232

Brazos de Santiago, Tex.,
collection-district 2578
deputy collector to reside at, powers of 2579
transshipment of merchandise from Brazos Harbor to Brownsville 2581

Breach of Duty,
penalty for, on merchant-vessels 4602

Bread for Navy,
how, may be procured 3727

Breech-Loading System,
what to be used for carbines and muskets for military service 1672
no royalty to be paid to officers or employés of United States for patent 1673

Bremen,
consulate, salary of 1690

Brevet,
not to entitle officers to increased pay 1264

Brewer,
definition of 3244
special tax of 3244
when to pay special tax as wholesale dealer. 3244
notice by 3335
bond of 3336
to keep books 3337
to render monthly statement, in duplicate, from his books 3337
books of, to be open at all times 3337
entries in books of, to be verified by oath ... 3338
fraudulently failing to make entry, &c., or making false entry 3340
evasion of tax by 3340
neglecting to keep books, or refusing to furnish account 3340
to obtain stamps from collector of district, and to affix and cancel same 3342
neglecting to affix or cancel stamps, or affixing false, &c 3342
selling, removing, &c., fermented liquors in packages without stamp, &c., or with false, &c 3343
drawing fermented liquor from packages without stamp, or with false, &c., or without defacing, &c 3344
when to stamp fermented liquor removed under permit 3345

Section.

Brewer—Continued.
how, may sell and remove sour or damaged fermented liquor 3347
selling at retail at brewery 3348
monthly statement of sales at brewery 3348
to mark, by branding, packages of fermented liquor 3349
permit to conduct business at another place on account of accident, &c 3350

Brewer's Books,
to be open at all times to inspection of internal-revenue officers 3337
entries therein 3337
entries in, to be verified by oath 3338

Brewery,
description of the premises of............... 3335
books to be kept at.......................... 3337
removal of fermented liquors from, without stamp or permit 3343
under permit.............................. 3345
brewer selling at retail at.................. 3348
bottling on premises of 3354

Bribery,
of officer of United States, &c., to influence decision or action, &c.................. 5451
acceptance of bribe by United States officer. 5501
penalty 5502

Bridges,
across Iowa River, in Iowa.................. 5248
across Maquoketa River, in Iowa............ 5250

Bridgeton, N. J.,
collection-district and port of entry 2541
collector in, to reside at.................... 2542

Brigade-Inspector,
one for each brigade of militia.............. 1631
duties of, in militia 1640

Brigades,
in State militia, regiments in 1630
officers in 1631
when called into United States service, how organized 1647

Brigadier-Generals,
number of................................... 1094
aids to...................................... 1098
pay of 1261
of aid to................................. 1261
allowance of forage to...................... 1271
one for each brigade of militia when called into United States service 1647
one for each brigade of militia as organized by each State 1631

Brindisi,
consul at, salary of......................... 1690

Bristol, Me.,
port of delivery............................. 2517

Bristol and Warren, R. I.,
collection-district and port of entry........ 2531
collector in, to reside at Bristol 2532

British North America,
consular fees for certifying certain invoices in 1721
imports from, entered, &c., at certain ports, to what ports transported for benefit of drawback, &c 3053
what imports may be exported from warehouse and transported to, &c 3054
what imports may be exported to 3056
provisions concerning lading and unlading of vessels from 3129

British Provinces,
imported merchandise for, arriving at certain ports, how entered and conveyed..... 3005
imports and domestic products, &c., how transported over territory of 3006
merchandise exported to, not to be landed in United States; penalty 3008

Section.

British Vessels,
may engage in coasting-trade on Saint Lawrence and Great Lakes, when 4347
suspension of privilege, when............ 4347

Bronze Coins,
how redeemed................................ 3529

Brothers,
when to have pensions 4707
when pension of, to begin.................... 4710

Brownsville, Tex.,
port of entry 2578
collector to reside at........................ 2579
transshipment of merchandise to, by Brazos Harbor 2581

Brunswick, Ga.,
collection-district and port of entry........ 2559
collector to reside at.................. ... 2560
collector at, may grant permits to unload vessels in Savannah collection-district, and appoint inspectors for such vessels. 2561

Brunswick, Me.,
port of delivery 2517

Bucksport, Me.,
port of delivery............................. 2517

Buenos Ayres,
consul at, salary of 1690

Buffalo, N. Y.,
port of entry................................ 2535
collector to reside at........................ 2536
additional inspectors for district of......... 2605
weighers, gaugers, measurers, and inspectors for 2606
transportation in bond extended to.......... 2997
inspectors of hulls and boilers for district .. 4414
their salaries.............................. 4414

Buffalo Creek, N. Y.,
collection-district 2535
collector and appraiser in, residence of 2536

Builder,
of vessel to engage in cooly-trade, penalty upon 2160
of recorded vessels, oath of, to obtain record. 4180
to countersign certificate of measurement .. 4181

Buildings, Public,
President may obtain assent of State legislatures to purchase of sites 1838

Bulbs,
third-class mail-matter 3878

Bullion,
deposits of, to be reported by mint superintendents 3503
for assay or coinage to be received, &c., by mint superintendents................. 3506
how paid for 3526, 3527
transfer of, for coinage ingots 3530
to be received and conveyed for United States in vessels belonging to citizens. 4204
to be promptly delivered on arrival 4204
compensation for conveying.................. 4204
shipper of, to notify carrier, &c 4281

Bullion Deposits,
to be received, valued, and accounted for... 3506
certain, may be refused...................... 3519
may be made for coinage 3519, 3520
what shall be the true weight............... 3521
how received and accounted for 3521
certain part of, to be delivered to assayers.. 3522
coinage, charge on.......................... 3524
delivery of coin for......................... 3544
at assay office, N. Y., where coined 3553

Bullion-Fund,
may be used to purchase silver bullion 3526
Secretary of Treasury to provide............ 3545

Bunting,
purchases of, for Navy, not subject to provisions as to advertising, &c......... 3721

Section.

Bunting—Continued.
of American manufacture, may be contracted for in open market by Secretaries of War, Navy, and Treasury 3729
Buoys,
materials for construction or repair of, how to be procured 4666
on coasts, bays, &c., how to be colored and numbered 4678
Burden of Proof,
when on claimant, in cases of seizure under impost or tonnage laws, &c 909
in case of seizure of distilled spirits 3333
Bureau of Currency,
expenses of, to be paid out of taxes on national-bank circulation 5173
Bureau of Military Justice,
in Army, authorized 1094
organization of 1198
Bureau of Mint,
establishment of; what embraced in 343
director of, appointment, term of office 343
clerks in, how appointed 345
Bureau of Statistics,
establishment of, superintendent of 334
for what purposes established 335
annual report of commerce and navigation . 336
what to contain as to coastwise trade 338
quarterly returns to, by collectors of customs, of facts relating to commerce and navigation 337
monthly reports of exports and imports to be published 339
annual statement of vessels 340
annual statement of merchandise 341
statistics of manufactures of United States. 342
Bureaus of Navy Department,
establishment and names of 419
to have custody of certain books, &c 420
chiefs of, how appointed 421
who eligible for 421–426
estimates for, to be furnished to Secretary by chiefs 430
title and relative rank of chiefs of 1471
relative rank of chief of, when line officer below rank of commodore 1472
of officers retired from chief of 1473
pay of chiefs of 1565
Burlington,
inspectors of hulls and boilers for district of. 4414
their salaries 4414
Burlington, Iowa,
port of delivery in district of New Orleans. 2568
surveyor to reside at, duties of 2569
Burlington, N. J.,
collection district and port of entry 2541
collector in, residence of 2542
Burlington, Vt.,
port of entry 2525
collector to reside at 2526
Business Cards,
penalty for printing, &c., in imitation of, or upon, national-bank notes 5188
Business Paper,
national banks not limited as to certain 5200
Bushel,
what to constitute, in grain imports 2919
Butter for Navy,
purchases of, not subject to provisions as to advertising, &c 3721
contracts for, may be made for periods longer than one year 3721
may be in such manner and with such restrictions as Secretary deems proper. 3726

Section.

Buying,
public property unlawfully, by persons not in military or naval service 3490
by any person 5438
valuable inclosure stolen or embezzled from mail, &c., knowing, &c 5470
By-Laws,
directors of national banks may prescribe ... 5136

C.

Cadet Engineers,
formation of class at Naval Academy 1522
appointment of 1523
pay of 1556
Cadet Midshipmen,
students at Naval Academy to be styled 1512
number allowed 1513
appointed contrary to law, not to be paid ... 1518
academic course of 1520
education of, as constructors and engineers .. 1522
pay of 1556
(see *Naval Academy*.)
Cadets,
at Military Academy, part of Army 1094
(see *Military Academy* and *Naval Academy*.)
Cadiz,
consul at, salary of 1690
Cahawba River,
in Alabama, tolls on 5244
Cairo, Ill.,
port of delivery in district of New Orleans. 2568
surveyor to reside at, duties of 2569
Calais, Me.,
port of delivery 2517
deputy collector to reside at 2518
may enter and clear vessels, &c 2521
Calcutta,
consul-general at, salary of 1690
California,
salary of district attorney for 770
fees retainable by clerks of courts in 840
jurisdiction of district courts of, over certain offenses in Alaska 1957
appointment of Indian superintendent for tribes in 2046
of Indian agents 2052
appointment of surveyor-general 2207
salary of 2210, 2211
fifty per cent. addition to certain fees of registers and receivers in 2238
augmented rates allowed for survey of certain public lands in 2405
Geodetic surveys in, may be continued 2409
surveying in, paid for by day 2411
collection districts, ports of entry and delivery in 2582
officers in 2583
remission of fines, penalties, &c., in 5293
California Volunteers,
appropriation to pay traveling expenses of .. 3689
Callao,
Consul at, salary of 1690
Called Bonds,
interest on, to cease in three months 3697
when lost or destroyed, how paid 3702, 3703
Camboose,
for vessel carrying other than cabin passengers between Europe and United States 4258
penalty for failure to provide 4259
Cambridge, Mass.,
port of delivery 2527
Cambridge, Md.,
port of delivery 2548

Section.

Camden, Me.,
port of delivery 2517
Camden, N. J.,
port of delivery in Philadelphia collection-district 2543
assistant collector to reside at, duties 2544
enrollment and license of vessels by 4341
Camp Equipage,
allowance of, in militia, when in United States service 1650
Camphene,
not to be carried on steam passenger-vessel 4472
how packed and marked for shipment 4475
penalty for shipping, contrary to law 4476
Canada, Dominion of,
consular officers not to collect tonnage-fees from vessels touching at ports of 1722
certain fish and fish-oil, produce of fisheries of, free of duty 2506
merchandise imported from, in steamers on Lake Champlain, when and in what districts may be landed 3128
lading and unlading of vessels from 3129
vessels of, may engage in coasting-trade on lakes, &c., under treaty of Washington, when 4347
suspension of privilege by President 4347
exemption from tonnage-duties of certain vessels on inland waters trading with 4221
Canadian Mail,
when, may be carried through United States 4012
Canals,
Postmaster-General may contract for carrying mail on 3967
Canal-Boats,
licensed, &c., not subject to libel for wages 4251
steam, exempted from provisions regulating steam-vessels 4400
Cancellation,
contrary to law, penalty for 3316
of stamps for distilled spirits 3322
of stamps for fermented liquors 3342
of permits for removal of fermented liquors 3345
of stamps for tobacco and snuff 3369
of adhesive stamps 3423
method of, how prescribed 3424
penalty for failure to make 3423
of stamps from private dies 3423
instruments for, how prescribed 3445
of certificates of registry of vessels where new issued 4170
of certificates of registry of lost, &c., vessels 4174
of bond for registry of vessel 4175
Cancelled Notes,
of national banks, burning of, certificate of burning 5184
Candia,
consul at, salary of 1690
Canton,
consul at, salary of 1670
Capacity of Distillery,
to be ascertained by survey 3264
reduction of 3311
Cape Cod,
appointment of keepers for life-saving stations at 4247
employment of crews of surfmen at 4247
Cape Haytien,
consul at, salary of 1690
Cape of Good Hope,
duties on articles produced east of 2501
Cape Porpoise, Me.,
port of delivery 2517
Cape Town,
consul at, salary of 1690

Section.

Cape Vincent, N. Y.,
collection-district and port of entry 2535
collector in, to reside at 2536
Capital,
of banks, &c., internal-revenue tax on 3408
borrowed from day to day, tax on 3408
invested in United States bonds, exempt from tax 3408
Capital Offense,
limitation of time for finding indictment of, wilful murder excepted 1043
(see *Consular Courts.*)
Capital Stock,
of national banks, organization-certificate to state amount of and number of shares 5134
minimum amount of 5138
how divided and transferred, rights of holder 5139
how paid in 5140
proceedings on failure to pay installment 5141
proceedings to increase 5142
to decrease 5143
holders to have a vote for each share 5144
circulation to be in proportion to, &c 5171
proportion of surplus fund to 5199
not to be purchased by bank; loans not to be made on 5201
liabilities of banks not to exceed, except 5202
not to be created by use of bank's own notes, &c 5203
no portion of, to be withdrawn by bank, except 5204
proceedings on failure to pay up, or impairment of 5205
to pay duty on certain part of 5214
shall make returns to Treasurer of United States, penalty for default 5215
duties on, how assessed in default of return 5216
how collected, in default of payments 5217
Capitol,
supervision of improvements, repairs, &c., of furniture, &c., for, how purchased 1816
Capitol Police,
organization and compensation 1821, 1822
how members of, may be suspended 1823
uniform and arms of 1824
at whose expense furnished 1825
supervision by, extended to Botanical Garden; employment of additional force in 1826
Captains in Army,
for batteries of artillery 1100
for troops of cavalry 1103
for companies of infantry 1107
pay of 1261
allowance of forage to 1271
Captains in Navy,
number of, on active list 1363
pay of 1556
Captains of Vessels,
(see *Masters.*)
Captivity,
pay of non-commissioned officers, &c., during 1288
Captors,
of prizes proper, shares of 4630
how distributed 4631
doing any act relating to bringing in, custody, sale, &c., of property captured as prize, or to documents, &c., with intent to defraud or delay, &c 5441
Captures,
as prize, provisions concerning 4613, 4652
property employed in aid of insurrection, when subject of, &c 5308
proceedings in cases of, on account of use, &c., in aid of rebellion, where may be had, and how instituted 5309, 5311

Section.

Captures—Continued.
doing any act relating to bringing in, custody, sale, &c., of property captured as prize, or to documents, &c., with intent to defraud, &c., United States or any captor 5441
Captured and Abandoned Property,
jurisdiction of Court of Claims, of claims for proceeds of, as provided by act of 12th March, 1863........ 1059
appropriation to return proceeds 3689
contracts for collection of........ 3755
prohibition upon trade in, persons to give notice of, to Treasury agent, penalty, &c. 5313
Carbines,
system to be used by Ordnance Department in manufacture of 1672
no royalty to be paid to officers and employés of the United States for........ 1673
Cards,
to be third-class mail-matter........ 3878
Cards, Playing,
imported, to be stamped as prescribed in schedule A........ 3435
tax on, (see *Schedule A.*)
Cargo,
of vessels arriving from foreign ports, where to be entered and unloaded 2770
penalty for unlading, without permit; exceptions, &c........ 2867
of vessels in distress, of perishable nature, &c., when and how disposed of........ 2892
when delivery of, does not agree with master's report, penalty........ 2893
of vessels seeking port, in distress, not disposed of, how reladen, charges, &c.... 2894
of Spanish vessels seeking port in distress, provisions concerning unlading and relading of........ 2895
articles separate from, customs officers what to do, penalty for breaking seals, &c.. 3069
provisions concerning sales of, prior to arrival, &c........ 2104
Carondelet Canal, La.,
vessels for Bayou Saint John may unlade at, after making report, &c........ 2571
departing from, for foreign ports, how cleared 2575
Carpenter in Post-Office Department,
salary of........ 393
assistant........ 393
Carpenters in Navy,
number and appointment of........ 1405
assimilated rank to........ 1491
pay of 1556
Carpenter's Certificate,
as to building, &c., of vessel applying for register........ 4147
Carriage-makers,
enlistment of, for Ordnance Department.... 1162
Carrying Mail,
on established post-roads shall be provided for 3965
to court-houses shall be provided for........ 3966
on navigable canals........ 3967
on plank-roads 3968
in steamboats, &c........ 3969
in steamships........ 3970
to officers not on established routes........ 3971
on routes not established by law 3975
on vessels in foreign trade 3976
on steamboats not in regular mail-service... 3977
on vessels not in mail-service 3978
route-agents, &c., engaged in, to receive certain letters, &c........ 3980
in foreign-bound vessels, &c., illegally...... 3987
in arriving vessels; delivery; oath........ 3988
unlawfully; search of vessels........ 3989

Section.

Carrying Mail—Continued.
seizing letters, &c........ 3990
disposition of seized letters, &c........ 3991
by private hands, &c., when allowed........ 3992
when in stamped envelopes, &c........ 3993
separating letters for expedition in........ 3994
pay for, on railways 3998
on railway-routes, by horse-express........ 3999
on any train required........ 4000
on land-grant, &c., railways........ 4001
on railways, re-adjustment of pay for........ 4002
refusal of railway company to provide postal-cars for........ 4003
additional pay for postal-car for........ 4004
to foreign countries, in steamships........ 4008
pay for........ 4009
contractors for, may be fined........ 4010
of foreign countries through United States.. 4012
rates of postage on, when carried in foreign vessels 4015
(see *Contracts for Carrying Mail.*)
Cars,
(see *Railroad Cars.*)
Carson Mint,
legal designation of........ 3495
officers of........ 3496
salaries of officers........ 3498
assistants, clerks, &c 3499
to be place of deposit of public money...... 3592
superintendent of, to be assistant treasurer.. 3594
Cartage,
customs, appropriation of........ 3687
Carthagena,
consul at, salary of 1690
Carts,
lost in military service to be paid for........ 3483
Cashier,
in office of Treasurer, salary of 235
assistant 235
in office of assistant treasurers........ 3601–3612
Cashiers of National Banks,
when to report "outstanding liabilities" to Secretary of Treasury 310
directors to appoint, &c 5136
shall certify payment of installments on capital stock 5140
Comptroller shall require oaths of, as to organization, &c 5168
penalty for embezzlement, &c., by 5209
shall cause to be kept, &c., list of shareholders 5210
reports to be verified by oath of........ 5211
reports of dividends to be verified by oath of. 5212
Casks,
containing imported spirits, when and how marked 2885
emptied, marks on, to be effaced; penalty.. 2886
change from, of imported distilled spirits, &c., how made 3029
capacity of, for distilled spirits drawn from receiving-cisterns 3287
to be marked by gauger 3287
affixing of stamps to 3287
spirits drawn into other, to be gauged and branded 3323
mark, brand, or stamp on, to be effaced at time of emptying........ 3324
seizure, &c., of empty, from which marks, &c., not obliterated, &c 3324
railroad or transportation company transporting empty, having brand, &c 3324
buying or selling with inspection-marks, after use for distilled spirits 3325
fraudulent use of any, having stamp on 3326
changing, &c., marks, stamps, or brands ... 3326
(see *Empty Casks.*)

Section.

Castine, Me.,
collection-district and port of entry 2517
collector in, to reside at 2518
Catalogues,
of sale of merchandise remaining in public store, &c., how distributed 2973
of prize-property, United States marshal to circulate, before sale 4628
Cattaraugus Creek, N. Y.,
port of delivery 2535
deputy collector at 2536
Cavalry,
in Army, regiments, number of 1094
composition of 1102
troops, number of 1102
composition of 1103
troops of, how formed in militia, and how armed and provided 1632
privileges of, not incorporated with militia . 1641
when and how organized in militia 1646
Cedar Keys, Fla.,
port of entry 2562
collector to reside at 2563
Cedar Point, Md.,
port of delivery 2548
Cellars,
(see *Warehouse.*)
Cemeteries, National,
lands for, may be purchased by Secretary of War 4870
may be taken by him in certain cases without leave of owner 4870
appraisement by courts, of lands so taken . 4871
when fee-simple vests in United States 4872
jurisdiction of United States over 4872
payment of appraised value 4872
superintendents of, how appointed 4873
porters' lodges to be erected for 4873
salary of 4875
quarters and fuel of 4875
to be visited annually by officer detailed by Secretary of War 4876
inclosure of, to be of stone or iron 4877
head-stones 4877
register of burials 4877
who may be buried in 4878
soldiers, sailors, and marines dying in United States service 4878
honorably discharged, dying destitute 4878
production of honorable discharge sufficient authority for burial 4878
cemetery near City of Mexico, care and preservation of 4879
to be subject to same rules as military cemeteries in United States 4880
penalty for injuring, defacing, &c., any 4881
superintendent authorized to arrest and prosecute 4881
jurisdiction of United States over 4882
Census,
to be under control of Secretary of Interior. 443
to be taken by marshals 2176
marshals to cause inhabitants to be enumerated 2176
to collect all other statistical information. 2176
compensation of; fees 2197
minimum compensation allowed 2197
allowance for clerk-hire 2197
may perform duties of assistant 2197
compensation in such case 2197
compensation of assistants; fees 2198
how computed and ascertained 2198
fees for farms returned 2199
for establishments of productive industry 2199
for social statistics, &c. 2199
strict observance of instructions required. 2199

Section.

Census—Continued.
no allowance for unauthorized returns, &c. 2199
fees for making out and returning copies of original returns 2200
Superintendent of, appointment, duties, and compensation of 2204
clerks of, number and classification of 2205
Certificate, (Commerce and Navigation,)
of cancellation of bills of sale, &c., by whom and how recorded, &c. 4193
Certificate, (Coasting Trade,)
penalty for forging, altering, &c 4375
Certificate, (Customs,)
masters of vessels failing to obtain from collector, when going to other district, &c., penalty 2784
accompanying casks of imported spirits, when to be cancelled, refusing to deliver, penalty 2886
of appraiser of customs, and revenue officer, what deemed to be 2950
of consignee, &c., of exported merchandise, when to discharge export bond 3044
of consul, officer verifying same, confirmation of 3045
of clearance of vessels on northern, &c., frontiers 3116
form and execution of 3124
for debenture of goods exported from district other than that of importation ... 3041
of exportation, bond to be given for delivery of merchandise at a foreign port before receipt of 3043
of landing of exported merchandise, when cannot be procured, other proofs, &c. 3047
forging, altering, &c., certificate of entry, knowingly using counterfeited, &c ... 5417
(see *Invoices.*)
Certificate, (Internal Revenue,)
of Commissioner that all reports, &c., have been received from collector 3147
of purchase of real estate 3198
of deposit, payments to Commissioner to be made by 3210
of due diligence of collector by Commissioner to First Comptroller 3218
of collectors, for tobacco-manufacturer 3355
to tobacco-peddler 3383
of collectors, for cigar-manufacturer, of the number of cigar-makers 3387
of drawback of internal-revenue tax ... 3441, 3442
Certificate, (Lands,)
forging, altering, &c., of land-warrant, uttering false, as true, &c 5420
Certificate of Curning,
of worn-out, cancelled, &c., national-bank notes, who to make disposition of, &c. 5184
Certificate of Character,
of discharged seamen 4553
ertificate of Citizenship,
shall be furnished to seamen; form of; fee for 4588
list of, to Secretary of State 4591
(see *Citizenship.*)
Certificate of Deposit,
for United States notes, may be issued; may be part of reserve fund 5193
included in words "obligation or other security of United States" 5413
for public money due to Secretary of Treasury 3621
of coin and bullion, how regulated 254
imitating or printing, &c., on, to be punished 3708
Certificate of Disability,
of invalid pensioners 4771

Section.

Certificate of Disability—Continued.
of two unappointed surgeons not to be taken, except 4773
Certificate of Discharge,
authority of Secretary of War to supply loss of 224
loss of, by survivors, &c., of war of 1812, other proof for pensions 4740
shall be given to seamen 4550
form of 4612
Certificate of Enrollment,
(see *Vessels.*)
Certificate of Indebtedness,
of United States, business cards imitating, penalty 3708
included by words "obligation or other security of United States" 5413
Certificate of Inspection,
(see *Inspection of Steam-Vessels.*)
Certificate of Labor,
of surveyor-general, to be filed with register of land-office by applicant for mineral lands 2325, 2326
Certificate of License,
(see *Vessels.*)
Certificates of Merit,
to soldiers for distinguished conduct 1216
pay of enlisted men, who receive 1285
Certificate of Ownership,
(see *Vessels.*)
Certificate of Pensions,
shall be forwarded to pension-agent; notice to pensioner, fees 4768
Certificate of Record of Vessels,
(see *Vessels.*)
Certificate of Registry of Vessels,
(see *Vessels.*)
Certificate of Salaries and Accounts,
for traveling-expenses of members and delegates, effect of 48
Certificates,
making or using, by persons not in military or naval service, of false, to obtain approval, &c., of claim against United States, action for 3490
delivery, by such persons of less money or property, to be used in military, &c., service, than described in 3490, 5438
giving unlawfully, by such persons, for public property, to be used in military, &c., service 3490, 5438
falsely making, altering, uttering, &c., with fraudulent intent 5421
making or using of false, to obtain approval, &c., of claim against United States 5421
having in possession false, &c., with intent to defraud United States 5422
Certified Balances,
to be conclusive upon executive branch of Government 191
head of Department may submit evidence to Comptroller in regard to 191
Certified Checks or Drafts,
shall accompany certain bids for mail-contracts, as guarantee 3953
Certifying Checks,
penalty for, where deposit is not sufficient .. 5208
Ceylon,
consul at, salary of 1690
Chambers,
what orders, &c., may be made in, by district judge, in admiralty and equity causes. 574
Champagne,
wines made in imitation thereof 3328

Section.

Champlain, N. Y.,
collection-district of 2535
collector in, residence of 2536
additional inspectors for district of 2605
Chancellor of Smithsonian Institution,
(see *Smithsonian Institution.*)
Chaplains,
to Senate, salary 52
to House of Representatives, salary 53
of Congress, salaries of, how payable 55
in Army, post and regimental 1094
number and appointment of 1121
rank, tenure of office, &c. 1122
pay of 1261
forage allowed to 1271
when pension to dependent relative of, to begin 4710
in Navy, number and appointment of, on active list 1395
relative rank of, on active list 1479
pay of 1556
Chargés d'Affaires,
appointed to foreign country, compensation of 1676
appointment of; not to be paid except 1684
salary of secretary of legation acting as 1685
salaries of, term for which payable 1740
shall be deemed diplomatic officers 1674
Charges on Bullion,
to be covered into Treasury 3552
Charleston, S. C.,
collection district and port of entry 2557
officers of customs in, residence of 2558
transportation in bond extended to 2997
assistant treasurer at, appointment, &c., of 3595–3597
clerks, &c., in office of 3608
collectors, &c., shall pay public money to. 3615
inspectors of hulls and boilers for 4414
balances with national banks in, may be part of reserve 5192
redemption agencies 5195
Charlotte, N. C.,
assay-office at, legal designation of 3495
Charterer,
of vessel deemed owner, when 4286
Charts,
of northwestern lakes, sale of 226
Chatham, Mass.,
port of delivery 2527
Chatham, Conn.,
port of delivery 2533
Charwoman,
in Bureau of Statistics, salary of 235
Checks,
stamp-tax on bank 3418
duplicates of lost, how procured 3646, 3647
included by words "obligation or other security of United States" 5413
Cheese for Navy,
may be purchased without advertising, &c. 3721
contracts for, may be for periods longer than one year 3721
may be in such manner and with such restrictions as Secretary deems proper .. 3726
Chelsea, Mass.,
to be part of port of entry of Boston 2527
inspector of customs for 2529
Chemical Preparations,
(see *Medicines and Medicinal Preparations.*)
Chemnitz,
consul at, salary of 1690
Cherokees of North Carolina,
payment of interest to 3689

Section.

Cheroots,
held to be cigars 3387
inspection of, and tax on 3394, 3396

Cherrystone, Va.,
collection-district and port of entry 2552
collector to reside at 2553

Chesapeake City, Md.,
deputy collector of customs to reside at.... 2549
enrollment and license of vessels by..... 4343

Chester, Pa.,
port of delivery 2543
inspector of customs to reside at, powers of. 2544

Chicago, Ill.,
collection-district and port of entry........ 2601
collector and appraiser to reside at......... 2602
additional inspectors for district of......... 2605
weighers, gaugers, measurers, and inspectors for 2606
transportation in bond extended to......... 2997
assistant treasurer at, appointment, &c., of 3595–3597
clerks, &c., in office of.................... 3611
appropriation for payment of coin, &c., destroyed at............................ 3689
appropriation for drawback on building-material for, burned.................. 3689
inspectors of hulls and boilers for.......... 4414
their salaries............................. 4414
reserve of national banks in 5191
balances with banks in, may be part of reserve 5192
redemption agencies....................... 5195

Chief Clerks in Departments,
duties of..................................173, 174
(see *Clerks.*)

Chief Constructor,
Chief of Bureau of Construction and Repair, to have title of....................... 1471

Chief Coiner,
(see *Coiner.*)

Chief Engineers, Navy,
number and rank of........................ 1390
relative rank of, on active list............... 1476
pay of 1556

Chief-Justice of United States,
salary of 676
to constitute one of board of managers of National Home for Disabled Volunteer Soldiers............................... 4825
to nominate and recommend registers in bankruptcy 4993

Chief Medical Purveyor,
of Army, rank of 1168
to give bonds 1191

Chief Musicians,
for regiment of artillery 1099
of cavalry............................... 1102
of infantry 1106
pay and allowances of.................... 1279

Chief of Engineers,
duties of................................. 1152
to employ engineers, for surveys and improvements of rivers 5253
to furnish offices for Office of Education.... 519
employés in office of, in charge, &c......... 1799
to have charge of aqueduct and public works in District of Columbia......... 1800
no compensation for services in charge of public buildings, &c.................. 1807
apartments, stationery, &c., for............ 1808
to have supervision of old Hall of Representatives 1814
to control electrical apparatus jointly with Architect of Capitol................ 1817

Chief of Ordnance,
(see *Ordnance Department.*)

Section.

Chief Signal-Officer,
of Army.................................. 109
authority of, to sell surplus maps and publications of Signal-Office.............. 227

Chief Supervisor of Elections,
circuit-court commissioner to be appointed as 2025
(see *Elections.*)

Chief Trumpeter,
for regiment of cavalry.................... 1102

Children,
of colored soldiers, who deemed to be....... 2037
when half-pay allowed to, of officer, private, &c., in militia, dying in United States service, &c.......................... 1656
when to have pensions, term of 4702
increase of pension on account of 4703
pension to, when abandoned by mother, &c. 4706
limitation as to commencement of pension not to apply to....................... 4709
when pension of, to begin...............4709, 4710
of persons in late rebellion not to receive pensions 4716
when to receive accrued pension........... 4718
of pensioners may revive pension when unclaimed................................. 4719
of certain Missouri State militiamen to have pensions 4722
half-pay pensions to, under former acts, continued 4725
to continue until sixteen 4726
not to exceed what rate 4727
of naval officers, &c., to have pension 4729
of soldiers, &c., of Mexican war to have pension 4731
of soldiers, &c., of war of 1812 and Indian wars to have pension................. 4732
on pension-rolls to have pension, &c., under pension Title 4733
of revolutionary soldiers not to have claim for pension allowed after April 2, 1862, when, &c............................ 4732

Chili,
salary of minister to....................... 1675

China,
salary of minister to....................... 1675
secretary and interpreter of legation to... 1680
interpreters at consulates in, salaries, &c., of. 1692
subjects of, not to be transported in American vessels as Coolies.............2158–2161
voluntary emigration of subjects of, not impeded, (see *Cooly-Trade*)............... 2162
postal agents authorized in................. 4023
marshal for consular courts in 4111
rent of prisons for American convicts in.... 4121
rent of prison, &c., at Shanghai 4122
hire of constables at other ports............ 4122
wages of keepers and care of offenders in, (see *Consular Courts*)................. 4122

Chincoteague Island, Va.,
deputy collector of customs at.............. 2553

Chin-Kiang,
consul at, salary of 1690

Chippewa Indians of Michigan,
unoccupied lands of, opened to homestead entry by certain...................... 2313
time, place, and manner of making entry. 2313
selection of homesteads for minor children of, how made......................... 2314

Chose in Action,
jurisdiction of circuit courts................ 629

Cienfuegos,
consulate at, may be established; salary of consul................................ 1694

Section.

Cigar-Boxes,
fraudulently stamped, selling from, or having in possession 3376
number of cigars to be packed in 3392
labels on 3393
stamps on emptied, to be destroyed 3406
destruction of empty, upon which a cigar-stamp shall be found 3406
giving away, accepting, selling, buying, or using empty stamped 3406

Cigarettes,
held to be cigars 3387
inspection of, and tax on 3394, 3396

Cigar-Lights,
imported, to be stamped as prescribed in Schedule A 3435
tax on, (see *Schedule A*.)

Cigar-Makers,
to be registered with collector 3244
manufacturer employing unregistered; penalty 3244
collector's certificate of number of, to be employed by manufacturer 3387
record of, to be kept by collector 3389

Cigar-Manufacturer's Book,
form of entries in 3390

Cigar Stamps,
(see *Stamps for Cigars*.)

Cigars,
package of, for importation, storage, and stamping of 2804
internal-revenue officer interested in manufacture of, penalty for 3168
penalty for manufacturing without paying special tax 3242
manufacturer of, special tax on 3244
definition of manufacturer 3244
makers of, to be registered 3244
abandoned, condemned, or forfeited, not to be sold for less than tax, but destroyed 3369
sold or removed, not properly stamped, may be assessed within two years 3371
peddlers of 3381–3384
exportation of, without payment of tax 3385
drawback on, exported 3386
manufacturer's statement, bond, and certificate 3387
cigarettes and cheroots held to be 3387
manufacturer's sign 3388
record of manufacturers of, to be kept by collector internal revenue 3389
manufactories to be numbered by collector.. 3389
manufacturer's inventory, book, and abstract 3390
how to be packed 3392
sale of, at retail 3392
label on boxes 3393
tax on, to be paid by manufacturer 3394
stamps for 3395
inspection of 3396
buying, &c., on which tax has not been paid. 3397
packing, in a box bearing a false, fraudulent, or counterfeit stamp 3397
removal of, without properly boxing, stamping, or branding 3397
removing, &c., stamps from boxes of 3397
absence of proper stamp, notice and evidence of non-payment of tax 3398
manufactured on shares, commission, &c 3399
selling, &c., without properly boxing and stamping 3400
falsely representing to have been made and tax paid prior to July 20, 1868 3401
imported, to be stamped and boxed, same as domestic 3402

Cigars—Continued.
imported, to pay internal-revenue tax, in addition to import duties 3402
selling imported, not packed and stamped, as required by law 3403
after April 1, 1869, all, to be taken to be manufactured or imported after July 20, 1868, and stamped 3403
purchasing, &c., not branded or stamped.... 3404
buying, &c., not stamped or branded, from a manufacturer who has not paid special tax 3405
taxes on, extended to all produced within boundaries of United States 3448
penalty on manufacturer for violation of law, where no specific penalty 3456

Cincinnati, O.,
port of delivery in district of New Orleans.. 2568
surveyor and appraiser, duties of 2569
weighers, gaugers, measurers, and inspectors for 2606
transportation in bond extended to 2997
assistant treasurer at, appointment, &c., of..3595–3597
clerks, &c., in office of assistant treasurer at. 3612
inspectors of hulls and boilers for collection-district of 4414
their salaries 4414
reserve of national banks in 5191
balances with banks in, may be part of reserve 5192
redemption agencies 5195

Circuit Court Commissioners,
(see *Commissioners*.)

Circuit Courts,
organization of 607–628
terms of, in southern district of New York, for criminal business; compensation of judge of eastern district for holding 613
clerks of, how appointed, general rule 619
number and appointment of, in Kentucky... 620
in western district of North Carolina 621
in western district of Virginia 622
in western district of Wisconsin 623
deputy clerks of, how appointed 624
at what places appointed, duties and powers of, in Indiana 625
compensation of 626
commissioners of, how appointed, powers of. 627
no marshal or deputy marshal to be, or exercise duties of 628
jurisdiction of 629
removal from State court into, of personal action by alien against civil officer, &c., non-resident in State 644
what final judgments or decrees of, may be reviewed, &c., by Supreme Court on writ of error or appeal 691–693, 699
criers of, appointment and compensation ... 715
power of, to enforce awards of foreign consuls, &c., in differences between captains and crews of vessels, &c 728
number of commissioners of, to be increased for certain purposes 1983
jurisdiction of, in suits for possession of office. 2010
to be opened on application of citizens prior to elections, when 2011
appointment of supervisors of elections by.. 2011
to be kept open until after election 2012
power of judge at chambers 2012
appointment of chief supervisors by 2025
judge of, to certify fees of chief supervisor.. 2031
jurisdiction and condemnation in, of vessels employed in the cooly-trade 2159

Section.

Circuit Courts—Continued.
admission of alien seamen to citizenship by. 2174
(see *Naturalization.*)
power of, to appoint, remove, and regulate shipping-commissioners 4501
masters of vessels to be accountable for effects of deceased seamen to 4540
shipping-commissioners shall pay proceeds of effects, &c., of deceased seamen to. 4543
distribution by, of proceeds of deceased seamen's effects, &c 4544
disposal by, of proceeds of deceased seamen's effects, &c., when unclaimed 4545
jurisdiction of, in penalties, &c., under Title MERCHANT SEAMEN 4610
may be adjourned to another place in consequence of contagious or epidemic disease 4799
may grant injunction in case of national banks in hands of receiver; effect of.. 5237
power of, to adjudge forfeiture of franchises, &c., of national banks 5239
jurisdiction in mandamus to Union Pacific Railroad Company 5262
condemnations in, of property seized on account of use, &c., in aid of rebellion 5309, 5311
Circuit Judges,
appointment, powers, salary, and residence of 607
duties of, in regard to importation of obscene articles, &c 2492
to fix, &c., bonds of shipping-commissioners. 4502
Circuit Justice or Judges,
when, may grant injunction or permit appeal in case of distress-warrant against delinquent collector, &c 3637
Circulars,
postage on, at free-delivery offices 3872
Circulating Notes of National Banks,
(see *National Banks.*)
Circulation,
(see *National Banks.*)
Cisterns, (Distillery,)
receiving, to be erected by distiller......... 3267
construction and capacity of 3267
to be in charge and under lock and seal of gauger 3267
time and manner of drawing spirits from... 3267
Cistern-Rooms, (Distillery,)
opening door of, or gaining access to, in absence of proper officers, penalty for... 3268
Commissioner may require fastenings, &c., to be put on 3270
Commissioner may require changes of or additions to 3270
Citizens of United States,
final judgments or decrees in suits to redress deprivation of rights of, reviewed in Supreme Court 699
dying abroad, duty of consular officers as to estate of 1709
notice of death to be published, &c....... 1710
diplomatic officers who are not, not to receive compensation 1744
deserters to forfeit rights of.............1996–1998
not to build, equip, &c., vessels for transporting coolies 2158
forfeiture of vessels belonging to, engaged in the cooly-trade 2159
penalty for building, navigating, &c., vessels of, employed in cooly-trade 2160
penalty of, for receiving on board or transporting coolies 2161
examination and seizure of suspected vessels of 2163

Section.

Citizens of United States—Continued.
alien seamen may become, in what manner.. 2174
commanders and officers of vessels of United States must be 4131
vessels of United States must be owned by. 4131
usually residing abroad, registry of vessels owned by, when 4133
(see *Consular Courts.*)
Citizenship,
forfeiture of rights of, by deserters.....1996, 1998
for avoiding draft 1998
admission of alien seamen to 2174
(see *Naturalization.*)
certificates of, to be furnished to seamen by collectors, &c 4588
lists of, to be furnished by collectors to Secretary of Treasury 4591
certain soldiers and sailors, deserters, relieved of disabilities from loss of 4749
City Point, Va.,
port of entry, to extend from Petersburgh to, &c 2552
Civil Engineers,
employment of, in surveying rivers 5253
in Navy, appointment of, at navy-yards 1413
relative rank of 1478
pay of 1556
Civil Office,
officers of Army on active list forbidden to hold 1222
(see *Office.*)
Civil Rights,
jurisdiction of district courts of suits for damages by conspiracy against 563
or to redress deprivation of, under color of law, &c 563
duties of United States officers as to prosecutions for crimes committed against. 1982
speedy arrest and examination of offenders. 1983
United States commissioners, number of, to be increased 1983
powers and duties of 1983
may appoint persons to execute process... 1984
authority of persons so appointed 1984
warrants of, where to run and be executed 1984
fees of district attorneys, marshals, and clerks under title CIVIL RIGHTS 1986
of persons appointed to execute process .. 1987
how made up and paid 1987
to be recovered from defendant 1987
(see *Elective Franchise* and *Crimes.*)
Civil Service,
regulations for appointment in, and examiners for 1753
persons honorably discharged from military or naval service preferred for appointment in 1754
persons in, may receive pension, &c 4724
Civil Surgeons,
when biennial examinations may be made by. 4773
may be appointed examining surgeons 4777
Claim-Agents,
not to have fees for application for arrears of pension 4711
Claimant,
delivery to, of vessel, goods, &c., seized under customs-revenue laws, &c 938
may be ordered by judge, in vacation..... 940
delivery to, by marshal, in cases of arrest in admiralty, other than seizures for forfeiture 941
of property seized, &c., to pay his own costs before possession given, on recovering judgment, &c 979
prosecuting claims before Departments to take oath 3478, 3479

Section.

Claims,
by or against United States,
to be settled and adjusted at Treasury Department ... 236
against United States,
for Indian depredations ... 466
jurisdiction of district courts of suits to recover forfeiture or damages for presenting, &c., false or fraudulent ... 563
jurisdiction of Court of Claims over ... 1059
reference of, to Court of Claims, by heads of Executive Departments ... 1063
by Secretary of Treasury, on certificate of Auditor or Comptroller ... 1063
proceedings in cases of, referred, &c ... 1064
judgments on, how paid ... 1065
growing out of treaty stipulations, &c, not within jurisdiction of Court of Claims ... 1066
commissioner, and commissions to take testimony concerning ... 1075
demand for information or papers concerning, from Departments ... 1076
forfeited by fraud in proof, statement, establishment, or allowance of ... 1086
new trial, on motion of United States ... 1088
judgment for, how paid ... 1089
interest on judgment for ... 1090
interest on, before judgment ... 1091
payment of judgment for, a full discharge, &c. 1092
final judgment on, against claimant, a bar, &c. 1093
penalty for presenting or allowing, for salary of civil officer suspended, &c ... 1762
members of Congress and public officers not to receive compensation for services relating to, before any Department or commission; penalty ... 1782
due colored soldiers and sailors, laws providing for collection and payment ... 2032
use of retained bounty-fund for payment of certain ... 2036
for Indian supplies purchased without authority not to be paid ... 2085
for property seized under customs laws, what to state, &c ... 3076
transfer, &c., null and void, unless ... 3477
persons prosecuting before Departments must take oath ... 3478, 3479
of disloyal claimants not to be paid ... 3480
for horses, &c., steamboats, &c., lost in military service, provisions relating to, 3482–3487, 3489
for collecting, &c., volunteers not to be paid, unless ... 3489
knowingly making false ... 3490, 5438
making or using false receipt, voucher, &c., in obtaining approval of ... 3490, 5438
conspiracy to defraud United States by obtaining approval, &c., of false ... 3490, 5438
carrying away from place where kept any paper prepared, &c., to be used to procure payment of ... 5454
presenting paper so taken, &c., in order to procure payment of ... 5454
officer of United States, or person connected with Executive Department, or either House of Congress, not to act as agent, &c., in prosecuting; penalty ... 5498
for prize share,
how to be made ... 4616
for pension,
evidence of injury, &c., when claim not prosecuted to successful issue within five years from time of filing ... 4717
of Indians, time for prosecuting extended ... 4721
Clearance Fees,
what vessels not to pay ... 2793

Section.

Clearing-House Balances,
may be paid in certificates of deposit for United States notes ... 5193
Clearing-House Certificates,
may be part of national-bank reserve-fund. 5192
Clearances,
blank, to be kept for sale by certain collectors of customs ... 2648
Clearance of Vessels,
from certain ports, laden with live-oak timber, conditions of ... 2463
ship's papers to be returned upon ... 2790
ferry-boats not required to clear ... 2792
on northern, &c., frontiers ... 3116
in foreign and coasting trade, departing for ports where no custom-house ... 3118
in foreign trade, not to be granted until mails have been received ... 3976
oath as to letters required before granting .. 3987
bound to foreign port, how granted ... 4197
penalty on master for departing without ... 4197
oath by master to obtain ... 4198
form of report and manifest to obtain ... 4199
manifests of shippers to obtain ... 4200
oath of master, owner, shippers, and consignors, before granting ... 4200
form of ... 4201
not to be granted until State inspection laws complied with ... 4202
until mails received on board ... 4203
until bullion, coin, securities, &c., of United States offered by Government received on board ... 4204
not granted to vessels from certain ports laden with live-oak timber until, &c. 4205
not to be granted until all fees paid ... 4206
rates of fees of consular and diplomatic officers to be attached to ... 4207
of steamboat going from Lake Champlain to province of Quebec ... 4208
of foreign vessel to be produced on entry ... 4209
penalty on master failing to produce ... 4209
exception as to vessels of certain nations ... 4210
production of, to foreign consul to obtain papers ... 4211
penalty on foreign consul delivering papers without production of ... 4211
licensed yachts exempt from, when ... 4214
foreign yachts exempt from, when ... 4216
fees for, (see *Fees*) ... 4381, 4382
not to be granted until master has furnished crew-list ... 4573
Secretary of Treasury may refuse, to vessels suspected to be bound for insurrectionary ports; attempting to depart, &c., without, forfeiture ... 5320
when bond may be taken upon, that cargo shall not be used in aid of insurrection ... 5321
falsely making, forging, altering, &c., uttering as true any false, &c ... 5423
Clerks, (Congress,)
of Senate and Senate committees, salaries of. 52
in House, salaries of ... 53
Clerks of Courts,
supervision of accounts of, by Attorney-General ... 368
of district courts, appointment of ... 555
number of, in western district of Arkansas ... 556
in Kentucky ... 557
of circuit courts, how appointed, general rule ... 619
number and appointment of, in Kentucky. 620
in western district of North Carolina ... 621
in western district of Virginia ... 622

Section.
Clerks of Courts—Continued.
in western district of Wisconsin ... 623
of circuit and district courts, statement by, to Solicitor of Treasury ... 797
fees ... 828
rule as to per-diem allowance to, for attendance, &c ... 831
semi-annual return to be made by, to Attorney-General of fees, &c ... 833
amount of fees retainable by ... 839
in California, Oregon, and Nevada ... 840
of district court, additional compensation for services in prize-causes ... 842
of district and circuit courts, allowance to, for each year to be made from fees, &c., of same year ... 843
surplus fees to be paid into Treasury ... 844
accounts of, examination by Attorney-General ... 845
to be certified by district judge, subject to revision, &c ... 846
fees of, in cases where United States liable, how to be paid ... 856
in other cases, how to be recovered ... 857
bill of fees of, how taxed, and when included in judgment ... 983
bill of costs of, how proven before taxed by judge or allowed by accounting-officers ... 984
fees of, in civil-rights cases ... 1986
of district courts, duties in prize-cases ... 4644
compensation of, for such services ... 4644
failure of, to deposit with Treasurer, &c., money belonging to registry; conversion, &c., by, of moneys belonging, &c. 5504
knowingly receiving from, as deposit, loan, &c., moneys belonging to registry ... 5505
Clerk of Court of Claims,
appointment and oath of ... 1053
salary of ... 1054
bond of ... 1055
power of, to disburse contingent fund; accounts of ... 1056
annual report by, to Congress, of judgments; decisions transmitted by, to heads of Departments ... 1057
Clerk of Supreme Court,
how appointed ... 677
Clerks of Territorial Courts,
of supreme courts, how appointed, &c ... 1870
of district courts, appointment, &c., of ... 1871
one only in each district to be entitled to compensation ... 1871
fees and costs allowed to ... 1883
of supreme court of Arizona, mileage of, at adjourned terms ... 1934
Clerks, (Custom-House,)
in office of appraiser of customs at Boston .. 2530
at New York ... 2539
at Philadelphia ... 2545
employed by customs officers ... 2634
at New York ... 2745
Clerks in Departments,
provisions concerning ... 163–176
of State ... 201
of War ... 215
of Treasury ... 235
of Justice ... 351
of Post-Office ... 393
of Navy ... 416
of Interior ... 440
of Agriculture ... 522, 523
in General Land-Office, prohibited from being interested in purchase of public lands. 452
in Pension-Office, may be detailed to investigate frauds, &c ... 474, 4744

Section.
Clerk of House of Representatives,
salary of ... 53
bond of ... 58
where deposited ... 59
to advertise for stationery ... 65–68
may contract for separate parts of stationery ... 68
fees of, for transcripts from journals ... 71
duty of, to transmit petitions, &c., for private claims to Court of Claims ... 1060
printing, binding, &c., for the House done upon requisition of ... 37, 89
duty of, to select papers in certain States, in which laws, treaties, and advertisements to be published, and to fix rates. 3823
to notify such selection to heads of Departments and judges ... 3824
Clerks in Post-Offices,
allowances for ... 3859, 3860, 3863
in railway post-offices, salaries, &c., of ... 4025
Clerk's Office,
what orders, &c., may be made in, by district judge, in admiralty and equity causes. 574
Cleveland, O.,
collector and appraiser of customs ... 2604
weighers, gaugers, measurers, and inspectors for ... 2606
transportation in bond extended to ... 2997
inspectors of hulls and boilers for ... 4414
reserve of national banks in ... 5191
balance with banks in, may be part of reserve ... 5192
redemption agencies ... 5195
Clifton,
consul at, salary of ... 1690
Clippings,
of bullion, disposal of ... 3540
Clippings and Cuttings,
of tobacco, when may be sold without payment of tax ... 3362
Clothing,
Army,
punishment for spoiling or losing ... 1342
of soldiers, not to be sold, bartered, &c. 1242, 3748
for the Army, to be prescribed by the President ... 1296
not allowed to sergeants of ordnance ... 1297
gratuitous issues of, to soldiers who have had contagious diseases ... 1298
deductions and allowances for overdrawn and undrawn ... 1302
balances accumulating to soldiers' credit ... 1308
prisoner discharged from military prison to be furnished with ... 1355
what, allowed in militia, when in service of United States ... 1650
purchases of, for Army not to exceed necessities of year ... 3732
Navy,
for students at Naval Academy ... 1527
proceeds of sale of condemned, not to be covered into Treasury ... 3618
lost in Navy, appropriation for ... 3689
provisions concerning contracts for ... 3718
purchases, &c., not to exceed necessities of year ... 3732
seamen's,
vessels shall carry for winter use ... 4572
to be forfeited for desertion ... 4596
disposal of, when forfeited by desertion ... 4604
Coal,
of steam-vessels, exempt from duty ... 2798
imported, where stored ... 2958
Coal and Salt,
time for unlading extended to vessels laden with ... 2881

Section.

Coal and Wood,
for Government use in District of Columbia . 3711–3713
Coal Depots,
establishment of, for Navy . . . 1552
Coal-Heavers,
pay of, in Navy, how fixed . . . 1569
additional to seamen, &c., doing duty as . . . 1570
Coal-Lands,
who may make entry of . . . 2347
limit of amount which individual may enter . 2347
price, how regulated . . . 2347
persons who have opened, &c., mines to have preference right of entry . . . 2348
certain associations may enter 640 acres, when . . . 2348
Coal-Oil,
not to be carried on steam passenger-vessels . 4472
how packed and marked for shipment . . . 4475
penalty for shipping contrary to law . . . 4476
Coasting Districts,
coast of United States divided into three great . . . 4348
Coasting Steam-Vessels,
to carry what lights . . . 4233
Coasting Trade,
enrolled, &c., vessels engaged in, on northern, &c., frontiers, not liable to entry-fees, &c . . . 2793
vessels qualified to carry on the, deemed vessels of United States . . . 4131
vessels, belonging to citizens, engaged in, exempt from tonnage duties . . . 4220
what vessels may engage in . . . 4311
enrolled and licensed vessels on northern, &c., frontier may engage in . . . 4318
form of enrollment for vessels engaged in . . . 4319
licensed to engage in, how obtained . . . 4320
bond for . . . 4320
form of license . . . 4321
enrollment and license of vessels for, at Jersey City . . . 4340
at Camden, N. J . . . 4341
at Wilmington, N. C . . . 4342
at Chesapeake City, Md . . . 4343
at ports authorized by Secretary of the Treasury . . . 4344
at Cold Spring, Greenport, and Port Jefferson . . . 4345
foreign vessels not to engage in . . . 4347
British vessels may engage in, on Saint Lawrence River and Great Lakes . . . 4347
suspension of privilege by President . . . 4347
suspension of, when export duty levied on timber cut in Maine and floated to sea in New Brunswick . . . 4347
between neighboring districts, manifests and permits for . . . 4349
penalty for departing without manifest, &c . . . 4350
delivery of manifest before unlading . . . 4351
penalty for non-delivery . . . 4352
between remote districts, manifests and permits for . . . 4353
penalty for departing without manifest, &c . . . 4354
delivery of manifest before unlading . . . 4355
penalty for non-delivery . . . 4356
between Long Island and Rhode Island, privileges of vessels in . . . 4357
between Alaska and other districts, how regulated . . . 4358
masters of certain vessels engaged in, to carry manifests . . . 4359
penalty for not exhibiting, &c . . . 4360

Section.

Coasting Trade—Continued.
registered vessels engaged in, subject to provisions governing licensed vessels . . . 4361
vessels in putting into port other than destination, to report, &c . . . 4366
penalty for not reporting, &c . . . 4366
penalty on vessel carrying on, not enrolled or licensed . . . 4371
forfeiture of, and of merchandise . . . 4371
Coast of United States,
divided into three great districts . . . 4348
Coast Survey,
preliminary surveys, under direction of superintendent . . . 4663
President authorized to cause survey of coasts of United States to be made . . . 4681
to cause banks and shoals beyond twenty leagues, &c., to be examined . . . 4682
appropriations for Coast Survey, how to be expended . . . 4683
officers of Army and Navy employed in; departments of work; no extra pay . . . 4684
maps, books, apparatus, &c., belonging to United States; employment of astronomers, &c . . . 4685
use of public vessels in actual service . . . 4686
officers of Army and Navy to be employed in, as far as practicable . . . 4687
allowance for subsistence to officers and men . 4688
salary of superintendent . . . 4689
report to Congress . . . 4690
disposal of maps and charts . . . 4691
Coastwise Vessels,
provisions as to shipping-articles not to apply to . . . 4513
shipping-articles for . . . 4520
penalty for illegally shipping seamen . . . 4521
Coaticook,
consul at, salary of . . . 1690
Cobija,
consul at, salary of . . . 1690
Cod-Fishery,
form of license to carry on . . . 4321
agreement for shares with fishermen . . . 4391
penalty for violation of . . . 4392
recovery of shares of fish under . . . 4393
vessels liable for shares, &c . . . 4393
discharge of vessel on bond . . . 4394
Cohasset, Mass.,
port of delivery . . . 2527
Coin,
and bullion, regulations for deposit of, in United States Treasury . . . 254
consular and diplomatic fees shall be collected in coin of United States, or its value in exchange . . . 1746
customs-duties payable in . . . 3009, 3473
internal-revenue returns stated in, to be reduced to legal tender . . . 3178
other than standard, when receivable for public dues . . . 3474
limit of abrasion of . . . 3505
superintendents of mints to deliver, &c . . . 3506
denomination, weight, and fineness . 3511, 3513–3515
certain abraded, in Treasury to be recoined . . 3512
denomination, &c., of minor . . . 3515
of denominations not authorized, not to be issued . . . 3516
devices and legends on . . . 3517
silver exchangeable for gold at par . . . 3527
provisions concerning . . . 3527
deviations allowed in, from standard . . . 3535–3537
pieces for annual trial . . . 3539
delivery of, to superintendents . . . 3539
delivery of, to depositors . . . 3544
foreign, not legal-tender in payment of debts . 3584

Section.

Coin—Continued.
of United States to be legal tender...... 3585–3587
faith of United States pledged to pay notes and bonds in 3693
application of, received from duties on imports 3694
Secretary of Treasury may sell surplus...... 3699
may purchase 3700
shipper of, to notify carrier, &c 4281
falsely making, forging, &c., coin current in United States 5457
knowingly passing, uttering, &c., falsely-made, forged, &c 5457
knowingly selling, bringing into United States, or having in possession falsely-made, forged, &c 5457
falsely making, forging, &c., minor coinage of United States; uttering, selling, bringing in, &c., or having in possession such coin 5458
fraudulently defacing, mutilating, diminishing, &c., coin current in United States 5459
debasement of, or making of less than lawful weight or value, by employés, any coin struck at United States Mint 5460
embezzlement of, by officers, &c., at any mint or assay office 5460
making, without authority, or passing such unauthorized coin 5461, 5462

Coinage,
gold, silver, and minor, to be reported by mint superintendents 3503
charge, memorandum of, to depositors 3506
report by assayer to form basis of 3523
rates of 3524
money arising from, to be covered into Treasury 3552
recoinage of certain foreign coin required 3566
regulation and expenses of 3568

Coiner,
office created 3496
salaries 3498
to give bond 3501
to take oath 3500
power to nominate subordinates 3504
duties of 3509
as to ingots 3532
as to coins 3538
as to annual trial 3539
as to clippings 3540
as to annual settlement 3541
as to defacing working-dies 3550
at Philadelphia may strike medals 3551

Cold Spring, N. Y.,
port of delivery 2535
merchandise for, to be entered and duties paid at New York 2540
enrollment and license of vessels by surveyor at 4345

Collecting Revenue from Customs,
appropriation for 3687

Collecting Volunteers,
claims for, not to be audited, unless 3489

Collection Districts, (*Customs*,)
of United States; ports and officers 2517–2612
in Maine, where no boundaries are prescribed 2519
vessels arriving and departing from port before making report or entry 2773
on northern, &c., boundaries, merchandise how imported into 3096
entry of merchandise in, &c 3097

Collection Districts, (*Internal Revenue*,)
two or more States or Territories may be united in one district 3141
to be divided by the President 3141
limitation of the number of 3141

Section.

Collection Districts, (*Internal Revenue*)—Cont'd.
additional, in California 3141
may be altered by the President 3141
when two or more are united in one 3142
collector to be appointed for each 3142

Collection of Abandoned Property,
contracts may be made for 3755

Collections, (*Internal Revenue*,)
all to be paid daily into the Treasury 3210
Secretary may extend time for such payment 3210
monthly statement of, by collector 3212

Collectors of Customs,
where to reside 2518–2604
regulations for, in making quarterly returns to Bureau of Statistics, as to commerce and navigation 337
to select homestead-lands for certain minor children of Ottawa and Chippewa Indians 2314
duties of, at certain ports respecting clearance of vessels laden with live-oak timber 2463, 4205
at New York, assistant collector at Jersey City, to act under 2535
to instruct, &c., assistant collector at Jersey City 2536
at Richmond, Va., may clear vessels loaded at Petersburgh, in certain cases 2554
for districts of Savannah and Brunswick, Ga., may grant permits to unload vessels, appoint inspectors, &c., in both those districts 2561
at New Orleans, La., when to appoint temporary inspectors, number of, &c 2576
may appoint head gaugers 2577
at Astoria, Oregon, duties of, in cases of vessels bound for Portland 2588
in cases of vessels for Astoria and Portland 2590
to administer oaths to special examiners of drugs, &c 2611
duties of, in districts where no examiners of drugs provided 2612
term of office 2613
appraiser at New York to transmit certain reports to 2615
oath of, before whom taken 2617
of officers of customs taken before 2617
bonds of 2619
by whom approved and where filed 2620
duties of 2621–2625
duties of, in ports where no naval officer, and when naval officer is disabled 2622
where neither naval officer nor surveyor 2623
when surveyor may be appointed by 2624
in case of death or disability of, who to perform duties 2625
liability of estate of 2625
to authorize fit persons to perform duties of surveyor in case of disability or death 2629
to employ deputy collectors who may act, &c., responsibility of 2630
when to authorize officer or clerk to act in his place as disbursing agent, bond to cover, &c 2631
number and compensation of clerks of 2634
to keep posted table of fees, &c., receipts 2635
to keep account of fees, &c., and make annual returns to Commissioner 2639
personal attention, &c., of, duties of, in respect to accounts 2640
accounts of, what to include and how rendered 2639–2941, 2643, 2645, 2647
to render list of clerks, their duties and compensation, account of stationery, office-rent, &c 2643

Section.

Collectors of Customs—Continued.
of the northern, &c., frontier districts to forward list of employés, &c., and make certain estimates 2644
books, blanks, &c., how furnished to 2646
to render quarterly accounts of moneys collected for fines, penalties, forfeitures, rents, storage, &c., excess of $2,000 in certain cases to be paid into Treasury 2647
in certain districts to keep for sale blanks 2648
fees of 2654
where naval officer at same port 2655
drawback fees, how shared, &c., by 2656
fees of, for entry on northern, &c., frontiers 2658
allowances and percentages of 2659
salaries and commissions of 2647, 2660–2685
at Paso del Norte to pay into Treasury annual excess of $2,000 2671
at certain other places 2675
division of commissions on death or resignation of 2686
when entitled to pro-rata compensation only 2687
limit to compensation of 2688
compensation exclusive of expenses of 2689
limit to emoluments of, at certain ports 2690
at other ports 2691
when fees, &c., insufficient for compensation of 2692
at New York, responsible for assistant, &c. 2694
to direct officers of revenue-cutter service 2760
may employ small open boats, &c 2763
when to put in suit re-exportation, &c., bonds 2778
when to grant to masters of vessels departing for other districts copies of manifests, certificates, &c 2780
when to take bond from agents, factors, &c., for account of merchandise by owner 2787
imperfect entry of merchandise 2789
to certify separate entry of distilled spirits 2794
excess of sea-stores 2796
examination of baggage, &c 2801
delivery to, of baggage in transit for foreign countries, &c 2803
to administer oaths 2805
goods intended for transportation in bond 2826
to certify duplicate manifests of 2827
not to permit entry of merchandise, when duties exceed bond 2831
to take possession of merchandise when invoices not correct 2840
when to certify invoices 2852
when to notify consular officer to transmit copy of invoice 2857
to administer oath to officers, &c., of vessels, in case of unlading by accident, &c 2867
to make estimate of duties, and grant permit to land 2869
to grant license to unload at night, compensation for unlading 2871
penalty for unlawfully unlading, &c 2873
to put inspectors on board of vessels going from one district to another 2875
inspectors' books to be deposited in office of 2876
to take possession of merchandise not reported by master of vessel; delivery by order of 2880
to extend time for unlading of vessels laden with salt or coal 2881
to compare returns of delivery of merchandise 2889
vessel seeking port in distress; when to appoint inspector and grant permit to unlade, &c 2891

Section.

Collectors of Customs—Continued.
storage of goods landed from vessels in distress under direction of; disposal of perishable cargo 2892
vessels obstructed by ice 2896
tare on imports 2898
delivery of goods on bond before appraisal 2899
opening package without consent of, violating bond, &c 2899
appraisal of market value of goods in additions to entries 2900
to designate number of packages to be opened, &c., forfeiture, remission 2901
estimating value and quantity of imports 2902
appraisal of market value of merchandise at time of exportation 2906
Secretary of Treasury to furnish, with standard of sugar 2914
to examine upon oath owners, &c., as to value of merchandise, and require production of papers; evidence to be retained in office of, &c 2922
bond to produce evidence of class and value of merchandise 2925
to designate bonded warehouse for merchandise of which entry is not complete 2926
when to order re-appraisement 2929
persons appointed by, to re-appraise goods, disagreements, final decision 2930
decisions of, as to rate of duties, fees, charges, &c., final, unless protest and appeal are made 2931, 2932
re-examination of drugs, medicines, &c 2936
when analysis of imported drugs, medicines, &c., sustains examiner's report 2937
at New York, how to direct appraisements 2939
powers of, to lease or hire stores at certain ports 2953
when to lease stores in certain ports 2955
use of warehouse hired by 2956
not to enter into contract for use of warehouse before completion 2957
deposit of imported merchandise in public stores and bond for duties 2964
charges and duties on unclaimed merchandise sold 2965
deposit in bonded warehouse of importations in steamers 2966
to sell merchandise remaining in public store beyond one year, proceedings 2973
to pay into Treasury overplus of sales of unclaimed merchandise, papers transmitted by, to exonerate master of vessel, &c 2974
to sell unclaimed perishable merchandise in public warehouse 2976
permit for exportation, without payment of duties 2979
lien for freight on merchandise in warehouse 2981
quarterly reports of warehoused merchandise, by 2988
to permit entry for warehouse and transportation 2990
priority in time of examination of certain merchandise, &c 2991
sureties on transportation bond, how to justify before, certificate of, as to sufficiency 2992
transfer of merchandise for immediate transportation 2995
immediate-transportation merchandise, remaining in warehouse more than ten days 2996
money paid under protest, &c., for duties, to be deposited 3010

Section.

Collectors of Customs—Continued.
to retain one per centum on amount of drawbacks 3017
ten per centum on amount of certain drawbacks 3019
fees on gaugeable merchandise 3023
on weighable articles 3024
to appoint officer to inspect change from casks, &c., of distilled spirits and sugars 3029
when to permit merchandise entitled to debenture, to be changed into other packages 3030
when to appoint inspector to superintend transfer, &c 2031
invoice of merchandise for drawback to be deposited with, and preserved by, &c. 3032
inspection of merchandise entitled to drawback, and comparison of invoices, &c 3033
to certify copy of cost of merchandise for drawback from invoice, &c 3034
inspection of merchandise notified for exportation, permit for landing 3035
refusal of, to pay debenture, suit, how brought 3039
certificate of exportation from port other than of importation, and debenture .. 3041
in case of error or fraud to refuse debenture, and represent case to Secretary of Treasury 3042
proofs of landing abroad other than exportation certificates 3047
to pay debentures, drawbacks, &c 3048
penalty for fraud or error in relation to drawback 3049, 3050
not incurred if error is accidental 3051
duplicate list and appraisement of property seized 3074
to publish notice of seizures 3075
bond of claimant in seizure cases 3076
sale of seized property, deposit of proceeds, adjournments of sale 3077
advertisement and sale of perishable articles seized, &c 3080
release of seized merchandise on payment of appraised value 3081
report of seizures to Solicitor of Treasury ... 3083
report of fines, &c., to district attorney, penalty for failure, &c 3084
to have custody of goods seized, &c 3086
when to cause commencement of suits; receipt and distribution of amount recovered 3087
may examine papers, &c., seized by warrant of district judge 3093
in northern, &c., frontier districts, manifests to be delivered to 3098
when to search certain stores, warehouses, &c 3107
excess of sea-stores of vessels on northern, &c., frontiers 3112
license, &c., to vessels in foreign and coasting trade 3115
clearances to be indorsed on manifests of vessels on northern, &c., frontiers 3116
to furnish registered vessels with certified manifests 3126
exportation for drawback of distilled spirits. 3329
distilled spirits exported without payment of tax 3330
internal-revenue tax on imported tobacco and snuff 3377
on imported cigars 3402
public money 3639
President may increase penalty of, bonds of. 3639

Section.

Collectors of Customs—Continued.
naval officer and surveyor shall examine books, &c., of 3650
shall act as disbursing agents 3657
shall require oath as to letters before clearing vessels leaving United States 3987
shall search vessels for letters illegally conveyed 3989
may seize such letters 3990
disposal of letters seized 3991
to appoint persons to measure vessels for register tonnage, when 4148
for other tonnage, when 4154
to make and keep in books registry of vessels 4155
to grant certificates of registry 4155
to fill up, sign, and seal certificates of registry 4158
to administer oath to owner 4159
to issue new certificates of registry, when ... 4160
to issue new certificate of registry to agent or attorney of owner, when 4161
to transmit old certificate to collector who granted it 4162
to issue certificate of register to vessel sold under legal process, when 4164
to issue new certificate in place of one lost or destroyed, when 4167
to issue new register where vessel sold or changed in form or burden 4170
to transmit old certificate to Register of Treasury for cancellation 4170
to indorse changes of masters of vessels on certificates of registry 4171
to transmit certificates of registry delivered on loss, &c., of vessel to Register of Treasury 4174
to cancel bond for registry on delivery of certificates, &c 4175
to number certificates of registry, how 4176
recording of vessels in office of 4180
oath of builder of vessel to obtain record ... 4180
to be recorded in books 4180
to cause survey or measurement of vessels for record 4181
to grant certificates of record 4182
to record such certificates 4182
to transmit copy to Register of Treasury .. 4182
to indorse on certificates of record change of master or name of vessel 4183
to record such change in record-book 4183
to transmit transcript to collector granting certificate 4183
to transmit duplicate to Register of Treasury 4183
fees of, for granting certificate of registry .. 4184
for indorsements on certificates 4184
for taking any bond 4184
for granting certificate of record 4185
for indorsements on certificate 4185
for taking any bond 4185
penalty upon, for making, &c., false register or record, &c 4187
for receiving reward, &c., for registering or recording 4187
bills of sale, hypothecations, mortgages, and conveyances of vessels to be recorded. 4193
record of discharges of, to be kept 4193
to keep what items concerning, in books .. 4193
to certify what items concerning, on bills, &c 4193
to keep an index of such records 4194
index and records open to inspection 4194
to furnish certificates, relating to 4194
fee of, for furnishing certificates 4194

Section.

Collectors of Customs—Continued.
fee of, for furnishing certified copy of record 4195
manifests of vessels foreign-bound to be delivered to, by master 4197
clearance of, to be granted by, when 4197
form of manifest to be delivered to 4199
manifest to be delivered to, by owners, shippers, &c., of cargo 4200
oath before, concerning 4200
to observe State inspection laws in granting clearances 4202
duties of, in Florida, Alabama, Mississippi, and Louisiana in clearing vessels laden with live oak 2463, 4205
not to grant clearances until fees paid 4206
to annex table of consular fees to clearances of registered vessels 4207
to grant clearance to vessels going from Lake Champlain to province of Quebec, how 4208
to transmit to Secretary of Treasury copies of receipts by consular officers for fees paid abroad 4213
statement of all certified invoices, &c 4213
what statement to specify 4213
to require sail-vessels to be furnished with proper signal-lights 4233
to direct inspection and report passenger-vessels arriving from abroad 4264
effect of report as evidence when approved by 4264
to make quarterly return to Secretary of State of lists of passengers arriving from abroad 4267
to examine emigrant vessels on arrival 4272
to report to Secretary of Treasury, concerning 4272
to furnish passports to vessels of United States, departing for foreign ports 4306
to furnish unregistered vessels, &c., letter with passport 4308
to issue license for coasting trade or fishery. 4320
may enroll and license registered vessels 4322
may register enrolled and licensed vessels .. 4322
exchange when made in another district .. 4323
to transmit surrendered enrollments, licenses, and registers to Register of Treasury 4323
to grant new license in place of one lost or destroyed 4326
to renew licenses 4326
to issue or renew enrollment or license of vessel from another district 4328
to number and record licenses, how 4333
to grant registers to enrolled or licensed vessels going abroad 4337
where vessel is in another district 4338
at Wilmington, N. C., may register, enroll, and license vessels 4342
to certify manifests of vessels trading between neighboring districts 4349
permit for unlading of vessel from neighboring district 4351
to certify manifest and permit vessels to proceed 4353
permit for unlading of vessel from remote district 4355
to certify manifest and permit vessel to proceed 4355
of Philadelphia may grant permits for land-transportation of foreign merchandise. 4362
of New York may grant, &c 4362
of Maryland or Virginia 4363
penalty for illegally enrolling or licensing vessels 4373

Section.

Collectors of Customs—Continued.
for receiving reward or gratuity for, &c ... 4373
advertisement of seizure of vessel 4379
to post conspicuously table of fees, &c 4383
when to act as shipping-commissioners 4503
shall not grant clearance to vessels not having shipping-commissioner's certificate as to effects, &c., of deceased seamen .. 4539
when, shall inspect provisions, &c., on vessels 4565
when complaint of crew reported to be false; penalty 4566
crew-list shall be furnished to 4573
shall examine and certify crew-list, shall preserve copy, &c 4574
shall report to Secretary of Treasury violations of provisions respecting crew-lists, &c 4575
duty of, as to crew-lists of arriving vessels .. 4576
shall collect hospital-tax 4585
shall not grant enrollment until hospital-tax is paid 4587
shall keep register of, and give citizenship certificates to seamen 4588
shall inform masters of vessels of the provisions of law relating to certificates of citizenship and impressments 4590
shall send list of certificates of citizenship, &c., to Secretary of State 4591
assignment to, of superintendence of light-houses, beacons, light-ships, buoys, &c.; compensation 4672
two per cent. of prize-money and salvage to be paid to, for privateer pension fund. 4759
shall deposit the two per cent. in Treasury .. 4760
to transmit transcripts from privateers' journals to Secretary of Navy 4763
discharge of vessels in quarantine 4793
to designate warehouse for storage of cargo 4793
joint custody of goods, &c 4795
to grant permits for receiving merchandise in such cases 4795
to deposit moneys collected for marine-hospital fund 4803
monthly returns of such collections 4803
not to clear foreign vessel until hospital-dues paid 4805
detention of vessel built for warlike purposes, &c 5290
in insurrectionary district, removal of custom-house 5315
may require bond before clearing vessels, that cargo, &c., shall not be used in aiding insurrection 5321

Collectors of Internal Revenue,
appointment of 3142
to give bond 3143
to act as disbursing agent when so directed. 3144
salary and commissions of 3145
further allowances in certain cases 3145
commissions of, on articles shipped in bond. 3145
annual compensation not to exceed $4,500 ... 3145
no salary unless confirmed by Senate 3145
adjustment of accounts of 3146, 3147
no payment of salary or commissions without certificate of Commissioner 3147
authorized to appoint deputies, and require bonds from them 3148
responsibility for deputies 3148
case of sickness, &c 3149
case of a vacancy in the office of 3149
may designate temporary store-keeper 3155
to supervise duties of gaugers 3156
duties of superintendent of export and drawback to devolve upon 3161

Section.
Collectors of Internal Revenue—Continued.
may have charge of exportation and drawback 3161
to administer oaths and certify papers relative to export and drawback 3162
may be suspended for fraud, &c 3163
to report violations of law to district attorneys 3164
may administer oaths and take evidence 3165
not to do duties of other collectors 3166
to cause deputies to canvass districts 3172
may summon persons to be examined relative to returns 3173
may make list or return 3176
may allow time for return 3176
may enter brewery, distillery, manufactory, &c., in day-time 3177
to reduce returns to legal-tender currency .. 3178
to collect all taxes imposed by law 3183
to give receipt for all sums collected 3183
to give demand-notice in case of neglect to pay taxes within ten days 3184
if tax not paid within ten days of service of demand-notice, to add penalty and interest 3184
to distrain in case of non-payment 3187, 3188
to make return of tax on property distrained, on which no assessment has been made 3191
to pay surplus proceeds of sale under distraint into Treasury 3192
may sell property purchased in sales under distraint 3192
to render account of charges incurred in such sales 3192
may purchase property sold under distraint, for United States 3192
may retain five per cent. commission from proceeds of sale under distraint 3193
may seize and sell real estate 3196
may seize and sell lands in any district in State 3200
to keep record of sales of real estate 3203
to deliver record to successor 3203
to make entry in record, of redemption of real estate 3204
may transmit list to district of person liable. 3209
duty on receiving list from another district. 3209
to make monthly statement of collections to Commissioner 3212
to render accounts as often as required 3212
to prosecute for recovery of sums forfeited .. 3213
failing to account 3217
proceedings against property of delinquent. 3217
what he shall be charged with 3218
what credited with 3218
transfer of lists and accounts of uncollected taxes to successor for collection 3219
to collect tax on spirits removed without deposit in warehouse, &c 3253
to retain and preserve one registry of stills, &c., and forward one to Commissioner. 3258
may refuse to approve distiller's bond 3260
may require new bond 3260
may accept bond of distiller in lieu of consent of owner of site of distillery 3262
plan of distillery, &c., how to be made 3263
survey of distillery 3264
or gauger to have charge of keys of distillery 3267
to have control of distillery warehouse 3271
to seize and sell merchandise not transferred from unsafe warehouse, &c 3272
to sign distillery-warehouse stamps 3287
delivery of spirits after withdrawal entry, and payment of tax 3294
to sign tax-paid stamps 3295

Section.
Collectors of Internal Revenue—Continued.
to account for locks and seals 3310
to send notices of distillery suspension and resumption to Commissioner 3310
duties as to suspension and resumption of work at distilleries 3310
limitation and reduction of producing capacity of distillery 3311
use of stamps for payment of tax on spirits. 3313
accountability for stamps for spirits 3314
to make monthly return of 3314
to return books of stubs to Commissioner ... 3314
commission of one-half of one per cent. on tax from spirits 3314
books of stamps, other than tax-paid, may be intrusted to gauger by 3314
to collect amount due for stamps for spirits, other than tax-paid 3314
to sign stamp for rectified spirits 3320
to sign wholesale liquor-dealer's stamp 3321
to furnish stamps for exportation of spirits without payment of tax 3330
permit for removal and transportation of spirits for exportation 3330
to obliterate, &c., tax-paid stamps on condemned spirits sold 3334
to keep two months' supply of stamps for fermented liquors 3341
to keep account of stamps sold to brewers and permits delivered 3341
permits for removal of fermented liquors 3345
stamps for malt-liquors removed 3345
permit to brewer, in case of accident, to carry on business elsewhere 3350
to approve tobacco or snuff manufacturers' bonds 3355
to issue certificate to such manufacturer .. 3355
to keep record of such manufacturers 3357
to number manufactories of tobacco and snuff 3357
to examine and verify tobacco manufacturer's inventory 3358
to make examination in case dealers in leaf-tobacco make no statements or false ones 3359
stamps for tobacco, snuff, and cigars, sold under distraint, abandoned, condemned, or forfeited, sold by order of court or Government officer 3369
to keep supply equal to three months' sales of tobacco and snuff stamps 3369
to keep account of sales 3369
to issue certificate to tobacco peddlers 3383
to issue permits for removal of tobacco, snuff, and cigars for exportation 3385
to issue certificate to cigar-manufacturer of number of cigar-makers bonded ... 3387
record of cigar-manufacturers and makers .. 3389
to examine and verify cigar-manufacturer's inventory 3390
to keep two months' supply of cigar-stamps. 3395
to keep account of sales 3395
may stamp instruments issued without proper stamps 3422
to supply deputies and others with adhesive stamps 3427
to render bonded account monthly 3444
to seize property, &c., forfeited 3453
to appraise property perishable, &c., returned to owner on bond 3459
seizure and sale 3460
Colleges,
articles imported for, free of duty 2505
alcohol may be withdrawn from bond by, for scientific purposes, without payment of tax 3297

Section.

Colombia,
salary of minister to 1675
Colonels,
of artillery regiments 1099
of cavalry regiments 1102
of infantry regiments 1106
pay of 1261
maximum pay of 1267
allowance of forage to 1271
Colonization Societies,
vessels of, subject to provisions relating to transportation of passengers 4271
Colorado Territory,
number of members of council and house of representatives of 1922
contingent executive expenses of, annual appropriation for 1935
legislative expenses of, provision for 1939
penitentiary in, care and custody of 1936
maintenance of prisoners 1937
mileage of members of assembly 1942
appointment of surveyor-general for, authorized 2207
salary of 2210
fifty per cent. addition to certain fees of registers and receivers in 2238
(see *Territories.*)
Colored Emigrants,
vessels transporting, to Africa subject to provisions as to transportation of passengers 4271
Colored Soldiers and Sailors,
bounty, prize-money, &c 2032
evidence of marriage under pension-laws ... 4705
Colored Soldiers,
enrolled as slaves to have pension 4723
retained bounty-fund of 2035, 2036
wives and children of, who deemed to be 2037
Colors,
taken by Navy from enemies, disposition of. 1554
regimental, how provided in militia 1633
Columbia Institution for Deaf and Dumb,
(see *Deaf and Dumb, Columbia Institution for.*)
Columbia River,
jurisdiction over offenses committed on 1950
Commandant of Cadets,
(see *Military Academy.*)
Commandant of Military Prison,
(see *Military Prison.*)
Commanders, (Navy,)
number of, on active list 1363
pay of 1556
Commanders of Vessels,
to furnish collectors with copy of receipts for fees paid consuls abroad 4213
Commanding Officers of Navy,
to send home men at expiration of enlistment. 1422
authorized to exercise consular powers 1433
of vessel taking prize, duties of 4615
to make claim for share in prize 4616
share in prize-money of a fleet 4631
not entitled in certain cases 4633
of division of fleet 4631
of single vessel 4631
Commerce,
laws relating to, extended over Alaska 1954
Commerce and Navigation,
statements of condition of, by whom made, and to whom submitted 251
Commercial Agents,
(see *Consuls-General, Consuls, Commercial Agents, and Consular Officers.*)
Commercial Intercourse,
when to cease between States in insurrection, &c.; forfeitures 5301
Commercial Intercourse—Continued.
in parts of State not declared to be in insurrection 5302
provisions relating to suspension of, in cases of insurrection 5303
licenses and permits by President, with part of State in insurrection 5304
Commercial Information,
Secretary of State to publish, in newspapers. 211
consular officers shall procure, &c 1712
Commercial Paper,
national banks not limited as to certain 5200
Commercial Relations,
consular officers shall furnish information respecting 1712
number of copies to be printed 3798
Commerce with Contiguous Countries,
provisions relating to 3095–3129
Commissaries of Subsistence,
jurisdiction of Court of Claims of claim by, for relief, &c 1059
when loss of funds, &c., without fault, credit to be allowed 1062
for regiments of artillery 1099
number and rank of 1140
acting assistant, pay of 1261
articles purchased from, on credit by officers 1299
by enlisted men 1300
for militia called into United States service. 1647
Commissary-General of Subsistence,
rank of 1140
President may increase, &c., bonds of 3639
Commissary Sergeants,
selection, duties, and pay of 1142
Commissary Stores,
proceeds of certain sales of, not to be covered into Treasury 3618
disposal of proceeds of, sales of, to officers .. 3692
Commission to Take Testimony,
power of Court of Claims to issue 1075
for use in courts in foreign countries, proceedings in 4071
Commissioned Officers,
pension according to rank at time of disability 4696
Commissioner of Agriculture,
appointment and salary of 521
to appoint chief clerk, and certain scientific persons 523
chief clerk to act in absence of 523
bond of 524
to have custody of property, records, &c., of Department 525
duties of 526
what seeds, plants, &c., may be purchased by 527
annual reports of 528
shall direct expenditures for his Department 3677
Commissioner of Customs,
balances certified by, in public accounts, subject to revision only by Congress and courts 191
appointment and salary of 316
duties of 317
report to Secretary of Treasury, of forms, &c. 318
reference of accounts to Court of Claims upon certificate of 1063
proceedings in such cases 1064
oaths of customs officers to be sent to 2618
to approve bonds of 2620
to report to Congress abstract of returns of. 2639
Commissioner of Education,
appointment and salary of 517
duties of 518

Section.

Commissioner of Fish and Fisheries,
how appointed ... 4395
qualifications ... 4395
salary ... 4395
Executive Departments to aid investigations of ... 4397

Commissioner of General Land-Office,
examination of accounts of, by First Comptroller ... 269
appointment and salary of ... 446
in case of vacancy or absence, how duties of, to be performed ... 448
general duties of ... 453
to have custody of seal of office ... 454
to make plats of land surveyed, and to give information to President or Congress. 455
all returns as to lands to be made to ... 456
to audit and settle all accounts relative to lands, and transmit to First Comptroller ... 456
receivers to make returns to ... 2245
to send quarterly accounts-current to ... 2245
to fix minimum price for reservations ... 2364
to approve and order contracts for surveys .. 2398
to fix price per mile for surveys ... 2400
to direct manner of keeping accounts of cost of surveys, &c., of private land-claims. 2400
may allow augmented rates for surveys in Oregon ... 2404
in California and Washington Territory .. 2405
to prescribe regulations for geodetic surveys in Oregon and California ... 2409
to make allowance for compensation for surveying in Oregon and California ... 2411

Commissioner of Indian Affairs,
(see *Indians.*)

Commissioner of Internal Revenue,
appointment and salary of ... 319
designation by, of chief clerk ... 320
duties of ... 321
statement to, by district attorneys, of suits, &c ... 774
report to, of facts, when attorney decides against prosecution for fine, &c ... 838
collector's bond, to prescribe amount of ... 3143
to prescribe further conditions to ... 3143
to certify to receipt of reports of collectors .. 3147
to prescribe notice of appointment of deputy collectors ... 3148
to prescribe fees of tobacco and cigar inspectors ... 3151
may employ and assign agents ... 3152
to determine compensation of store-keepers. 3153
to assign store-keepers to warehouses ... 3154
may transfer store-keeper ... 3154
to prescribe gaugers' fees ... 3157
may authorize officer to seize ... 3166
to prescribe form and regulations for return of taxes ... 3173
to prescribe form of notice of taxes due ... 3185
to assess tax on property distrained ... 3191
to prescribe regulations for resale of property purchased by collectors for United States ... 3192
to determine fees and charges in distraint and seizure ... 3206
to have charge of real estate ... 3208
may sell at public vendue ... 3208
may release to debtor ... 3208
to authorize suits before commencement ... 3214
to establish regulations relative to suits ... 3215
shall certify due diligence of collector to First Comptroller ... 3218
to remit taxes erroneously assessed and collected, &c ... 3220

Section.

Commissioner of Internal Revenue—Continued.
to repay to officers moneys recovered of them for official acts ... 3220
to compromise cases with consent of Secretary 3229
to make regulations for registry of death, removal, &c., of persons having paid special tax ... 3241
to adopt hydrometers, saccharometers, weighing and gauging instruments, &c ... 3249
may prescribe rules for inspection, weighing, marking, and gauging spirits ... 3249
to assess tax on spirits removed without deposit in warehouse ... 3253
to exempt distillers from fruits ... 3255
may prescribe form of notice to be given of intention to carry on business ... 3259
may require new bond of distiller ... 3260
to prescribe form of distiller's bond ... 3260
decision final on appeal by distiller from collector's refusal to approve bond ... 3260
acceptance of bonds of distiller in lieu of consent of owner of site of distillery. 3262
may prescribe manner of appraising value of site of distillery ... 3262
may order resurvey of distillery ... 3264
to prescribe manner of constructing receiving-cisterns ... 3267
to provide locks and seals at expense of United States ... 3267
may require any fastenings on still, tub, &c. 3270
may require changes of distilling apparatus, &c ... 3270
to approve distillery warehouse ... 3271
may discontinue warehouse and require transfer of merchandise ... 3272
to prescribe manner of marking spirits removed into warehouse ... 3287
to prescribe rules, &c., for deposit of spirits in warehouse ... 3293
to prescribe form of book for store-keeper's record of distillery operations ... 3302
to prescribe form of distiller's book ... 3303
to prescribe rules, &c., in cases of involuntary suspension of distillery ... 3310
to prescribe means to prevent lighting of fire, &c., in suspended distillery ... 3310
to furnish locks and seals to collector ... 3310
to prescribe precautions to reduce capacity of distillery ... 3311
to issue stamps for spirits to collectors ... 3312
to assess amount of stamps used other than tax-paid ... 3314
to prescribe rules for restamping spirits from which stamps have been lost or destroyed ... 3315
to prescribe form of rectifiers' and wholesale liquor-dealers' book ... 3318
to prescribe regulations for affixing, cancelling, and covering stamps on spirits .. 3322
to provide stamps for compound liquors, imitation wines, &c., and prescribe manner of affixing and cancelling ... 3328
to procure stamps for special taxes, and to make rules relative thereto ... 3328
to prescribe bonds, bills of lading, &c., for exportation of spirits without payment of tax, and marks for such spirits ... 3330
to prepare stamps and permits for fermented liquors ... 3341
to allow deduction on sales of stamps to brewers ... 3341
to prescribe rules for removal of fermented liquors under permit ... 3345
to prescribe manner of affixing and cancelling such permits ... 3345

Section.
Commissioner of Internal Revenue—Continued.
to prescribe rules for purchasing fermented liquors by brewers 3349
for issuing permits for brewer to conduct business elsewhere 3350
for transfer and sale of unfermented worts. 3351
to prescribe form of tobacco or snuff manufacturer's inventory 3358
of books to be kept by such manufacturers. 3358
to prescribe regulations for keeping leaf-tobacco dealer's book 3360
for packing tobacco, snuff, and cigars in wood, metal, paper, &c 3362
for sale of fine-cut shorts, refuse, sweepings, &c., of tobacco 3362
for using stamps for tobacco, snuff, and cigars, condemned, forfeited, &c 3369
to provide revenue stamps for tax on tobacco and snuff, and prescribe mode of affixing and cancelling 3369
to prescribe regulations for destruction of worthless tobacco, snuff, and cigars... 3369
for refunding taxes on tobacco, &c 3379
to prescribe bonds, bills of lading, &c., for exportation of tobacco, &c 3385
to prescribe regulations for drawback on tobacco, &c 3386
may prescribe form of bond to be given for return of goods seized 3459
of cigar-manufacturer's inventory 3390
of book to be kept by cigar-manufacturer. 3390
to prepare stamps for tax on cigars 3395
to prescribe rules for inspecting cigars, cheroots, and cigarettes, and collecting tax 3396
to prescribe form and manner of returns from banks, &c 3414
to approve private dies 3423
to describe method of cancelling adhesive stamps 3424
authorized to sell adhesive stamps and allow commission 3425
may supply stamps on credit to manufacturers of matches 3425
may regulate allowance for stamps spoiled, &c. 3426
may furnish stamps to officers for sale without prepayment 3427
may make regulations for supplying adhesive stamps 3428
for exportation of matches 3430
to assess tax on articles sold not properly stamped, and certify same to collector. 3437
to prescribe regulations for ascertaining drawback 3441
with Secretary, may change stamps, prescribe instruments, &c., for attaching, protecting, and cancelling same; also, marks and labels 3445, 3446
to dispose of forfeited spirits 3450
may pay for detecting and punishing violations 3463
shall estimate for expenses of collecting, &c. 3671
Commissioner of Patents,
appointment of 476
nominations by 476
salary of 477
bond of 479
general duties of 481
to regulate business of Patent-Office 483
to have models, &c., classified and arranged. 484
may return, &c., models on rejected applications 485
may exclude patent-agents for misconduct.. 487
may require papers to be printed at expense of party filing 488

Section.
Commissioner of Patents—Continued.
may print copies of claims, laws, decisions, &c., for public information 489
may print, and place in State capitals, &c., copies of specifications and drawings. 490
may print copies of specifications, &c., for sale 491
may fix price of copies of specifications and drawings 493
annual reports of 494
to have charge of collections of exploring expeditions 495
Commissioner of Pensions,
appointment and salary of 470
duties of 471
by whom to be performed, in case of death, resignation, or absence of 472
may appoint person to sign certificates or warrants for bounty-lands 473
to prescribe regulations for proving service by claimant for bounty-lands 2431
may prescribe additional evidence 2432, 2435
may detail clerks to investigate frauds.. 474, 4744
certificate of examining surgeons, &c., subject to approval of 4698½
duty of, as to arrears 4711
may designate persons before whom declaration may be made 4714
may suspend payment under special act 4720
shall forward certificate to agent, notice to pensioner, fees 4768
duplicate certificate of biennial examination to be filed with 4771
may require more frequent examinations ... 4772
may organize boards of examining surgeons. 4774
may require boards to make special examinations 4775
medical referee to be under direction of 4776
shall fix attorneys' fees 4785
duplicate articles of agreement to be filed with, &c 4786
shall cause commutation for artificial limbs, &c., to be paid 4789
Commissioners, Diplomatic,
shall be deemed diplomatic officers 1674
compensation of 1676
term for which payable 1740
Commissioners, District Court,
appointment of, to swear appraisers of vessels or goods, seized for breaches of law... 570
Commissioners of Circuit Courts,
how appointed, powers of 627
no marshal or deputy marshal to be, or exercise duties of 628
may enforce awards of consuls, &c., in differences between captains and crews 728
accounts of, to be certified by district judge. 846
fees of 847
when United States liable, how paid 856
in other cases, how recovered 857
taxation of witness fees in criminal case 981
bill of fees of, how proven before taxed or allowed 984
may administer oaths and take acknowledgments 1778
to institute prosecutions under civil-rights laws 1982
number of, may be increased 1983
power of, in civil-rights cases 1983
may appoint persons to execute process.. 1984
powers of persons so appointed 1984
warrants of, where to run 1984
fees of, in civil-rights cases 1986
fees of appointees to execute process 1987
chief supervisors of election to be appointed from 2025

Section.

Commissioners of Circuit Courts—Continued.
may summon master of vessel in cases of seamen's wages 4546
Commissioners, Prize,
(see *Prize*.)
Commissioners, Railroad,
payment of, by corporations receiving land-grants or subsidies 5259
Commissioners of Territorial Courts,
fees of 1833
number of, may be increased, for protection of civil rights 1983
Commissions,
of marshals of fines on militia 1660
of registers and receivers 2238
of collectors, and surveyors acting as collectors, of customs 2659, 2663, 2664, 2667, 2675, 2682, 2683, 2685, 2720
to be accounted for 2644
on bonded goods to be divided between collector resigning and his successor who collects them 2686
included in maximum compensation 2688
of naval officers of customs 2704
of surveyors of customs 2720
of collector of internal revenue 3145
to be apportioned, in case of two or more in same year 3147
no payment of, without certificate of Commissioner 3147
on distilled spirits 3314
in cases of distraint 3193
on adhesive stamps sold 3425
on stamps from private dies 3425
internal-revenue officers to make statement of, when required 3158
to brewers on sales of stamps 3341
amount of sales of stamps to brewers to be included in estimating, of collector .. 3341
allowance of, to marshal in the disposal of prize property 4645
to auctioneer making sale of prize property 4650
of assignee in bankruptcy 5100
(see *Fees*.)
Commissions and Inquiries,
expenses of, to be paid only from special appropriations therefor 3681
Commissions, Official,
to revenue officers, where made, &c., how sealed and signed 238
President to deliver, after adjournment of Senate, to officers confirmed 1773
civil, made and recorded by Secretary of State; affixing of seal 1794
Committees of Congress,
Court of Claims to have use of reports of .. 1076
Commodores,
number of, on active list 1363
pay of 1556
Common Carrier,
to carry merchandise entered for immediate transportation in bond; bond of 2993
vehicles of, not forfeited in certain cases under customs laws 3063
non-liability for gold, bullion, jewelry, &c., on steamers 4281
for loss by fire on steamers 4282
limit on liability for merchandise lost on steamers 4283
transfer of interest to trustees for benefit of shippers 4285
after such transfer proceedings against owner to cease 4285
charterer of vessel deemed owner 4286

Section.

Common Carrier—Continued.
remedies against masters, owners, &c., for embezzlement, negligence, fraud, &c., reserved 4287
provisions of Title XLVIII not applicable to canal-boats, &c., or vessels in river or inland navigation 4289
Common Law,
jurisdiction of district courts of suits at, brought by United States or any officer. 563
remedies of, not excluded by admiralty jurisdiction of district courts 563
jurisdiction of circuit courts of suits at, where United States or officer is plaintiff 629
Companies, Incorporated,
(see *Incorporated Companies* and *Corporations*.)
Compensation,
for double duties or extra services 1764
of marshals, for care, &c., of territorial penitentiaries 1893, 1894
statement of, by internal-revenue officers, when composed, wholly or in part, of fees 3158
estimates for, shall be founded on express provisions of law 3662
not to be paid from contingent, &c., appropriations 3682
appropriation for, of employés in customs service 3687
of southern claims commission 3689
of steamboat inspectors 3689
of persons employed in plate and seal engraving and printing of money in Treasury 3689
of persons employed in insurrectionary States, (internal-revenue) 3689
of Kansas military organizations 3689
for payment of tax on salaries and 3689
of California and Nevada volunteers, for travelling expenses 3689
for allowance for reduction of, under eight-hour law 3689
of persons employed in Smithsonian Institution 3689
of postmasters 3852–3857
postal accounts to show expenditures for, of postmasters 4049
of letter-carriers 4049
of blank-agents and assistants 4049
of clerks 4049
of marshals of consular courts 4111
for conveyance of mails by vessels to or from foreign ports 4203
of United States securities 4204
in prize cases to clerk of district court 4644
to district attorney and prize commissioner. 4646
maximum 4647
of special counsel 4648
of assignee in bankruptcy 5099
commissions allowed to 5100
(see *Salaries*, *Fees*.)
Company,
term, includes what 5
Complaint,
for warrant of district judge, in customs cases, what to set forth 3092
of offenses against navigation laws, how made 4301
to be read to accused 4301
plea or answer to 4301
Compound-Interest Notes,
legal tender for face except 3590
Compound Liquors,
tax on 3328

Section.

Compound-Liquor Stamps,
(see *Stamps.*)

Compromise,
in internal-revenue cases 3229
of claims in favor of United States 3469

Comptroller of Currency,
to be chief officer of Currency Bureau 324
appointment, term of office, and salary 325
oath and bond of 326
employment of clerks by 328
not to be interested in national banks 329
seal of office of 330
examination of banks of District of Columbia by, and report on, to Congress 332
annual report by, to Congress 333
jurisdiction of the circuit courts of all suits by national banking associations to enjoin, &c. 629
proceedings by national bank to enjoin, in what district shall be had 736
papers sealed, &c., and copies certified, &c., in office of, received in evidence 884
copy of articles of association of banks to be sent to 5133
title assumed by banks subject to approval of 5134
organization certificate to be sent to, &c 5135
banks not to begin business of banking until authorized by 5136
payments of instalments on stock to be certified to 5140
increase of stock to be valid only on his approval 5142
decrease of stock to be approved by 5143
oaths of directors to be sent to, &c 5147
shall determine as to capital, surplus of certain State banks, &c.; when may compel bank to close 5151
shall receipt for bonds deposited by banks .. 5162
shall keep a register of bonds transferred by Treasurer 5163
shall notify banks of transfers, &c 5164
shall have access to books of Treasurer, &c. 5165
comparison of bonds of banks with books of. 5166
collection of interest on bonds, additional bonds, exchange of bonds, returning bonds on surrender of circulation, &c. 5167
shall satisfy himself of correctness of organization of banks, &c 5168
may permit banks to commence business ... 5169
issuance of circulation to national banks ... 5171
shall cause notes to be engraved, &c 5172
shall have custody of plates, &c 5173
annual examination of plates, &c 5174
equalization of apportionment of circulation. 5180
removal of banks from one State to another. 5181
shall replace worn-out notes 5184
when shall issue gold-notes to banks 5185
to notify banks to make good reserve; when may appoint receiver, &c 5191
selection of redemption agencies; when may appoint receiver 5195
shall require banks to make good impaired capital; proceedings on refusal 5205
list of shareholders to be sent to 5210
reports to be made to; may call for special reports 5211
dividend reports shall be sent to 5212
may levy fine for failure to make reports ... 5213
vote to go into liquidation shall be certified to 5221
duty of, on failure to redeem notes 5226
appointment of receivers 5234
shall give notice of 5235
dividends to creditors of banks 5236

Section.

Comptroller of Currency—Continued.
may be enjoined in proceedings against banks 5237
forfeiture of franchises to be at suit of 5239
may appoint occasional examiners, pay, &c., of 5240

Comptrollers of Treasury,
balance certified by, in public accounts, subject to revision only by Congress and courts 191
reference of certain accounts to Court of Claims upon certificate of 1063
proceedings in such cases 1064
duty as to fines assessed against militia in United States service 1660
to certify accounts of disbursing-officers failing to account, and pay over balances. 3633
(see *First Comptroller* and *Second Comptroller.*)

Concealed Debtor,
claims of United States against, to have priority in cases of attachment 3466

Conception,
articles to prevent, not to be imported 2491

Concurrent Jurisdiction,
Oregon and Washington to have, over offenses on Columbia River 1950

Condemnation,
jurisdiction of district courts of proceedings for, in cases of capture as prize under Title INSURRECTION 563
of circuit courts 629
proceedings of district court after appeal from decree of, in prize causes 565
proceedings after, of vessels, &c., seized under customs laws 939
may be had before judge in vacation 940
of property taken as prize, on account of use, in aid of rebellion 5308
proceedings for 5309, 5311
claims of loyal creditors to be provided for. 5322

Condemned Property,
certain proceeds of sale of, to be deposited and covered into Treasury 3618
certain, not to be 3618
disposal of proceeds of, not deposited and covered in 3692
horses, when to be paid for 3485
proceeds of sale of, to be stated in book of estimates 3672
condemned vessels, extra wages not required for seamen discharged from 4583

Confederate States,
collection of moneys, &c., due to 3755

Confiscation,
of property taken as prize, on account of use, in aid of insurrection 5308
proceedings for 5309, 5311

Congress,
fuel for, by whom provided 73
debates of, to be printed 78
Delegates to, in Territories 1862
engravings for documents ordered by, to be printed 3779
printing and binding for, where to be done. 3786
on whose requisition 3789
regular number of bills, &c., to be printed. 3791
"usual number" of documents ordered by, to be printed 3792
number to be printed of certain documents. 3798
of acts, resolutions, and treaties 3807
bribery of officers of 5451
penalty on member of, for accepting bribe .. 5502

Congressional Directory,
compilation of 77

Section.

Congressional Printer,
Congressional debates to be printed by..... 78
qualifications and election of.............. 3758
salary and bond of.......................... 3759
general duties of........................... 3760
appointment of foremen of printing and binding.......................... 3761
clerks...................................... 3762
employés.................................... 3763
printing at night........................... 3764
advertisement for proposals for paper....... 3767
proceedings in case of default of contractor for paper....................3775, 3777
purchase of paper in open market............ 3778
engravings, &c., for maps, diagrams, &c. 3779, 3780
lithographing maps for Land-Office report.. 3781
to preserve samples of paper for engravings, and enforce compliance with contract, &c.. 3782
to charge himself with and be accountable for material............................ 3783
form and style of printing and binding, &c., for Departments.......................... 3790
copies of documents in addition to "usual number,"..................................... 3796
to keep account with each Department, of printing, &c., not to exceed appropriation.................................... 3802
printing of acts, resolutions, &c., under direction of Secretary of State.......3805, 3806
extra copies of documents to private persons...................................... 3809
delivery of report of Secretary of Treasury on national banks....................... 3811
estimates of, to Register of Treasury....... 3814
quarterly account to Secretary of Treasury. 3815
advances of money to........................ 3816
settlement of accounts...................... 3817
deposit of moneys received from sales....... 3818
monthly statements to, by foremen........... 3819

Connecticut,
collection-districts, ports of entry and delivery in...................................... 2533
officers in................................. 2534

Consignee,
in Alaska, bond on landing of arms, &c.... 1955
of imported goods, bond for production of invoice..................................... 2848
deemed to be owner.......................... 3058

Consignees of Vessels,
penalty on, of vessel carrying away live-oak or red-cedar timber from lands reserved by United States......................... 2462
to cause to be indorsed on certificate of record change of name or master of vessel.. 4183
to furnish collectors copy of receipts for fees paid to consuls........................... 4213
when may perform duties of shipping-commissioners.................................. 4504

Consolidated Land Districts,
additional fees to registers and receivers of. 2239

Consolidation,
deposits to redeem circulation, by national banks winding up for purpose of..... 5223

Conspiracy,
of revenue officer with others to defraud.... 3169
to defraud United States by false or fraudulent claims by persons not in military or naval service, action for........... 3490
by any person, punishment for.............. 5438

Constables,
allowance for hire of, &c., at ports in China and Japan..........................4122, 4123
may assist in arresting seamen deserters... 4599

Section.

Constantinople,
consul-general at, to be secretary of legation. 1677
salary of................................... 1690

Constitution of United States,
force and effect of, in Territories......... 1891

Construction and Repair,
relative rank and title of Chief of Bureau.. 1471
of retired Chief of Bureau................. 1473

Consular Agents,
(see *Consuls General, Consuls, &c.*)

Consular Certificate,
as to prices of articles purchased for Navy on foreign stations........................ 3723

Consular Clerks,
(see *Consuls General, Consuls, &c.*)

Consular Courts,
marshals of, number and appointment of... 4111
their salary and fees...................... 4111
bond of................................... 4113
suits upon.............................. 4114
production of original.................. 4115
fees for judicial services, tariff of........ 4120
by and to whom payable.................... 4120
proceeds, how applied..................... 4120
regulation of accounts.................... 4120
prisons, allowance for expenses of.......... 4121
limit to allowance for.................... 4121
number of, authorized...................... 4121
ports at which may be hired............... 4121
limit to expenses of, at Bangkok.......... 4121
allowance for, at Shanghai................ 4122
for hire of constables, &c., at other ports in China............................ 4122
for rent of prison, &c., at Kanagawa... 4123
for constables, &c., at other ports in Japan................................. 4123
for court-house and jail at Jeddo....... 4124
words "minister" and "consul" to include what officers............................ 4130

Consular Fees,
(see *Fees, Consular.*)

Consuls-General, Consuls, Consular Officers, and Commercial Agents,
jurisdiction of district courts in suits against. 563
enforcement of awards of foreign, between masters and crews......................... 728
title includes what.....................1674, 4130
general provisions respecting...........1689–1739
application of provisions of Title XVIII to.. 1689
appointment, salaries, and locations of...... 1690
consuls-general may be appointed instead of consuls, and consuls instead of commercial agents, and *vice versa*.......... 1690
not to hold two consulates.................. 1691
interpreters to, in China, salaries, &c., of... 1692
at Bangkok, salary, &c., of............... 1693
at Trinidad de Cuba may be discontinued, and appointed at Cienfuegos.......... 1694
territory of consulate to be defined, appointment of vice-consuls, deputies, &c., salaries of............................ 1695
allowances to vice-consulates, &c........... 1696
bonds of..............................1697, 1698
certain, not to transact business, &c........ 1699
where salary exceeds $1,000, not to transact business; prohibition may be extended to any consul, &c...................... 1700
penalty for illegally transacting business, recovery................................ 1701
compensation where fees exceed $3,000..... 1702
compensation of deputies, vice-consuls, &c. 1703
consular clerks, appointment, &c., of....... 1704
examination and removal of.............. 1705
expenses of office-rent..................... 1706
may receive protests or declarations, copies of, to be evidence....................... 1707

Section.

Consuls-General, Consuls, Consular Officers, and Commercial Agents—Continued.
record of seamen, vessels, &c. 1708
estates of deceased Americans 1709
shall publish, &c., notice of deaths 1710
shall procure and transmit commercial information 1712
shall furnish Treasury Department with prices-current 1713
shall not certify invoices unless, &c 1715
fee for certifying invoices, penalty for excessive fees 1716
not to grant certificate for goods from countries adjacent to United States, when they have passed a consulate after purchase 1717
shall be paid legal fees; liability of masters, &c., for; papers may be retained until paid 1718
shall not receive fees, &c., from extra wages, &c., of seamen 1719
fees from vessel making regular trips 1720
for certifying invoices in British North American provinces 1721
in Canada not to collect tonnage-fees . . . 1722, 4222
penalty for exacting excessive fees, recovery . 1723
penalty for failure to collect fees, remission . 1724
shall make returns of fees 1725
shall give receipt for fees 1726
shall number and record receipts 1727
transcript of fee-book with accounts of 1728
not mentioned in Schedules B and C, shall account for fees 1729
shall have fees for compensation 1730
shall keep fee-list conspicuously posted in consulate 1731
not mentioned in Schedules B and C, limit of fees to 1732
fees in excess of $1,000 a year 1733
penalty for embezzlement by 1734
for neglect of duty 1735
to seamen 1736
performance of diplomatic functions 1738
pay when performing 1739
salaries of, term for which payable 1740
when absent from post, &c 1742
compensation of, to be in full payment for services, &c 1743
no compensation to certain consuls-general if not citizens 1744
President may regulate fees and salaries 1745
tariff of fees to be reported to Congress 1745
fees to be collected in United States coin or its value in exchange 1746
to be accounted for 1747
stationery, &c., to be furnished to 1748
dying abroad, allowance to widow, &c. 1749
President may make regulations, &c., governing 1752
in China, Japan, &c., to give certificates of voluntary emigration 2162
what to state in certificate 2162
to be personally satisfied by evidence before giving 2162
certificate on declaration of American artist abroad 2505
oaths to invoices 2843–2845
authentications by foreign 2844
fees for verification of invoices 2851
invoices, when to be produced to 2854
declaration of persons producing, and duty of 2855
invoices of merchandise from countries adjacent to United States 2856
when to transmit to collector of customs certified copy of invoice 2857

Section.

Consuls-General, Consuls, Consular Officers, and Commercial Agents—Continued.
when not to grant certificates to invoices in customs cases 2861
to exact proof of invoice 2862
to report fraudulent verification of invoice . . 2863
certificate of landing of goods abroad, oath of master 3045
fees for administering oath and granting such certificates; forfeiture for excessive fees 3046
may require mails to be carried in vessels bound for the United States 3976
may pay postage on letters held in foreign countries 4014
registry of vessels owned by 4133, 4134
when merchant-seamen shall be engaged in presence of, &c 4517
penalty for illegally engaging merchant-seamen where there are 4518
table of fees to be attached to clearances of registered vessels 4207
copy of receipts given for fees, to be furnished collector on entry 4213
duties of, in protecting vessels stranded on foreign shores 4238
restriction of authority when master, owner, or consignee present 4238
to return papers to vessels on production of clearance 4309
seamen to be engaged in presence of 4517
duty of, respecting effects, &c., of deceased seamen 4539, 4541
seamen's wages paid by direction of, to be in gold 4548
shall cause survey of vessels on proper complaint 4559
approval by, of report of survey 4560
may discharge crew with extra wages 4561
shall certify charges for survey, &c 4562
inspection of provisions, &c., on merchant-vessels 4565
complaint found to be false; penalty 4566
may demand crew-list and shipping-articles . 4575
discharge of seamen by, not to forfeit bond of master 4576
destitute seamen, to provide for return to United States of 4577
may require masters to carry 4578
at ports where there is no consular officer . 4579
may discharge seamen and require extra wages 4580
penalty for neglect to require such wages . . . 4581
extra wages on sale of vessel 4582
when may remit 4583
how to dispose of 4584
shall collect hospital-tax on vessels sold 4586
reclamation of deserters; discharge of deserters with extra wages 4600
pension declarations may be made before . . . 4714
two per cent. for privateer pension fund to be paid to 4759
to be deposited in Treasury 4760
penalty for falsely certifying papers 5442

Consular Receipts,
appropriation to return to heirs proceeds of estates, &c 3689

Consular Regulations,
President may make, shall be obeyed 1752

Consular Service,
officers of Army and Navy forbidden to enter 1223, 1440

Consular Territory,
may be defined, consular agencies, &c. 1695

Section.

Consulate,
goods having passed in adjacent countries, after purchase for shipment, not to be certified by consular officer....... 1717, 2861

Contingent Expenses,
of Senate, when paid, how moneys appropriated for, disbursed.................... 56
of Senate and House, restrictions on use of appropriations for.................... 3680
of pension-agents, allowances for........... 4781

Contingent Funds,
of Senate and House, payments from, how regulated.............................. 76
of House, expenses of contested elections not to be paid out of..................... 130
of Departments, annual report of expenditure of, to contain what............... 193
of Department of State, annual report of expenditures of, to contain what........ 209
of Mint, transfer of bullion to be paid from.. 3553
shall not be used for compensation of clerks, &c................................ 3682
of Departments, restriction as to use of, for purchases............................ 3683

Continuance,
when granted in suits or criminal proceedings under internal-revenue laws.... 3231

Contraband of War,
for Navy, purchased without advertising, &c. 3721

Contractors,
for carrying mail, statement of account of, certified by Sixth Auditor, received in evidence............................ 889
for furnishing goods, &c., to Indians, restriction on payment to.................. 2107
for carrying mail to foreign countries, may be fined, &c............................ 4010

Contracts,
with Post-Office Department, form of........ 403
for carrying mail, duplicates of, to be delivered to Sixth Auditor................ 404
no person in Post-Office Department to be interested in.......................... 412
made by Secretaries of War, Navy, and Interior, to be filed in returns office....... 512
members of Congress and public officers accepting consideration for procuring; penalty.............................. 1781
receiving compensation for services relating to, before Department or commission; penalty........................ 1782
for surveys to be approved by Commissioner General Land-Office.................. 2398
what instructions to be deemed a part of.... 2399
construction of, when payable in pounds sterling............................ 3565
construction of, in metric equivalents of United States weights and measures..... 3570
limit as to payments on, with United States.. 3648
not to be made in excess of appropriations.. 3679
for supplies, to be advertised for........... 3709
of Navy Department, when reservations on, may be relinquished.................. 3730
not to be in excess of appropriations, except in War and Navy Departments....... 3732
for public buildings and improvements not to exceed appropriations.............. 3733
with United States shall not be transferred. 3737
what ones to be deposited in office of First Comptroller......................... 3743
for collection, &c., of abandoned, &c., property.............................. 3755
for paper for Government Printing-Office... 3767–3778
for engraving and lithographing for Government Printing-Office............ 3779–3782

Contracts—Continued.
what advertisements for, to be made in District of Columbia.................. 3826
for apparatus or buildings, &c., for light-house service...................... 4665
for materials for construction or repair of light-houses, beacons, buoys, &c...... 4666
for erection of light-houses................ 4667
knowingly making, to pay for erection, or repair of public building, amount larger than appropriated.................. 5503

for carrying mail,
advertising for bids for................... 3941
with railways............................. 3942
with steamboats, &c....................... 3943
shall be awarded to lowest bidder; except... 3949
failure to enter into, proceedings on......... 3951
certified check as guarantee of proposal..... 3953
limit of term of............................ 3956
omission of route from advertisement for... 3957
change of, proceedings on.................. 3958
payment on.............................. 3959
additional services under.................. 3960
allowance for increased expedition under... 3961
deductions from pay under................. 3962
assignments of, void...................... 3963
through foreign countries may be made, revocation, indemnity.................... 4006
to foreign countries may be made............ 4007
special stipulations in...................... 4011

with Indians,
(see *Indian Contracts*.)

Contract Surgeons,
when to have pension...................... 4693
rate of total-disability pension to........... 4695
pension to dependent relative of, when to begin.............................. 4710

Contributions,
not to be required or requested of employés of yards for political purposes......... 1546

Convention,
attempting to negotiate with Indians, except for United States, penalty............. 2116

Conversion to his own use,
of public moneys, by disbursing officer...... 5488
by person charged with safe-keeping..... 5490
what shall constitute..................... 5496

Conveyances,
by Indians of lands, titles, or claims to be void.................................. 2116
of vessel not valid unless recorded.......... 4192
to be recorded by collectors of customs.... 4193
certificates discharging, to be recorded.... 4193
what record to be kept in books.......... 4193
what to be certified on.................. 4193
fee for recording..................... 4193, 4382
not to be recorded until acknowledged, &c. 4193
collectors to keep index of records of..... 4194
index and record of, to be open to inspection.............................. 4194
collectors to furnish certificates relating to. 4194
fee for furnishing such certificate........ 4194
fee for furnishing certified copy of record. 4194

Convicts,
military prison for, established.............. 1344
sentenced under territorial laws, may be received in penitentiaries.................. 1895

Conviction,
of seamen and punishment inflicted to be entered in log-book...................... 4290

Cooking-Range,
for vessel carrying other than cabin-passengers between Europe and United States.............................. 4258
penalty for failure to provide................ 4259

Section.

Cooly-Trade,
building or equipping vessels for, prohibited. 2158
forfeiture of vessel, &c., employed in. 2159
penalty for building or fitting out, &c. 2160
penalty for receiving or transporting coolies. 2161
voluntary emigration from Oriental countries not affected. 2162
certificate of, to be given by consular officer 2162
examination of vessel suspected. 2163
disposal of vessel found engaged in. 2163
Coosa River, Ala.,
tolls on. 5244
Coos Bay, Oreg.,
port of entry. 2586
Copano, Tex.,
port of delivery. 2578
surveyor to reside at. 2579
Copartnerships,
to pay but one special tax. 3234
Copies,
of papers in General Land Office, duty of Secretary of Interior to furnish; authentication of. 460
duty of Commissioner to furnish; fees for. 461
of books, records, papers, in Executive Departments, when evidence. 882
in office of Solicitor of Treasury. 883
in office of Comptroller of Currency. 884
of organization certificate of national bank, when evidence. 885
of bonds, contracts, &c., annexed to Treasury transcripts, when evidence. 886
of any return in returns office of Interior Department, when evidence. 888
of postmaster's return, when evidence. 889
of papers in office of Sixth Auditor, when evidence. 889
of statement of postmaster or special agent, that he had mailed letter of demand to delinquent postmaster, when evidence. 890
Copper Coins,
how redeemed. 3529
Copper-Nickel Coins,
how redeemed. 3529
Copyright,
custody, &c., of records and other things relating to, required by law to be preserved. 4948
general duty of Librarian of Congress as to. 4948
fees. 4958
Cordials,
manufacture of, in bonded warehouse for exportation without stamps. 3433
Cork,
consul at, salary of. 1690
Corporals,
for battery of artillery. 1100
troop of cavalry. 1103
company of infantry. 1107
Corporations,
included in "persons". 1
proceedings by United States against debtors of, as garnishees. 935–937
no officer or agent of, to act as officer or agent of United States in transactions with same. 1783
religious, &c., in Territories, limit to power of, to hold real estate. 1890
when real estate of, forfeited. 1890
fee to be paid on location of land-grants by. 2238
unlawful re-issue, or uttering, as money, by officer, agent, &c., of bills, &c., of expired corporation created by United States. 5437
(see *Incorporated Companies.*)

Section.

Corporators of Smithsonian Institution,
(see *Smithsonian Institution.*)
Corps of Engineers,
(see *Engineer Corps.*)
Corpus Christi, Tex.,
collection district and port of entry. 2578
collector in, to reside at. 2579
Corrected Proof-sheet,
third-class mail-matter. 3878
Costa Rica,
minister resident at. 1682
(see *Gautemala.*)
Cosmetics,
manufacture of, in bonded warehouse for exportation without stamps. 3433
imported, to be stamped. 3435
tax on, (see SCHEDULE A). 3437
Costs,
when United States not subject to, in suits under internal-revenue laws. 969
not allowed claimant, in cases of seizure with probable cause. 970
when double costs allowed defendant, in action against officer, &c., making seizure under impost laws, &c. 971
of prosecution for fine or forfeiture, to be paid by defendant when judgment against him. 974
for other offenses not capital, to be paid at discretion of court. 974
when informer is liable for defendant's costs. 975
what, to be allowed on several libels against vessel and cargo which might have been joined. 978
on several libels or informations against cargo, &c., seized as forfeited for same cause. 978
claimant of property seized, &c., to pay his own costs before possession given, on recovering judgment, &c. 979
only one bill of, to be paid district attorney for several suits, prosecutions, &c., which should be joined. 980
bill of, in favor of clerk, marshal, district attorney, or commissioner, how verified and proven, before being taxed or allowed. 984
bond for, not given when error or appeal taken by United States or Departments. 1001
what, payable from contingent fund of Department. 1001
when single or double, may be allowed to respondent in error. 1010
what portions, in certain cases of revenue seizures and sales, to be applied to payment of. 3089
of internal-revenue suits, United States not subject to, in certain cases. 3214
in suits for making false claims against United States. 3493
in prize cases, security may be required for. 4638
to be paid from proceeds of property. 4639
court may order payment, when. 4640
when to order final payment. 4640
payable by the United States, when. 4640
in bankruptcy proceedings, justices of Supreme Court to regulate. 4990
to have priority in order for dividend. 5101
to be paid in full. 5101
expenses of register to form part of. 5125
Cotton,
loose, not to be carried on steam passenger-vessels. 4472
baled, how to be secured when so carried. 4472
penalty for carrying, contrary to law. 4473

Section.

Cotton and Cotton Goods,
customs duties on 2504
thread, yarn, warps, &c. 2504
spool-thread 2504
cords, gimps, &c., and other manufactures of. 2504
of different qualities in same package, how appraised 2911

Councils, Legislative,
in Territories, of what numbers to consist .. 1922

Counsel,
special, to aid district attorneys 363
for Departments to be provided by Attorney General 364
compensation of 365
appointment, commission, oath 366
names and compensation to be reported to Congress 385
in prize causes, may be employed by Secretary of Navy 4620
compensation to be allowed by court 4648
when no allowance to be made 4648
fees of, to be paid out of what fund 4649

Counter-Claim,
jurisdiction of Court of Claims of on part of United States 1059
enforcement of judgments of Court of Claims for, in favor of United States 1061

Counterfeiting,
wine or compound-liquor stamps 3328
stamp, &c., for fermented liquors 3346
stamp from private dies 3423
adhesive stamps 3429
"obligation or other security of the United States" 5414
note in imitation of national-bank note 5415
certificate of entry required by customs laws. 5417
bid, proposal, guarantee, official bond, public record, &c., to defraud United States 5418, 5479
military bounty-land warrant, &c 5420
deed, power of attorney, order, receipt, &c., to obtain money, &c., from United States 5421
fraudulently having in possession false deed, power of attorney, &c 5422
abstract, official copy, or certificate of registry, or enrollment of, or license to vessel, passport, sea-letter, clearance, permit, debenture, &c 5423
coin or bars in similitude of coin or bars coined or stamped at United States Mint or assay offices, or of foreign coin current in United States 5457
coin in similitude of minor coinage of United States 5458

County,
includes what 2

County Courts, Territorial,
may be held by justices of supreme court ... 1874
what cases may be tried in 1874
expenses, how payable 1874

County Officers, Territorial,
how appointed or elected 1857

Coupon Bonds,
provisions concerning duplicate for lost, &c. 3702, 3703
registered bonds in exchange for 3706
belonging to national banks to be exchanged for registered 5161

Coupons,
imitating or printing, &c., on, to be punished. 3708
on stamps for payment of tax on spirits 3313
all unused, to remain attached to stub 3313
no value when detached from stamp and stub. 3313
included by words "obligation or other security of the United States" 5413

Section.

Court-Houses,
mail shall be carried to, &c 3966
at or near Jeddo, in Japan, rent of, &c., authorized 4124
limit to annual cost of 4124
term and renewals of lease 4124

Court of Claims,
when evidence to be furnished to, by Departments 188
appeals from judgments of 707, 708
judges of, appointment, tenure of office, oath, salary 1049
clerks, bailiff, and messenger of, appointment and removal 1053
salaries of clerks, bailiff, and messenger 1054
bond of chief clerk of 1055
contingent fund of 1056
chief clerk of, to transmit statement of judgments to Congress, and decisions to heads of Departments, &c 1057
general jurisdiction of 1059
when and how private claims before Congress transmitted to 1060
judgment of, in favor of United States, on set-off, &c., how enforced against claimant 1061
decree of, finding loss of funds, &c., by paymaster, &c., to be without fault; credit by accounting officer 1062
reference to, by Departments, of claims and accounts 1063
proceedings in such claims or accounts ... 1064
judgments or decrees in, how paid 1065
jurisdiction of, not to extend to claims growing out of treaty stipulations 1066
when suit pending in another court, claim not to be prosecuted in 1067
nor in Supreme Court on appeal 1067
aliens may prosecute claims in 1068
limitation on suits in 1069
may appoint commissioners to take testimony, and to issue commissions, &c .. 1075
may call upon Departments for information or papers 1076
fees of commissioners appointed by 1085
judgment by, of forfeiture of claim by fraud. 1086
new trial granted by 1088
judgment in favor of claimant, how paid ... 1089
interest on 1090
to operate as a discharge, &c 1092
against claimant, a bar 1093
when interest before judgment allowed by .. 1091
railroad company may sue in, for freight or transportation withheld by Secretary of Treasury 5261

Courts of Bankruptcy,
justices of Supreme Court to prescribe rules, &c., for 4990
(see *Bankruptcy.*)

Courts-Martial, (Army,)
reporter to 1203

Courts-Martial, (Militia,)
how composed 1658
fines against militia in United States service, how certified to marshals and Comptroller of Treasury 1659

Courts-Martial, (Navy,)
may inflict loss of pay 1624

Courts of United States,
when to have exclusive jurisdiction 711
salary of judges after resigning 714
may require production of books, &c., in actions at law; judgment on non-compliance 724
deposit of moneys paid into, or to officer of. 995
how withdrawn from deposit 996

Section

Courts of United States—Continued.
penalty on judge of, for accepting bribe.... 5502
failure of clerk, &c., of, to deposit moneys; conversion, &c., of same.............. 5504
knowingly receiving from clerk, &c., of, as deposit, loan, &c., moneys........... 5505
Courts, Territorial,
(see *Supreme, District,* and *Probate Courts.*)
Credit,
payment for purchases on, by Army officers. 1299
by enlisted men of Army................ 1300
not allowed to purchasers of public lands.. 2356
Creditors in Bankruptcy,
may require bond of assignee to United States.................................. 5036
Crew,
maltreating of, on American vessel......... 5347
Crew-Lists,
to be furnished by master before clearance.. 4573
to be examined and certified by collector of customs.............................. 4574
rules respecting duplicate................. 4575
discharge of seamen deserters by consul, &c., to be entered on................. 4600
Criers,
appointment of, by circuit and district courts; compensation of............... 715
Crimes and Offenses,
jurisdiction over, of district courts........ 563
of circuit courts........................ 629
courts of United States to have exclusive cognizance of, against United States. 711
committed on high seas, where tried....... 730
begun in one district and completed in another, where tried and punished...... 731
duty of distict attorneys to prosecute delinquents for........................ 771
costs, on conviction for, not capital........ 974
pardon or remission of one or two punishments................................ 5330
causing death on steamboat, &c., by negligence.................................. 5344
maltreating crew of American vessel....... 5347
nitro-glycerine, &c., transporting in passenger-vessel............................ 5353
without proper marks.................... 5355
causing death by explosion of............ 5354
plundering vessel in distress, wrecked, &c.. 5358
forcing officer or mariner on shore, leaving him in foreign port, &c.............. 5363
"obligation or other security of United States," what included in, in Title CRIMES.............................. 5413
counterfeiting, altering, &c., such obligation or security...................... 5414
national-bank circulation-notes.......... 5415
certificate of entry of goods.............. 5417
bid, guarantee, official bond, &c.....5418, 5479
bounty-land warrant, certificate of purchase, location, &c................... 5420
deed, power of attorney, certificate, receipt, &c............................ 5421
having in possession counterfeited deed, &c., with intent to defraud United States. 5422
counterfeiting, altering, &c., certificate of registry, enrollment, license, passport, sea-letter, clearance, permit, debenture, &c., of vessel.................. 5423
unlawfully using genuine plates, &c., for printing United States obligations, &c.................................. 5430
unlawfully engraving plate, &c., in likeness of plate designed for printing United States obligations, &c............... 5430
having in possession, &c., such plate..... 5430

Section.

Crimes and Offenses—Continued.
printing, engraving, &c., in likeness of United States obligation.............. 5430
bringing into United States such plate or engraving, &c........................ 5430
uttering counterfeited, &c., United States obligations.......................... 5431
taking impression from implement for printing United States obligations........ 5432
having in possession such impression....... 5433
buying, selling, &c., counterfeited United States obligations.................... 5434
national-bank notes..................... 5434
personation of holder of public stocks or person entitled to pension, prize-money, &c............................... 5435
demanding public stocks, or pension, prize-money, &c, under forged, &c., power of attorney......................... 5436
director or officer uttering as money bills of of expired corporation............... 5437
presenting claim against United States, knowing it to be false, &c........... 5438
using false voucher, &c, to obtain payment, &c., of claim against United States.. 5438
conspiring to defraud United States by obtaining payment, &c., of fraudulent claim................................. 5438
delivering less money or property for military or naval use than described in receipt or voucher for................ 5438
giving receipt or voucher, &c., for property for military or naval use, without knowing truth thereof, and with intent to defraud United States........ 5438
purchasing, &c., from soldier, officer, sailor, &c., not having right to sell, &c., arms, equipments, stores, &c.......... 5438
defrauding captor, or claimant of prize, or United States, relative to such property, or to documents.................. 5441
consul, &c., falsely certifying invoice...... 5442
concealing or destroying invoice, &c., of goods imported, &c.................. 5443
officer admitting goods on payment of less than lawful duty..................... 5444
effecting entry of goods at less than true weight, on false classification, or on payment of less than lawful duties.. 5445
rescuing property detained by revenue officer............................... 5446
resisting, &c., officer of customs in making seizures or searches.................. 5447
staving, throwing overboard, &c., property, &c., to prevent seizure, &c.......... 5447
falsely assuming to be revenue-officer and demanding or receiving money, &c., as such............................... 5448
bribing officer of United States, &c........ 5451
giving or offering presents to revenue officer by importer........................ 5452
secreting, embezzling, carrying away implement for printing United States obligations............................ 5453
material for such printing................ 5453
unlawfully taking away or using, &c., papers relating to claims against United States............................... 5454
counterfeiting, &c., United States coin or bars................................ 5457
foreign coins current in United States.... 5457
uttering, &c., such coins.................... 5457
having in possession, &c.................. 5457
counterfeiting, &c., minor United States coins.............................. 5458

Section.
Crimes and Offenses—Continued.
fraudulently mutilating, &c., United States or current foreign coin ... 5459
debasing or diminishing coins by officers of Mint, using false weights, &c ... 5460
embezzlement of metals, coins, or medals, &c., by Mint or assay officers ... 5460
unauthorized making, or uttering of, coins as money ... 5461
of minor United States coins ... 5462
receiving, &c., valuable inclosure stolen from mail or post-office ... 5470
counterfeiting, forging, or uttering, presenting false bond, bid, public record or other paper in order to defraud United States ... 5479
extortion by United States officer, under color of office ... 5481
inspector of steamboats receiving illegal fees ... 5482
payment by disbursing officer to employé of United States of less than lawful sum, and requiring receipt for amount larger than paid ... 5483
receiving money, &c., under threat of informing, or for not informing, of violation of internal-revenue law ... 5484
pension-agent, &c., taking fee from pensioner ... 5487
disbursing officer depositing public money otherwise than authorized by law ... 5488
loaning public money ... 5488
withdrawing from depository, or unlawfully applying public money ... 5488
United States Treasurer, or depositary, failing to keep safely moneys deposited, &c ... 5489
loaning, using, &c., improperly depositing, &c., by person charged with safe-keeping of public moneys ... 5490
failure of officer, &c., having public money, &c., to render accounts ... 5491
failure to deposit, &c., public moneys when required by head of proper Department ... 5492
application of sections 5488–5492 ... 5493
transcript from Treasury, evidence of balance due on trial for embezzlement ... 5494
refusal to pay or transfer public money when required prima-facie evidence of embezzlement, on trial ... 5495
non-paid receipt or voucher evidence of conversion, &c., of public money ... 5496
person not authorized receiving public money on deposit or loan ... 5497
using, converting, &c., public money ... 5497
United States officer acting as agent in prosecuting claim against United States ... 5498
United States officer accepting bribe ... 5501
penalty ... 5502
officer contracting beyond appropriation for erection, repair, &c., of public building or improvement ... 5503
officer of United States court failing to deposit or converting money belonging to registry ... 5504
receiving from officer of United States court, on loan or deposit, money belonging to registry ... 5505
expenses of transporting, and of execution of sentence upon, prisoners under United States law, to be paid out of United States Treasury ... 5536
marshal may procure temporary jail ... 5537
or make other temporary provision ... 5538

Section.
Crimes and Offenses—Continued.
only reasonable cost of subsisting prisoner, to be paid by Attorney-General ... 5545
Attorney-General to prescribe regulations for marshals, &c., as to prisoners ... 5545
may designate place for imprisonment, transportation, expenses ... 5546
to contract for subsistence, proper employment of prisoners ... 5547
of juvenile offenders ... 5550
court may order sentence executed in house of correction or reformation ... 5548
juvenile offenders under sixteen years, where to be imprisoned ... 5549
to give notice to United States courts of places provided ... 5550
committed on Guano Islands, how cognizable and punished ... 5576
prosecution of, committed prior to repeal by Revised Statutes ... 5598
Crisfield, Md.,
port of entry ... 2548
collector to reside at ... 2549
Cumberland, Va.,
port of delivery ... 2552
Currants,
grown in United States, exemption from tax, of wine, liquors, &c., made from ... 3328
Currency Bureau,
establishment of ... 324
rooms, furniture, &c., for ... 331
expenses of, to be paid out of taxes on national-bank circulation ... 5173
Cushing, Me.,
port of delivery ... 2517
Custom-House Dues,
Brazilian-mail steamships exempt from ... 4232
duration of such exemption ... 4232
Custom-Houses,
samples of wool and hair to be deposited in ... 2916
when to be shipping-offices ... 4503
removal by Secretary of Treasury or First Comptroller during epidemics ... 4797
by President ... 4798
by President, in insurrectionary district, residence of collector, &c ... 5315
Customs,
duty of district attorneys, as to fines, penalties, and forfeitures ... 838
report by, to Secretary of Treasury, in case of non-prosecution ... 838
Customs-Appropriations,
permanent ... 3689
(see *Appropriations.*)
Customs-Duties,
(see *Duties on Imports.*)
Customs-Fees,
(see *Fees.*)
Customs Laws,
(see *Revenue Laws.*)
Customs-Officers,
to receive no salary until they make oath that they have received no gifts, &c ... 1790
in Alabama ... 2565
in Alaska ... 2592
in California ... 2583
in Connecticut ... 2534
in Delaware ... 2547
in District of Columbia ... 2550
in Florida ... 2563
in Georgia ... 2560
for Indiana and Illinois ... 2602
in Louisiana ... 2569
in Maine ... 2518
in Maryland ... 2549
in Massachusetts ... 2529

Section.

Customs-Officers—Continued.
in Michigan 2600
in Minnesota 2596
in Mississippi 2567
in New Hampshire 2523
in New Jersey 2542
in New York 2536
in North Carolina 2556
in Ohio 2604
in Oregon and Washington Territory 2587
in Pennsylvania 2544
in Rhode Island 2532
for San Diego, Cal 2607
in South Carolina 2558
in Texas 2579
in Vermont 2526
in Virginia 2553
in Wisconsin 2598
term of office of 2613
additional oath of 2616
bonds of 2619
by whom approved and where filed 2620
penalty of, may be increased by President .. 3639
qualifications, pay, and duties of 2613–2746
penalty for demanding or receiving excessive fees 2636
for certifying shipment of goods for drawback, &c., without inspection 2637
not to own vessels, &c., nor engage in importation 2638
books, blanks, &c., how furnished to 2646
to follow instructions and decisions of Secretary of Treasury 2652
subordinate offices of, may be abolished 2653
pro-rata pay for part of year's service 2687
to administer oaths 2805
demand by, of manifests of vessels 2811
of vessels arriving in port of discharge 2812
neglecting to certify production of manifests, penalty 2814
report by, for failure to produce manifests .. 2815
to board vessels at New Orleans for Natchez or Vicksburgh, powers and duties of .. 2832
expenses of, to be paid by such vessels 2833
in appraisal department at New York not to engage in mercantile business 2941
not to contract for use of warehouse before completion 2957
to have charge and supervision of private warehouse 2960
powers of, for discovery of frauds and seizure of merchandise relanded contrary to law 3049
when to board vessels and make searches and arrests 3059
how to obtain warrant to search dwelling-house, &c 3066
when to board vessel, demand manifest, make searches, &c., powers of 3067
master of vessel, obstructing, penalty, &c ... 3068
what to do, where articles found separate from cargo 3069
when to make known character; power of, to demand assistance, &c.; refusal to assist, penalty 3071
when and where to make seizures of vessels, &c 3072
when sued, &c., may give special matter in evidence under the general issue 3073
what proportion of fines, penalties, and forfeitures to be distributed to 3090
powers and duties of, in northern, &c., frontier districts 3097
when to retain baggage, &c., from contiguous foreign countries, and examine; forfeiture 3101

Section.

Customs-Officers—Continued.
when to seal vessels and cars to avoid inspection at first port of arrival 3102
appropriation of fees paid for services of 3687
shall require oath as to letters before granting clearances 3987
shall search for letters illegally conveyed ... 3989
may seize, &c., such letters 3990
disposal of letters, &c., seized by 3991
shall aid in collection of postage, &c., on letters, &c., carried in foreign vessels ... 4015
to observe State inspection-laws in clearing vessels 4202
to pay fees of marshals and witnesses in investigations by steamboat inspectors. 4451
to enforce provisions of Title REGULATION OF STEAM-VESSELS 4496
penalty for neglect 4497
shall require certificate as to effects of deceased seamen before granting clearance 4539
two per cent. for privateer pension-fund to be paid to 4759
shall deposit same in Treasury 4760
when appointed to carry into effect licenses, &c., relating to supplies in parts of State in insurrection, how compensated 5305
knowingly admitting to entry any goods, &c., upon payment of less than lawful duty 5444
assaulting, resisting, &c., in execution of duty 5447
rescuing property seized by 5447
discharging weapon at, or using, &c., in resisting 5447
offering present to, by person importing, &c., or interested in entry of goods, &c ... 5452
(see *Revenue-Officers*.)
Customs Revenue,
appropriation for expenses of collecting 3687
Cuttings of Plants,
to be third-class mail-matter 3878
Cuyahoga, O.,
collection-district 2603
officers of customs in, residence of 2604
additional inspectors for district of 2605
Cypress,
consul at, salary of 1690

D.

Dakota Territory,
number of members of legislature 1922
contingent expenses of executive department of, appropriation for 1935
legislative expenses of, provision for 1939
mileage of members of legislature of 1942
appointment of surveyor-general for, authorized 2207
salary of 2208
(see *Territories*.)
Damaged Goods,
imported, appraisers to certify rate of percentage of; deductions, how made; proof of, where lodged 2927
appraisal, &c., at New York 2943
Damages,
for delay, to respondent in error 1010
payment for, to arms, &c., in Army 1303
to military supplies 1304
Damaging Vessel or Cargo,
punishment of seamen for 4596
Dams,
may be constructed across Iowa River, in Iowa, north of Wapello 5248

Section.

Danvers, Mass.,
port of delivery ... 2527
Darien, Ga.,
port of delivery ... 2559
deputy collector to reside at ... 2560
Day's Work,
of laborer, &c., to be eight hours ... 3738
Dead Letters,
action of Post-Office Department as to foreign ... 401
containing valuables, disposition of ... 3938
accounts to show amount derived from ... 4049
account to show expenditures for ... 4049
unclaimed money in, to be deposited as postal revenues ... 4050
Dead-Letter Office,
valuable letters to be registered in ... 3938
Deaf and Dumb, Columbia Institution for,
corporation to have perpetual succession .. 4859
property of, not to be devoted to other purpose ... 4861
real estate of, to be sold only by authority of Congress ... 4861
admission of pupils from States and Territories ... 4865
not to be supported by United States ... 4865
from District of Columbia ... 4864
education of blind, provision for ... 4869
Dealers in Cigars,
who have paid special tax, sales by ... 3392
Dealers in Leaf-Tobacco,
carrying on business without paying special tax ... 3242
special tax of ... 3244
definition of ... 3244
no exemption from special tax of, except in case of farmer or planter selling, &c. 3244
to sell only to certain classes of persons ... 3244
to render statement of sales when demanded. 3359
book to be kept by ... 3360
Dealers in Liquor,
when liable as rectifiers ... 3244
special tax on ... 3244
definition of ... 3244
purchase by, of more than 20 gallons liquor.. 3319
retail, doing business without paying special tax ... 3244
wholesale doing business, without paying special tax ... 3242
spirits delivered on promises of, to be gauged and stamped ... 3321
stamp of, form of ... 3321
penalty for violations of law ... 3456
Dealers in Malt Liquors,
definition of ... 3244
special tax of ... 3244
payment by brewer of special tax as wholesale dealer ... 3244
Dealers in Tobacco,
penalty for carrying on business without payment of special tax ... 3242
special tax of ... 3244
definition of ... 3244
retail, to keep a book ... 3244
entries in ... 3244
to make inventory of tobacco and snuff on hand July 20, 1868, unstamped, and monthly thereafter ... 3378
Death,
in case of, of person having paid special tax, rights of representatives ... 3241
happening on vessel to be entered in log-book ... 4290
Debasing of Coin,
at United States mints, penalty for ... 5460

Section.

Debates of Congress,
how to be printed ... 78
Debentures,
(see *Drawback of Customs Duties.*)
Debentures and other Charges,
appropriation for refunding ... 3689
Debentures and Drawbacks,
customs, appropriation for ... 3689
Debenture-Certificates,
fee for, on northern, &c., frontier ... 4382
Debt,
contracted by sale of articles with intent to evade tax, void ... 3454
Debtor,
deceased, insufficient estate of, United States claims to have priority ... 3466
surety, &c., on bond of, to United States, when to have priority ... 3468
Debts, Bankrupt,
what, entitled to priority in order for dividend ... 5101
fiduciary, or by defalcation of public officer, not released by discharge ... 5117
(see *Bankruptcy.*)
Debts by or to United States,
provisions concerning ... 3466–3494
what shall be a legal tender in payment of ... 3588–3590
Debts by United States,
payable in national-bank notes, when ... 3475
in interest-bearing Treasury notes, when. 3476
in United States notes, except for duties and interest on public debt ... 3588
in demand Treasury notes, under acts July 17, 1861, and February 12, 1862 ... 3589
in Treasury notes, under acts March 3, 1863, and June 30, 1864, for face value, excluding interest ... 3590
(see *Public Debt.*)
Debts to United States,
who to superintend recovery of, and direct suits for ... 269
to have priority ... 3466
priority of, in assigments, attachments, and bankruptcy ... 3466
when executor, &c., liable for ... 3467
priority of surety on bond to United States, who pays ... 3468
compromise of ... 3469
in what payable ... 3473, 3588–3590
none but standard coin receivable for, except ... 3474
in what sums fractional currency receivable for ... 3574
Deceased American Citizens,
duty of consular officers as to estate of ... 1709
Deceased Debtor,
(see *Debtor.*)
Deceased Seamen,
(see *Seamen.*)
Deceased Soldiers,
(see *Soldiers.*)
Deceased Officers and Soldiers,
(see *Officers of Army* and *Soldiers.*)
Decimal System,
of money, established ... 3563
Decisions of Supreme Court,
appropriation for three hundred copies ... 3689
Deck-Passengers,
on river-steamers, provisions for safety and accommodation of ... 4484–4485
penalty for failure ... 4486
Declaratory Statement,
fee for each, filed with register and receiver of land-office ... 2238

Section.

Decrees,
from what final, of circuit court, appeal allowed to Supreme Court 692
on certificate of division of opinion 693
statement of, by clerks of circuit and district courts to Solicitor of Treasury .. 797
of foreign courts as to lands claimed by or under United States, how authenticated and admitted in evidence 907
to include fees of officers, witnesses, &c., where costs are recoverable by prevailing party 983
Decree of Distribution,
in prize cases to be made by the court 4634
what it shall recite 4634
Deductions,
from salaries of members and delegates in Congress 40–42
from pay of Army officers or soldiers ... 1299–1304
of 7½ per cent. on stamps for fermented liquors 3341
from bullion to be covered into Treasury ... 3552
from wages of seamen, enforcement of 4603
table of 4612
Deed,
of real estate sold for internal-revenue taxes 3198, 3199
given by marshal on sale of real estate of delinquent internal-revenue collector . 3217
falsely making, altering, forging, &c., with intent to defraud United States; uttering false as true, &c 5421
having false, &c., with intent to defraud United States 5422
Deer Island, Me.,
port of delivery 2517
Defacing Notes and Drafts,
of national banks, penalty 5189
Defalcation,
of public officer, discharge in bankruptcy not to release debt created by 5117
Defaulter's Bid for Naval Supplies,
may be rejected 3722
Deficiencies,
of military supplies, delinquents to be charged for in Army 1304
Deficiency,
assessment on distillers for 3309
to be a lien on distillery, &c 3309
Definitions,
of words as used in Revised Statutes 1–6
of official designations of diplomatic and consular officers 1674
of word "ton," as used in Title COLLECTION OF DUTIES 2951
of words "value" and "valued," as used in Title COLLECTION OF DUTIES 2952
of "minister" and "consul," in Title FOREIGN RELATIONS 4130
of "master," "vessel," "owner," in Title MERCHANT SEAMEN 4612
of "obligation, or other security of United States," in Title CRIMES 5413
Delaware,
collection-district of, ports of entry and delivery in 2546
collector in, residence of 2547
permit for land-transportation of foreign merchandise across 4362
Delaware City, Del.,
port of delivery 2546
Delawares,
appointment of agent for 2052
Delegates in Congress,
salary of 35
right of Territories to send 1862
not to be interested in contracts 3739–3742
Delinquent Mail-Contractors,
may be fined 3962
Delivery,
of cargoes, inspector to attend to 2877
copies of accounts of, to be returned to collector, &c., and what to comprise 2888
of vessel in distress not agreeing with master's report, penalty 2893
from custody of customs officers, imported goods to be inspected and appraised before 2899
of merchandise in bulk, from warehouse 2980
of imports for transportation, time of, penalty for failure 3001
(see *Unlading.*)
Delivery Bond,
(see *Bonds.*)
Delivery of Letters,
from vessels in foreign trade 3976
from steamboats 3977
Demand Notes,
customs duties may be paid in 3009, 3473
legal tender to what extent 3589
Demand Notice,
for internal-revenue taxes 3184, 3185
Demerara,
consul, salary of 1690
Denmark,
salary of minister to 1675
Denominations,
of coin, depositors of bullion to receive such as they desire 3544
of United States notes 3571
of fractional currency 3573
Denver Mint,
legal designation 3495
business of 3558
officers of 3559
to be place of deposit of public money 3592
Departments,
(see *Executive Departments.*)
Department of Agriculture,
design and duties of 520
Commissioner of Agriculture, appointment and salary of 521
clerks and employés in, salaries, &c., of 522
chief clerk, appointment, salary, duties in absence of Commissioner 523
bonds of Commissioner and chief clerk 524
custody of property, records, &c., of 525
duties of Commissioner 526
purchase and distribution of seed, &c., by .. 527
annual reports of Commissioner 528, 529
expenditure of appropriations for, by whom directed 3677
Department of Interior,
Secretary of Interior to be head of 437
Assistant Secretary, appointment, salary ... 438
duties of 439
clerks and employés in 440
general duties of Secretary of 441
Secretary of, to exercise powers as to territories, formerly exercised by Secretary of State 442
supervisory and appellate powers of Secretary of, as to census 443
requisitions of, to be signed by Secretary ... 444
annual reports of Secretary of 445
provisions respecting General Land-Office . 446–461
Commissioner of Indian Affairs 462–469
Commissioner of Pensions 470–474
Patent-Office 475–496
Superintendent of public documents ... 497–511
Returns Office 512–515
Office of Education 516–519
permanent appropriations for 3689

Section.

Department of Justice,
to furnish counsel and advice to heads of Departments 189
provisions concerning 346–387
Attorney-General to be head of 346
Solicitor-General, appointment, duties, salary 347
Assistant Attorneys-General 348
solicitors, assistant solicitors, examiner of claims 349
to perform duties under control of Attorney-General 350
chief clerk, law clerk, and examiner of titles, disbursing clerk, &c., salaries of. 351
rooms provided for 352
seal of 353
solicitors and officers of, to perform duties required by Attorney-General 360
general duty of officers of 361
special counsel to be provided for Departments by 363–366, 385
officers of, may be sent by Attorney-General to any State or district, to attend to suits, &c 367
money requisitions for, by whom signed 369
traveling expenses of officers of 370
disbursement of moneys drawn for, by whom 371
suits for money due Post-Office Department, to be under control of 381
power of, to direct proceedings in equity in cases of debts due Post-Office Department 382
to be charged with distribution to judges, of Statutes and Reports of Supreme Court 386
register of distribution of Statutes and Reports to be kept, &c 387
copies of Statutes and Supreme Court Reports to be furnished to, for distribution 498
statement to, by district attorneys, of suits for moneys due Post-Office Department 775
(see *Attorney-General.*)

Department of the Navy,
accounts of, how to be kept 283
questions of law to be sent by, to Attorney-General 357
Secretary of Navy, to be head of 415
clerks and employés in, salaries of 416
general duties of Secretary 417
custody of books, &c., of 418
bureaus in 419
custody of books and records of bureaus 420
chiefs of bureaus in, how appointed 421
who eligible for office of 422–426
to have use of engraved plates of Wilkes's Expedition 427
flags captured by Navy to be collected in 428
annual reports of Secretary 429
estimates of expenses, by whom prepared .. 430
Hydrographic Office in 431
maps prepared at 432
moneys from sale of 433
pay of officer in charge of Naval Observatory 434
meridian of Washington to be used for astronomical purposes 435
meridian of Greenwich for nautical purposes. 435
supervision of the Nautical Almanac 436
to defray expenses of revenue cutters when under direction of Secretary 2757
estimates for expenditures by, in what details given; expenditures of appropriations for, how accounted for in detail. 3666
money appropriated for, how drawn 3673
appropriations for, to be under control of, and expended by Secretary 3676

Department of the Navy—Continued.
for each bureau of, to be kept separate in Treasury 3676
permanent appropriations for 3689

Department, Post-Office,
(see *Post-Office Department.*)

Department of State,
Secretary of State to be head of 199
Assistant and Second Assistant Secretaries, appointment and salaries of 200
subordinate officers in, salaries of 201
duties of Secretary of State 202–211
passport-clerk in, to administer oath without fee 212
fees for copies of records in 213
registration in, of names of persons in service of foreign ministers 4065
Secretary to transmit names to marshal of District of Columbia 4065

Department of the Treasury,
provisions concerning 233–345
Secretary of Treasury to be head of 233
Assistant Secretaries of, appointment and salaries 234
subordinate officers in 235
claims and accounts to be settled in 236
fiscal year of Treasury 237
commissions of revenue officers, issued from and recorded in 238
internal-revenue accounts kept in 239
contingent expenses of, how allowed 240
expenditures for furniture and repairs, how allowed 241
temporary clerks in 242
officers and clerks of, restricted as to certain kinds of business 243, 244
provisions relating to Secretary of 245–267
Comptrollers 268–275
Auditors 276–300
Treasurer 301–311
Register 312–315
Commissioner of Customs 316–318
of Internal Revenue 319–323
Comptroller of the Currency 324–333
Bureau of Statistics 334–342
of the Mint 343–345
transcript from books, &c., of, made evidence in suits against delinquents accountable for public money 886
in trial of indictment for embezzling public money 887
accounts of disbursements for government of Territories to be settled at 1886
permanent appropriations for 3689
what binding may be done at 3787

Department of War,
Secretary of War to be the head of 214
subordinate officers in 215
general duties of Secretary 216
custody of books and property in 217
captured flags, collection of 218
purchase and transportation of supplies, regulation of 219
transportation of troops, &c., control and supervision of 220
meteorological observations, storm-signals, provision for, by Secretary 221
reports and signals for benefit of agriculture and commerce 222
connection of signal-stations by telegraph-lines 223
authority to furnish duplicates of lost certificate of discharge 224
officers detailed in, to administer oaths 225
sale of surplus charts of lakes 226
sale of surplus maps, &c., of Signal-Office .. 227

Section.

Department of War—Continued.
report to Congress of appropriations and unexpended balances 228
annual statement of contracts and contingent expenses 229
reports of bids for works 230
reports on river and harbor surveys 231
abstract of returns of State adjutant-general 232
accounts of, how to be kept 283
questions of law to be sent by, to Attorney-General 357
money appropriated for, how drawn 3673
permanent appropriations for 3689

Departure of Vessels,
(see *Vessels.*)

Dependent Relatives,
when to have pension 4707
when pension of, deemed to accrue 4710
of persons in late rebellion not to receive pensions 4716

De Pere, Wis.,
port of delivery 2597
deputy collector to reside at 2598

Deposits,
authority of Secretary of Treasury to receive, of gold coin, &c 254
of outstanding liabilities 306
by settlers for survey of townships 2401
excess to be returned to settlers 2402
to be deemed and credited to, appropriation for surveys 2402
to go in part payment for lands 2403
tax on, in banks, &c 3408
in savings and provident institutions 3408
national banks, power of, to receive 5136
proportion of reserve to 5191
may be liable for, in addition to capital 5202
not to certify checks in excess of 5208
shall pay duty on 5214
shall make returns of, to United States Treasurer; penalty 5215
duty on, how assessed in default of return 5216
duty on, how collected in default of payment 5217
of bullion, reports of, by mint-superintendents 3503
to be received, &c 3506
what may be refused 3519
for gold coinage 3519, 3520
for surveying public lands, appropriation to repay excess of, by individuals 3689
of postal revenues may be made with national banks 3847
when, with assistant treasurers, &c 3848
of money-order funds, where may be made 4046

Depositaries,
to report "outstanding liabilities" to Secretary of Treasury, when 310
receipt to collector of internal revenue, voucher in his accounts 3211
how silver coin shall be sent to 3527
how may redeem copper, &c., coins 3529
shall exchange United States notes for fractional currency 3574
may appoint deputies in case of sickness 3613
duties as to public money 3639
penalty of bonds of, may be increased by President 3639
shall keep separate accounts of Post-Office Department money 3642
to render accounts of receipts and payments 3644
shall pay duplicate checks 3646
examination of 3649, 3650
compensation of 3655
limit of 3656
when to pay duplicate pension-checks 4770

Section.

Depositaries—Continued.
when national banks to be; security; duties 5153
failing safely to keep moneys deposited by officer, or other person having moneys of United States 5489
banker, &c., not being, receiving public moneys from disbursing officer, &c., on deposit, loan, &c 5497

Depositories,
to be designated by Secretary for keeping of internal-revenue collections 3211
public money in, subject to draft of United States Treasurer 3593

Depositions,
making or using, by civilians, of any false, to obtain claim against United States; civil liability for 3490
making or using, by any person, of false, to obtain approval, &c., of claim against United States; punishment 5438

Depots,
for coal and fuel for the Navy 1552

Depreciated Currency,
when original cost of imports exhibited in, who to establish regulations for estimating duties 2903

Depredations by Indians,
to be paid for only from special appropriations 2098

Deputy Assistant Treasurer,
at New York, appointment, &c., of 3602, 3603

Deputy Clerks,
of district courts 558
number of, in Indiana 559
in Iowa 560
compensation of 561
of circuit courts, how appointed 624
in Indiana, where appointed 625
compensation of, how paid and allowed 626
of Supreme Court, how appointed 678

Deputy Collectors of Customs,
ports at which appointed 2518–2602
at Calais, Me., when to enter and clear vessels, &c 2521
when to perform duties of collector 2625
collector to appoint, duties of 2630
when empowered to act as principal, bond of 2633
salaries of, at New York, Boston, Philadelphia, Baltimore, New Orleans, Portland, Me., and San Francisco 2697
at Eureka and Vallejo, Cal 2698
at Potomac 2699
at Shreveport 2700
at Saint Paul, what to include; duties of 2701
at Ellensberg, Port Orford, and Gardiner 2702
at Vallejo, Cal., when to exercise powers of surveyor 2824
in northern, &c., frontier districts, certain oaths to be administered by 3098
when to search certain stores, warehouses, &c 3107
when to act as shipping-commissioners 4503

Deputy Collectors of Internal Revenue,
collector authorized to appoint 3148
bonds may be required of 3148
duties and powers of 3148
collector responsible for 3148
in case of sickness, &c., of collector, duties may devolve upon 3149
oldest, to act in case of vacancy of office of collector 3149
Secretary may designate who shall act in certain cases 3149
bond of, available to legal representatives and sureties of collector 3149

Section.

Deputy Collectors of Internal Revenue—Cont'd.
compensation of, while acting as collector during vacancy 3150
authorized to administer oaths and take evidence 3165
to canvass district 3172
general duties of, relating to returns 3173
may make list of taxable property, &c., for persons 3173
to serve summons 3174
may enter brewery, manufactory, distillery, &c 3177
duty of, as to taxable property of non-resident 3180
to give receipts for all sums collected 3183
to make returns of sales of real estate to collector 3203
to transmit notice of distiller or rectifier to collector 3259

Deputy-Commissioner of Pensions,
appointment, duties, and salary of 472
to act in absence of Commissioner 472

Deputy-Comptroller of Currency,
appointment, salary, duties, oath, and bond of 327
not to be interested in national banks 329

Deputy-Commissioners of Internal Revenue,
two, to be employed under direction of Secretary of Treasury; salary 235
one, to be appointed by President; salary .. 322
duties of 323

Deputy Consuls,
title to denote what; shall be deemed included as consular officers 1674
not to be appointed except under regulations 1695
prohibition to trade may be extended to 1700
(see *Consuls General, Consuls, &c.*)

Deputy Inspectors of Customs,
fees of 2657

Deputy Marshals,
not to be, or exercise duties of, commissioner of circuit court 628
appointment and removal of 780
per diem for attendance, &c 831
proportion of fees, &c., allowed to, by Attorney-General, in accounts of marshal .. 841
duties and fees of, in civil-rights cases .. 1982, 1986
appointment of special, for election purposes 2021
duties of 2021
number of, not to be increased 2030
compensation of special deputies 2031
may seize, &c., letters, &c., illegally carried. 3990
disposal of such letters 3991
(see *Marshals of United States.*)

Deputy Naval Officers,
salaries of, at New York, Boston, Philadelphia, Baltimore, New Orleans, San Francisco, and Portland, Me., how payable 2705
additional compensation of, at San Francisco 2746

Deputy Paymasters-General,
of Army, number and rank of 1182

Deputy Provost-Marshals,
when to have pension 4693
rate of total-disability pension to 4695
pensions to widows, &c., of, when to begin . 4710

Deputy Shipping-Commissioners,
appointment, duty, &c., of 4505

Deputy Surveyors of Customs,
salaries of, at San Francisco 2721
at New York, Boston, Philadelphia, Baltimore, New Orleans, Portland, Me., how payable 2722
at Savannah 2723

Section.

Deputy Land-Surveyors,
surveyors-general to engage a sufficient number of skilful surveyors as 2223
to give bond 2230
bond of, to be approved by surveyor-general 2230

Derby, Conn.,
port of delivery 2533

Derelict Property,
collection, &c., of 3755

Deserters,
from military or naval service prior to March 3, 1865, loss of citizenship of .. 1996
to be incapable of holding office, &c 1996
certain men absent without leave not to be held as, &c 1997
penalty hereafter incurred by 1998
penalty for avoiding draft 1998
from mercantile marine, penalty for deserting 4601
certain soldiers and sailors not to be deemed; forfeiture of pension 4749

Desertion of Merchant Seamen,
(see *Seamen.*)

Desiccated Vegetables for Navy,
how may be procured 3726

Designated Depositaries,
(see *Depositaries.*)

Designated Depositories,
(see *Depositories.*)

Des Moines River,
United States property, or persons in United States service, free of toll on 5246

Destitute Seamen,
(see *Seamen.*)

Destroyed Checks,
duplicates of, how procured 3646, 3647

Destruction,
of stills, &c., in cases of forfeiture 3332
of tobacco, snuff, and cigars, abandoned, condemned, or forfeited, which will not bring price equal to tax 3369
of empty cigar-boxes having stamps 3406

Details,
of enlisted men of Army as artificers and laborers 1235
extra pay of such men 1287

Detention,
of enlisted persons in Navy beyond term 1572
extra pay to 1572

Detention of Spirits,
power of internal-revenue officer to make, for forty-eight hours, on suspicion 3298

Detroit, Mich.,
collection-district and port of entry 2599
officers of customs in, residence of 2600
weighers, gaugers, measurers, and inspectors for 2606
inspectors of hulls and boilers for 4414
salaries of 4414
reserve of national banks in 5191
balances with banks in, may be part of reserve 5192
redemption agencies in 5195

Diamonds,
shipper of, to notify carrier, &c 4281

Dies,
of national character may be executed at Mint 3551

Dime-piece,
weight and fineness of 3513, 3514
devices and legends on 3517
deviation in adjusting 3536

Diplomatic Fees,
(see *Fees, Diplomatic.*)

Section.

Diplomatic Functions,
when consular officers may perform 1738
pay to, when performing 1739

Diplomatic Officers,
term defined 1674
salaries of.............................. 1675
salaries of commissioners and chargés d'affaires 1676
consul-general to be secretary of legation at Constantinople 1677
interpreter of legation to Turkey, salary of 1678
Japan, salary of....................... 1679
China, salary of....................... 1680
minister to Uruguay accredited also to Paraguay 1681
but one minister to Guatemala, Costa Rica, &c., residence of 1682
to Hayti and Liberia, titles and salaries of.. 1683
chargé d'affaires or secretary of legation, appointment and compensation of...... 1684
secretary of legation, salary of, when acting as chargé d'affaires 1685
compensation of person filling two offices.. 1686
fees collected at legations to be accounted for 1687
salaries of, term for which payable......... 1740
salaries when absent from post............ 1742
compensation to be in full for services, &c.. 1743
not to receive compensation when not United States citizen 1744
fees, regulation, &c., of.................. 1745
shall be collected in United States coin or its value in exchange.............. 1746
stationery, &c., for, shall be provided 1748
dying abroad, allowance to widow, &c 1749
President may make regulations, &c., governing 1752
may require mails to be carried in vessels bound to the United States 3976
table of fees allowed to, to be attached to clearances of certain registered vessels. 4207

Diplomatic and Consular Officers,
Title XVIII............................1674–1752
provisions common to both 1740–1752

Diplomatic Service,
officers of Army accepting appointment in. 1223
of Navy................................ 1440

Director of the Mint,
appointment and term of office of........... 343
salary and expenses of..................... 344
power and duties of 345
to estimate, annually, value of foreign coins receivable for public lands............ 2366
to determine certain salaries.............. 3499
to approve bonds of assistants, &c......... 3501
to approve appointments to act in case of absence, &c 3502
Secretary of Treasury to designate acting .. 3502
superintendent's control to be subject to approval of.......................... 3503
to prescribe time and form of reports of superintendents 3503
reports to be made to...................3503, 3504
to approve all appointments of assistants, &c., in mints 3504
may engage artists, &c 3510
shall fix price of silver in gold deposits..... 3520
to fix coinage charge on trade-dollars 3524
shall propose regulations for sending silver coins 3527
shall approve purchase of metal for minor coinage 3528
discretion as to free delivery of minor coinage in cities, &c..................... 3529
copy of trial-piece, record to be sent to..... 3539
may prescribe tests of coins................ 3539

Section.

Director of the Mint—Continued.
balance-sheet of annual settlement to be sent to 3543
duty as to annual settlement................ 3543
to prescribe rules for exchange of fine bars for imported bullion................. 3546
shall approve regulations for striking, &c., medals 3551
shall estimate value of foreign coins 3564
may prescribe regulations respecting certain Spanish and Mexican coins.......... 3568
shall examine books, &c., of treasurers of mint 3650

Directors,
national banks to have board of............ 5136
of national banks, when may sell shares of delinquent holder 5141
votes, &c., in selection of................ 5144
election, &c., of 5145
qualifications of......................... 5146
oath of 5147
filling vacancies in board of............... 5148
proceedings when election is not had on proper day 5149
shall elect president...................... 5150
of State banks may convert organization into national bank, proceedings, &c.. 5154
of national banks, oath of, required as to facts in relation to organization...... 5168
penalty for embezzlement, &c., by 5209
reports to be signed by 5211
shall give notice of vote to go into liquidation, to Comptroller and public 5221
penalty for violation, &c., of laws by, personal liability of 5239
payment of, by corporations receiving land-grants or subsidies from United States with right reserved to appoint, &c... 5259

Direct Taxes,
appropriation to repay purchasers evicted.. 3689
to refund purchase-money of redeemed lands 3689
to refund taxes illegally collected........ 3689

Disability not provided for,
proportionate rate of pension for........... 4699

Disabled,
in militia while in United States service, how cared for 1639

Disabled Seamen,
(see *Seamen.*)

Disabled Volunteers,
appropriation for asylum for............... 3689
National Home for, provisions concerning ..4825, 4837

Disbursements,
of Patent-Office, by whom to be made...... 496
duty of engineer superintending construction of public work to disburse moneys applicable to same 1153
no extra allowance for, by officer having salary, unless appropriated for by Congress 1765
of appropriations for government in Territories, regulation of.................. 1886
in Washington, Idaho, and Montana........ 1940
security to be given by territorial officers... 1951
of appropriations for Government Hospital for Insane, regulation of............. 4858

Disbursing Agent,
designation of, by Secretary of Treasury, to pay moneys appropriated for construction of public buildings 255
of Navy for foreign stations............... 1650
internal-revenue collectors to act as........ 3144
bonds of 3144
special, to give bonds...................... 3614

Section.

Disbursing Agent—Continued.
duplicate checks of, how procured 3646
shall not exchange funds 3651
of appropriations for construction of buildings, collectors of customs shall act as. 3657
appointment of, where no collector.......... 3658
superintendent for Government Hospital for the Insane to be....................... 4839
(see *Disbursing Officers.*)

Disbursing Officers,
under Secretary of Senate and Clerk of House of Representatives, statements and receipts by, for moneys expended 62
in Departments, appointment, bond, duties, and salaries of 176
to make statement of expenditures to head of Department 193
payment of lost check issued by, in case of death of................................ 300
accounts of, of moneys covered into Treasury 309
to report outstanding liabilities to Secretary of Treasury, when 310
jurisdiction of Court of Claims of claim by, for relief, &c.......................... 1059
when loss of funds, &c., found by Court of Claims to be without fault, credit to be allowed by accounting-officers 1062
penalty for trading in public funds or property 1788
for Indians, annual settlement of accounts by 2091
delinquents to be reported to Congress... 2091
names, date of appointment, and salaries of, to be reported to Congress 2091
restrictions on advances to................. 2091
shall deposit public money in Treasury, &c. 3620
shall render accounts monthly, &c 3622
proceedings by distress warrant against, when delinquent.................3633, 3634
under War and Navy Departments, President may increase, &c., bonds of........... 3639
duplicate checks of, how procured......3646, 3647
advances may be made to.................... 3648
shall not exchange funds 3651
shall account for premiums on drafts, &c... 3652
extra expenses for clerks, &c................ 3653
estimates on information from, to be distinguished.................................. 3660
to pay expenses of commissions, &c., only from special appropriations........... 3681
depositing, converting, &c., loaning, withdrawing from deposit or applying public money for illegal purpose........ 5488
failing to render accounts as provided by law, &c 5491
failing to deposit public moneys with Treasurer, &c., when required by head of proper Department.................. 5492
evidence of balance against, of public moneys 5494
prima-facie evidence of embezzlement by... 5495
what constitutes conversion, &c., by....... 5496

Discharge,
received by militia from United States service, pay for travel to residence 1652

Discharge-Certificate,
to be returned to officers and men of Army, on settlement of accounts.............. 282
loss of, not to deprive survivors, &c., of war of 1812, of pensions, other proof....... 4740

Discharge of Seamen,
(see *Seamen.*)

Discharge in Bankruptcy,
fiduciary debts or debts incurred by fraud of public officer, not released by......... 5117
liability of other persons not released by.... 5118

Section.

Discipline,
in militia, system used in Regular Army to be enforced.............................. 1637
reports relating to.......................... 1635
returns of brigade-inspector concerning... 1640

Discontinuance,
of prosecution of distiller for fraud......... 3230

Discount and Exchange,
power of national banks to do business in .. 5136

Discriminating Duties,
(see *Duties, Discriminating.*)

Discriminating-Tonnage Duties,
(see *Duties, Discriminating-Tonnage.*)

Disease Contracted in Service,
who to have pension for...................... 4693
after July 27, 1868, must have been received in line of duty........................ 4694

Disloyal Claimants,
payment of claims of......................... 3480

Dismissals,
for cowardice or fraud, in Army, form and publication of sentence 1342

Disqualification to Hold Office,
of Secretary, and certain Heads of Bureaus of Treasury, when interested in certain business transactions 243
of members of Congress and Government officers for receiving, &c., consideration for procuring contract, office, or for voting.................................. 1781
of persons offering such consideration....... 1781
of members of Congress, heads of Departments, and officers for receiving, &c., compensation for services in claims, &c 1782
of United States disbursing officers trading, &c., in funds, debts, or property of United States, or of State 1788
of deserters from military or naval service failing to return, &c., under proclamation of 11th of March, 1865............ 1996
when not to apply.......................... 1997
for unlawfully unlading imported goods..... 2873
of revenue officers for unlawfully disclosing operations of manufacturers, &c...... 3167
of customs officers for making false register, or papers for vessels, taking illegal fees, reward, &c., and falsely measuring and describing vessels for registry. 4187
of customs officers for wilfully neglecting to perform duties prescribed by Title COMMERCE AND NAVIGATION.......... 4188
of persons making, uttering, &c., false sea-letter, Mediterranean passports, and certificates of registry, or availing themselves of same..................... 4191
of collectors of customs and persons appointed by or under them, for knowingly making records, granting papers, taking illegal fees, &c., contrary to provisions of Title VESSELS IN DOMESTIC COMMERCE......................... 4373
of surveyors of customs and measurers of vessels for wilfully delivering to collector or naval officer false description for enrollment and license of vessel... 4373
of officers named in Title VESSELS IN DOMESTIC COMMERCE, for neglect, &c., of duties 4374
of members of Congress for accepting bribe for vote, &c........................... 5502
of officers of, and persons acting for United States, &c., or Congress or committees thereof, for accepting bribe 5501, 5502

Section.

Dissolution and Receivership,
of national banks, provisions concerning 5220–5243

Distilled Spirits,
regulation of importation, &c., of, in Alaska . 1955
customs duties on, to be collected according to hydrometer proof ... 2918
internal-revenue officer becoming interested in the production, &c., of ... 3168
destroyed by accidental fire, &c., abatement or refunding of taxes on ... 3221
forfeiture of, for certain violations of law ... 3242
definition of ... 3248
when tax attaches to ... 3248
what shall be proof ... 3249
inspection, &c., of ... 3349
gallons of, as used in sales ... 3250
proof-gallon ... 3250
tax on ... 3251
fractional parts of gallon, how taxed ... 3251
who are liable for tax on ... 3251
tax, to be a first lien on ... 3251
in bonded warehouse August 1, 1872 ... 3251
adding substances to, to create fictitious proof ... 3252
assessment of tax on, removed without deposit in warehouse, as required by law . 3253
all products of distillation containing, to be considered and taxed as ... 3254
evading payment of tax on ... 3256
to be drawn from receiving-cisterns and removed, &c ... 3267
distillery warehouse for storage of ... 3271
tax on, to be paid before removal from ... 3271
receiving, carrying, &c., to or from distillery, rectifying establishment, &c., where sign not kept ... 3279
drawing off, gauging, marking of casks, and removal of, to warehouse ... 3287
not to remain on distillery premises after tax paid; forfeiture ... 3288
entry for deposit of, in distillery warehouse .. 3293
for withdrawal from ... 3294
tax-paid stamps to be placed on, before removal ... 3295
power of officer to detain packages of, for forty-eight hours, on suspicion ... 3298
unlawfully removed from distillery or warehouse, forfeited ... 3299
assessment for deficiencies in production of . 3309
production of, when deemed to have commenced ... 3310
preparation, form, and use of stamps for . 3312, 3313
accountability of collectors for stamps for ... 3314
restamping of, in certain cases ... 3315
purchases in quantities greater than twenty gallons by rectifier or liquor-dealer ... 3319
rectified, gauging, and stamping ... 3320
stamp for rectified, form of ... 3320
gauging and stamping of, on premises of wholesale liquor-dealer ... 3321
wholesale liquor-dealer's stamp for ... 3321
affixing and cancellation of stamps for ... 3322
drawn into new packages, containing ten gallons or more, to be gauged and branded ... 3323
to be removed only between sunrise and sunset, in packages of more than ten gallons ... 3327
may be withdrawn from warehouse, without payment of tax, for exportation in original casks ... 3330
compound, imitation, tax on ... 3328
burden of proof in case of seizure of ... 3333
sold by order of court, or under process of distraint, subject to tax ... 3334

Section.

Distilled Spirits—Continued.
laws imposing taxes on, extended to exterior boundaries of United States ... 3448
shipping, under false name or brand ... 3449
forfeited, to be disposed of by Commissioner of Internal Revenue ... 3450
manifest of, when carried by vessels in coasting trade between neighboring districts ... 4349–4352
transported by vessel between remote districts, without manifest and permit ... 4353–4356
by vessel of less than twenty tons burden .. 4359, 4360

Distilled Spirits or Wines,
report of vessel arriving with ... 2775
separate entry of, by importer, &c., how subscribed and certified, and to whom transmitted ... 2794
for different districts, how to be inserted in manifests of cargoes ... 2808
imported, not to be removed from wharf before proof of, &c.; forfeiture ... 2882
permit for unlading; penalty for unlading without permit ... 2883
under whose inspection to be landed ... 2884
when and how casks, &c., containing imported, to be marked ... 2885
imported, where and how stored ... 2958
change from casks of imported, how made, drawback on ... 3029
tax on imitation wines ... 3328
shipping wines under false name or brand .. 3449

Distiller,
definition of ... 3247
liability of, to tax on spirits ... 3251
assessment to be made on, for tax on spirits removed without deposit in warehouse, &c ... 3253
of brandy from apples, peaches, or grapes ... 3255
penalty and forfeiture for defrauding, &c., United States of tax on spirits ... 3257
notice of changes in business ... 3259
penalty for not giving notice, or giving false notice ... 3259
to give bond ... 3260
notice of intention to do business of ... 3260
may appeal to Commissioner if collector refuses to approve his bond ... 3260
may be required to give new bond ... 3260
forfeiture, &c., for refusing to give or renew bond, or giving false bond ... 3260
bond not to be approved until law, &c., complied with ... 3261
when may give bond in lieu of written consent of owner of fee that land may be used ... 3262
must be owner in fee of land on which distillery is situated, or have written consent, &c ... 3262
shall cause to be made plan of distillery, &c. 3263
to verify plan ... 3263
not to use any still, boiler, &c., in certain places ... 3266
penalty on, for not keeping pipes properly painted ... 3269
to provide warehouse ... 3271
to furnish to collector keys to gates, &c., of distillery ... 3275
hindering, &c., officer from entering, &c., distillery by night or day ... 3276
to furnish facilities for examination of distillery ... 3277
to put up sign ... 3279
not to carry on business until law is complied with ... 3280

Section.

Distiller—Continued.
not to do business less than 600 feet from rectifying premises 3280
penalty, &c., for doing business without giving bond, or engaging in business with fraudulent intent 3281
penalty for refusal, &c., to empty and cleanse worm-tubs 3286
to enter spirits for deposit in warehouse on first day of each month, &c 3293
to give bond in duplicate for tax on spirits so deposited 3293
may withdraw spirits from warehouse on application to collector, &c 3294
books to be kept by 3303
entries in 3303
to be kept at distillery and open to inspection, and preserved two years, &c 3304
penalty for false entries in, omitting to provide books, &c 3305
for doing or omitting certain acts with regard to, &c 3305
to render account taken from, in duplicate 3307
oath of, to monthly return 3307
returns to be made by 3307, 3308
assessment for deficiencies 3309
notice of suspension of work by 3310
of resumption 3310
penalty for doing business, &c., after time fixed in notice of suspension 3310
to give notice to collector of intention to reduce capacity of distillery 3311
penalty, &c., for violating law relative to business, &c., when no specific penalty imposed 3456

Distillery,
tax on spirits to be a first lien on 3251
plan and description of, to be made by distiller 3263
alterations in, to be shown on original or supplemental plan, &c 3263
survey of 3264
true producing capacity of, to be ascertained 3264
not to be within 600 feet of rectifying establishment 3266
fences and walls around premises of, height of 3275
keys of, to be furnished collector 3275
to be accessible to officer, &c., having key 3275
right of officer to enter and examine, &c., by night or by day 3276
power of officer to break open, to effect entrance 3276
facilities for examination of, to be furnished by distiller 3277
officer, &c., may break up ground or wall, &c., to search for hidden pipes, &c 3278
sign to be placed on 3279
forfeiture of, for violation of law 3281
no spirits to remain on premises of, after tax paid 3288
spirits unlawfully removed from, forfeited 3299
record to be kept by storekeeper 3302
assessment of deficiency-tax to be lien on, &c 3309
suspension of work at 3310
resumption 3310
reduction of capacity of 3311
how released after seizure and before judgment 3331
judgment against, having capacity of less than 150 gallons, or because no bond given 3332

Distilling-Apparatus,
set up, to be registered 3258
forfeited if not 3258

Section.

Distilling-Apparatus—Continued.
plan and description of, to be made by distiller 3263
Commissioner may order changes of 3270
storekeeper to have charge of 3273
forfeiture of, for violation of law 3281
release of, before judgment 3331
destruction of, in case of seizure and judgment 3332

Distillery-Warehouse,
spirits in, August 1, 1872 3251
assessment of tax on spirits removed without deposit in 3253
spirits to be directly removed into, after being drawn from receiving-cistern 3267
to be provided at expense of distiller 3271
to be situated on and constitute part of distillery premises 3271
use of 3271
not to be dwelling-house; no doors, &c., allowed in walls leading into distillery, &c 3271
to be approved by Commissioner 3271
when declared to be United States bonded warehouse 3271
to be under direction, &c., of collector and in charge of storekeeper 3271
tax on spirits to be paid before removal from 3271
may be discontinued by Commissioner when unsafe 3272
transfer of merchandise therein 3272
seizure, sale of, &c., in case of failure to make such transfer 3272
distillery-warehouse stamp, form of 3287
entry for deposit in 3293
bond for tax on spirits deposited in 3293
entry for withdrawal from 3294
withdrawal of alcohol from, for scientific purposes 3297
of spirits for exportation without payment of tax 3330
spirits removed from, in violation of law 3299
book to be kept by storekeeper 3301

Distillery-Warehouse Stamp,
how placed on cask on removal to warehouse 3287
how to be signed 3287
serial numbers and form of 3287

Distillery-Warehouse Book,
how to be kept by storekeeper, what to contain 3301

Distraint for Internal-Revenue Taxes,
property exempt from 3187
subject to 3187
proceedings 3188
books relating to property, &c., subject to, to be exhibited 3189
notice of, in newspaper 3190
sale, adjournment of 3190
disposition of proceeds of 3191–3193, 3195
taxes on property sold under, how assessed and collected 3191
property purchased by collector in sales under, may be sold 3192
collector to render account of charges incurred in sale 3192
when property sold under, may be purchased for United States 3192
goods under, to be restored on payment of tax 3193
effect of certificate of sale under 3194
stocks sold under 3194
when property not divisible, the whole may be sold 3195
fee and charges in cases of, to be prescribed by Commissioner 3200

Section.

Distraint for Internal-Revenue Taxes—Cont'd.
sale of spirits under process of 3334, 3458
of tobacco, snuff, and cigars under, stamps, &c., for 3369, 3458

Distraint,
exemption from, of arms, &c., of militia-men 1628

Distress-Warrant,
against delinquent collector, &c., proceedings, &c., under 3625–3635

Distributing-Offices,
Postmaster-General may designate; allowances at, for clerical services 3859

Distribution in Prize-Causes,
decree of, how far to be made by district court after appeal 565
method of 4631

Distribution in Bankruptcy,
what claims entitled to priority in 5101

Distributive Shares of Fines, &c.,
under customs-revenue laws 3090
appropriation to pay 3689

District Attorneys,
accounts of, for services where United States is interested, how settled 299
to aid in examining titles to land to be purchased by United States 355
general direction of, by Attorney-General 362
counsel to aid, how retained 363
supervision of accounts of, by Attorney-General 368
to conduct suits respecting national banks in which United States is interested 380
to obey Department of Justice in suits for money due Post-Office Department 381
where to be appointed 767
in Alabama, where to perform duty 767
in Georgia 767
in South Carolina 767
in Iowa 768
term of office and oath of 769
salaries of 770
general duties of 771
statement by, to Solicitor of Treasury 772, 773
to Commissioner of Internal Revenue 774
to Department of Justice 775
vacancy, how filled temporarily 793
compensation for services in defence of revenue offices 827
per diem for attendance 831
for southern district of New York, sum to be paid to, &c 836
additional compensation of, in prize-causes. 836
when to prosecute for fines, penalties, and forfeitures under revenue laws; compensation 838
report by, to Secretary of Treasury or Commissioner of Internal Revenue, when declining to prosecute 838
compensation of, for each year, to be allowed from fees, &c., of same year 843
accounts to be certified by district judge, &c., subject to revision, &c 846
to be paid but one bill of costs for several suits, prosecutions, &c., which should be joined 980
to proceed against marshals not paying into Treasury fines assessed against militia in United States service 1660
to proceed by quo warranto against persons illegally holding office, &c 1786
in Territories, appointment and term of office of 1875
salary of, and how payable 1880, 1882
to prosecute for violation of civil-rights laws, &c 1982

Section.

District Attorneys—Continued.
proceedings for condemnation of property seized under customs laws 3076
collectors of customs to make report to, of fines, &c 3084
of internal revenue 3164
proceedings in customs cases; compensation 3085
accepting gift, &c., for settlement of violation of internal-revenue law 3170
report of, in compromise of claim of United States 3469
suits for false claims against United States. 3492
President may increase penalty of bonds of. 3639
United States property under attachment, stipulation, &c 3753
duties of, in trying offenses against navigation laws 4300
amendment of complaint by 4302
compensation of, in prize-causes 4646
maximum allowed 4647
to render account to Attorney-General 4647
to pay excess into Treasury 4647
duties in cases of prize of insurrectionary property 5311
fees of, (see *Fees*.)

District Courts,
clerks of, how appointed 555
number of, in western district of Arkasas. 556
in Kentucky 557
deputy clerks of 558
number and duties of, in Indiana 559
in Iowa 560
compensation of 561
jurisdiction of 563
for what purposes always open, as courts of admiralty and equity 574
in Florida, as court of admiralty 575
in Wisconsin, as court of admiralty 576
clerks of, how appointed, and number of, in western district of North Carolina 621
in western district of Virginia 622
in western district of Wisconsin 623
writs of prohibition to, when proceeding as courts of admiralty, issued by Supreme Court 688
criers of, appointment and compensation 715
power of, to enforce awards of foreign consul, &c., in differences between captains and crews of vessels, &c 728
jurisdiction of certain, over violations of revenue laws, &c., in Alaska 1959
jurisdiction of, in suits for possession of office 2010
prosecution and condemnation in, of vessels employed in cooly-trade 2159
admission of alien seamen to citizenship by. 2174
to have jurisdiction of suits against civilians for making false claims against United States 3491
special term of, may be held to try offenses against navigation laws, when 4300
prize-commissioners to be appointed by 4621
may direct transfer of prize property to another district for sale 4629
shall order testimony to be taken for determining prize-shares 4634
shall make decree of distribution in prize-causes 4634
what such decree shall recite 4634
to make order for payments from prize-fund. 4640
for payment of costs and charges 4640
shall order amount decreed for distribution to be paid into Treasury 4641
shall make distribution of prize-money in case of vessels not of Navy 4641

Section.

District Courts—Continued.
may appoint commissioner to make distribution 4641
shall determine the compensation of district attorney and prize-commissioner in prize-cases 4647
compensation of special counsel for captors may be allowed by 4648
may be adjourned to another place in case of contagious, &c., disease 4799
may enjoin receivers, &c., of national banks, effect of 5237
power of, to adjudge forfeiture of franchises, &c., of national banks 5239
condemnations in, of property taken as prize, on account of use, &c., in aid of rebellion 5309, 5311

District Courts of Territories,
clerks, designation and appointment of 1871
in New Mexico, jurisdiction over citizens of, and in revenue cases in, El Paso County, Texas 1928
to have jurisdiction over certain offenses committed in Alaska 1957
number of commissioners of, to be increased with reference to civil rights 1983
to have jurisdiction of suits against civilians for making false claims against United States 3491

District Judges,
appointment and residence of 551, 552
salaries of 554
what orders may be made by, in chambers or clerk's office, in admiralty and equity causes 574
designation of, to act in place or aid of another district judge in same circuit 596
duty of, to comply with 596
no additional compensation allowed for 596
expenses of, when designated to southern district of New York 597
to certify fees of persons appointed to execute warrants of commissioners 1987
to certify fees of chief supervisors 2031
duties of, in regard to importation of obscene articles 2492
when to issue warrant for seizure of books, &c., in revenue cases 3091
what papers subject to order of; examinations and retention by 3093
may grant injunction to stay proceedings on distress-warrant against delinquent collector, &c 3636
may issue summons to witnesses under letters rogatory 4071
for district of Florida may grant license to vessel for wrecking, &c., when 4241
proceeds, &c., of deceased seamen's effects, &c., to be sent to, by consuls 4541
may summon master to show cause why libel for wages should not issue 4546
unseaworthy vessel, complaint of, may be made to 4556
shall direct survey of alleged 4557
may punish seamen for refusal to sail, &c 4558
report of examination of provisions, &c., of merchant-vessels to be sent to 4565
to appoint registers in bankruptcy; in what manner 4993
to fix and approve bond of register 4995
summary inquiry by, in proceedings for remission of fines, penalties, or forfeitures, in certain cases 5292

District of Columbia,
banks in, to be examined by Comptroller of Currency 332

District of Columbia—Continued.
annual distribution of arms and equipments for militia of 1667
to be seat of Government 1795
what offices to be exercised in 1796
public buildings and grounds in, appropriations for, how expended 1798
public works and improvements in, under whose charge 1800
expenditures for, under direction of Secretary of War 1802
expense of laying main-pipes, what to be paid by 1805
board of public works in, provisions concerning liabilities contracted by 1813
collection-district in 2550
collector in, residence of 2551
supreme court of, to have jurisdiction of suits against civilians for making false claims against United States 3491
collectors, &c., in, shall pay public money to United States Treasury 3615

Dividend,
in bankruptcy, what claims entitled to priority in order for 5101
upon fiduciary debts, or debts accruing by fraud of public officer, how accounted 5117
national banks not to declare, when reserve is reduced 5191
nor when losses exceed undivided profits 5204
when and how declared 5199
liabilities for, may be in addition to capital 5202
shall report, to Comptroller 5212
penalty for failure to make report of 5213
to creditors of national banks by Comptroller, when and how made 5236

Division of Opinion,
final judgments or decrees of circuit court, on certificate of, reviewed by Supreme Court on writ of error or appeal 693

Divisions,
in State militia 1630
officers of 1631
companies of artillery and cavalry in 1632
of militia, when called into United States service 1647

Dock-Yards,
assent of State legislatures to purchase of land for 1838

Document-Room,
of Senate, officers and salaries in 52
of House of Representatives, officers and salaries in 53

Documents,
official, of customs, substantial compliance with prescribed forms 2769
number of, to be printed for Congress as "usual number" 3792
additional number of, printed by order of Joint Committee on the Library 3796
accompanying annual reports of Departments, number of, to be printed 3798
number of, to be printed and bound in addition to "usual number" 3798
printed by order of either House, number of additional copies for exchange in foreign countries 3799
extra copies of, how procured from Government Printing-Office by any person 3809
of vessels, (see *Vessels*.)

Dollar-piece,
deviation allowed in adjusting 3535, 3536

Door-Keeper of House,
salary 53
duty of, during recess of Congress 73

Section.

Door-Keeper of Senate,
salary ... 52
duty of, during recess of Congress ... 73
Dorchester, Mass.,
port of delivery ... 2527
Double-Eagle,
weight and fineness of ... 3511, 3514
deviation allowed in adjusting ... 3535
Double Pensions,
no person allowed to receive ... 4715
Double Postage,
when to be charged on letters ... 3898
on books, &c ... 3910
Doubler, (Distillery,)
space around and elevation of ... 3269
to be destroyed and materials sold in certain cases of forfeiture ... 3332
Double Salaries,
not allowed, unless authorized by law ... 1763
Dover, N. H.,
port of delivery ... 2522
Draft,
forfeiture of citizenship for avoiding ... 1998
Drafts,
drawn upon any bank, &c., at sight or on demand, tax on ... 3418
prompt presentation for payment required ... 3645
by or upon authorized officers of United States, included in words "obligation or other security of the United States" 5413
Draughtsman,
to verify plan of distillery ... 3263
Drawback,
of customs-duties,
jurisdiction of district courts of suits on debentures for, &c ... 563
of circuit courts ... 629
debentures, 6 per cent. interest allowed on, in suits ... 965
not allowed on oil-cake made from imported seed ... 2504
duty-paid merchandise may remain in warehouse and be entitled to ... 2977
no entry or exportation of goods withdrawn from custody of officers ... 2978
except on certain manufactures and salt for curing fish ... 3025
provisions relating to ... 3015–3057
allowance of, on imports exported ... 3015
restrictions on ... 3016
no allowance of, unless goods exported within three years ... 3017
1 per cent. of retained for United States ... 3017
drugs, medicines, and chemicals ... 3018
on articles manufactured wholly of imported materials, 10 per cent. of, retained for United States ... 3019
on manufactures, in part, of wood grown in United States ... 3020
on salt for curing fish ... 3022
how ascertained on saltpetre manufactured into gunpowder ... 3026
10 per cent. retained for United States ... 3026
of discriminating duties not allowed ... 3027
on articles imported in bulk ... 3028
on spirits and sugars changed from original packages ... 3029
goods entitled to, when may be changed into other packages ... 3030
notice of change, to whom given ... 3031
invoice to be deposited with collecter, &c. 3032
inspection of, entered for ... 3033
goods intended for, transported, to be accompanied by copy of cost from invoice, &c. 3034
proceedings before lading; oath of exporter. 3035

Section.

Drawback—Continued.
on merchandise transported to another district for exportation ... 3036
merchandise entered for, on incomplete entry, when extension of time, &c ... 3037
debentures for, in certain cases, at what time payable ... 3038
when payment of, refused by collector, protest of; suit, how brought ... 3039
how assigned, &c ... 3040
on certificate of exportation of merchandise from other than port of importation ... 3041
error or fraud; duties to be received before payment of ... 3042
bond to be given for delivery of merchandise at a foreign port before receipt of. 3043
appropriation for payment of, how expended; who to pay; certificates of, where receivable for customs ... 3048, 3689
on material to rebuild burnt district in Chicago ... 3689
falsely making, forging, altering, &c., uttering false as true, &c ... 5423
merchandise entered for, and relanded, seizure, forfeiture, and penalty ... 3049
false entry of, forfeiture ... 3050
when by accident or mistake ... 3051
imports from British North America entered, &c., may be transported, &c., for benefit of ... 3053
on imports exported from Lake Pontchartrain ... 3055
imports entered for, may be exported to British North America ... 3056
Secretary of Treasury to prescribe rules, &c., for ... 3057
fee for permit to load goods for export entitled to ... 4382
of internal-revenue taxes,
collector may be designated to have charge of ... 3161
appointment of superintendent of ... 3161
papers in bureau of, in respective ports, to be delivered to collector having charge of. 3161
on distilled spirits ... 3329
Secretary of Treasury to prescribe regulations in regard to, exported for ... 3329
duties of customs-officers relative thereto. 3329
on tobacco, snuff, and cigars ... 3386
Commissioner to prescribe regulations for ascertaining ... 3386
no allowance of, on tobacco less than $50 worth ... 3388
on certain articles exported ... 3441
Commissioner to make regulations concerning ... 3441
method of payment ... 3441
limitation of time as to claims ... 3441
no allowance of, on less than $10 worth ... 3441
certificates of, receivable for internal-revenue taxes ... 3442
fraudulent claim for ... 3443
appropriation for ... 3689
Drawing off,
distilled spirits ... 3267
water for purpose of cleansing worm-tub ... 3286
Drayage,
customs, appropriation of, receipts from ... 3687
Drilling Volunteers,
claims for, against United States ... 3489
Drop Letters,
rates of postage on ... 3904
Drugs, Medicines, and Chemicals,
(see *Examiner of Drugs, &c.*, and *Medicines and Medicinal Preparations.*)

Section.

Drunkenness,
penalty for, on merchant-vessels 4602
Dubuque, Iowa,
port of delivery in district of New Orleans. 2568
surveyor to reside at, duties of 2569
Du Luth, Minn.,
collection-district and port of entry 2595
collector to reside at 2596
Duncan City, Mich.,
port of delivery 2599
Dundee,
consul at, salary of 1690
Dunkirk, N. Y.,
collection-district and port of entry 2535
collector in, to reside at 2536
additional inspectors for 2605
Duplicate Bonds,
of United States, in lieu of destroyed bonds, 3702–3705
Duplicate Checks,
when and how issued 3646, 3647
for lost checks of disbursing officers in favor of postmasters 4046
in pension-cases, when and how issued 4770
Duplicates,
books, &c., exchange and disposal of, in library of Congress 86
agents for exchange of 87
Duties,
on imports,
schedules of special rates of 2503–2505
suits for, to be brought in name of United States 919
when special bail may be required in suits to recover 942
judgment in suit to recover, payable in coin.. 962
execution of, to be satisfied in coin, &c... 962
interest to be allowed in suits on bonds for. 963
dutiable articles not to be imported in public vessels 1342
on sealskins from St. Paul and St. George Islands, Alaska 1969
collection and payment of 1969
on non-enumerated articles 2499, 2516
"similitude clause" 2499
to be levied on reimportations 2500
on goods produced east of Cape of Good Hope. 2501
discriminating duties on importations in foreign vessels 2502
90 per cent. of regular duties, list of importations admitted at 2503
10 per cent. reduction of duties, articles entitled to 2503
tariff of 2504
free list 2505
certificate of consul or minister to be indorsed on American artists' declaration to admit works of art free, &c... 2505
certain fish and fish-oil admitted from Canada, Prince Edward's Island, and Newfoundland, free 2506
merchandise recovered from vessels sunk and abandoned, free of 2507
produce of forests of Maine, upon St. John River, sawed, &c., in New Brunswick, admitted free of 2508
of forests upon St. Croix River 2509
machinery for manufacture of beet-sugar to be exempt from 2510
imported for repair only, to be free of 2511
statuary and pictures for exhibition and not for sale, to be free of; bond for payment of, when not reëxported 2512
materials for construction, &c., of vessels in foreign and Atlantic and Pacific trade may be imported in bond 2513

Section.

Duties—Continued.
if used for such construction no duties to be paid 2513
such vessels not to engage in coastwise trade more than two months in a year. 2513
articles for repair of American vessels may be withdrawn from bonded warehouse free of 2514
peltries and proper goods, &c., of Indians, when admitted free of 2515
on non-enumerated articles, rate of....2499, 2516
cargoes for Greenport, N. Y., to pay at Sag Harbor 2537
for Cold Spring or Port Jefferson, N. Y., to pay at New York 2540
rates of, to be posted up in office of collectors, &c., receipts for, penalty, &c.... 2635
reëxportation, &c., bonds conditioned for payment of, suit on 2778
on merchandise for districts other than that of arrival, how paid 2779
to be paid only on goods landed 2779
when not paid in district of arrival, duty of master of vessel 2780
bond for, by master of vessel proceeding to another district 2782
when to be cancelled 2783
on excess of sea-stores.............2796, 3112, 3113
coal of steam-vessels exempt from 2798
baggage, on articles contained in 2801
concealing dutiable articles in, penalty... 2802
in transit to foreign country free from.... 2803
on merchandise transported to interior ports, bond of importer or consignee........ 2825
to be ascertained by collector, certificate of, to surveyor 2826
when greater than bond, no entry allowed; surveyor to collect, when ascertained. 2831
invoices of goods subject to ad-valorem, how and in what currency made out..2838, 2854
merchandise undervalued to be held by collectors 2840
proper value of, to be ascertained 2840
oaths of owner, consignee, agent, &c., forms of 2841
bond for production of invoice verified by oath of absent owner of goods subject to ad-valorem 2842
not to be liquidated until triplicate invoice is received 2857
collector and naval officer to estimate and secure, before granting permit to unlade 2869
weighing, gauging, &c., to be done before goods removed from wharf 2882
to be paid before sale of perishable cargo... 2892
20 per cent. additional on undervalued goods. 2900
on articles omitted in entry without fraud, to be collected 2901
President to establish regulations for estimating, in case of depreciated currency 2903
estimated upon value at date of shipment.. 2904
merchandise subject to ad-valorem, &c., appraised at foreign market value at time of exportation 2905, 2906
charges for transportation, packing, &c., to be added 2907
commission at usual rates, but not less than $2\frac{1}{2}$ per cent., to be added 2907
on wines, &c., how graded, &c 2907
charges a part of value for assessment of ... 2908
20 per cent. collected on additions for charges exceeding 10 per centum, &c., and on wools exceeding 12 cents per pound .. 2908
where appraisal exceeds 10 per centum of invoice value 2909

Section.

Duties—Continued.
on imports of different values invoiced at average price 2910
on wool in same bale, &c., of different qualities 2912
on vinegar, according to standard 2917
on distilled spirits, according to hydrometer proof 2918
on grain 2919
allowance made for deficiency of articles 2921
when bond required of owner, to give information to determine rate of 2925
decision of collector final, and no suit to be maintained for recovery of, unless protest and appeal are made 2931
additional, not deemed fines, penalties, &c., for purpose of distribution, &c 2948
stored merchandise, when sold for 2963
imports, how and where stored, upon nonpayment of 2964
amount and payment of, on goods withdrawn from warehouse for consumption 2970
on merchandise in public store unpaid, after one year, &c., proceedings to obtain 2973
paid on goods remaining in warehouse, returnable on exportation within three years, &c 2977
goods may be exported without payment of 2979
no abatement of, for injury to goods while in public warehouse 2983
refund allowed on goods destroyed, &c., by accident 2984
merchandise for immediate transportation not subject to liquidation of, at port of first arrival 2991
what, to be collected in case of failure to transport bonded merchandise in given time 3001
goods withdrawn from warehouse for exportation to Mexico without payment of 3002
through port of Lavaca, Tex 3003
through port of Indianola, Tex 3004
goods arriving at certain ports for British provinces and Mexico not to pay 3005
how collected and paid 3009
unascertained 3010
paid under protest, to be deposited 3010
may be recovered 3011
suits to recover, not to be maintained unless bill of particulars is served 3012
improperly collected, how refunded 3012½
refund of unascertained 3012½
in case of failure to appeal 3013
judgment for, what to recite, and payable in coin 3014
remitted on salt for curing fish 3022
on excess of sea-stores of vessels on northern, &c., frontiers, penalty, &c 3112
on saloon stores 3113
not to accrue because registered coasting-vessel touches at foreign place 3127
shall be paid in what 3473
United States notes not received in payment of 3588–3590
appropriation of, to interest on sinking-fund 3688
application of coin received from 3694
change of place of collection during prevalence of epidemic or contagious diseases 4397
States not to collect, without consent of Congress 4792
not to be deposited in national-bank depositories 5153
national-bank notes not receivable for 5182
President may cause, to be collected at port of delivery in case of insurrection, &c. 5314

Section.

Duties—Continued.
or at any place on land, or on a vessel 5315
when land and naval forces may be employed to prevent removal of vessel, &c., detained for payment of, in times of insurrection, &c. 5316
when port of entry may be closed by proclamation of President; forfeitures 5317
when President may employ vessels in addition to revenue-cutters in aid of collection of 5318
willfully concealing or destroying invoice, book, or paper relating to merchandise liable to 5443
drawback of, (see *Drawback.*)
discriminating,
to be levied on articles imported in certain foreign vessels 2502
no part of, allowed to be drawback 3027
appropriation to refund certain 3689
tonnage or impost, may be suspended or discontinued by President's proclamaton, when 4228
when suspension to take effect 4228
duration of suspension 4228
Prussian vessels exempted from 4229
duration of exemption 4230
Spanish vessels exempted from, when 4231
duration of exemption 4231
imports and tonnage,
superintendence of, collection of, by Secretary of Treasury 249
tonnage,
what vessels not to pay 2793
decision of collector of customs as to rate of, final, unless, &c 2931
foreign vessels in northern, &c., districts, when to pay 3110
on vessels entering from foreign port—
exemption of foreign yachts 4216
on vessels of United States 4219
built in United States but owned by foreigners 4219
exemption from, of registered, enrolled, and licensed vessels in coasting or fishing trade 4220
of vessels making daily trips on inland waters between United States and Canada, except, &c 4221
from tonnage-fees of vessels touching at Canadian ports, when 4222
to be paid but once in each year 4223
exception as to certain foreign vessels 4223
time of payment of, by vessels paying once a year 4224
"light-money," on vessels not of United States 4225
how payable 4225
unregistered vessels, owned by citizens and carrying sea-letter, exempt 4226
oath by owner on entry, when 4226
by master, when 4226
effect of failure to take 4226
rights, &c., of foreign nations under laws and treaties regarding, preserved 4227
suspension of, by President's proclamation 4228
on vessel licensed for coasting-trade or fisheries 4320
licensed vessel in coasting-trade or fisheries subject to, when 4335
States not to collect without consent of Congress 4792
Brazil, steamships carrying mail between United States and, exempted from port charges, &c 4232

Section.

Duties—Continued.
duration of exemption 4232
discriminating tonnage,
on certain foreign vessels 4219
on other vessels 4219
when discrimination against United States abolished 4219
rights of nations under laws or treaties not impaired 4219
Duxbury, Mass.,
port of delivery 2527
Dwelling-House,
customs-officers not to enter, in making searches 3065
warrant to search, how and by whom obtained, &c.; forfeitures 3066

E.

Eagle,
weight and fineness of 3511, 3514
deviation allowed in adjusting 3535
Eagle Pass, Texas,
inspector of customs to reside at 2580
Eastern District, Md.,
collection-district 2548
collector in, residence of 2549
East Greenwich, R. I.,
port of delivery 2531
East Haddam, Conn.,
port of delivery 2533
East Hartford, Conn.,
port of delivery 2533
East River, Va.,
port of delivery 2552
East Windsor, Conn.,
port of delivery 2533
Easton, Md.,
port of delivery 2548
Eastport, Me.,
port of entry and delivery 2517
collector to reside at 2518
Ecuador,
salary of minister to 1675
Edenton, N. C.,
port of entry 2555
collector to reside at 2556
Edgartown, Mass.,
collection-district and port of entry 2527
collector to reside at 2529
Edgecomb, Me.,
vessels owned at, may unlade there 2520
Education, Office of,
establishment and purposes of 516
Commissioner of, appointment and salary .. 517
duties of 518
rooms for 519
Effects of Deceased Seamen,
provisions in relation to 4538–4545
Egypt,
salary of agent and consul-general to 1675
judicial authority of United States minister and consuls in 4111–4120
(see *Consular Courts.*)
Eight-Hour Law,
appropriation for reduction of wages under. 3689
eight hours to constitute a day's work under. 3738
Elections,
contested, fees of witnesses and officers .. 128, 129
expenses of contestants 130
Presidential, mileage of electoral messengers 144
in Territories, of justices of peace and militia officers 1856
of township, district, and county officers. 1857

Section.

Elections—Continued.
right to hold office not impaired by denial to citizen of right to vote at 2010
person so deprived of office may bring suit for possession 2010
jurisdiction of courts in such cases 2010
of Representative to Congress, circuit court to be opened on application of citizens 2011
appointment of supervisors of election 2012
of special deputy marshals 2021
duties of 2021
designation of circuit court commissioner as chief supervisor 2025
duration of office of chief supervisor 2025
duties of 2026
limit to appointment of marshals and deputies 2030
fees of chief supervisor 2031
compensation of supervisors and special deputy marshals 2031
Elective Franchise,
removal of suits from State to circuit court, against officer, &c., for acts done under provisions of Title XXVI, "THE ELECTIVE FRANCHISE" 643
Electrical Apparatus,
for lighting hall of House, dome, &c., who to have charge of 1817
Elizabeth, N. J.,
port of delivery 2541
Ellensberg, Oreg.,
port of delivery 2586
deputy collector of customs to reside at 2587
Ellsworth, Me.,
port of entry 2517
collector to reside at 2518
Elsinore,
consul at, salary of 1690
El Paso County, Texas,
jurisdiction of district court of New Mexico over citizens of 1928
El Paso, Texas,
port of entry 2578
collector to reside at 2579
Embassadors,
(see *Diplomatic Officers.*)
Embezzlement,
by consular officers, penalty for 1734
of money-order funds, penalty 4046
of postal revenues, what shall be deemed 4053
of pension-money by guardians, penalty 4783
discharge in bankruptcy not to release debt created by 5117
of private or public property by persons in military or naval service 5306
of implement used, &c., in printing any bond, bill, note, certificate, coupon, postage-stamp, revenue-stamp, fractional-currency note, &c 5453
of paper, &c., intended, &c., to be used in making bonds, &c 5453
of paper, &c., printed and intended to be used as bond, &c 5453
of metals, coins, medals, &c., at United States mint or assay-office 5460
officer guilty of, who pays clerk, &c., less than lawful sum and requires receipt for sum greater than paid 5483
depositing moneys unlawfully, converting, &c., loaning, withdrawing from deposit, or applying same for unlawful purpose by disbursing-officer 5488
failure of Treasurer, depositary, &c., safely to keep moneys deposited, &c 5489

Section.

Embezzlement—Continued.
loaning, using, converting, &c., depositing in banks, exchanging, &c., of moneys, by person charged with safe-keeping, &c 5490
failure of officer, &c., receiving moneys, &c., to render accounts 5491
failure of person having United States moneys to deposit with Treasurer, &c 5492
application of sections 5488–5492 5493
evidence of balance, against defendant, on trial of indictment for 5494
prima-facie evidence of, against person charged with safe-keeping, transfer, or disbursement of public moneys 5495
receiving from disbursing-officer, &c., on deposit, loan, &c., or using, converting, &c., moneys, by banker, &c., not an authorized depositary 5497
by president, cashier, teller, director, &c., of bank or banking association 5497
Embezzling Cargo,
punishment of seamen for 4596
Emigration,
(see *Cooly-Trade.*)
Emoluments,
of collectors, naval officers, and surveyors at certain ports, limit of 2690
at other ports 2691
of surveyors of customs, limitation on 2719, 2720
Empty Casks,
of American manufacture exported full and returned empty, free of duty 2505
distilled spirits, marks, &c., must be obliterated 3324
forfeiture of 3324
transporting, failing to efface marks, &c 3324
buying or selling, with inspection-marks thereon 3325
Empty Cigar-Boxes,
stamps on, to be destroyed 3406
giving away, accepting, selling, buying, or using stamped 3406
destruction of, on which a stamp shall be found 3406
Empty Package,
stamped, of tobacco and snuff, selling or giving, buying or accepting 3376
putting tobacco or snuff into 3376
Enacting Clause,
form of 7
Enacting Words,
limitation of use of 9
Engineer Corps,
of Army,
component of Army of United States 1094
composed of what 1151
chief of, to determine supplies for battalion 1152
engineer superintending construction of fortification to disburse, &c 1153
battalion, composition of 1154
company, composition of 1155
superintendent and commandant of cadets to have local rank of colonel and lieutenant-colonel of engineers 1310
detail of officers from, to superintend construction, &c., of light-houses 4664
of Navy,
number and grades in, on active list 1390
Chief of Bureau of Steam-Engineering to have title of Engineer-in-Chief 1471
relative rank of, on active list 1476
education of midshipmen—engineers at Naval Academy 1522
pension 4693
rate of total-disability pension 4695

Section.

Engineer Soldiers,
(see *Battalion of Engineers.*)
Engineer in Department of the Treasury,
salary of 235
assistant 235
Engineer in Post-Office Department,
salary of 393
assistant 393
Engineers in Revenue-Marine Service,
rank and pay of 2750
Engineers, Licensed,
(see *Licensed Officers of Steam-Vessels.*)
Engineers,
in service of Senate, salary 52
of House of Representatives 53
chief, of House of Representatives, to have charge of electrical apparatus, &c 1817
civil, payment of, by corporations receiving land-grants or subsidies, with right reserved to appoint, &c 5259
Chief of, (see *Chief of Engineers.*)
England,
salaries of minister and secretaries to 1675
Engraver of Mint,
at Philadelphia; how appointed 3496
salary of 3498
power of, to nominate subordinates 3504
duties of 3510
may execute certain dies 3551
Engraving,
required by Commissioner of Patents; advertisement and contract for 492
on stamped envelopes, prohibited 3915
of United States notes, &c., Secretary of Treasury may provide for 3575, 3577
Engraving and Printing,
provisions relating to 3571–3579
United States notes in Treasury 3577
expenses of 3578
appropriation for 3689
Engravings,
of maps, diagrams, &c., to illustrate documents ordered by Congress, procured by Congressional Printer 3779
when by advertisement 3780
of maps of States, &c., accompanying annual report of Commissioner of General Land-Office 3781
samples of paper for, to be preserved by Congressional Printer; execution of contract for 3782
to be third-class mail-matter 3878
Enlisted Men,
of Army,
number of privates for batteries of artillery 1100
for troops of cavalry 1103
for companies of infantry 1107
number of, allowed 1115
term of service of 1119
of Engineer Corps, allowances and benefits for, &c 1155
of Ordnance Department, designations of 1162
pay of 1280
increased pay of 1281
re-enlistment pay of 1282
to be paid according to length of service 1283
pay of, re-enlisting under honorable discharge 1284
allowance of rations to 1293
deposits of savings by 1305
interest on 1306
regulations for 1307
when payable 1308
when to have pensions 4693
rate of total-disability pension to 4695

Section.

Enlisted Men—Continued.
not mustered, when pension to dependent relatives to begin 4710
of navy,
pay of, how fixed 1569
when to have pensions 4693
rate of total-disability pension to 4695
non-enlisted men in temporary service, when pension to dependent relative to begin 4710
Enlistment,
in Army, term of 1119
in Navy, number authorized 1417
men to be sent home at expiration of 1422
when petty officers, &c., may be detained beyond term of 1422
men detained to be subject to laws and regulations 1423
limit of detention after arrival in port 1424
in Marine Corps, term of 1608
Enrolled Vessels,
(see *Vessels.*)
Enrolling-Officers,
when to have pension 4693
rate of total-disability pension to 4695
pensions to widows, &c., of, when to begin. 4710
Enrollment in Militia,
who subject to 1625
by whom made 1629
notice of 1627
Enrollment and License,
(see *Vessels.*)
Ensigns,
number of, on active list 1363
pay of 1556
Ensign, or Flag,
of revenue-cutter service, who to prescribe. 2764
Entry,
for deposit in distillery warehouse to be made in triplicate 3293
for withdrawal of distilled spirits from warehouse to be made in duplicate, &c 3294
for exportation of distilled spirits entitled to drawback, form of 3329
drawback,
(see *Drawback.*)
of imports,
by owners, &c., when to be made and what to include 2785
to be verified by oath 2786
how made, when particulars of merchandise are unknown 2788
when imperfect, collector what to do 2789
of distilled spirits or wines separate, certificate and transmission of 2794
separate, of personal baggage, tools, &c., how and by whom made 2799
when not by owner, bond, &c 2800
of cigars, number in package, &c 2804
where made for Albany, N. Y 2816
for Augusta, Ga 2817
for Pilatka, Fla 2818
for Bayport, Fla 2819
for Selma, Ala 2820
for Houston, Tex 2821
for ports of delivery on Mississippi River and its tributaries 2822
for ports of delivery in district of New Orleans 2823
for Vallejo, Cal 2824
and permit for landing 2826
when duty on merchandise exceeds bond 2831
for Petersburgh and Richmond collection-districts, how made 2836
subject to ad-valorem duty, when bond required for production of invoice 2842

Section.

Entry—Continued.
of non-residents, subject to ad-valorem duty, how made 2843
of non-residents not acquired by purchase, &c 2845
when merchandise admitted to, without oath to invoice 2847
who to give bond prior to, and in what form 2848
where one of owners resides abroad, on whose oath may be made 2849
how made when change of destination of merchandise after production of invoice, and non-receipt of triplicate at port of arrival 2857
when impracticable, from accident, &c., to produce invoice at time of, who to authorize making of 2858
certain provisions concerning, not to apply to countries where there are no consular officers of United States 2859
when may be made without production of triplicate invoice, &c 2859
not to be made unless invoice in proper form. 2860
by means of false invoice, &c., how punished. 2864
under treaty of Washington, how made 2866
estimate of customs-duties to be indorsed on. 2869
in case of vessel seeking port in distress, to be made before sale of perishable cargo 2892
addition to cost or value, how and when made 2900
articles omitted from invoice to be added to, when no fraud &c 2901
additions made to value of, for charges, how regarded, and what duty collected on; exceptions as to certain wools 2908
appraisal before, of imported goods damaged and taken from wrecks 2928
imported into northern, &c., frontier districts, how made 3097
of saloon-stores of vessels on northern, &c., frontiers, penalty for failure, &c 3113
of equipments, penalty for failure, &c 3114
taken or delivered at intermediate port, by vessels in foreign and coasting trade, how made, &c 3117
fees for 4382
officer of revenue knowingly admitting to, or aiding, upon payment of less than lawful duty 5444
knowingly effecting, at less than true weight, or by payment of less than lawful duty 5445
of public lands,
(see *Lands, Public.*)
of vessels,
where to be made 2770
ship's papers to be produced to collector 2790
vessels of war and certain others not required to make 2791
ferry-boats not required to make 2792
when obstructed by ice, how made 2896
in foreign trade, mails to be delivered before. 3976
shall not be allowed until delivery of letters at post-office; oath, penalty 3988
of foreign vessels, production to collectors of register, clearance, &c., by master on 4209
deposit of papers with foreign consul 4209
penalty for failing to produce and deposit 4209
exceptions as to vessels of certain nations 4210
of vessels of United States, oath of master as to delivery of mails on 4212
licensed yachts exempt from, when 4214

Section.

Entry—Continued.
foreign yachts exempt from, when 4216
of yachts returning from foreign country... 4218
not to be allowed until hospital-tax is paid. 4585
until master has made oath as to impressment of crew 4590
fees for ,(see *Fees.*)
Envelopes,
(see *Postage Stamps and Envelopes.*)
Envelopes and Wrappers,
(see *Postal Envelopes and Wrappers.*)
Envoys Extraordinary,
shall be deemed included by words "diplomatic officers" 1674
salaries of, to Austria 1675
to Brazil 1675
to Chili 1675
to China 1675
to France 1675
to Germany 1675
to Great Britain 1675
to Italy 1675
to Japan 1675
to Mexico 1675
to Peru 1675
to Russia 1675
to Spain 1675
term for which payable 1740
Epidemics,
removal of offices from seat of Government in case of 4798
adjournment of Supreme Court in case of... 4799
of district and circuit courts 4799
removal of prisoners in case of 4800
"*E Pluribus Unum,*"
shall be inscribed on coins 3517
Equipage,
lost in military service to be paid for .3482, 3486, 3487
of horse condemned in military service, when to be paid for 3485
Equipments,
annual appropriation for, in militia 1661
of vessels, (see *Vessels.*)
Equity,
jurisdiction in, of district courts, to enforce liens for internal-revenue taxes, &c... 563
for what purposes district courts, so far as courts of, always open 574
jurisdiction of circuit courts, where United States are petitioners 629
appeals in cases of, within what time to be taken 1008
limitation to suits in, by and against assignee 5057
Erie, Pa.,
collection district and port of entry 2543
collector to reside at 2544
additional inspectors for district of 2605
Escheat,
to United States when real estate held by religious, &c., associations in Territories shall 1890
Esopus, N. Y.,
port of delivery 2535
Estates,
of citizens dying abroad, duty of consular officers as to 1709
liability of, on national-bank stock 5152
in bankruptcy, (see *Bankruptcy.*)
Estimates,
for Post-Office Department, when to be furnished to Secretary of Treasury 414
for permanent barracks, to be submitted to Congress before construction 1136
for public buildings and grounds in charge of Chief of Engineers, how approved and submitted 1798

Section.

Estimates—Continued.
of material for printing and binding, by foremen of printing and binding 3783
of expenses of Government Printing-Office to Register of Treasury 3814
of expenses, to be furnished by Light-House Board 4659
of cost of apparatus and buildings to be prepared for Light-House Board by engineer secretary 4665
manner of communicating 3660
for printing and binding for Departments, &c. 3661
for compensation of officers 3662
for public works 3663
to contain explanations of new items, &c... 3664
to state amount of outstanding appropriation 3665
for Navy Department 3666
for Post-Office Department 3668
all annual, to be submitted through Secretary of Treasury, and included in book of.. 3669
statement of appropriations of current year to be annexed to, by Secretary of Treasury 3670
of Commissioner of Internal Revenue 3671
statement of proceeds of old material to be included in appendix to book of 3672
for public buildings shall be approved before commencement 3734
Ethics,
professor of, at Naval Academy 1528
Eureka, Cal.,
port of delivery 2582
deputy collector to reside at 2583
vessels going to or from, how to report 2585
Europe,
goods may be transported in bond through United States from and to 2997
Evading Payment,
of tax on distilled spirits 3256
on fermented liquors 3340
Evansville, Ind.,
port of delivery in district of New Orleans.. 2568
surveyor and appraiser at, duties of 2569
weighers, gaugers, measurers, and inspectors for 2606
transportation in bond extended to 2997
inspectors of hulls and boilers for 4414
salaries of 4414
Evidence,
books and writings containing, &c., power of United States courts to require production of, in actions at law 724
what admitted, of value of merchandise in customs cases 2852
written, in customs cases where filed, &c... 2922
possession of goods imported contrary to law deemed sufficient, to authorize conviction 3082
how obtained under letters rogatory 4071
what shall be, of balance due from defendant, upon trial of indictment for embezzling public moneys 5494
what will be prima-facie, of embezzlement upon trial of indictment for, against person charged with safe-keeping, &c., public moneys 5495
Examination,
of clerks in Departments 164
in Navy, pay of officers delayed in 1562
of applicants for admission into civil service 1753
of emigrant vessels arriving 4272
report of, to Secretary of Treasury 4272
customs,
for appraisal, by customs officers, of importers, &c., how conducted 2922

Section.

Examination—Continued.
refusal of parties to answer, or to produce papers, penalty 2923
perjury on, forfeitures 2924
of imported drugs, medicines, &c., how made 2933
return upon 2935
appeal from, how made 2936
priority in, of goods for immediate transportation 2991
of books, &c., seized under customs laws, by warrant of district judge, by whom made 3093
internal revenue,
of distillery, &c., by revenue officer 3276–3278
of rectifying premises, &c 3278
by breaking up grounds, &c., of distillery, &c., to find concealed pipe, &c 3278

Examiner,
of claims for Department of State, appointment and salary of 349
of applicants for appointment in civil service 1753
of national banks, appointment, powers, duty, and pay of 5240
of customs at New York, number and appointment of 2538
compensation of 2745
how and when appointed, qualifications and oath of 2940
not to engage in mercantile business 2941
of drugs, &c., in collection-district of Boston and Charlestown, Mass 2529
at Philadelphia, Pa 2544
at Baltimore, Md 2549
at Charleston, S. C., residence of 2558
at New Orleans, La 2569
at San Francisco, Cal 2583
oath of, how administered 2611
salaries of 2743
at New York and San Francisco 2744
assistant appraiser at New York to perform duties of 2938

Examiners-in-chief,
in Patent-Office, appointment of 476
salary of 477
duties of 482

Examining Surgeons,
pension to commence at date of certificate of, certificate to be approved by Commissioner 4698½
of pensioners, biennial certificate of, required in case of invalid pensioners .. 4771
boards of, may be organized; duties, fees, &c 4774
may be required to make special examinations, fees of, in special cases 4775
in Pension-Office, may be appointed, &c .. 4776
civil surgeons may be appointed as; fees. 4777

Excess of Deposits,
for unascertained duties, appropriation to repay 3689

Exchange and Discount,
power of national banks to do business in .. 5136

Exclusive Jurisdiction,
of causes of admiralty 563
of courts of United States 711

Excursions,
special permit to steamers to carry additional passengers on 4466

Executions,
statement of proceedings upon, by marshals to Solicitor of Treasury 791
to Sixth Auditor 792

Section.

Executions—Continued.
issued on judgment for customs duties, &c., to require marshal to satisfy same in coin, &c 962
when not to issue against revenue officer, in suit for acts done, &c., or money exacted, &c 989
exemption from, of arms, &c., of militiaman. 1628
on judgment in customs cases, what to set forth, and how satisfied 3014
when United States may purchase on 3470
in bankruptcy, may be issued against petitioner, for register's fees, when 5124
against national banks not to issue from State courts, &c., before, &c 5242

Executive Clerks,
salary of 155

Executive Departments,
provisions applicable to all 158–198
what departments designated as 158
when included in word "Department" 159
salaries of heads of 160
regulations for, how prescribed 161
hours of business in 162
clerks in, how classified 163
examinations of 164
women may be 165
distribution of 166
and employés, salaries of 167
temporary, salaries of 168
number of, how regulated 169
extra services of, when to be paid for 170
extra, when to be employed 171
compensation of 171
subordinate assistants, restriction on employment of 172
chief clerks in, duties of 173–174
to report monthly to their superior officers. 174
duty of superior on receipt of report of ... 175
disbursing clerks in, duties, &c., of 176
vacancies in offices of heads of 177, 179–181
in office of chief of bureau in 178
no extra compensation to officer filling vacancy in office of head of Department or bureau 182
oaths administered by officers or clerks of, detailed to investigate frauds 183
witnesses in claims before, how subpœnaed. 184
fees of 185
how compelled to attend and testify 186
professional assistance, in examining witnesses or claims, how obtained by 187
evidence to be furnished by, in suits pending in Court of Claims 188
heads of, not to employ attorneys, &c 189
former employés in, not to prosecute claims pending when, &c 190
balances certified by Comptrollers or Commissioner of Customs conclusive upon executive branch of Government 191
may be revised by Congress or courts 191
newspapers in, expenditure for 192
annual report concerning contingent fund for 193
respecting clerks employed in 194
time of making 195
when to be furnished to printer 196
inventories of property in, by whom kept ... 197
biennial list of persons employed in 198
right of heads of, to require opinion of Attorney-General 356
copies of books, records, documents, &c., in, how made evidence 882
reference by, of claims against, to Court of Claims 1063
proceedings in such cases 1064

Section.

Executive Departments—Continued.
judgment in such cases, how paid........ 1065
Court of Claims may call on, for information or papers.............................. 1076
contracts of, for stationery and supplies, limited to one year...................... 3735
printing, binding, &c., for, where to be done. 3786
upon whose requisition.................. 3789
form of, by whom determined............ 3790
reports of bureau officers in, how printed... 3788
number to be printed of annual reports of, for use of members of Congress...... 3798
accounts for printing and binding to be kept with, by Congressional Printer, not to exceed appropriation................. 3802
advertisements for, on what authority made or paid for......................... 3828
giving or offering to officer of, money, or other thing of value, to influence decision or action............................. 5451
acceptance of bribe by officer of, with intent, &c.............................. 5501
forfeiture of, and disqualification for, office, by accepting bribe, with intent, &c.. 5502

Executive Proceedings in Territories,
copies to be transmitted to President....... 1844

Executors,
when to make oath to invoices in customs cases.............................. 2846
may carry on business without additional special tax........................ 3241
when liable for debts due United States.... 3467
holding national-bank stock, not to be individually liable...................... 5152

Exemptions,
of certain property from distraint for internal-revenue taxes................... 3187
of distiller of brandy from apples, &c., provision for........................... 3255
from stamp-tax, of official instruments, &c.. 3420
of certain medicines, drugs, or chemicals.. 3436

Exeter, N. H.,
port of delivery........................... 2522

Expenditures,
of Senate and House, when made up and reported............................... 63
estimates of, how communicated to Congress 3660
of Navy Department, how accounted for, in estimates........................... 3666
limited to objects for which appropriations are made.......................... 3678
to amounts of appropriations.......... 3679
of postal service, classification, &c., of..... 4049

Expenses,
of march to rendezvous of militia in United States service, how paid............. 1654
of national loan, appropriation for........ 3689
at post-offices, allowances for............. 3860
of postal service, may be deducted from receipts.............................. 3861
vouchers for, to be audited................ 3862
of prize sale, to be charge upon property... 4629
advanced by marshal, how re-imbursed..... 4629
of national currency, to be paid out of taxes, &c., on national banks............. 5173

Expenses of Collecting Revenue from Customs,
appropriations for......................... 3687
customs fees to be credited to..........2602, 3687
fees for storage, drayage, labor, and cartage.............................. 3687
sums received from fines, penalties, and forfeitures.......................... 3687

Expiration of Service,
seamen in Navy to be sent home at......... 1422
subject to laws, if detained after......... 1423
limit of detention of, after............... 1424

Section.

Expiration of Service—Continued.
shipping-articles of, to contain conditions as to................................ 1425

Explosive Articles,
excluded from mails....................... 3878
not to be carried on steam passenger-vessels. 4472

Exploring Expeditions,
proceeds of materials, &c., sold to, not to be covered into Treasury................ 3618

Exports,
of goods and merchandise under treaty of Washington........................... 2866
superintendent of, how designated......... 3161
stamps for spirits to be furnished by internal-revenue collector, &c.............. 3330
for tobacco, snuff, and cigars to be furnished to internal-revenue collectors. 3385
when condensed statement of amount of, to be furnished to Congressional Printer by Secretary of Treasury............ 3812

Exportation,
of fire-arms, ammunition, and spirits to Alaska, regulation of.............. 1955
of goods in bonded warehouse.............. 2971
of goods, when entitled to return-duties, &c. 2977
restriction upon entry and, for drawback... 2978
when permitted without payment of duties. 2979
what imported merchandise may be withdrawn from warehouse for, to Mexico. 3002
through port of Lavaca, Tex............ 3003
through port of Indianola, Tex.......... 3004
of drugs, medicines, &c., how made........ 3018
of articles imported in bulk, how made, &c. 3028
of merchandise, from district other than that of importation, certificate of.......... 3041
of bonded imports from warehouse within three years.......................... 3052
from warehouse, and transportation to British provinces........................ 3054
of duty-paid imports to British provinces... 3056
collector of internal revenue may be designated to have charge of.............. 3161
superintendent of, appointment of......... 3161
of distilled spirits for drawback........... 3329
of spirits withdrawn from warehouse, without payment of tax, in original casks. 3330
of fine-cut, shorts, refuse scraps, clippings, &c., of tobacco..................... 3362
of tobacco, snuff, and cigars, without payment of tax........................ 3385
of matches................................ 3430
of medicines, preparations, &c., manufactured in bonded warehouse........... 3433

Extension of Patents,
issued prior to 2d March, 1861...........4924, 4925

Extortion,
by internal-revenue officer................ 3169
by United States officer, under color of office. 5481
by receiving money, &c., under threat of informing, or for not informing, against violation of internal-revenue law.... 5484

Extra Compensation,
to soldiers detailed for labor.............. 1287
not allowed where salary is fixed, unless authorized by law, and stated in appropriation.........................1764, 1765
none to officers, &c., employed on public building, &c., at seat of government. 1835
none for signing, &c., United States notes.. 3578
limit of, for disbursements on construction of public buildings.................. 3654

Extra Copies,
order for, by Joint Committee on Library... 3796
of documents, how procured from Government Printing-Office................. 3809

Section.

Extra Copies—Continued.
moneys from sales of, where deposited, and to credit of what appropriation 3818
Extradition,
transportation and safe-keeping of person delivered by foreign government to United States to be tried for crime; use of land and naval forces, &c...... 2575
(see *Seamen, Foreign.*)
Extra Duty,
punishment by summary court-martial in Navy 1624
Extra Pay,
(see *Extra Compensation.*)
Extra Postage,
prohibited on mail-matter delivered, &c., by carriers 3873
Extra Services,
no compensation allowed for, unless expressly authorized by law 1764, 1765
Extra Sessions,
of legislative assemblies in Washington, Idaho, and Montana Territories 1923
Extra Wages,
(see *Seamen in Merchant Service.*)

F.

Fact,
issues of, how tried in district courts 566
Factors,
to give bond for account by owner on entry of imported goods 2787
Fairfield, Conn.,
collection district and port of entry 2533
collector to reside at 2534
Fairport, O.,
port of delivery 2603
Falkland Islands,
consul at, salary of 1690
Fall River, Mass.,
collection-district and port of entry 2527
collector to reside at 2529
Falmouth, Mass.,
port of delivery 2527
False Accounts,
penalty for keeping 5306
False Brand,
shipping, &c., spirituous or fermented liquors or wines under 3449
False Certificates,
by internal-revenue officer 3169
False Claims,
jurisdiction of district courts of suits to recover forfeiture or damages for presenting 563
False Entry,
by internal-revenue officer 3169
in books of distiller 3305
of brewer 3340
of tobacco-manufacturer 3372
of cigar-manufacturer 3400
False Lights,
holding out, with intent to bring vessels into danger, &c 5358
False Oath,
by owner, to obtain register of vessel 4143
by agent or attorney 4163
False Personation,
of lawful holder of public stocks or debts, or of persons entitled to annuity, pension, prize-money, wages, &c., in receiving money, &c 5435
of revenue officer, &c 5448
False Receipt,
(see *Receipt.*)

Section.

False Returns,
by persons in military or naval service, penalty 5306
False Statement,
by internal-revenue officer relative to fees, &c. 3158
by farmer or planter, relative to leaf-tobacco. 3361
by dealer in leaf-tobacco 3359, 3391
False Swearing,
(see *False Oath.*)
False Weights,
or measures used in ascertaining distillery materials 3306
Falsely Making or Altering,
(see *Forging.*)
Farriers,
for troop of cavalry 1103
pension to relatives of 4710
Farmer or Planter,
producing leaf-tobacco, special tax 3244
shall make statement of sales on demand ... 3361
penalty on, for not making, or making false 3361
Fastenings,
Commissioner of Internal Revenue may require, on stills, &c 3270
of distillery, breaking, injuring, or tampering with 3311
Fathers,
when to have pension 4707
when pension of, to begin 4710
Fayal,
consul at, salary of 1690
Fees,
for transcripts from journals of Congress ... 71
of witnesses and officers in contested elections 128, 129
of witnesses in claims pending in Departments 185
passport clerk to administer oaths without .. 212
for copies of records of State Department .. 213
for exemplification of papers by General Land-Office 461
attorneys may charge clients compensation, &c. 823
of attorneys, solicitors, and proctors 824
to district attorneys on moneys collected or realized in proceedings under revenue laws 825
in suits on bonds, &c 826
for defense of revenue officers 827
of clerks of United States courts 828
of marshals 829
for services rendered United States; for expenses, &c 830
per diem allowance to district attorneys, clerks, and marshals, &c., for attendance, &c 831
of marshal of Supreme Court 832
semi-annual return of, and of expenses, by district attorneys, clerks, and marshals, to Attorney-General 833
to what fees not to apply 834
district-attorneys, amount to be retained by. 835
for southern district of New York, what sum, in addition to, shall be paid for expenses 836
additional compensation in prize causes .. 836
of district-attorneys and marshals in Oregon and Nevada, to be double, &c 837
of district-attorney, in proceeding to recover fines, penalties, and forfeitures, in revenue cases 838
amount of, to be retained by clerks of circuit and district courts 839
in California, Oregon, and Nevada 840
by marshal 841

Section.

Fees—Continued.
of clerks and marshals in prize causes, as additional compensation 842
of district attorneys, clerks, and marshals, allowances from, how made 843
surplus of, to be paid into Treasury by ... 844
Attorney-General to cause returns of, to be examined, &c 845
and commissioners of circuit courts, accounts of, to be certified by district judge, &c 846
in cases where United States is liable .. 856
of commissioners of circuit courts 847
of witnesses 848
none to be paid to officer of United States court for attending as witness before court or commissioner where he officiates 849
expenses to be paid to United States officer sent away from place of business as witness for Government 850
to seamen, &c., sent to United States from foreign port, to testify 851
of jurors 852
of printers 853
folio, number of words in, in estimating 854
jurors and witnesses, in cases where United States is party 855
mentioned in chapter XVI of Title JUDICIARY, how to be recovered 857
when informer, &c., alone liable for, of clerks, marshals, and attorneys 976
district attorney to be paid but one bill of, for suits which should be joined 980
taxation of, for witnesses before commissioner of circuit court, in examination of criminal case 981
bill of, of officers, witnesses, &c., where costs are recoverable by prevailing party, to be taxed, &c., and included in judgment or decree 983
how proven before taxed or allowed 984
of commissioners taking testimony for Court of Claims, how paid 1085
judicial, &c., in Territories, how prescribed. 1883
of attorneys, marshals, and clerks, in civil-rights cases 1986
of commissioners in such cases 1986
of persons appointed to execute process .. 1987
how made up, certified, &c 1987
to be recovered from defendant 1987
of chief supervisor of elections 2031
to be payable at Treasury 2031
accounts for, how made out, certified, &c. 2031
of supervisors of elections, appropriation for. 3689
postal employés not to receive 3858
for registering letters, amount of, to be accounted for 3927
for money-orders, schedule of 4032
of witnesses under letters rogatory, how to be paid 4074
in consular courts how established 4120
proceeds, how to be applied 4120
regulation of accounts of 4120
of marshals for services to inspectors of steam-vessels 4451
for inspection of steam-vessels 4458
of shipping-commissioners, provisions relating to 4592–4595
allowances and commissions of marshals in disposal of prize-property 4645
in prize cases of district attorneys and commissioners 4646
maximum allowed 4647
to be accounted for to Attorney-General .. 4647
excess to be paid into Treasury 4647

Section.

Fees—Continued.
of special counsel, how to be paid 4649
of witnesses 4651
of examining surgeons of pensioners 4774, 4775
of pension-agents for preparing vouchers ... 4782
of attorneys and agents of pensioners 4785
in patent-cases 4934–4936
for witnesses in contested cases 4907
receiving illegal, by inspector of steamboats 5482
receiving or demanding, by pension-agent, &c., from pensioner, for services connected with payment of pension 5487

consular,
for certifying invoices to be in full payment; penalty, &c 1716
masters of vessels shall pay; shall be liable for; papers may be withheld until paid 1718
for certifying invoices in British North American provinces, rate of 1721
none on tonnage of vessels touching at Canadian ports 1722, 4222
may be paid in foreign coin in Canada 1722
penalty for exacting illegal 1716, 1723
for failure to collect, remission 1724
returns of, shall be made 1725
receipt shall be given for 1726
to be numbered and registered 1727
transcript of register of, shall be furnished with accounts 1728
collected by officers not in Schedules B and C shall be accounted for 1729
such officers to have, as compensation 1730
in excess of $2,500 a year, subject to draft of Secretary of Treasury 1732
tariff of, to be conspicuously posted in consulate 1731
received at vice-consulates and consular agencies, in excess of $1,000 a year, when subject to draft of Secretary 1733
penalty for embezzlement of 1734
President may prescribe rates of tariff of ... 1745
shall be collected in United States coin or its value in exchange 1746
received by officers in Schedules B and C to be subject to draft of Secretary of Treasury 1747
for verification of invoice and certificate 2851
in cases of drawback, forfeiture for excessive 3046
table of consular, &c., to be attached to clearances of registered vessels 4207
copy of receipts for, given by consuls, &c., abroad to be furnished collectors on entry 4213
collectors to transmit copies of, to Secretary of Treasury 4213

customs,
table of, to be posted up in office of, officers; receipts for, penalty, &c 2635
penalty for demanding, &c., excessive 2636
accounts of, to be kept and transmitted to Commissioner, &c., penalty 2639
collectors of northern, &c., frontier districts to account for 2644
of collectors, list of 2654
of collector and naval officer at same port, how divided and who to account for 2655
drawback fees, how shared, &c 2656
of surveyors, inspectors, and deputy inspectors, list of 2657
of collectors for entry on northern, &c., frontiers 2658
pro ta only for serving portion of year 2687

Section.

Fees—Continued.
of collectors and of surveyors acting as collectors, limit of 2688
to be credited to appropriation for expenses of collecting revenue from customs... 2692
entry and clearance 2793, 4381, 4382
decisions of collectors of customs as to, final, unless, &c.; no suit to be maintained for recovery of, unless protest and appeal are made 2932
sealed cars laden with goods in transit exempt from manifest-fees 3007
on gaugeable merchandise exported and withdrawn from warehouse, &c 3023
on weighable articles, &c 3024
appropriation of 3687
of collectors of customs for registering or recording vessels 4185
for indorsements on certificates 4185
for taking bonds 4185
of surveyors for measurement of vessels, &c. 4186
by whom paid 4186
limit upon, for measuring and certifying tonnage of vessels 4186
of collectors for furnishing certificate as to bills of sale, mortgage, hypothecations, and conveyances of vessels 4194
for furnishing certified copies of, &c 4195
due by vessels, to be paid before clearance.. 4206
of surveyors, for enrolling and licensing vessels 4346
of coasting vessels navigating by sea 4381
of vessels navigating on northern, &c., frontier, otherwise than by sea 4382
table of, to be conspicuously posted by customs-officers 4383
of vessels subject to enrollment or license.. 4384
exemption of lighters and boats 4385
diplomatic,
at legations, to be accounted for to Secretary of Treasury 1687
President may prescribe rates 1745
to be collected in United States coin or its value in exchange 1746
internal revenue,
of inspectors of tobacco and cigars 3151
of gaugers of internal revenue 3157
officers to make statement of, when required. 3158
of officers making sales of real estate 3197
in cases of distraint and seizure, to be prescribed by Commissioner 3206
of appraisers of goods seized 3460
in bankruptcy,
of register, by whom to be paid 5008
to have priority in order for dividend 5101
to be paid in full 5101
of register, schedule of 5124
to have priority over all other claims 5124
security to be deposited for 5124
when no assets, petitioner to pay 5124
payment by petitioner, how compelled 5124
of messenger, how payable 5126
schedule of 5126
justices of Supreme Court may reduce 5127
may prescribe tariff of, for other services .. 5127
Fees and Commissions,
of registers and receivers, for services relating to entry and purchase of public land.. 2238
in consolidated land-districts for transcripts and record information 2239
limit of 2240
for quarter or fractional part of quarter.. 2240
excess of, to be paid into Treasury 2241
no compensation to be paid for past services to those who have received illegal fees 2242

Section.

Fees and Commissions—Continued.
removal from office for receiving illegal fees 2242
when to commence 2242
not to be charged for administering oaths. 2247
(see *Commissions.*)
Fee-simple,
of purchaser of lands and tenements reverting from Indian reservations 2122
Female Inspectors of Customs,
how and by whom employed 3064
Female Laborers,
in Post-Office Department, salaries of 393
Feminine,
words of masculine gender to include feminine 1
Fences,
for distillery, height of 3275
Fermented Liquors,
internal-revenue officers interested in production of 3168
provisions of section 3282 not to apply to... 3282
brewer of, notice by 3335
bond of 3336
books and statements 3337
entries of, in brewery books to be verified by oath 3338
measure of contents of barrel 3339
rate of tax on 3339
by whom tax is to be paid 3339
fractional parts of barrel, how accounted... 3339
evasion of tax on 3340
fraudulently failing to make entry of, &c., of, or to do anything required, &c 3340
stamps for 3341, 3342
brewer to obtain, from collector 3342
mode of affixing and canceling 3342
selling, removing, &c., in packages without, or with false 3343
drawing, from packages without, or with false, or without defacing 3344
permits for removal of 3345
removal or transportation of, under 3345
becoming sour, &c., may be removed for manufacturing purposes without 3347
brewers selling, at retail, at brewery 3348
marking by brand, packages of 3349
purchases by one brewer from another with brand of purchaser 3349
unfermented worts for enlivening of 3351
possession of, after sale or removal from brewery, &c., not tax-paid 3352
absence of stamps from, to be notice that tax not paid 3352
removal or defacement of stamp or permit by other than owner 3353
withdrawing for bottling, from unstamped packages or bottling on brewery premises 3354
laws imposing taxes on, extended to exterior boundaries of United States 3448
shipping, &c., under false name or brand... 3449
Fermenting Tubs,
(see *Tubs.*)
Fernandina, Fla.,
collection-district and port of entry 2562
collector in 2563
Ferry-Boats,
not required to enter and clear 2792
what reports required of 2792
to carry what lights 4233
may be employed in United States by foreign railroad company 4370
Fiduciary Debts,
not released by discharge in bankruptcy 5117

Section.

Fifteen Months,
assessment of internal-revenue taxes within. 3182
Fifth Auditor,
examination of accounts of, by First Comptroller ... 269
immediate settlement by, of particular accounts ... 271
appointment and salary of ... 276
duties of ... 277
Fifty-Cent Piece,
weight and fineness of ... 3513, 3514
deviation in adjusting ... 3536
Final Decree,
and judgments of circuit court, appeal to Supreme Court ... 692
on certificate of division of opinion, reviewed by Supreme Court on appeal. 693
of State court, review of, by Supreme Court. 709
Financial Agents,
national banks may be employed as ... 5153
Fine Bars,
of gold may be made by mints ... 3518
of silver ... 3518
may be exchanged for imported bullion ... 3546
Fineness of Coins,
assay-commissioners to test ... 3547
Fines, Penalties, and Forfeitures,
jurisdiction of district courts of suits for ... 563
in what districts prosecuted for violation of Title INSURRECTION ... 564
jurisdiction of circuit courts of suits to recover ... 629
United States courts to have exclusive jurisdiction of suits for recovery of, incurred under United States laws ... 711
where pecuniary, may be sued for ... 732
seizures for, under United States laws, in what district to be prosecuted ... 734
district attorneys, statement by, of suits for recovery of, to Solicitor of Treasury .. 772
duty of, to prosecute for recovery of, under revenue laws; compensation ... 838
report by, to Secretary of Treasury or Commissioner of Internal Revenue of cases not prosecuted ... 838
suits for, to be brought in name of United States ... 919
special bail in prosecutions to recover pecuniary ... 942
when United States not subject to costs in suit for recovery of, under internal-revenue laws ... 969
costs to be paid by defendant in prosecution for, when judgment against him ... 974
within what time prosecution for, to be commenced ... 1047
assessed against militia in United States service, how certified to marshals, &c.; collection of and imprisonment for ... 1659
deposit of, in Treasury; marshal's commission on ... 1660
for what offenses, may be remitted by governors of Territories ... 1841
of real estate held by religious, &c., associations in Territories ... 1890
incurred in customs collection-district of Alaska, remission of ... 1958
limit to emoluments of customs-officers, not to extend to ... 2690, 2691
lien for freight to be paid from proceeds of sale of forfeited imports ... 2981
for smuggling ... 3062
in customs cases, suits, &c., for, when and by whom to be commenced ... 3085
who to cause commencement of ... 3087
Fines, Penalties, and Forfeitures—Continued.
deductions from proceeds of, distribution of balance ... 3090
under customs laws, appropriation of proceeds of ... 3687
appropriation to pay distributive shares of ... 3689
internal revenue, to be sued for by collector. 3213
collected without authority, to be abated or refunded by Commissioner ... 3220
sale of distilled spirits forfeited, to be subject to tax ... 3334, 3458
for various offenses ... 3443–3463
of boiler, stills, machinery, materials, &c., to be sold at public auction ... 3450
of spirituous liquors, to be disposed of by Commissioner ... 3450
to be enforced by proceedings in rem ... 3453
postal, accounts to show amounts derived from ... 4049
to be deposited as postal revenues ... 4050
how recovered ... 4059
on sailing vessels navigated in violation of navigation rules, how recovered ... 4234
for offenses against navigation laws, how recovered ... 4305, 4380
under Title LIII, MERCHANT SEAMEN, how recovered, application of ... 4610
relating to live-oak, recovery and distribution of, mitigation of ... 4751
of Navy officers, seamen, and marines, to be applied to Navy Hospital ... 4809
of soldiers, to Soldiers' Home ... 4818
of officers and soldiers, to National Home for Disabled Volunteers ... 4831
proceedings for remission of, on summary examination before district judge, under customs, navigation, &c., laws ... 5292
under methods prescribed by Secretary of Treasury ... 5293
under laws relating to steam-vessels ... 5294
witnesses interested in, may be examined in proceedings to recover, without deprivation of share ... 5295
distribution of, under laws relating to slave-trade ... 5565
incurred under statutes embraced in Revised Statutes, prior to repeal, &c., how prosecuted, &c ... 5598
(see *Cigars, Customs, Distilleries, Tobacco,* and *Vessels.*)
Fire-Arms,
into Alaska, regulation of importation, &c., of ... 1955
killing seal by use of, unlawful ... 1960
Fire-Buckets,
on river passenger-steamers ... 4483
Fire-Crackers,
storage of in public or private warehouse ... 2962
in bonded warehouse, exception of, in sales .. 2975
Fire-Extinguishers,
on steam-vessels ... 4479
Fire-Pumps and Hose,
on steam passenger-vessels ... 4471
Fireman and Blacksmith,
in Post Office Department, salary of ... 393
Firemen,
salary of, for Senate ... 52
for House ... 53
in Post Office Department ... 393
in Navy, enlistment of ... 1417
pay of, how fixed ... 1569
additional to seamen, &c., doing duty as .. 1570
First Auditor,
not to engage in certain business ... 243

Section

First Auditor—Continued.
examination of accounts of, by First Comptroller ... 269
immediate settlement by, of particular accounts ... 271
appointment and salary ... 276
duties of ... 277
First Assistant Engineers of Navy,
number and rank of ... 1390
relative rank of, on active list ... 1476
First Sergeants,
for battery of artillery ... 1100
for troop of cavalry ... 1103
for company of infantry ... 1107
First Comptroller,
to approve bond of Secretary of Senate ... 57
of Clerk of House ... 58
balances certified by, subject to revision only by Congress and courts ... 191
not to engage in certain business ... 243
appointment and salary ... 268
duties of ... 269
appeal to, from settlements made by Sixth Auditor ... 270
power of, to direct immediate settlement of accounts by First and Fifth Auditors. 271
annual report by, of officers failing to make settlement of accounts ... 272
reference of certain accounts to Court of Claims on certificate of ... 1063
proceedings in such cases ... 1064
to prescribe sum and form of internal-revenue collector's bond as disbursing agent .. 3144
duty of, in regard to delinquent internal-revenue collector ... 3217
shall institute suit for money due United States on settlement ... 3624
shall state and certify account of delinquent collector, &c., to Solicitor ... 3625
of delinquent disbursing officers ... 3633
shall keep appropriation accounts, &c ... 3675
shall be furnished copy of appointment of inspector of fuel ... 3712
what contracts shall be deposited in office of. 3743
discretion of, as to pay for carrying destitute seamen ... 4579
First-Class Mail Matter,
what shall constitute ... 3876
First Officer,
with majority of crew may demand inspection of vessel ... 4556
in foreign port ... 4559
Fiscal Agents,
public officers to perform duty as ... 3639
expenses of, for clerks, &c., may be allowed. 3653
Fiscal Year,
date of commencement of ... 237
accounts of expenditure of public money to be settled within ... 250
outstanding liabilities to be deposited at end of ... 306
to be observed in adjustment of accounts of internal-revenue collectors ... 3146
Fish and Fisheries,
(see *Fisheries*.)
Fish and Fish-Oil,
from Canada, Prince Edward's Island, and Newfoundland, free of duty ... 2506
Fisheries,
vessels qualified to engage in, deemed vessels of United States ... 4131
belonging to citizens engaged in, exempt from tonnage duties ... 4220
what vessels may engage in ... 4311
license to engage in, how obtained ... 4320
bond to obtain ... 4320

Section.

Fisheries—Continued.
form of ... 4321
enrollment and license of vessels for, at Jersey City ... 4340
at Camden, N. J ... 4341
permit for vessel engaged in, to touch at foreign port ... 4364
penalty for being within three leagues of coast, &c., without permission ... 4365
penalty on vessel engaged in, without license 4371
agreement with fishermen for voyage, what to specify ... 4391
penalty for violating agreement ... 4392
recovery of shares of fish under, &c ... 4393
vessel liable for master and fishermen's share ... 4393
discharge of vessel from process on giving bond ... 4394
Commissioner of Fish and, appointment of .. 4395
executive departments to aid in investigations of ... 4397
Five-Cent Piece,
weight and material of ... 3515
devices and legends on ... 3517
deviation in adjusting ... 3537
Five-Dollar Piece,
weight and fineness of ... 3511, 3514
deviation in adjusting ... 3535
Five per Cent. Fund to States,
appropriation of ... 3689
Five-Twenty Bonds,
redemption of ... 3697
Flags,
captured by Army, collection of ... 218
by Navy, collection of ... 428
disposition of ... 1554
and signs for diplomatic and consular officers ... 1748
revenue, form of ... 2764
Fleet,
share of prize-money allowed to captain of .. 4631
pay of engineer of ... 1556
of paymaster of ... 1556
of surgeon of ... 1556
Flexible Patterns,
third-class mail-matter ... 3878
Flogging,
forbidden on merchant-vessels ... 4611
Florida,
district court of southern district of, always open as court of admiralty ... 575
what benefits extended to militia and volunteers employed in suppressing Indian depredations in ... 1657
surveyor-general for, authorized ... 2207
salary of ... 2208
to be paid quarterly; to commence when. 2211
protection of live-oak and red-cedar timber in ... 2460
clearance, from ports in, of vessels laden with ... 2463, 4205
President may establish ports of delivery, and appoint surveyors in ... 2562
collection-districts, ports of entry and delivery in ... 2562
officers in ... 2563
disposal of property wrecked on coast of ... 4239
forfeiture of vessel conveying such property to foreign port ... 4240
Flour,
manufacture of, permitted at distillery only for distillation of spirits ... 3266
for Navy, how purchased ... 3727
Fog-Signals,
to be used on steam and sail-vessels, coal and canal-boats, &c ... 4233

Section.

Folding-Room,
of Senate, officers in, salaries 52
of House 53
Folio,
number of words in 854
Folly Landing, Va.,
port of delivery 2552
President may appoint surveyor at 2553
Foo-Chow,
consul at, salary of 1690
Forage,
for Army, allowance of, in kind 1270
to whom furnished 1271
on what conditions 1272
purchases not to exceed necessities of year. 3732
what allowed to mounted companies of militia when in United States service 1653
Forage-Masters,
employment of, by Quartermaster's department 1137
not to deal in public property on private account 1137
Foreign Affairs,
to be managed by Secretary of State under direction of President 202
number to be printed, of papers relating to, accompanying President's message ... 3798
Foreign and Coasting Trade,
(see *Vessels.*)
Foreign-built Vessels,
wrecked and repaired in United States, registry of 4136
Foreign Coins,
how estimated in payment of consular fees . 1722
may be received in payment for public lands. 2366
value, basis of, and how fixed 3564
recoinage of, before issue 3566
shall not be a legal tender 3584
counterfeiting of, current in United States .. 5457
passing, selling, bringing into United States, or having counterfeit 5457
mutilating, current in United States 5459
making, issuing, or passing coins resembling, as current money 5461
Foreign Consul,
deposit with, of register and papers of foreign vessel on entry 4209
exception as to certain vessels 4210
to return papers to master on production of clearance 4211
penalty for unlawful delivery 4211
Foreign Hydrographic Surveys,
restrictions on appropriations for publishing. 3686
Foreign Letters,
advertising undelivered 3931
carried in vessels leaving United States 3987
Foreign Mail,
rates of postage on 3912
contracts for carrying 4007
shall be carried in steamships, except 4008
pay for carrying 4009
fines on contractors 4010
stipulations in contract 4011
may be carried through United States, how. 4012
postage on, payment of, by consuls 4014
rates of, when carried in foreign vessels .. 4015
Foreign Merchandise,
in coasting-trade, carried by vessels between neighboring districts 4349–4352
between remote districts 4353, 4354
by vessels under twenty tons burden. 4355, 4356, 4359, 4360
permits for transportation of, by land, across New Jersey, Delaware, and Maryland. 4362
what to specify 4362
when not necessary 4362

Section.

Foreign Merchandise—Continued.
penalty for failure to report such merchandise on arrival 4363
Foreign Money,
rates at which receivable for consular fees .. 1722
Foreign Money-Orders,
provision may be made for 4028
Foreign Nations,
settlement of expenses of intercourse with. 291
adjoining United States, when mails of, may be carried through United States 4012
testimony may be obtained for use in suits in which any, &c., may be a party 4071
rights of, not impaired by provisions concerning tonnage-duties, &c 4227
(see *Letters Rogatory.*)
Foreign Postage,
on letters for United States, when may be paid by consuls 4014
Foreign Relations,
testimony for use in certain suits in foreign countries, how taken 4071, 4074
prisons for American convicts in foreign countries 4121–4124
judicial authority of United States ministers and consuls 4111–4130
in China, Japan, Siam, Egypt, and Madagascar 4111–4120
meaning of words "minister" and "consul". 4130
(see *Consular Courts* and *Letters Rogatory.*)
Foreign Seamen,
(see *Seamen, Foreign.*)
Foreign Stations,
supplies for vessels on, purchases of, out of United States 3721
contracts for, in United States 3723
Foreign Trade,
(see *Vessels.*)
Foreign Vessels,
(see *Vessels.*)
Foreign Vessels of War,
(see *Vessels.*)
Forfeitures,
(see *Fines, Penalties, and Forfeitures; Cigars; Customs; Distilleries; Tobacco;* and *Vessels.*)
Forging,
obligation or other United States security... 5414
note in imitation of national-bank notes 5415
certificate of entry of goods, &c 5417
bid, proposal, guarantee, official bond, public record, &c., to defraud United States. 5418, 5479
military bounty-land warrants, &c 5420
deed, power of attorney, order, receipt, &c., to defraud United States, &c 5421
knowingly, &c., having false, altered, &c., deed, power of attorney, &c 5422
abstract, official copy, or certificate of registry, or enrollment of, or license to, vessel, &c., passport, sea-letter, clearance, permit, debenture, &c 5423
United States coin or bars, or foreign coin current in United States 5457
minor coinage of United States 5458
Foremen,
of printing and binding, in Government Printing-Office, appointment and salaries of. 3761
to make estimates and file requisitions for materials 3783
what monthly statements to be made by, to Congressional Printer 3819
Form,
prescribed for customs documents, substantial compliance with 2769

Section.

Form—Continued.
for customs service in northern, &c., frontier districts ... 3124
Fort Covington, N. Y.,
port of delivery ... 2535
Fort Erie,
consul at, salary of ... 1690
Forts,
assent of State legislatures to purchase of land for ... 1838
Fourth Auditor,
accounts of, to be examined by Second Comptroller ... 273
appointment and salary of ... 276
duties of ... 277
duty as to requisitions of Navy Department ... 3673
Fox River,
(see *Wisconsin River*.)
Fractional Currency,
provisions relating to ... 3572–3581
issue, &c., by private parties prohibited ... 3583
printing, &c., business cards in imitation of, or upon ... 3708
letters from and to postmasters containing, to be registered free ... 3932
Fractional Gallons,
of distilled spirits, how taxed ... 3251, 3313
Fractional Parts of Barrel,
of fermented liquors, how accounted ... 3339
Fractional Notes,
provisions relating to ... 3572–3581
included by words "obligation or other security of the United States" ... 5413
France,
salary of minister and secretaries to ... 1675
Frankfort, Me.,
port of delivery ... 2517
collector and deputy collector to reside at ... 2518
Frankfort-on-the-Main,
consul-general at, salary of ... 1690
Frauds,
detail of clerks in Pension-Office to investigate ... 474, 4744
jurisdiction of district courts of suits for, against United States ... 563
power of Court of Claims to adjudge claims to be forfeited by ... 1086
on revenue to be reported by consuls, &c ... 2863
how punished in certain cases ... 2864
by internal-revenue officer ... 3168
in returns to collector of internal revenue ... 3179
in manufacture of tobacco and snuff on shares 3370
in manufacturing cigars on shares ... 3399
removal or concealment of goods, &c., with intent to defraud, forfeiture ... 3450
relative to execution or signing of documents required by internal-revenue laws ... 3451
taxable articles held by person with intent to defraud revenue ... 3453
Fraudulent Claims,
jurisdiction of district courts of suits for presenting, &c ... 563
for drawback on distilled spirits ... 3330
of internal-revenue taxes ... 3443
Frederica, Ga.,
port of delivery ... 2559
Fredericksburgh, Va.,
port of delivery ... 2552
surveyor to reside at ... 2553
Free Delivery,
of mail-matter, where authorized ... 3865
Free-Delivery Offices,
postage on drop-letters at ... 3904
Freedmen,
accounts for expenses incurred for, how settled ... 2034

Section.

Freedmen—Continued.
Hospital and Asylum in District of Columbia, supervision of ... 2038
restrictions upon expenditure of appropriation for ... 2038
Free of Duty,
list of importations ... 2505
machinery for manufacture of beet sugar ... 2510
railroad iron for repair under bond ... 3021
Freeport, Me.,
port of delivery ... 2517
Freetown, Mass.,
port of delivery ... 2527
Freight,
lien for, on imports in warehouse, payment of ... 2981
on forfeited imports, to be paid from proceeds of sale ... 2981
Freight-Boats,
steam-pressure allowed to, on Mississippi River and tributaries ... 4420
Frenchman's Bay, Me.,
collection-district ... 2517
collector in, residence of ... 2518
Friction-Matches,
(see *Matches*.)
Fuel,
for Congress, by whom provided ... 73
to officers of Army in kind ... 1270
purchased for use in distillery ... 3302, 3303
for Government use in District of Columbia, purchase, inspection, &c., of ... 3711–3713
for Navy, how purchased ... 3728
contracts for, for Army or Navy, not to exceed necessities of current year ... 3732
for seamen, vessels shall provide ... 4572
to be furnished superintendents of national cemeteries ... 4875
Fugitive from Justice,
limitation of time for indicting, &c., not to apply to ... 1045
Funchal,
consul at, salary of ... 1690
Fund,
for relief of sick and disabled seamen, custody and appropriation of ... 3689, 3692, 4545, 4585–4587, 4610, 4803
for Navy hospitals, deductions from pay to be applied to ... 4808, 4809
for support of Soldiers' Home, how derived ... 4818
for support of National Home for Disabled Volunteers, how derived ... 4831
Funeral Expenses,
allowance for, in Navy ... 1587
Fur-Bearing Animals,
in Alaska, killing of ... 1956
(see *Alaska*.)
Furlough,
in Navy, pay of officers on ... 1557
of officers retired on ... 1593
transfer from, to retired pay-list ... 1594
Furnaces, (Distillery,)
doors of, how to be constructed ... 3269
using, which have been locked ... 3311
Fur-Seal,
regulations for taking ... 1956–1976
(see *Alaska*.)
Fusible Plugs,
of boilers of steam-vessels, inspection of ... 4418

G.

Gaboon,
commercial agent at, salary of ... 1690
Galena, Ill.,
port of delivery in district of New Orleans ... 2568
surveyor to reside at, duties of ... 2569

Section.

Gallon,
of distilled spirits, definition of, as used in sales ... 3250
fractional, of distilled spirits, how taxed. 3251, 3313
Galveston, Tex.,
collection-district and port of entry ... 2578
collector to reside at ... 2579
inspectors of hulls and of boilers for ... 4414
their salaries ... 4414
Gangways,
for river-steamers carrying deck passengers. 4484
Gardner, Oreg.,
port of delivery ... 2586
deputy collector of customs to reside at ... 2587
Garnishees,
proceedings by United States, debtors of corporations may be summoned as ... 935
Gauge-Cocks,
of boilers of steam-vessels, inspection of ... 4418
Gaugers,
customs,
for certain ports ... 2606, 2607
extortion by, neglect of duty, and failure to make returns, &c., penalty ... 2637
salary of head gauger at New Orleans ... 2740
at New York, limitation on ... 2741
at Boston ... 2742
returns of goods gauged ... 2890
internal revenue,
appointment of ... 3156
to take oath and give bond ... 3156
duties to be under supervision of collector ... 3156
compensation of, to be by fees ... 3157
and traveling expenses to be verified by oath and paid monthly ... 3157
transfer or suspension by supervisor ... 3163
receiving-cisterns and room containing them to be under lock and seal of ... 3267
spirits from, to be drawn off under supervision of ... 3267
to gauge, prove, and mark spirits before removal from distillery to warehouse. 3287
to place distillery-warehouse stamp on cask. 3287
to sign such stamp ... 3287
penalties relating to ... 3290, 3292
to make daily return ... 3291
to stamp spirits removed from warehouse ... 3295
to sign tax-paid stamps ... 3295
to mark cask at time of affixing stamp, and erase, &c., when cask is empty ... 3295
to make daily report to collector, of stamps other than tax-paid, used ... 3314
to return book of stubs to collector ... 3314
to gauge and stamp rectified spirits ... 3320
to sign stamp for ... 3320
to gauge and stamp distilled spirits on premises of wholesale liquor-dealer ... 3321
to sign such dealer's stamp ... 3321
to gauge and brand spirits drawn into new packages containing ten gallons or more ... 3323
Gauging,
customs,
imported merchandise not to be removed from wharf before, &c., forfeiture ... 2882
of imports, when at expense of owner, &c. 2920
internal revenue,
of distilled spirits, Commissioner to prescribe rules for ... 3249
instruments for, to be prescribed by ... 3249
before removal from distillery to warehouse. 3287
of distilled spirits drawn into new packages of not less than ten gallons ... 3323
General Issue,
special matter under, in customs cases ... 3073

Section.

General Land-Office,
Commissioner of, appointment, salary ... 446
recorder of, appointment, salary ... 447
principal clerks of public lands and private land-claims ... 448
chief clerk of, to perform duties of Commissioner in his absence ... 448
principal clerk of surveys, appointment, salary ... 449
secretary to sign President's name to land-patents ... 450
assistant ... 450
clerks, &c., not to be interested in purchases of public lands ... 452
duties of Commissioner of ... 453
custody of seal and books of ... 454
to make plats, and furnish information, &c., to President or either House ... 455
duties and powers as to accounts relating to public lands ... 456
warrants for military lands to be recorded in. 457
patents, how issued and signed ... 458
duties of recorder of ... 459
papers in, authenticated copies to be furnished ... 460
fees for exemplification, &c., of ... 461
General of Army,
authorized ... 1094
office of, to cease ... 1094
title of ... 1095
aids to ... 1096
pay of ... 1561
General Postal Agency,
in China or Japan, authorized ... 4023
Genesee, N. Y.,
collection-district and port of entry ... 2535
collector in, residence of ... 2536
additional inspectors for ... 2605
Genesee River, N. Y.,
collector of customs to reside on ... 2536
Geneva,
consul at, salary of ... 1690
Genoa,
consul at, salary of ... 1690
Geodetic Surveys,
may be continued in Oregon and California. 2409
regulations for, how prescribed ... 2409
restrictions upon, and upon charges for ... 2409
Georgetown, D. C.,
collection-district and port of entry ... 2549
collector at ... 2550
Georgetown, Me.,
port of delivery ... 2517
Georgetown, S. C.,
collection-district and port of entry ... 2557
collector at ... 2558
Georgia,
district judge in, appointment and residence. 552
district attorney and marshal of southern district of, to perform duty in northern ... 767, 776
office of marshal in northern district of, where to be kept, mileage, &c ... 777
collection-districts, ports of entry and delivery in ... 2559
officers in ... 2560
collectors of customs at Savannah and Brunswick, may grant permits to unload vessels, appoint inspectors, &c., in each other's district ... 2561
Germany,
salaries of minister and secretaries to ... 1675
Gibraltar,
consul at, salary of ... 1690

Section.

Gifts,
penalty for soliciting or receiving, from employés in Government service, by superiors in office ... 1784
acceptance of, by inspector, gauger, weigher, or measurer of customs ... 2637
by internal-revenue officers for compromise, &c., of violation of law ... 3169
by marshals or district attorneys for compromise, &c ... 3170
by officers of customs for services under Title XLVIII, COMMERCE AND NAVIGATION; penalty ... 4187
for services under Title L, VESSELS IN DOMESTIC COMMERCE; penalty ... 4373
making or offering by persons engaged in importation or entry of goods, to ... 5452

Glasgow,
consul at, salary of ... 1690

Glass,
excluded from mail ... 3878

Glastenbury, Conn.,
port of delivery ... 2533

Gloucester, Mass.,
collection-district and port of entry ... 2527
collector and surveyor to reside at ... 2529

Glonoin or Glynoin Oil,
(see *Nitro-Glycerine.*)

Gloves,
imported kid and other, how appraised ... 2913

Goderich,
consul at, salary of ... 1690

Gold,
other than standard coin, when receivable in payment of dues ... 3474
bars, how may be cast by mints ... 3518
bullion may be deposited for coinage, &c.; certain may be refused ... 3519
coinage-charge on ... 3524
coinage to be reported by mint superintendents ... 3503
silver in deposits of, for coinage, to be paid for ... 3520
dollar, devices and legends on ... 3517
ingots, deviation allowed in ... 3533
notes, establishment of associations to issue ... 5185
redemption of, issued by gold-banks ... 5186
sales authorized as to surplus ... 3699
and gold dust, shipper of, to notify carrier, &c ... 4281
coin, (see *Coin.*)

Gold-Banks,
authorized ... 5185
reserve of, redemption by ... 5186
of San Francisco, not required to redeem notes in New York ... 5195
not required to take notes of currency banks at par ... 5196

Government Aid,
pay for carrying mail on railways receiving, how fixed ... 4001

Government Property,
proceeds of sale of old or condemned material, &c., shall be covered into Treasury ... 3618

Government Printing-Office,
estimates for printing and binding at, for Departments ... 3661
to be under management of Congressional Printer ... 3758
materials, &c., for, by whom to be purchased ... 3760
foremen of printing and binding in, appointment and salaries of ... 3761
clerks in, appointment and salaries of ... 3762
employés in, appointment and wages of ... 3763
when printing to be done at night, &c ... 3764

Section.

Government Printing-Office—Continued.
standards of paper for, how fixed ... 3767
advertisements for proposals to furnish paper for ... 3767
approval of contract ... 3772
contractor for paper, default of, how new contract made, and temporary supplies procured ... 3775
liable for increased cost in procuring ... 3776
report of, and prosecution of ... 3777
purchases in open market of paper ... 3778
engravings for documents ordered by Congress ... 3779
when procured by advertisement ... 3780
of maps for annual report of Commissioner of General Land-Office ... 3781
payment for engraving, &c ... 3782
foreman of, to make estimates and file requisitions for materials ... 3783
what printing and binding not to be done at ... 3785
what printing and binding to be done at ... 3786
printing of reports of officers in charge of bureaus, &c ... 3788
form and style of printing, &c., for Departments, how determined ... 3790
accounts for printing, &c., at, kept with Departments ... 3802
extra copies of documents, on what terms printed at, for private persons ... 3809
foremen of printing and binding in, to furnish monthly statements for Congressional Printer ... 3819

Grain,
customs duties on, how estimated ... 2919
how stored in customs bonded warehouse ... 2959
quantity of mash to represent one bushel of ... 3264
may be ground into meal or flour on distillery premises for purposes of distillation ... 3266
penalty for delivery of, at distillery having no sign ... 3279
not to be mashed at distillery between 11 p. m. Saturday and 1 a. m. Monday ... 3283
fifty-six pounds of, to be a bushel in determining quantity used at distillery ... 3309

Grand Gulf, Miss.,
port of delivery ... 2566

Grand Haven, Mich.,
port of entry ... 2599
collector to reside at ... 2600

Grapes,
brandy made from, exempt from certain provisions of internal-revenue laws ... 3255
grown in United States, exemptions from tax, of wine, &c., made from ... 3328

Gratuity,
to seamen in Navy, receiving medals of honor ... 1407
(see *Gifts.*)

Great Britain,
salaries of minister and secretaries to ... 1675
gold coins of, receivable for public lands ... 2366
par of exchange with ... 3565
vessels of, may engage in coasting-trade on lakes, &c., under Treaty of Washington, when ... 4347
suspension of privilege by President, when ... 4347

Great Districts,
division of sea-coast of United States into three ... 4348
coasting-trade between ... 4349–4361

Great Egg Harbor, N. J.,
collection-district ... 2541
collector in, residence of ... 2542

Greece,
salary of minister to ... 1675

Section.

Green Bay, Wis.,
port of delivery 2597
deputy collector to reside at 2598
Greenport, N. Y.,
port of delivery 2535
surveyor to reside at 2536
cargoes for, to be entered and duties paid at Sag Harbor, N. Y 2537
enrollment and license of vessels by surveyor at 4345
Greenwich, Conn.,
port of delivery 2533
Groton, Conn.,
port of delivery 2533
Guano Islands,
when considered as appertaining to United States 5570
notice of discovery and proofs to be furnished to Department of State 5571
proof, how completed, in case of death of discoverer 5572
privilege of discoverer, rate of charges, &c. 5573
restrictions on exportation, bond, penalty, &c. 5574
regulation of guano trade 5575
crimes and offenses committed on 5576
President to employ land and naval forces for protection of discoverer's rights .. 5577
right of United States to abandon, after guano removed 5578
Guarantee of Bid,
for naval supplies, sureties, &c 3719–3722
for carrying mail, shall be by certified check, &c., in certain cases 3953
Guaranteed Stocks,
held by United States, to be protected 3481
Guardians,
when increased pension to be paid to 4703
when pension to be paid to 4706, 4766
pension to joint pensioners having different. 4707
penalty for embezzling ward's pension 4783
holding national-bank stock not to be individually liable 5152
Guatemala,
salary of minister to 1675
minister to be accredited to Costa Rica, Honduras, Salvador, and Nicaragua, also. 1682
Guayaquil,
consul at, salary of 1690
Guaymas,
consul at, salary of 1690
Guilford, Conn.,
port of delivery 2533
Gun-Boats,
when persons serving on, to have pensions .. 4693
rate of total disability, pension to 4695
when pension to relatives of persons killed, &c., in, to begin 4710
Gunpowder,
in bonded warehouse, when to be sold 2975
storage of, in public or private warehouse .. 2962
drawback on foreign saltpeter manufactured into, &c 3026
for Navy, purchases of 3721
penalty for shipping, without notice 4288
license to carry, on steam passenger-vessels. 4422
penalty for carrying, contrary to law 4424
not to be carried on steam passenger-vessels except, &c 4472
how packed and marked for shipment 4475
penalty for shipping, contrary to law 4476
Gunners,
in Navy, number and appointment of 1405
pay of 1556
assimilated rank to 1491

H.

Section.

Habeas Corpus,
seamen committed for refusal to sail not to be discharged on writ of, for want of form, &c 4558
Haddam, Conn.,
port of delivery 2533
Hair,
(see *Wool.*)
Hakodadi,
consul at, salary of 1690
Half-Eagle,
weight and fineness of 3511–3514
deviation in adjusting 3535
Half-Dime,
weight and material of 3515
devices and legends on 3517
deviation in adjusting 3537
Half-Dollar Piece,
weight and fineness of 3513–3514
deviation in adjusting 3536
Half-Pay Pensions,
(see *Pensions.*)
Halifax,
consul at, salary of 1690
Hallowell, Me.,
port of delivery 2517
Hamburg,
consul at, salary of 1690
Hampden, Me.,
port of delivery 2517
Hampton, Va.,
port of delivery 2552
Hankow,
consul at, salary of 1690
Hardwicke, Ga.,
port of delivery 2559
surveyor of customs to reside at 2560
Harness,
lost in military service, to be paid for 3483
Harpswell, Me.,
port of delivery 2517
Hartford, Conn.,
port of delivery 2533
Harwich, Mass.,
port of delivery 2527
Havana,
consul-general at, salary of 1690
resident mail-agent at, authorized 4021
Haverhill, Mass.,
port of delivery 2527
Havre,
consul at, salary of 1690
Havre-de-Grace, Md.,
port of delivery 2548
Hawaiian Islands,
salary of minister to 1675
Hay,
loose, not to be carried on steam passenger-vessels 4472
Hayti,
salary of minister, &c., to 1675
minister to, shall be consul-general also 1683
Heads of Departments,
salaries of 160
to prescribe regulations for Departments ... 161
to appoint board for examination of clerks .. 164
to regulate distribution of clerks 166
to employ clerks and employés 169
to employ extra clerks, when 171
to amend defects reported by chief clerk 175
to appoint disbursing clerks in Departments. 176
death, absence, &c., of, how provided for .. 177–182
may have witnesses subpœnaed, when 184
may obtain professional assistance, how 187
not to employ attorneys or counsel 189

Section.

Heads of Departments—Continued.
duties of, respecting certified balances...... 191
to make annual reports of expenditure of contingent fund.............................. 193
of clerks employed........................ 194
time of making annual reports.............. 195
when to furnish annual reports to printer .. 196
to keep inventories of property............. 197
to file biennial list of clerks and employés in Interior Department.................. 198
may require opinion of Attorney-General... 356
prohibited to receive compensation for services in claim, &c., before Department or commission; penalty............... 1782
to aid investigations by Commissioner of Fish and Fisheries.......................... 4397

Health, Public,
United States officers to observe quarantines and health laws of the States........ 4792
to aid in execution of such laws; in what manner.................................. 4792
States not to collect tonnage or impost duties, by reason of health-laws, without consent of Congress.......................... 4792
discharge of vessel elsewhere than at port of entry..................................... 4793
warehouses to be erected for deposit of merchandise................................. 4794
cargo to be deposited in such warehouse as collector may designate................ 4795
to be under joint custody of collector and owner................................... 4795
to remain until it may be safely removed. 4795
collector to permit owners, &c., to receive merchandise............................ 4795
rate of storage, how fixed.................. 4795
extension of time for entry of vessels subject to quarantine......................... 4796
no cargo to be unladen except as allowed by law...................................... 4796
in case of contagious or epidemic disease revenue officers may remove from port... 4797
to perform same duties as at original port. 4797
public notice of removal to be given...... 4797
public offices may be removed from seat of government........................... 4798
Supreme Court may adjourn to another place.................................. 4799
marshal to publish notice of such removal.................................... 4799
circuit and district judges may adjourn court.................................... 4799
United States prisoners may be removed.. 4800
such removals to be at expense of United States............................... 4800

Headstones,
in national cemeteries, requirements for.... 4877

Heirs,
of diplomatic or consular officers dying abroad, allowance to.................. 1749
of colored soldiers and sailors, collection and payment of bounty, &c., due to....... 2032

Hemp,
statistics in regard to, to be embraced in census returns......................... 2184
loose, not to be carried on steam passenger-vessel.................................. 4472
baled, how carried.......................... 4672
penalty for carrying, contrary to law..... 4473
for Navy, provisions concerning contracts for.........................3718–3722
American growth or manufacture to be preferred.............................. 3725

High Seas,
offenses committed upon, where to be tried. 730

Section.

Hingham, Mass.,
port of delivery............................ 2527

Hioga and Osaka,
consul at, salary of........................ 1690

Hogshead,
of fermented liquors, contents of........... 3339

Homestead,
chiefs, &c., of Stockbridge Munsee Indians may acquire.......................... 2310
Ottawa and Chippewa Indians may enter certain lands as...................... 2313
entries, how made..................... 2313
selection of, for minor childen of......... 2314
on lands reserved as mineral, settlers' rights. 2341
applicant, commissions to be paid by....... 2238
fee for testimony establishing right of.... 2238

Home for Disabled Volunteers,
(see *National Home, &c.*)

Honorable Discharge,
certificate of, to be returned by accounting officer to officers and men of Army.. 282
pay of men re-enlisting in Army under..... 1284
in Navy................................ 1573

Honolulu,
consul at, salary of........................ 1690

Honduras,
minister-resident at........................ 1682
(see *Guatemala.*)

Hong-Kong,
consul at, salary of........................ 1690

Horses,
allowance of forage for, in Army........... 1271
of militia in United States service........ 1653
punishment of soldier for losing or selling.. 1342
condemned, to be paid for.................. 3485
lost in military service, provisions concerning.........................3482–3487, 3489
appropriation to pay for.................. 3689

Horse-Express,
mail may be carried on railway-routes by.. 3999

Hospitals,
may be prepared on passenger-vessels...... 4254
when used, to be counted as passenger space................................. 4254

army,
allowance of sick-diet in.................. 1175
employment of women as nurses........... 1238
of matrons in............................ 1239
pay of matrons and nurses at.............. 1277

freedmen's,
in District of Columbia, supervision, &c., of. 2038

insane,
to be located in District of Columbia....... 4838
superintendent of, how appointed.......... 4839
salary and bond of........................ 4839
qualifications and duties of.............. 4839
to be disbursing agent of................. 4839
to be ex-officio secretary of board of visitors.................................. 4839
office of visitor to be honorary and without compensation........................... 4840
admission of persons in military or naval service............................... 4843
admission of persons having property, but not enough to defray all expenses.... 4849
authority of board of visitors in such cases. 4849
of persons accused of crime.............. 4851
of private patients........................ 4853
disbursement of appropriations for 4858

marine,
proceeds of sale of, not to be covered into Treasury........................... 3618
disposal of.............................. 3692
appropriation for..3689, 3692, 4545, 4585–4587, 4610
tax, assessment and collection of.......... 4585
on vessels sold abroad.................... 4586

Section.

Hospitals—Continued.
no documents to be granted till paid 4587
to be deducted from seamen's wages 4587
regulations for collection to be prescribed by Secretary of Treasury 4587
President may receive gifts in aid of 4801
supervising-surgeon of, to be appointed 4802
duties and salary of 4802
to make monthly reports to Secretary of Treasury 4802
deposits to credit of fund for relief of sick and disabled seamen, by collector of customs 4803
monthly returns to be made 4803
appropriation and employment of fund... 4803
persons employed on canal-boats in coasting-trade excluded from benefit of ... 4804
sick foreign seamen may be admitted on application of master of vessel 4805
charges per diem in such case 4805
to be paid by master 4805
collector not to grant clearance until paid 4805
officer in charge of hospital to render account of, to collector 4805
buildings, &c., for, may be leased or sold... 4806
exception of those at Cleveland, O., and Portland, Me 4806
other exceptions 4806
navy,
deduction from pay of marines for fund 1614
Secretary of Navy to superintend 4807
deduction of pay from officers and men for fund of 4808
fines imposed on 4809
purchase and erection of.................. 4810
asylum for aged and decrepid officers and men to be provided at one of......... 4810
how governed 4811
pay of clerk to paymaster at............ 1556
disabled sailors and marines may have half pay in lieu of home in, at Philadelphia 4756
allowance of rations to 4812
pensions to be deducted during stay in..... 4813
Hospital-Tax,
(see *Hospitals*.)
Hospital-Stewards,
number authorized 1094
enlistment or appointment of, for posts..... 1179
for permanent attachment to medical corps 1180
grading of 1181
pension to relatives of, when to begin 4710
Houlton, Me.,
port of entry 2517
collector to reside at 2518
Hours of Business,
in Executive Departments 162
Household-Furniture,
to amount of $300, exempt from distraint for internal-revenue taxes 3187
House Contingent-Fund,
restrictions on use of 3680
House of Representatives,
officers and employés in, salaries.......... 53
expenditures of, when made up and reported. 63
furniture and carpets for, how purchased... 1816
every Territory may send Delegate to 1862
Houses,
on deck of vessel transporting other than cabin-passengers between United States and Europe 4256
booby-hatches may be used in lieu of....... 4256
penalty for failure to provide 4259

Section.

Houston, Tex.,
port of delivery 2578
surveyor to reside at 2579
merchandise for, where entered 2821
Hudson, N. Y.,
port of delivery 2535
Hulls of Steam-Vessels,
(see *Inspection of Steam-Vessels.*)
Huron, Mich.,
collection-district 2599
collector in, residence of................ 2600
inspectors of hulls and boilers for.......... 4414
their salaries 4414
Husband,
of vessel to give bond for registry.......... 4145
Hydrographic Office,
to be attached to Bureau of Navigation 431
maps, charts, &c., to be prepared at........ 432
Hydrographic Surveys,
restrictions on appropriations for publishing foreign 3686
Hydrometers,
Secretary of Treasury to adopt, for proof of imported liquors 2918
to be adopted and prescribed for use by Commissioner of Internal Revenue 3249
Hydrostatic Pressure,
to be used in testing boilers of steam-vessels. 4418
Hypothecation,
of vessel not valid, except, &c., unless recorded, &c 4192
to be recorded by collectors of customs... 4193
certificates discharging, to be recorded ... 4193
what record of, to be kept in books....... 4193
what to be certified on.................. 4193
fee for recording 4193
not to be recorded until acknowledged, &c. 4193
collectors to keep index of records 4194
index and records open to inspection 4194
collectors to furnish certificates relating to, &c 4194
fee for such certificates 4194
for certified copy of record of 4194
for recording 4382

I.

Ice,
vessels prevented from getting to port by... 2896
used in distillery 3303
Idaho Territory,
number of members of council and house of representatives of 1922
extra sessions of legislative assembly of, how called 1923
penitentiary in, care and custody of 1936
maintenance of prisoners by................ 1937
contingent expenses of executive department of, annual appropriation for........... 1935
legislative expenses of, provision for........ 1940
salaries of governor, &c., of, not payable until duties entered upon 1941
mileage of members of legislative assembly of 1943
Indian agencies, &c., in, continued.......... 1949
disbursing officers in, to give security, in what manner 1951
appointment of surveyor-general for 2207
salary of 2210
fifty per cent. addition to fees of registers and receivers in 2238
collection-district, what to comprise......... 2593
collector in 2594
(see *Territories*.)
Illinois,
collection-district, port of entry, and ports of delivery in 2601

Section.

Illinois—Continued.
officers in ... 2602

Imitation Wines,
internal-revenue tax on ... 3328

Immediate Transportation,
(see *Transportation.*)

Immigration, (*Cooly*,)
involuntary, of persons from oriental countries prohibited ... 2158
voluntary, not affected by prohibition ... 2162
States not to impose unequal charges upon, of particular persons ... 2164

Immoral Articles,
not to be imported ... 2491

Importation,
of dutiable articles, in public vessels, forbidden ... 1624*
of fire-arms, ammunition, and spirits, in Alaska, regulation of ... 1955
prohibited, of obscene, &c., articles ... 2491
of liquors, except in certain quantities, packages, &c., Schedule D ... 2504
of cigars, except in certain quantities and packages ... 2804
of merchandise into United States, how to be made ... 3095
into northern, &c., collection-districts ... 3096

Import Duties,
(see *Duties on Imports.*)

Imported Cigars,
(see *Cigars.*)

Imported Tobacco and Snuff,
provisions relative to ... 3377

Imports,
superintendence of collection of duties on, by Secretary of Treasury ... 249
jurisdiction of circuit courts of suits under laws providing revenue from ... 629
when prohibited in foreign vessels, forfeiture ... 2497
prohibition not to apply, when ... 2498
discriminating duty on, when levied, &c ... 2502
duties on non-enumerated articles, rate of ... 2516
tare on, how estimated ... 2898
duty on, subject to be levied on market-value, &c., how estimated and collected ... 2904
deposited in Government warehouse, at whose risk, &c ... 2961
custody of, not unladen in time ... 2969
at New York, Philadelphia, Boston, Baltimore, Portland, Me., Port Huron, Detroit, New Orleans, Toledo, and San Francisco, destined for certain ports, how entered for warehouse and transportation ... 2990
in bond, products, &c., of United States, how transported over certain foreign territory and how treated ... 3006
when condensed statement of amount of, to be furnished to Congressional Printer by Secretary of Treasury ... 3812

Impost,
(see *Duties on Imports.*)

Impressment of Seamen,
(see *Seamen.*)

Imprisonment,
in territorial penitentiaries, how regulated ... 1894, 1895
proceedings to discharge poor debtor from, by Secretary of Treasury ... 3471
by President ... 3472
from malice and without cause, of crew of American vessel ... 5347

Section.

Incidental Appropriations,
shall not be used for compensation ... 3682

Incompetent or Orphan Indians,
payments to, of moneys due, how made ... 2108

Incorporated Companies,
registry of vessels owned by, how made ... 4137
new registry on death, &c., of president or secretary of ... 4138
oath by, before registry ... 4139
enrollment and license of vessels of ... 4313–4315
(see *Corporations.*)

Increase of Capital,
of national banks authorized, maximum to be fixed by Comptroller ... 5142

Increase of Pension,
(see *Pensions.*)

Increased Expedition,
allowance for, on mail-contracts ... 3961

Increased Salaries,
statements of, by Secretary of Senate and Clerk of House ... 64

Indecent Articles,
not to be imported ... 2491

Indefinite Appropriations,
statement of, shall be annexed to estimates ... 3670

Indemnity,
appropriation for, for clothing lost in Navy ... 3689
for swamp-lands to States ... 3689

Indemnity Bond,
required for lost, &c., bonds ... 3703, 3705

Independent Treasury,
provisions respecting ... 3591–3613

Indiana,
deputy clerks at New Albany and Evansville ... 559
of circuit court in, for what places appointed ... 625

Indiana and Illinois,
collection-district, port of entry, and ports of delivery in ... 2601
officers in ... 2602

Indianola, Tex.,
port of entry ... 2578
collector to reside at ... 2579
what imports may be withdrawn, &c., for exportation to Mexico, &c., through ... 3004

Indians,
instruction of ... 2071
employés of United States not to be concerned in trade with ... 2078
who to be present at and witness delivery of goods and disbursements to ... 2088, 2089
annual settlement of accounts for disbursements to ... 2091
restrictions on appropriations for education of ... 2099
no payment to tribes engaged in hostilities ... 2100
report to Congress of, hostilities ... 2100
holding captives, not to be paid until surrender ... 2102
restrictions on payments to contractors for goods, &c., furnished ... 2107
payment to orphan and incompetent ... 2108
reports as to number of Indians present and receiving food, &c ... 2109
rations, when may be issued to ... 2110
purchases or grants, &c., of lands from, void ... 2116
penalty for attempting such negotiations ... 2116
adjustment by State agent of claims for lands extinguished by treaty ... 2116
Indians trespassing on lands of civilized Indians ... 2120
suspension of chief for such trespass ... 2121

* NOTE.—"No person connected with the Navy shall, under any pretense, import in a public vessel any article which is liable to the payment of duty."—*Sec.* 1624, "*Articles for the Government of the Navy*," *Art.* 12; (*sec.* 10, *act of July* 30, 1846, *ch.* 74.)

Section.

Indians—Continued.
sale of buildings on lands reverting to United States 2122
what may be sold with buildings 2123
penalties under this Title, how recovered ... 2124
proceedings against goods seized 2125
competent as witnesses in relation to distilled spirits 2140
chiefs, warriors, &c., of Stockbridge Munsees may acquire homesteads, when 2310
Ottawas and Chippewas of Michigan may enter homesteads of their unoccupied lands, &c 2313, 2314
peltries and proper goods, &c., of, when admitted free of duty 2515
pension-claimants, declarations of, may be made before United States agent 4714
limitation as to pension-claims of, extended, validity of evidence in, &c., not required to take constitutional oath 4721

agents,
appointment of, for certain tribes, States, and Territories 2052
services of, to be dispensed with when practicable 2053
may be required to perform additional duties. 2053
to report direct to Commissioner, when 2054
salary of 2055
term of office 2056
bond 2057
military officers may be required to perform duties of 2062
not to receive extra compensation 2062
restrictions on compensation of, performing extra services 2063
appointment of sub-agents 2065
their duties, compensation, and bonds 2065
of special agents 2067
restrictions on advances to 2092
payments on receipts of, how restricted 2107
to sell cattle of Indians for their benefit, when 2127
evidence in pension cases, taken before, to be valid, &c.; how taken before, hereafter 4721

agencies,
in Idaho and Montana, continued 1949
may be discontinued or transferred, when .. 2059
limits of, how established 2066
of sub-agencies 2066

annuities,
under treaties, may be paid in coin, when ... 2081
President may cause to be paid in goods, when 2082

commissioner of Indian affairs,
appointment and salary of 462
to have management of Indian affairs 463
duties of, as to accounts 464
regulations by President 465
regulations as to claims for depredations 466
rules for prohibiting sales of arms, &c., in territory of uncivilized Indians 467
annual reports of 468, 469
to consult with commissioners in making purchases 2041
to direct purchases 2083

commissioners,
board of, appointment; qualifications 2039
to serve without pecuniary compensation. 2039
secretary to, appointment and compensation 2040
to supervise expenditure of appropriations 2041
to inspect all goods purchased 2041
member of, may investigate contracts, expenditures, and accounts of service ... 2042
to have access to all books and papers 2042
examination of vouchers and accounts by, not a pre-requisite to payment 2042

Section.

Indians—Continued.
special, when may be appointed by Secretary of Interior 2067

contracts,
to be in writing, &c 2103
how to be executed and approved 2103
what to embrace 2103
limit of time 2103
certificate of execution 2103
made in violation of this section void 2103
recovery of over-payments 2103
restrictions upon payments under 2104
penalty for receiving money under prohibited contracts 2105
assignments of, restricted 2106
to be endorsed, how 2106

country,
trading with Indians in 2128
selling spirituous liquors in, penalty 2139
search for and destruction of 2140
setting up distillery in, penalty 2141
distilleries in, to be destroyed 2141
military force, employment of, in enforcement of laws in 2150
detention and treatment of persons apprehended by 2151
reparation to friendly Indians in, for injury to property by whites 2154
payment by United States when offender unable 2155

depredations,
benefits extended to militia and volunteers employed in suppressing, in Florida .. 1657
to be paid for, only from special appropriations 2098

funds,
restrictions upon application of 2097

inspectors,
not exceeding five may be appointed 2043
term of office of 2043
salary and allowances of 2044
statement of expenses of each, to accompany report of Secretary of Interior 2044

interpreters,
one to be allowed to each agency 2068
one for each tribe, when allowed 2068
to be nominated to Department by agents .. 2068
suspension of, from pay and duty 2068
preference of Indians, in appointment of, &c. 2069
salaries of 2070

lands,
disposal of proceeds of sales of 2093
reservations, how to be surveyed 2115

scouts,
in Army 1094
enlistment of 1112
pay of 1276

soldiers and sailors,
evidence of marriage in case of, under pension-laws 4705

superintendencies,
in Idaho and Montana continued 1949
limits of, how established 2066

superintendents,
appointment of, for certain tribes, States, and Territories 2046
offices of four, abolished 2047
appropriations unexpended for salaries of, &c., how applied 2047
assignment or discontinuance of remaining four by President 2047
term of office of 2048
bond of 2049
temporary clerks for 2051
disbursements of moneys to be made by 2089

Section.

Indians—Continued.
restrictions on advances to 2092
supplies,
in place of money annuities, how purchased and disbursed 2083
restrictions on purchases of 2084
claims for unauthorized purchases of, not to be paid 2085
modes of distributing 2086
not to be distributed to Indians intoxicated, &c 2087
who to be present and certify to delivery of. 2088
to fulfill treaty stipulations, how disbursed. 2089
report to be made of number of Indians present and receiving 2109
rations to Indians visiting military posts, &c. 2110
treaties,
jurisdiction of Court of Claims not to extend to claims growing out of 1066
appropriation to carry out, ceding lands, &c. 2094
investments of stock required by, how made. 2095
special accounts of funds of, to be kept... 2095
investment of proceeds of sales of land ceded by 2096
what interest investments to bear 2096
wars,
what widows, &c., of soldiers in, to have pensions 4732

Indictment,
limitation of time for finding, of capital offense, willful murder excepted 1043
of offenses not capital 1044
not extended to fugitives from justice.... 1045
under revenue or slave-trade laws 1046
evidence of balance due, upon trial of, against embezzlers 5494
prima-facie evidence of embezzlement upon trial of 5495

Indigent Blind,
appropriation for instructing 3689
provision for education of 4869

Indigent Deaf and Dumb,
of District of Columbia, admission of, to Columbia Institution for 4864

Individual Liability,
of shareholders of national banks 5151

Indorser,
discharge in bankruptcy not to affect liability of, when 5118

Infantry,
regiments, number of 1094
composition of 1106
companies, number of 1106
composition of 1107
corps of States, not incorporated with militia, what privileges to retain 1641

Inferior Disability,
pension shall be granted for 4692

Inflammable Materials,
shippers of, to notify carrier of character... 4288

Informations,
what costs to be allowed on several 978
limitation of time for instituting, of offenses not capital, except, &c 1044
of crimes arising under revenue or slave-trade laws 1046
proceedings under, in cases of prize of property used in aid of insurrection 5311

Informers,
when liable for defendant's costs 975
when alone liable to clerk, marshal, and attorney for fees of prosecution 976
share of, of fines, penalties, and forfeitures, under customs-revenue laws 3090
moiety to, of fines collected for violation of laws for transportation of passengers. 4273

Section.

Informers—Continued.
of fines collected for unlawful shipment of dangerous articles on vessels 4476
of fines collected for violation of regulations of steam-vessels 4499
may be examined as witness in proceedings to recover fine, &c., without loss of share in 5295

Ingots for Coinage,
who shall make 3530
assay, &c., of 3531
deviation from standard 3533

Injunctions,
proceedings for, against Comptroller of Currency by national banks, in what district shall be had 736
not granted to restrain collection of taxes.. 3224
to stay proceedings on distress-warrant against delinquent collector, &c..3636, 3637
upon Comptroller of Currency and receivers, &c., of national banks; how obtained; effect of 5237
against national banks not to issue from State courts, &c., before, &c 5242

Injury Received in Service,
who to have pension for 4693
after July 27, 1868, must have been received in line of duty 4694

Inland Waters,
vessels navigating, to carry what lights 4233
property taken upon, by naval forces, not to be regarded as maritime prize 5310

In Rem,
certain internal-revenue forfeitures to be enforced by proceedings 3453

Insane, Government Hospital for,
(see *Hospitals.*)

Insane Persons,
term includes what 1
provision for, of Navy, care and treatment of. 1551
limitation as to commencement of pension not to apply to 4709

Insolvency,
(see *Bankruptcy.*)

Insolvent Debtor,
claims of United States against, to have priority 3466
when surety of, on bond of, to United States, to have priority 3468

Insolvents,
when oath to invoices in customs cases administered to assignees of 2846

Inspection,
of damaged military stores 1241
surveyor of customs when to cause, of cargo, and compare with manifests 2830
imported merchandise liable to; not to be delivered without 2899
of merchandise, baggage, &c., imported from contiguous foreign countries, when, how, and by whom made 3100
forfeiture for obstructing 3101
proceedings to avoid, at first port of arrival. 3102
of distilled spirits 3249
of cigars, &c 3396
of fuel purchased by officers in District of Columbia 3711, 3713
of steam-vessels,
United States and foreign public vessels exempt from 4400
supervising inspector-general, appointment of 4402
qualifications 4402
salary 4402
duties 4403
supervising inspectors, appointment of..... 4404

Section.

Inspection—Continued.
qualifications 4404
salary and allowances 4404
board of supervising inspectors, how formed. 4405
meetings of 4405
assignment of supervising inspectors to districts by 4405
establishment of regulations by 4405
regulations of, to have force of law, when. 4405
supervising inspector of Pacific coast to attend meetings of, when 4405
supervising inspectors, duties of, in their districts 4406
licensed officers to answer inquiries 4406
duties of, as to violations of law 4407
to investigate failure of licensed officers to perform duties 4407
supervision of local boards by 4408
of districts not having inspectors, by... 4409
reports by, to annual meeting of board of. 4410
board of supervising inspectors to examine into action of supervising inspectors and local boards 4410
to correct mistakes, &c 4410
regulations by, as to furnishing information to local inspectors 4411
to furnish regulations for steam-vessels passing each other 4412
to furnish each vessel two copies of regulations 4412
penalty on pilots violating such regulations 4413
inspectors of hulls and of boilers to be appointed for certain collection-districts. 4414
their salaries 4414
assistant inspectors may be appointed by Secretary of Treasury, when 4414
their salaries 4414
traveling expenses of inspectors, how allowed and paid 4414
appointment of inspectors of hulls and of boilers, how made 4415
qualifications 4415
inspector of hulls and inpector of boilers to constitute a board of local inspectors. 4415
who are not eligible as inspectors 4416
inspection of hulls, how often to be made, and what to embrace 4417
of boilers, when made 4418
to be subjected to hydrostatic pressure. 4418
water and steam-pipes, &c 4418
safety-valves 4418
gauge-cocks and steam-registers 4418
low-water gauges 4418
fusible plugs 4418
supply of water 4418
means of blowing out mud and sediment 4418
maximum low pressure 4418
high 4418
diminution of pressure 4418
unsafe boiler not to be approved 4418
test of, constructed of plates inspected under section 4430 4418
safety-valves and steam-registers, how controlled 4419
freight and tow-boats on Mississippi River, &c., what to be deemed maximum pressure on 4420
exception as to certain 4420
certificate of inspection, when granted 4421
when refused 4421
license to carry gunpowder, when local inspectors may grant 4422
certificates of inspection, originals to be retained on file at custom-house 4423
three copies to master or owner 4423

Section.

Inspection—Continued.
two copies to be conspicuously posted on vessel, &c 4423
penalty for receiving passengers on vessel not having certificate, &c 4424
for carrying gunpowder without certificate 4424
inspector certifying falsely, penalty 4425
ferry-boats, canal-boats, yachts, &c., propelled by steam, inspection of 4426
provision for security of life on 4426
certificate of inspection for, when granted. 4426
must have licensed engineer and pilot 4426
tug and freight-boats, how inspected 4427
officers of, must be licensed 4427
boilers to be constructed of stamped plates, &c 4428
penalty for constructing otherwise, &c... 4429
when boilers otherwise constructed may be used 4429
inspection of boiler-plates 4430
plates not inspected not to be used 4430
stamping boiler-plates 4431
record of stamps to be kept by inspectors 4431
counterfeiting, &c., stamps for boiler-plates, penalty 4432
pressure allowed for boilers constructed of stamped plates 4433
split-calking not permitted 4433
thickness of boiler-plates 4434
space around flues of certain boilers 4434
feed and connecting-pipes 4435
protection against sparks or flames 4435
safety-valves and gauge-cocks 4436
low-water indicator and fusible plugs 4436
Banca tin, plugs of 4436
penalty for obstructing safety-valves, &c. 4437
penalty for employing or serving as officer without license 4438
license and classification of officers by inspectors 4438
of captain 4439
of chief mate 4440
of engineer 4441
of pilot 4442
of captain or mate as pilot 4443
revocation of licenses 4439–4442
State regulations of pilots, restricted 4444
oath of licensed officers 4445
license of officers to be exhibited, when 4446
renewal of license of officers 4447
licensed officers to assist inspectors in examinations, penalty 4448
revocation of license for refusal to serve 4449
local boards to investigate conduct of officers, &c 4450
may compel attendance of witnesses 4450
may administer oaths and examine witnesses 4450
may suspend or revoke officer's license, when 4450
payment of marshal and witnesses 4451
appeal from, on refusal to grant license, to supervising inspector 4452
to furnish supervising inspector record of doings in cases appealed to him 4452
supervising inspector to examine anew cases of refusal of license appealed 4452
powers and duties in such cases 4452
additional inspections by local inspectors... 4453
notice for repairs needed 4453
where repairs may be made 4453
penalty for failure to make repairs 4454
jurisdiction of inspectors confined to their own districts, except 4455

Section.

Inspection—Continued.
inspection in districts without inspectors... 4456
records and reports by local inspectors..... 4457
fees for inspection........................ 4458
bond of supervising and local inspectors.... 4459
instruments, stationery, &c., for supervising inspectors and local boards.......... 4460
payment of salaries and expenses of inspection officers, how made.............. 4461
permanent appropriation for.............. 4461
Secretary of Treasury to make regulations for carrying out.......................... 4462
penalty on inspectors for receiving illegal fees.................................. 5482
of surveys,
to be made by surveyor-general............ 2223
may be made by confidential agent.......... 2223
allowance for.............................. 2223
of vessels,
of passenger-vessels arriving from abroad... 4264
of enrollment or license of vessel by revenue officer................................ 4336
provisions relating to, of alleged unseaworthy vessels.....................4556–4563
Inspection Laws,
of States, to be observed by customs officers clearing vessels........................ 4202
Inspector-General's Department,
of Army, authorized........................ 1094
number and rank in...................... 1131
Inspectors,
of armories,
compensation of............................ 1663
to be paid quarter yearly................ 1664
of customs,
for Chelsea, Mass., appointment of.......... 2529
at Chester, Pa., to have powers of deputy collector................................ 2544
appointment of temporary, at New Orleans, La., when number of................. 2576
in Texas, appointment, number, residence, and duties of......................... 2580
in California, how appointed............... 2583
additional, may be appointed by Secretary of Treasury for certain collection-districts................................ 2605
for certain ports.......................2606, 2607
penalty for extortion by, and for certifying shipment of merchandise entitled to drawback, &c., without inspection, &c. 2637
services of occasional inspectors to be specified in accounts........................ 2642
fees of.................................... 2657
of deputy inspectors..................... 2657
per-diem compensation of................... 2733
salary of, at San Antonio, Eagle Pass, Presidio del Norte, and San Elizario, and certain places on routes to Mexico..... 2734
at Monterey, Sacramento, Benicia, Stockton, San Pedro, and Santa Barbara... 2735
compensation of, at Chester, Pa............ 2736
Secretary of Treasury may increase compensation of................................ 2737
per-diem compensation of persons performing duties of............................ 2738
when to examine baggage, &c................ 2801
when to accompany vessels bound for certain ports in Connecticut and New Jersey; penalty for masters refusing to receive. 2834
not to deliver merchandise disagreeing with description in permit.................. 2870
to examine and superintend delivery of cargoes of vessels, &c.; who to empower to accompany vessels into another district.................................. 2875
duties of; books of, to whom transmitted... 2876

Section.

Inspectors—Continued.
to attend to delivery of cargoes; penalty for neglect, &c............................ 2877
not to perform duties other than, &c.; compensation of, proceeding from one district to another, by whom defrayed; provisions and accommodations for... 2878
compensation of, in case of delay in delivery of cargo, by whom paid; accounts of, to whom rendered..................... 2879
wages of, in extended time for unlading cargoes of salt and coal, by whom paid.. 2881
when distilled spirits to be landed under inspection of............................ 2884
to sign returns of delivery of merchandise.. 2889
appointed to oversee unlading of vessels seeking port in distress, to keep an account. 2891
to be stationed along route in cases of transportation in bond of imports.... 2994
special agents as, to superintend transfers between Atlantic and Pacific ports in foreign territory....................... 2999
compensation of.......................... 2999
female, how and by whom employed.......... 3064
on board of vessel, duties of.............. 3070
when to inspect merchandise and baggage imported from contiguous foreign countries.................................. 3100
of boilers,
(see *Inspection of Steam-Vessels.*)
of fuel,
in District of Columbia, appointment, bond, duty, and fees of...................... 3711
of hulls,
(see *Inspection of Steam-Vessels.*)
of steam-vessels,
(see *Inspection of Steam-Vessels.*)
of tobacco and cigars, (internal revenue,)
appointment of............................. 3151
to give bond in $5,000...................... 3151
fees of, to be paid by owner of articles inspected................................ 3151
none to be appointed except of tobacco, snuff, and cigars............................ 3152
may be transferred or suspended by supervisor.................................. 3163
may enter manufactory of taxable articles.. 3177
Insubordination,
consular officers shall discountenance, of seamen................................. 4600
Insurance,
on distilled spirits destroyed by accidental fire; when tax not remitted........... 3223
Insurrection,
jurisdiction of district courts in cases of, prize and capture, under title of........... 563
proceedings for certain forfeitures under laws concerning, in what district prosecuted................................. 564
jurisdiction of circuit courts, of proceedings for condemnation of property taken as prize, under laws relating to.......... 629
prize and captures under laws relating to, in what district may be condemned..... 735
power of President to call forth militia to suppress............................. 1642
militia called forth to suppress, subject to rules and articles of war............. 1644
Title LXIX.............................5297–5322
when President may declare State to be in; suspension of commercial intercourse; forfeitures.............................. 5301
part of State not declared to be in, under control of insurgents, &c.; suspension of commercial intercourse................ 5302

Section.

Insurrection—Continued.
provisions relating to suspension of commercial intercourse between States in, how, &c., to apply 5303
President to license, &c., commercial intercourse with part of State in, in certain cases, and to what extent 5304
compensation of officers designated or appointed to carry into effect licenses for taking supplies into insurrectionary States 5305
trading without license in State declared to be in, or obtaining license by fraud, &c.; penalty 5306
Secretary of Treasury to institute investigations to prevent frauds, &c., in trade between loyal States and States in; witnesses, &c 5307
confiscation of property employed in aid of. 5308
proceedings for, where had and how instituted 5309–5311
Secretary of Treasury may prohibit transportation of property when believing it for aid of rebellion; to require security, &c 5312
in case of, President may change port of entry; duties, how collected; appointment of officers; provisions of law applicable, &c 5314
removal of custom-house in case of; collector, where to reside; duties of collector ... 5315
vessels detained in districts in, not to be taken from customs-officers; enforcement of provisions 5316
close of port of entry by proclamation of President in districts in, forfeiture of vessels attempting to enter, &c 5317
vessels found at sea, &c., belonging to inhabitants of States in, when forfeited. 5319
vessels suspected to be bound for ports in, not to be cleared, &c 5320
collectors of customs may require bond that cargo shall not be used in aiding 5321
claims of loyal creditors to be provided for in condemnations of vessels, &c., under laws relating to 5322
Insurrectionary States,
appropriation for compensation of persons employed in 3689
Intercourse with Foreign Nations,
settlement of expenses of 291
Interest, Personal,
of internal-revenue officer in manufacture, &c., of tobacco, snuff, cigars, or liquors. 3168
Interest, (per cent.,)
what, to be allowed, in suits on bonds for duties 963
in suits for balances due Post-Office Department 964
in suits on debentures 965
in United States courts, same as allowed on judgments in State courts 966
on judgments of Court of Claims in favor of claimant 1090
on claims, prior to judgment, when allowed by Court of Claims 1091
rate of, on investments of money for Indians. 2096
on money held for incompetent or orphan Indians 2108
rate of, on internal-revenue taxes overdue 3184, 3185
in cases of stamping instruments by collector, where stamp-duty exceeds $50. 3422
on loans,
by national banks, rate allowed may be taken in advance 5197

Section.

Interest, (per cent.)—Continued.
penalty for usurious 5198
to North Carolina Cherokees,
appropriation for payment of 3689
on public debt,
permanent appropriation for 3689
coin from duties set apart to pay 3694
shall be paid out of any money in Treasury. 3698
Secretary of Treasury may anticipate 3699
national-bank notes not receivable for 5182
on sinking fund,
amount of, shall be applied to redemption of debt 3696
on state stocks,
due United States, how received 3481
on treasury notes,
when credit shall be given for 3473
on United States bonds,
given to Pacific Railway, appropriation for .. 3689
called in, to cease in three months 3697
belonging to national banks, semi-annual duties and penalty to be deducted from, when 5217
Interest-bearing Notes,
to be legal tender for face, except, &c 3590
Interior Department,
(see *Department of Interior.)*
Intermediate Ports,
provisions concerning lading or unlading of vessels at, in foreign and coasting trade on northern, &c., frontier 3117
Intermediate Service,
difference in cost of, to be charged to defaulting mail-contractor 3951
Internal Revenue,
regulations for enforcement of laws, prescribed by Secretary of Treasury 251
jurisdiction in equity of district courts to enforce liens for taxes of 563
jurisdiction of circuit courts of suits arising under laws providing 629
where taxes may be sued for 733
duty of district attorneys as to prosecution for fines, penalties, forfeitures, &c 838
report by, when not prosecuting, to Commissioner 838
suits for taxes, penalties, or forfeitures provided by laws of, to be brought in name of United States 919
when United States not subject to costs, in suit for penalty or forfeiture under laws relating to 969
no payment to be made to officers or clerks of, until they make oath that they have received no moneys, &c 1790
stamps on imported cigars, Secretary of Treasury to provide, &c 2804
appropriation for compensation of persons employed in insurrectionary States ... 3689
for redemption of stamps 3689
for refunding tax illegally collected 3689
national-bank notes shall be received in payment of 5182
receiving money, &c., under threats of informing or for not informing 5484
(see *Commissioner of Internal Revenue, Collector of Internal Revenue, Distilled Spirits, Tobacco, Cigars, Fermented Liquors, Banks, Stamps, &c.,)*
Internal-Revenue Drawbacks,
(see *Drawback.)*
Internal-Revenue Fees,
(see *Fees.)*
Interpreters,
of legations in Turkey, salary of; need not be United States citizen 1678

Section.

Interpreters—Continued.
Japan, salary of 1679
China, salary of, when secretary of legation acts as 1680
at consulates in China, appointments, salaries, &c 1692
at consulate of Bangkok, salary of 1693
of legations and consulates, term during which salary of, shall be payable 1740
(see *Indian Interpreters.*)

Interrogatories,
specific written, to accompany letters rogatory 4071

Invalid Pensions and Pensioners,
(see *Pensions.*)

Invasion,
power of President to call for militia to repel 1642

Inventories,
of property in Departments, by whom kept 197
to be made by manufacturers of tobacco, snuff, and cigars, annually, or on commencing or concluding business 3358, 3390
dealer in manufactured tobacco to make, of tobacco and snuff on hand, July 20, 1868, and monthly thereafter 3378
of ship's papers, to be made by commanding officer taking prize 4615
to be sent into court 4615
when prize property is taken for use of United States, how made 4624

Invoices,
consular officers not required to certify, unless 1715
if goods shipped from countries adjacent to United States have passed a consulate after purchase, certificate to, shall be refused 1717, 2861
exacting excessive fees for verification of, penalty 1716
of goods shipped from British North America, consular fee for certifying 1721
original to be produced to collectors, &c., and by what officers to be signed 2785
when entry imperfect for want of 2789
what weights and measures used in 2837
of merchandise subject to ad valorem duty, how made out 2838, 2854
of merchandise to be according to actual cost 2839
when incorrect, collectors of customs what to do 2840
oaths of owners, &c, to accompany 2841
bond for production of; how verified 2842
of merchandise of non-residents, how verified 2843
not acquired by purchase, &c 2845
oath to, in customs cases when made by executors, administrators, and assignees 2846
when merchandise not accompanied with, admitted to entry 2847
bond to be given for production of, in certain cases of entry without 2848
of merchandise manufactured by one of owners residing abroad, how verified 2849
effect of omission of verification of, by non-resident 2850
fees for verification of, and what articles included in 2851
when merchandise admitted upon, collector to certify, evidence 2852
how made and by whom signed 2853
when to be produced to consul, declaration indorsed on, by whom signed, and what to contain 2854
indorsement on, by consuls, &c., what to contain; delivery, filing, and transmission of 2855

Section.

Invoices—Continued.
of goods from countries adjacent to United States may be sworn to before consular officer nearest port of clearance 2856
change of destination after production of, and non-receipt of triplicate at port of arrival, entry how made 2857
when impracticable from accident, &c., to produce, at time of entry 2858
when triplicate, not required to be produced 2859
how goods admitted to entry without 2860
consular officers may exact proof of 2862
to report fraudulent verifications of 2862
entry of merchandise on false, &c., how punished 2864
attempting to pass false, forged, &c 2865
when tare on imports may be estimated according to 2898
duties not to be assessed on value less than that stated in 2900
who to designate on, number of imported packages to be opened, examined, &c., articles not specified in, when forfeited, remissions 2901
charges incurred in purchase of, how distributed in appraisal, &c 2907
of imports of same material at an average price, duties how assessed on 2910
officers of customs may require production of, in examinations 2922
in absence of, imported goods deposited in public warehouse 2963
of imports entered with right of drawback, deposited with collector, how preserved, &c 3032
inspection, and comparison with, forfeiture 3033
copy from, of cost, &c., of goods subject to ad valorem duty transported; variance from, forfeiture 3034
Secretary of Treasury to make rules concerning authentication of, &c 3103
consul, &c., knowingly and falsely certifying to; penalty 5442
canceling or destroying, after inspection demanded, or to suppress evidence of fraud 5443

Involuntary Bankruptcy,
(see *Bankruptcy.*)

Involuntary Suspension,
of distillery 3310

Iowa,
deputy clerks for judicial divisions of district 560
district attorney for district of, to perform duty in all divisions of district of 768
marshal for, to perform duty and keep offices in all divisions, &c.; mileage, &c 778
appointment of surveyor-general for Nebraska and, authorized 2207
salary of 2208

Iowa River,
north of Wapello, not deemed navigable 5248

Ipswich, Mass.,
port of delivery 2527

Islands of St. Paul and St. George,
(see *Alaska.*)

Issues of Fact,
how tried in district courts 566

Italy,
salary of minister and secretary to 1675

J.

Jail,
(see *Prisons for American Convicts.*)

James River, Va.,
vessels bound up, what to do 2835

Section.

Japan,
salary of minister and secretary to 1675
interpreter of legation in 1679
subjects of, not to be transported in American vessels as coolies 2158, 2161
voluntary emigration, not impeded 2162
postal agents authorized in 4023
judicial authority of United States minister and consuls in 4111–4120
marshal for consular court in 4111
hire of prison for American convicts in..... 4121
rent of prison, &c., at Kanagawa 4123
hire of constables at other ports 4123
wages of keepers and care of offenders 4123
rent of court-house and jail at Jeddo 4124
Jeffersonville, Ind.,
port of delivery in district of New Orleans.. 2568
surveyor to reside at, duties of 2569
merchandise imported into Louisville for, where and how landed, &c............ 2967
Jersey City, N. J.,
port of entry and delivery, assistant collector in, how to act..................... 2535
powers and duties of........................ 2536
enrollment and license of vessels at 4340
Jerusalem,
consul at, salary of 1690
Jewelry,
shipper of, to notify carrier, &c.............. 4281
Joint Committee on Public Printing,
appointment by, of editor of "accompanying documents" 75
direction by, of printing debates........... 78
to fix upon standards of paper for public printing 3767
approval by, of contract for paper, &c...... 3772
default of contractor for paper reported to; new contract and purchase of temporary supplies directed by............. 3775
power of, to authorize purchases of paper in open market 3778
power of, as to advertisements, lithographing, and engraving........................ 3780
as to sale of extra copies of documents... 3809
Joint Committee on Library,
powers of, as to library 82, 86, 87, 94
to give Navy Department use of plates of Wilkes's Expedition.................. 427
to direct printing of additional number of any document......................... 3796
Joint Contractor,
discharge in bankruptcy not to affect liability of 5118
Joint Resolution,
what number of, to be printed when ordered by either House, &c................... 3791
Journal Clerk,
of House of Representatives................ 53
Journals,
of Congress, fees for transcripts from....... 71
of Senate and House, transmission of, to executives of States, for distribution 503
number to be printed....................... 3798
Judge-Advocate General,
in Army, rank of 1198
Judge-Advocates,
in Army, number of....................1094, 1200
rank of 1200
may employ reporter 1203
Judges,
of territorial courts, term of office of....... 1864
to appoint or designate clerk of district courts 1871
may hold county courts..................... 1874
salaries of, how payable 1879, 1882

Section.

Judges—Continued.
in Washington, Idaho, and Montana, salaries 1941
of United States courts, when to receive salary after resigning 714
penalty for acceptance of bribe 5501, 5502
Judgments,
compromise of, for debts due Post-Office Department 295
of circuit court, reviewed, &c., by Supreme Court on writ of error................. 691
on certificate of division of opinion........ 693
statement of, by clerks of circuit and district courts to Solicitor of Treasury 797
interest on, when and at what rate allowed, and levied under execution 966
to include bill of fees of officers, witnesses, &c., in cases where costs are recoverable by prevailing party............. 983
of Court of Claims, in favor of claimant, how paid 1089
interest on................................ 1090
interest prior to, when allowed........... 1091
in favor of claimant, a discharge, &c..... 1092
against claimant, a bar 1093
of non prosequitur rendered in customs cases, if no bill of particulars served....... 3012
in customs cases, what to recite and how payable, execution on, to set forth what.. 3014
for internal-revenue taxes, &c., to be paid to collector 3216
Judicial Circuits,
judges of, appointment, powers, salary, and residence of 607
Judicial Districts,
appointment of district judges for.......... 551
of district attorneys...................... 767
of marshals.............................. 776
Judicial Process,
employment of military and naval forces, to execute 1984
Judicial Sales,
of spirits 3319, 3334
of tobacco, snuff, and cigars................. 3369
Jurisdiction,
of district courts.........................563–570
of circuit courts....................629, 643, 644
of Supreme Court.........................687–709
of diplomatic and consular officers in certain countries 4111–4130
no light-house, beacon, pier, or land-mark to be built on site until cession of, to United States 4661
when cession deemed sufficient........... 4662
of United States over national cemeteries.4872–4882
(see *Exclusive Jurisdiction.*)
Jurors,
fees and mileage of 852
in the Territories, fees of................... 1883
Justices of the Peace,
in Territories, manner of election of........ 1856
when, may be appointed by governor..... 1857
when, to issue search-warrant to customs officers 3066
jurisdiction of, in suits against seamen for breach of articles..................... 4522
power of, to summon master of vessel in cases of seamen's wages 4546
complaint of unseaworthy vessel may be made to 4556
shall direct survey of vessel................ 4557
may punish seamen for refusal to sail, &c .. 4558
may issue warrant for and punish seamen deserters 4598
may punish persons for unauthorized boarding of vessels 4606

Section.

Justices of the Supreme Court,
to frame, rescind, and vary general orders in bankruptcy 4990
(see *Associate Justices.*)

K.

Kanagawa,
consul at, salary of 1690
Kansas,
appointment of Indian agents for tribes in.. 2052
appointment of surveyor-general for 2207
salary of 2208
Kansas City, Mo.,
port of delivery in district of New Orleans.. 2568
surveyor to reside at, duties of 2569
Kansas Military Organizations,
appropriation to pay 3689
Keepers,
of prisons for American convicts in China, Japan, &c., allowances for wages of. 4121–4124
of life-saving stations on coasts of Long Island and New Jersey 4243
compensation of 4243
Kennebunk, Me.,
collection-district and port of entry 2517
collector in, to reside at 2518
Kenosha, Wis.,
port of delivery 2597
deputy collector to reside at 2598
Kentucky,
clerks of district court of 557
of circuit court in, at what places and how appointed 620
Keokuk, Iowa,
port of delivery in district of New Orleans.. 2568
surveyor to reside at, duties of 2569
Keys,
of distillery-locks to be in charge of collector of internal revenue or gauger 3267
to be furnished by distiller to collector ... 3275
Key West, Fla.,
collection-district and port of entry 2562
collector to reside at 2563
Kickapoos,
appointment of agent for 2052
Killingsworth, Conn.,
port of delivery 2533
Kinderhook, N. Y.,
port of delivery 2535
Kingston, Mass.,
port of delivery 2527
Kingston, Canada,
consul at, salary of 1690
Kingston, Jamaica,
consul at, salary of 1690
Kittery, Me.,
port of delivery 2522
goods for, may be entered, &c., at Portsmouth, N. H., or York, Me 2524

L.

Labels,
on tobacco and snuff 3364
on cigars 3393
Commissioner of Internal Revenue may make changes in 3446
Labor,
storage, &c., in customs service, appropriation of amounts received for 3687
Laborers,
in Senate, salaries 52
in House of Representatives 53
in Army, designation of 1162
detail of working-parties of soldiers as 1235
day's work of, to be eight hours 3738

Section.

La Crosse, Wis.,
port of delivery in district of New Orleans.. 2568
surveyor to reside at, duties of 2569
Lading,
of merchandise notified for exportation, how performed 3035
provisions concerning, of vessels from British provinces 3129
Lager-Beer,
(see *Fermented Liquors.*)
Laguayra,
consul at, salary of 1690
Lahaina,
consul at, salary of 1690
Lake Champlain,
imports from Canada in steamboats on, when and where may be landed 3128
clearance of steamboats on, going to province of Quebec 4208
Lake-going Vessels,
provisions as to shipping-articles not to apply to 4513
Lake Pontchartrain,
provisions concerning drawback on imports exported from 3055
Lakeport, La.,
port of delivery in district of New Orleans.. 2568
surveyor to reside at, duties of 2569
vessels bound for, may unlade at, after making report, &c 2572
bound from, to foreign ports, how cleared. 2573
Lamberton, N. J.,
port of delivery 2541
collector to reside at 2542
Land and Naval Forces,
persons appointed to execute process may call aid of 1984
President may employ, to enforce neutrality laws 5287
to compel departure of foreign vessels, when forbidden by laws of nations or treaties to remain, &c 5288
in aid of collection of duties 5316
to protect rights of discoverer of guano island 5577
Land-Districts,
appointment of register and receiver for each. 2234
when President may discontinue and annex to other 2250
Land-Grants,
railways receiving, how pay for carrying mail on, shall be fixed 4001
payment of directors, engineers, commissioners, &c., by corporations receiving, from United States 5259
Landing,
of passengers, cargo, &c., from foreign vessel, permit to be obtained 3121
Land-Office,
(see *General Land-Office.*)
Land-Offices,
discontinuance by President, when 2250
may be annexed to adjoining districts 2250
allowance for office-rent and clerks for consolidated offices 2255
employment of clerks at, to be sanctioned by Secrerary of Interior 2255
registers and receivers to reside where offices established 2235
Land-Patents,
secretary of President to sign 450
assistant secretary of President to sign 451
how signed, countersigned, and recorded 458
for mineral lands, how obtained 2325
to different claimants for portions of mining-claim 2326

Section.

Land-Patents—Continued.
for mining-claims under former laws may issue, when ... 2328
heretofore issued, what right to convey ... 2328
for placer-mining claims ... 2329
containing lode-claim ... 2333
for private land-claims, not to issue until expense of surveying, &c., paid ... 2400
for military bounty-lands, to issue, when ... 2423

Land-Warrants,
falsely making, forging, &c., military bounty, uttering false as true, &c ... 5420

Lands,
examinations and proceedings in purchases of, by United States, for forts, public buildings, &c ... 355
erroneously sold, appropriation to refund for ... 3689
purchase of, on account of United States, restricted ... 3736

Lands, Public,
bounty-lands,
for soldiers in certain wars ... 2418
for certain soldiers serving less than 12 months ... 2419
for certain volunteers, militia, and State troops ... 2420
for widows ... 2424
fees,
to be paid registers and receivers for declaratory statement filed, or service on pre-emption claim ... 2238
commissions on receipts ... 2238
on homestead applications ... 2238
on lands entered for growth of timber ... 2238
for locating military-bounty land warrants ... 2238
for final certificates in donation cases ... 2238
in location of land-grants to States and corporations ... 2238
for superintending public-land sales ... 2238
for patent or adverse claim for mineral lands ... 2238
for services in preëmption claims ... 2238
for reducing testimony to writing ... 2238
fifty per cent. additional on certain ... 2238
in addition to salary ... 2238
in consolidated districts for transcripts and record information ... 2239
maximum of compensation ... 2240
excess of, to be paid into Treasury ... 2241
receiving illegal fees, not to receive compensation for past services ... 2242
to be removed from office ... 2242
homesteads,
chiefs and heads of families of Stockbridge Munsee Indians may enter ... 2310
unsold lands of Ottawa and Chippewa Indians opened to them ... 2313
selection of, for minor children ... 2314
mineral lands, &c.,
not subject to entry under homestead law ... 2302
patents for, how obtained ... 2325
adverse claims for, proceedings on ... 2326
pending applications for, how decided ... 2328
placer-claims, entry and patent of ... 2329
proceedings to obtain patent for, for placer-claim ... 2333
where no valuable mines discovered, open to homestead entry ... 2341
additional land-districts and officers authorized ... 2343
coal-lands, entry of ... 2347
miscellaneous provisions,
live-oak and red-cedar timber-lands to be explored and reserved, when ... 2458
surveyors for such lands may be appointed ... 2459
lands selected to be reserved for timber for Navy ... 2459

Section.

Lands, Public—Continued.
protection of, by land and naval forces, when ... 2460
cutting or destroying, &c., timber on, penalty ... 2461
vessel carrying away such timber, forfeited ... 2462
penalty on master, owner, or consignee ... 2462
clearance of vessels laden with, from certain ports ... 2463, 4205
depredations on, how prosecuted ... 2463, 4751
mitigation of penalties for depredations on naval timber-lands ... 4751
appropriations to States from proceeds of sales of ... 3689
to indemnify States for swamp-lands sold as ... 3689
to refund for, erroneously sold ... 3689
of deposits for surveying ... 3689
national-bank notes shall be received in payment for ... 5182
pre-emption,
of coal-lands ... 2348
other lands appropriated for deficiency in school-lands ... 2275
military-bounty land warrants receivable in payment for ... 2277
agricultural-college scrip receivable ... 2278
rights, not impaired by homestead laws ... 2299
registers and receivers,
may hold over, after expiration of term of office ... 2222
bond to hold good for time so holding over ... 2222
President may transfer duties of, to surveyors-general ... 2227
appointment of, for each land-district ... 2234
to reside where land-office is kept ... 2235
bond ... 2236
salary ... 2237
compensation to commence, when ... 2243
term of office ... 2244
President may increase bonds of ... 3639
receiver to make monthly returns to Secretary of Treasury of moneys received ... 2245
to pay over moneys as instructed by him ... 2245
to make like returns to Commissioner of General Land-Office ... 2245
to transmit to Commissioner quarterly accounts-current ... 2245
register to publish notice of application for mineral land ... 2325
for patent for mining claim ... 2325
duty in case of adverse claim to mineral land ... 2326
shall examine books of receiver ... 3650
sale and disposal,
payments to be in full at public sale; no credit allowed ... 2356
price of public lands ... 2357
lands offered by order of President, how to be advertised ... 2359
purchase-money, repayment of, when sale cannot be confirmed ... 2362
when invested in stocks, stocks may be sold 2363
when reservation brought into market, Commissioner to fix minimum price ... 2364
what foreign coins receivable in payment ... 2366
location under treaty of September 30, 1854 ... 2368
not over three sections may be entered in any township with agricultural-college scrip ... 2377
survey,
contracts for, not binding until approved, &c. 2398
certain instructions deemed part of contract ... 2399
prices of surveys, how established ... 2400
of township on application of settlers ... 2401

Section.

Lands, Public—Continued.
deposit for cost of 2402
deposits to go in part payment for lands .. 2403
California and Oregon, augmented rates for, in 2404, 2405
geodetic method, when may be used in ... 2409
compensation for, by day, in 2411
surveyors-general and surveying,
appointment of, for certain States and Territories 2207
establishment of surveying districts 2207
appointment, &c., of deputy surveyors 2223
inspection of surveys in field by surveyor-general, &c 2223
allowance for clerk-hire in offices of 2226
for office-rent, fuel, books, &c 2227
President may transfer duties of registers and receivers to 2227
town-sites, &c.,
military and other reservations reserved 2393

Landsmen,
in Navy, performing duty of firemen, compensation 1570

Lanthala,
commercial agent at, salary of 1690

La Rochelle,
consul at, salary of 1690

Lascivious Books, &c.,
importation of, prohibited 2491

Laundresses,
women may accompany troops as 1240
rations to 1295

Lavaca, Tex.,
port of delivery 2578
surveyor to reside at 2579
what imported merchandise may be withdrawn, &c., for exportation to Mexico, &c., through port of 3003

Law Library,
expenses of, from what appropriation paid .. 83
books for, by whom to be purchased 84

Law of Nations,
jurisdiction of district courts of suits by aliens for torts in violation of 563

Laws,
publication of, in newspapers 79
to be promulgated by Secretary of State 204
copies of, to be furnished to Congressional Printer 210
transmission of, to President and Congress .. 1844
publication of 1844
of United States, force and effect of, in Territories 1891
relating to customs, navigation, &c., extended over Alaska 1954
authorizing expenditures shall be referred to in estimates 3660
printing of; number of, for Secretary of State, "usual number" 3805
number of, printed for Congress at close of session 3807
for Secretary of Interior 3808
to be published in certain States in papers selected by Clerk of House 3823
rates for publishing 3825
how published in District of Columbia 3826

Lawful Money,
United States notes declared, and a legal tender 3588, 3589
demand-notes declared to be 3589
meaning of term, in case of gold banks 5186

Lawful-Money Reserve,
(see *National Banks.*)

Leaf Tobacco,
(see *Tobacco.*)

Section.

Lease,
of Islands of St. Paul and Saint George. 1963–1972
of distillery, value of lot, building, apparatus, &c., to be appraised, and bond given . 3262

Leavenworth, Kan.,
port of delivery in district of New Orleans .. 2568
surveyor to reside at, duties of 2569

Leave of Absence,
to consular and diplomatic officers 1742
to persons in Indian service, limit of 2074
not to be paid if absent without 2074

Leeds,
consul at, salary of 1690

Legacies and Successions,
tax on 3438, 3439
assessment of 3440

Legal Tender,
no foreign coins shall be 3584
what shall be 3585–3590

Legal-Tender Currency,
lists furnished to collector of internal revenue must be made in 3178
returns, if made in coined money, to be reduced to 3178

Legations,
(see *Diplomatic Officers.*)

Leghorn,
consul at, salary of 1690

Legitimate Children,
who to be deemed, under pension laws 4704

Legislative Assemblies and Council.
(see *Territories.*)

Legislative Power,
in Territories, how vested 1846
extent and limit of 1852

Legislative Printing,
in Territories, limit to annual expense of 1887

Legislatures, State,
assent of, to be procured to purchase of land for forts, &c 1838

Leipsic,
consul at, salary of 1690

Lemon-Juice,
shall be served on merchant vessels 4569
penalty for neglect to serve 4570

Letter-Balances,
accounts to show expenditures for 4049

Letter-Boxes,
provisions relating to 3865–3874
where, may be established 3868
expenses of, how limited 3874

Letter-Carriers,
provisions relating to 3865–3874
where, shall be employed 3865
salaries of 3866
bonds of 3870
rates of postage on newspapers, &c., at letter-carrier offices 3872
not to receive fees or perquisites 3873
expenses of, how limited 3874
shall receive way-letters for mailing, &c 3980
postage on drop-letters delivered by 3904

Letter-Envelopes,
third-class mail-matter 3878

Letter-Mail,
when separated, &c., from other mail 3994
when carried by horse-express or railway routes 3999

Letter-Postage,
accounts to show amount derived from 4049

Letters,
mailable matter of first class 3875
postage on, must be prepaid, except, &c 3896
rates of postage on matter of which rates are not specified 3903, 3904
stamped envelopes for 3915

Section.

Letters—Continued.
registered ... 3926, 3927
containing fractional currency for United States Treasurer ... 3932
accounts to show amount received from ... 4049
unclaimed, list of to be published ... 3930
addressed to foreigners ... 3931
compensation for publishing list of ... 3934
extra postage on, when advertised ... 3935
delivery of, to postmaster when brought by vessels in foreign trade ... 3976
by steamboats ... 3977
pay for carrying ... 3978
shall be received, &c., by route agents, &c., when prepaid ... 3980
shall not be carried by stage coaches, &c., except in mail, penalty ... 3987
shall be delivered at post-office before entry of vessel is made; oath, penalty ... 3988
illegally carried, may be seized ... 3990
disposal of, when seized ... 3991
may be conveyed by private hands, without compensation ... 3992
in stamped envelopes, may be sent otherwise than by mail ... 3993
may be separated from other mail for expedition ... 3994
for United States held for postage in foreign countries, consuls may pay for ... 4014

Letters of Marque,
persons disabled, &c., on vessels carrying, to have pension, rate of ... 4761
commanders of vessels carrying, to enter on journal name, &c., of disabled officers and seamen ... 4762

Letters Rogatory,
issued by foreign court to be accompanied by specific written interrogatories ... 4071
proceedings upon production of, before district judge ... 4071
summons to witness ... 4071
examination of ... 4071
not compelled to appear or testify, except upon interrogatories ... 4071
fees and mileage of witnesses ... 4074

Lewd Books,
importation prohibited ... 2491

Liabilities of National Banks,
(see *National Banks.*)

Liabilities, Outstanding,
(see *Outstanding Liabilities.*)

Libel,
what costs to be allowed on several libels, against vessel and cargo, which might have been joined ... 978
on several libels against cargo, &c., seized as forfeited for same cause ... 978
when vessel subject to penalty, &c., to be proceeded against by ... 3088
vessels on northern frontiers, when subject to, for neglect, &c., of master ... 3125

Liberia,
salary of minister, &c., to ... 1675
minister to, shall be consul-general also ... 1683

Librarian,
in office of Secretary of Senate ... 52
in library of House ... 53

Librarian of Congress,
purchase of law-books by ... 84
appointment of ... 88
bond of ... 89
salary of ... 90
employment, &c., of assistants by ... 91
control by, of records; general duty, &c., relating to copyrights ... 4948

Section.

Librarian of Congress—Continued.
bond of, to account for moneys ... 4950
fees to be paid to, in respect of copyrights ... 4958

Library of Congress,
departments of ... 81
expenditures of appropriations for ... 82
incidental expenses of law-library ... 83
purchases of books for law-library ... 84
duplicates, injured and wasted books in ... 86
by whom books may be taken out ... 94

Library of Smithsonian Institution,
(see *Smithsonian Institution.*)

License,
or permit, special, to unlade steamships at night ... 2871
to carry gunpowder on steam passenger-vessels, when granted ... 4422
(see *Vessels.*)

License to Trade,
(see *Insurrection.*)

Licensed Officers of Steam-Vessels,
(see *Inspection of Steam-Vessels.*)

Licensed Vessels,
(see *Vessels.*)

Lien,
jurisdiction in equity of district courts to enforce, for internal-revenue taxes ... 563
for freight on imports in warehouse ... 2981
when goods forfeited, to be paid from proceeds ... 2981
penalty on vessel, owner, or master to be, on vessel, in customs cases ... 3088
unpaid tax to be, in favor of United States ... 3186
bill in chancery to enforce, of United States on real estate ... 3207
tax on distilled spirits to be, on what ... 3251
assessment for deficiencies on distillers to be, on distillery, premises, &c ... 3309
of United States against lands, &c., of delinquent collectors, &c., by levy of distress-warrant ... 3629
injunction not to impair ... 3636
by bottomry, not impaired by requirement to record conveyances ... 4192
on vessels, for penalties for violating passenger laws ... 4270
on steam-vessels, for penalties for carrying unlawful number, or failing to keep list of passengers ... 4469
for wages of seamen not to be forfeitable except ... 4535
upon vessels condemned under laws relating to insurrection, how satisfied, &c ... 5322

Lieutenant-Colonels,
of artillery regiments ... 1099
of cavalry regiments ... 1102
of infantry regiments ... 1106
pay of ... 1261
maximum of pay of ... 1267
allowance of forage to ... 1271

Lieutenant-Commanders,
number of, on active list ... 1363
promotion to grade of, suspended ... 1363
pay of ... 1556

Lieutenant-General,
of Army authorized ... 1094
office of, when to cease ... 1094
aids to ... 1097
military secretary to ... 1097
pay of ... 1261

Lieutenants,
army,
for batteries of artillery ... 1100
for troops of cavalry ... 1103
for companies of infantry ... 1107
pay of ... 1261

Section.

Lieutenants—Continued.
allowance of forage to 1271
navy,
number of, on active list 1363
pay of 1556
Lieutenants of Watchmen,
in Department of Treasury, salary of 235
Life-Saving Apparatus, Boats, and Preservers,
(see *Inspection of Steam-Vessels.*)
Life-Saving Stations,
establishment of, on coasts of Long Island and New Jersey 4242
appointment of keepers for each, &c 4243
of superintendents for, &c 4243
employment of crews of surfmen at 4244
at light-houses, when 4245
light-keepers to have charge of, &c 4245
purchase and location of boats for 4246
appointment of keepers for, on coasts of Cape Cod and Block Island 4247
supervision of, at Narragansett Pier and Block Island 4248
establishment of, on coasts of Maine, New Hampshire, Massachusetts, Virginia, and North Carolina 4249
supervision of construction of, hereafter 4250
Lighters,
and boats not masted, or, if masted, not decked, employed in harbors, not subject to Title L 4385
Light-House Board,
provisions relating to 4653–4680
Light-Houses,
appropriations for, how long available 3685
life-saving stations may be established at .. 4245
keepers of, to take charge of boats, &c ... 4245
provisions relating to 4658–4680
Light Infantry,
companies of, how formed in militia 1632
Light-Money,
on what vessels to be levied 4225
how levied and collected 4225
exemption of certain vessels from 4226
oath by owner or master 4226
Light-Ships,
preliminary surveys 4663
materials for construction or repair of 4666
when light-houses, on pile foundations, may be substituted for; from what appropriation, &c 4668
power of Light-House Board to place, over wreck or temporary obstruction 4676
Lights,
to be carried by vessels between sunset and sunrise 4233
non-exhibition of, by vessels of war 4233
holding out false, or extinguishing true, with intent to endanger vessel 5358
Lime Juice,
shall be served on merchant-vessels 4569
penalty for neglect to serve 4570
Limitations,
of time for finding indictment for capital offense, wilful murder excepted 1043
of offenses not capital, except under revenue and slave-trade laws 1044
not to apply to fugitives from justice 1045
of crimes arising under revenue or slave-trade laws 1046
of time for commencing suits or prosecutions for penalties or forfeitures 1047
civil or criminal proceedings, how affected by rebellion 1048
suits in Court of Claims 1069
for homestead entry by Indians of Ottawa and Chippewa lands in Michigan 2313

Section.

Limitations—Continued.
for filing certificate of work and affidavit by applicant for mining-claim 2325
adverse mining-claim 2325
of suits for recovery of internal revenue taxes 3227
on presentation of claims for refunding internal-revenue taxes 3228
of time for bringing suits by and against assignees in bankruptcy 5057
acts of, embraced in Revised Statutes and covered by repeal; time of commencement of suits and prosecutions 5599
Line-Officers, (Navy,)
grades of, on active list 1362
number in each grade 1363
relative rank of, with Army 1466
Liquidation,
of national banks 5220
shall give notice and make publication of intention to go into 5221
national banks in, shall deposit to redeem circulation 5222
for purposes of consolidation, not to deposit, &c 5223
reassignment of bonds, redemption of notes, &c., of 5224
destruction of notes of 5225
Liquids,
shall be excluded from mail 3878
Liquor Dealers,
(see *Dealers in Liquors.*)
Liquors,
customs duties on, and wines imported 2504
forfeiture of certain, entered as wine 2504
additional duty on importations in bottles, &c 2504
brandy, standard for proving, &c 2504
imported in casks of less than 14 gallons forfeited 2504
(see *Distilled Spirits* and *Fermented Liquors.*)
Lisbon,
consul at, salary of 1690
Lists of Internal-Revenue Taxes,
to be made by collector or deputy, in certain cases 3173, 3176
amounts on, to be estimated in legal-tender currency only 3178
of taxable property of non-residents 3180
annual, monthly, and special 3181
may be transmitted by collector to another district, where person liable resides or has property 3209
uncollected, to be transferred by collector to successor for collection 3219
Lists of Passengers,
to be furnished collector by master of vessel arriving from foreign port 4266
to be transmitted by collector, quarterly, to Secretary of State 4266
of steam-vessels 4467
penalty for failure to keep 4468
Lithographing,
required for publication of specifications and drawings by Commissioner of Patents. 492
stamped envelopes not to contain, except... 3915
(see *Engravings.*)
Little & Brown,
edition of laws and treaties published by, made evidence, &c 908
Little Egg Harbor, N. J.,
collection-district 2541
collector in, residence of 2542
Live-Oak Timber,
(see *Lands, Public.*)

Section.

Liverpool,
consul at, salary ... 1690
Living Persons,
portraits of, not to be placed on bonds, notes, &c ... 3576
Llewellensburgh, Md.,
port of delivery ... 2548
surveyor to reside at ... 2549
Loans and Discounts,
national banks not to make, when reserve is reduced, except ... 5191
rate of interest on, which may be charged by national banks ... 5197
penalty for usury, recovery ... 5198
of national banks to individuals, &c., limit of ... 5200
national bank not to make, on its own stock ... 5201
Loans on Personal Security,
power of national banks to make ... 5136
Local Acts,
not repealed by incorporation in Revised Statutes of parts of ... 5596
Local Inspectors of Steam-Vessels,
(see *Inspection of Steam-Vessels.*)
Local Letters,
rates of postage on ... 3904
Lockers,
cargo carried on deck or in cabins of passenger-vessels to be in, &c ... 4254
space occupied by, not allowed as passenger space ... 4254
measurement of ... 4254
Lock Post-Office Boxes,
box-holders may provide ... 4052
Locks and Seals,
customs,
on vehicles for goods entered for transportation ... 2994
removing, or aiding to remove; penalty for ... 2998
on packages separate from cargo; penalty for breaking ... 3069
secured by inspector on board vessel, liability of master for breaking, &c ... 3070
on vessels and cars, to avoid inspection at first port of arrival, &c ... 3102
who to regulate, &c ... 3103
breaking, opening, &c., attached to imports, how punished ... 3105
forfeiture of vessel, package, &c., from which removed ... 3106
internal revenue,
distillery, to be provided by Commissioner at expense of United States ... 3267
breaking, injuring, or tampering with, penalties for ... 3268, 3311
Commissioner may require such, on stills, &c., as he may deem necessary ... 3270
to be furnished to collector by Commissioner 3310
Log-Books,
what vessels to carry ... 4290
what entries to be made in ... 4290
manner and time of making entries in ... 4291
penalty for omitting to make entries in, &c ... 4292
entries to be made in, respecting deceased seamen ... 4538
master may be required to produce, in suit for wages ... 4547
deductions from seamen's wages to be entered on ... 4550
shipping commissioners may require production of, in proceedings relating to wages, &c ... 4555
statement of examination of provisions, &c., to be entered in ... 4565
entry of offenses, &c., to be made in, copy, &c., to offender ... 4597

Section.

London,
consul-general at, salary of ... 1690
Long Island,
establishment of life-saving stations on coast of ... 4242
appointment of keepers for ... 4243
employment of crews of surfmen at ... 4244
privilege of coasting-vessels trading between, and Rhode Island ... 4357
Losses and Bad Debts,
deducted from profits of national banks before dividend is declared ... 5204
Lost Checks,
settlement with owner of, in certain cases, by accounting-officers ... 300
duplicates of, how procured ... 3646, 3647
of disbursing-officers in favor of postmasters, duplicates of ... 4046
in pension cases, duplicates of ... 4770
Louisiana,
appointment of surveyor-general for, authorized ... 2207
salary of ... 2208
clearance from ports in, of vessels laden with live-oak timber ... 2463, 4205
collection-districts, ports of entry and delivery in ... 2508
officers in ... 2569
all navigable rivers in former territory of, to remain public highways ... 5251
Louisville, Ky.,
port of delivery in district of New Orleans ... 2568
surveyor and appraiser to reside at, duties of ... 2569
weighers, gaugers, measurers, and inspectors for ... 2606
merchandise imported into port of, for Jeffersonville, where and how landed, &c ... 2967
transportation in bond extended to ... 2997
inspectors of hulls and boilers for ... 4414
their salaries ... 4414
reserve of national banks in ... 5191
balances with banks in, may be part of reserve ... 5192
redemption agencies ... 5195
Louisville and Portland Canal,
assumption of control of, by Secretary of Treasury on behalf of United States ... 5255
reduction of tolls on ... 5255
Lower Marlborough, Md.,
port of delivery ... 2548
Low-Water Gauges,
of boilers of steam-vessels, inspection of ... 4418
penalty for obstructing ... 4437
Loyal Citizens,
certain assignments of disloyal contractors to, may be recognized ... 3480
Lumber,
imported, yards for storage of ... 2958
from forests of Maine on Saint John river, sawed, &c., in New Brunswick, to be admitted free of duty ... 2508
from forests upon Saint Croix river ... 2509
Lunatic,
includes what ... 1
Lyme, Conn.,
port of delivery ... 2533
Lynn, Mass.,
port of delivery ... 2527
Lyons,
consul at, salary of ... 1690

M.

Machias, Me.,
collection-district and port of entry ... 2517
collector in, to reside at ... 2518

Section.

Machinery,
for manufacture of beet-sugar to be exempt from customs-duties ... 2510
imported for repair to be free of duty, rules, &c., respecting importation of ... 2511
distillery, Commissioner may require changes of ... 3270
sale of, at public auction ... 3450

Machinist and Gas-Fitter,
in Treasury Department, salary of ... 235

Mackerel-Fishery,
form of license to carry on ... 4321
vessels engaged in, may catch cod or other fish, &c ... 4377
agreement for shares with fishermen engaged in ... 4391
penalty for violation by fishermen ... 4392
recovery of shares under ... 4393
vessels liable for ... 4393
discharge of vessel on bond ... 4394

Mackinaw, Mich.
port of delivery ... 2599
deputy collector to reside at ... 2600

Madagascar,
judicial authority of United States minister and consuls in ... 4111–4120
(see *Consular Courts.*)

Madison, Ind.,
port of delivery in district of New Orleans ... 2568
surveyor to reside at, duties of ... 2569

Magazines, Military,
assent of State legislatures to purchase of land for ... 1838

Magazines, Periodical,
regularly issued, &c., second-class mail-matter ... 3877
transient ... 3878
postage on, when sent to subscribers ... 3905
payable quarterly in advance ... 3906

Magnolia, Fla,
port of delivery ... 2562

Mahé, Seychelles,
consul at, salary of ... 1690

Mail,
provision relating to ... 3829–4061
to be conveyed by certain vessels going to or coming from foreign port ... 4203
to be promptly delivered on arrival ... 4203
compensation for carrying ... 4203

Mail-Agents,
on certain steamers authorized ... 4022

Mail-Carriers,
for Senate, salary of ... 52
for House of Representatives, salaries ... 53

Mail Contracts,
(see *Contracts.*)

Mail-Matter,
free delivery of, authorized ... 3865
divided into three classes ... 3875–3878
weight of ... 3879
metric balances for weighing ... 3880
prepayment of postage on ... 3896, 3897
postage on, paid by stamps ... 3914
registration of valuable, authorized ... 3926
-fee, &c., for ... 3927
shall be received by route-agents, &c., when prepaid ... 3980
letters may be separated from other mail for expedition ... 3994
shall be carried by railway companies on any train ... 4000

Mail-Routes,
what, to be published in papers of District of Columbia ... 3827

Mail-Steamers,
agents in charge of mail on certain, authorized ... 4022

Mail-Transportation,
(see *Carrying Mail.*)

Maine,
certain produce of forests of, on Saint John River, sawed, &c., in New Brunswick, to be admitted free of duty ... 2508
of forests on Saint Croix River ... 2509
collection-districts, ports of entry and delivery in ... 2517
officers in ... 2518
where no boundaries are prescribed ... 2519
goods for Kittery or Berwick in, may be entered at York, Me., or Portsmouth, N.H. 2524
life-saving stations on coast of ... 4249

Major-Generals,
number of ... 1094
aids to ... 1098
pay of ... 1261
of aids to ... 1261
allowance of forage to ... 1271
number of, in militia, as organized by each State ... 1631
as organized by President, when called into United States service ... 1647

Majors,
of artillery regiments ... 1099
of cavalry regiments ... 1102
of infantry regiments ... 1106
pay of ... 1261
allowance of forage to ... 1271

Malaga,
consul at, salary of ... 1690

Malfeasance,
by consular officers, penalty for ... 1736
by persons named in Title REGULATION OF VESSELS IN DOMESTIC COMMERCE, penalty ... 4374

Malta,
consul at, salary of ... 1690

Malt Liquors,
wholesale dealers in ... 3244
retail dealers in ... 3244
(see *Fermented Liquors.*)

Managing Owner,
of vessel, to give bond for registry, when ... 4145

Manchester, England,
consul at, salary of ... 1690

Manchester, Mass.,
port of delivery ... 2527

Manchester, Va.,
port of entry to extend from Richmond and, to Bermuda Hundred, Va ... 2552

Mandamus,
to compel Union Pacific Railroad Company to operate as required by law ... 5262

Manifests,
of vessels bound for Portland, Oreg., copies of, where deposited ... 2588
clearing from ... 2589
masters of, failing in duty, penalty ... 2589
blank, to be kept for sale by certain collectors of customs ... 2648
of merchandise for re-exportation, when to be delivered to collector ... 2776
of vessels departing for other districts with foreign goods, copies of, to be given to master ... 2780
not required of ferry-boats ... 2792
to specify sea-stores ... 2795
when excess of sea-stores appears by, duties to be collected ... 2796
forfeiture of sea-stores not included in ... 2797

Section.

Manifests—Continued.
no merchandise to be brought into United States in vessel without 2806
what to contain 2807
packages destined to different districts, and spirits and wines, how to be inserted in 2808
merchandise not included in, forfeiture and penalty 2809
when lost or mislaid without fraud, &c., no forfeitures 2810
master of vessel to produce and deliver copies of, to boarding-officer 2811
production of, on arrival; duty of boarding-officer 2812
how many copies of, to be delivered to boarding-officer 2813
masters failing to produce, &c., and customs-officers neglecting to certify, penalty 2814
of goods for interior ports 2827
penalty for not producing 2828
delivery of, to surveyor of interior port; oath of master; penalty for neglect, &c. 2829
cargoes to be compared with, when indorsement to be made on 2830
of cargoes of vessels bound for Connecticut and Burlington, N. J. 2834
of vessels arriving within district of Petersburgh or Richmond, Va 2836
merchandise not agreeing with, penalty 2887
returns of delivery of goods to be compared with 2889
goods imported into northern, &c., frontier districts, to be accompanied by, &c. 3097
when and to whom delivered, verification of. 3098
refusal, &c., to deliver, forfeiture and penalty 3099
Secretary of Treasury to regulate, of sealed cars, vehicles, &c. 3103
of vessels in foreign and coasting-trade on northern, &c., frontiers 3116
lading or unlading of goods to be entered on. 3117
when going to place where no custom-house 3118
when coming from such place 3122
form of, &c., prescribed by Secretary of Treasury 3124
of registered vessels in combined foreign and coasting-trade 3126
of vessels for foreign ports, to be delivered to collectors before clearance 4197
of owners, shippers, or consignors of cargo 4200
of steamboat going from Lake Champlain to province of Quebec 4208
for vessels in coasting-trade, to be signed by naval officer, when 4332
surveyors certifying or receiving certified, to make monthly return to collector 4332
of vessels departing for neighboring districts, carrying distilled spirits, sugars, or foreign merchandise 4349
penalty for proceeding without 4350
delivery of, on arrival, before unlading 4351
penalty for not delivering 4352
of vessels departing for remote districts, what to specify 4353
penalty for proceeding without, if having on board distilled spirits or foreign merchandise 4354
if carrying no cargo 4354
delivery of, by vessel arriving from remote district before unlading 4355
penalty for not delivering, &c 4356
exemption of vessels of less than 20 tons from above requirements 4359
what manifests carried by such vessels 4359
when to be exhibited 4359
penalty for not exhibiting, &c. 4360

Section.

Manifests—Continued.
forfeiture of merchandise, when 4360
for registered vessels carrying foreign merchandise from one district to another. 4361
of foreign vessels bound coastwise 4367
delivery of, on arrival 4368
penalty for not delivering, &c. 4369
of vessels entering insurrectionary district, destination may be changed in, &c., by master 5315

Manslaughter,
officers, employés, owners, inspectors, &c., of vessels, guilty of, by whose misconduct, &c., life is destroyed 5344

Manufacturer of Cigars,
(see *Cigars*)

Manufacturer of Matches,
(see *Matches*.)

Manufacturer of Stills,
(see *Stills*.)

Manufacturer of Tobacco,
(see *Tobacco*.)

Manufactures of Wool,
imported in an unfinished condition, how appraised 2902

Maps,
third-class mail-matter 3878
engravings of, &c., to illustrate documents ordered by Congress 3779
when procured by advertisement 3780
of States, &c., accompanying report of Commissioner of General Land Office 3781

Maps and Charts,
to be prepared at hydrographic office 432
disposal of moneys from sale of 433

Maquoketa River,
bridges across, Iowa 5250

Maranham,
consul at, salary of 1690

Marblehead, Mass.,
collection-district and port of entry 2527
collector to reside at 2529

Marine Band,
(see *Marine Corps*.)

Marine Corps,
compensation for loss of effects of officers of, in case of loss of vessel 290
appropriation to pay for 3689
number and constitution of 1596
credits to officers of, for volunteer service 1600
rank of commandant of 1601
staff, rank of 1602
term of enlistment in 1608
pay and allowances of 1612
extra pay to members of Marine Band 1613
deduction of pay for hospital-fund 1614
rations to enlisted men of 1615
conditions of retirement in 1622
collection and payment of bounty, prize-money, &c., due colored marines 2032
when officers, &c., of, to have pension 4693
rate of total-disability pensions to persons in 4695
officers of, to have pension according to rank, &c 4696
persons in, not to draw both pay and pension. 4724
disabled by age, &c., to have half-pay from Navy-pension fund 4756
certain, may have aid from surplus income of Navy-pension fund 4757
admission of persons belonging to, to Government Hospital for Insane 4843

Marine Hospitals,
(see *Hospitals, Marine*.)

Marine-Hospital Tax,
(see *Hospitals, Marine*.)

Section.

Marine Officers,
(see *Marine Corps.*)
Mariner,
(see *Seamen.*)
Marks, (Internal Revenue,)
by gauger on casks of spirits removed into warehouse ... 3287
on distilled spirits, drawn into new packages of 10 gallons or more ... 3323
to be effaced on emptying casks of ... 3324
changing, &c., on ... 3326
intended for exportation ... 3330
on packages of fermented liquors ... 3349
on wooden packages of tobacco ... 3362
Commissioner may change form, &c., of ... 3446
on articles sold under distraint or forfeiture, to be affixed by officer selling ... 3458
Marquette, Mich.,
port of entry ... 2599
collector to reside at ... 2600
Marriage,
of colored soldiers, what shall be deemed proof of ... 2037
on board vessel, to be entered in log-book ... 4290
of negroes and Indians, what evidence of, required under pension-laws ... 4705
Married Woman,
bond, &c., of, when appointed postmaster ... 3834
Marseilles,
consul at, salary of ... 1690
Marshals,
of consular courts,
at consulate of Bangkok, to receive no salary ... 1693
(see *Consular Courts.*)
of United States supreme court,
how appointed ... 677
salary, duties, and powers of ... 680
fees and account of ... 832
duties of, when court adjourns in consequence of epidemic, &c ... 4799
of territories,
appointment of ... 1875, 1876
salary of, and how payable ... 1881, 1882
fees and costs allowed to ... 1883
to have control of penitentiaries ... 1892
to cause regulations for, to be enforced ... 1893
compensation for services in care of ... 1893
from what fund payable ... 1894
maximum, not to be increased by ... 1894
of United States,
general direction of, by Attorney-General ... 362
supervision of accounts of, by Attorney-General ... 368
not to be, or exercise duties of, commissioner of circuit court ... 628
appointment by, of persons to attend on juries ... 715
duty of, to serve process, &c., in enforcement of awards of consuls ... 728
not to act as attorney, &c., within district ... 748
penalty ... 749
one to be appointed in each judicial district, except, &c ... 776
of southern district of Alabama, where to perform duty ... 776
of Georgia, southern district ... 776
of South Carolina, eastern district ... 776
office of, in northern district of Georgia ... 777
in Iowa, where to perform duty and keep offices ... 778
term of office of ... 779
deputies of, appointment and removal ... 780
salaries of, for extra services ... 781
suits on bond, by whom may be brought, &c. 784
statement by, to Solicitor of Treasury ... 791

Section.

Marshals—Continued.
to Sixth Auditor ... 792
vacancy in office of, how filled temporarily ... 793
power of, to stay warrant of arrest, to release, in admiralty causes, other than seizures for forfeiture ... 941
to pay fines assessed against militia, into Treasury, &c.; commissions of ... 1660
duty of, under civil-rights laws ... 1982
appointment of special deputies by ... 2021
number of, not to be increased ... 2030
vessels seized for transporting coolies to be delivered to ... 2163
how to satisfy execution in customs cases ... 3014
when to enter premises and seize papers, &c., in revenue cases ... 3091
accepting gift, &c., for settlement of violation of internal-revenue law ... 3170
to levy on property of delinquent collector of internal revenue ... 3217
to execute deed of real estate sold of delinquent collector of internal revenue ... 3217
to obliterate, &c., tax-paid stamps on sale of condemned spirits ... 3334
duties relative to goods seized under internal-revenue law ... 3458
when to make conveyance of lands, &c., to United States ... 3470
duty concerning distress-warrants against delinquent collectors, &c ... 3627–3632
may seize, &c., letters illegally carried ... 3990
disposal of such letters ... 3991
to safely keep all prize-property under warrant of court ... 4623
to report to court such property requiring to be stored or sold ... 4623
to insure same according to his judgment ... 4623
to keep custody of persons sent in as witnesses in prize-cases ... 4623
to report to Secretary of Navy, when required, condition of prize-causes ... 4623
sale of prize-property to be conducted under supervision of ... 4628
duties of, with reference to such sale ... 4628
duties of, when transfer is made to another district ... 4629
expenses advanced by, to be reimbursed ... 4629
allowances and commissions of, in disposal of prize-property ... 4645
witness-fees in prize-causes to be paid by ... 4661
to be reimbursed for such payment ... 4651
fees of, (see *Fees.*)
Marshfield, Mass.,
port of delivery ... 2527
Maryland,
collection-districts, ports of entry and delivery in ... 2548
officers in ... 2549
Masculine,
words of masculine gender to include feminine ... 1
Mash or Wort,
ratio of, to grain and molasses ... 3264
restriction on production of, fit for distillation; penalty ... 3282
none to be made between 11 p. m. Saturday and 1 a. m. Monday ... 3283
Massachusetts,
collection-districts, ports of entry and delivery in ... 2527
officers in ... 2529
establishment of life-saving stations on coast of ... 4249
"Master,"
who to be included under name of, as used in Title COLLECTION OF DUTIES ... 2768

Section.

"Master"—Continued.
who deemed to be, in construction of Title MERCHANT SEAMEN ... 4612

Master-Armorers,
at national armories, appointment of ... 1662
pay of ... 1663
to be made quarter-yearly ... 1664

Masters,
in navy,
number of, on active list ... 1363
pay of ... 1556
licensed, of steam-vessels,
(see *Inspection of Steam-Vessels.*)
of gunboats,
when to have pension ... 4693
rate of total disability-pension to ... 4695
of vessels,
shall pay consular fees, liability for, papers may be withheld until paid ... 1718
penalty for carrying away live-oak or red-cedar timber on lands reserved by United States ... 2462
in combined foreign and coasting-trade ... 3126
oath of, as to letters, &c ... 3987, 3988
of registered vessel, oath by, to obtain register ... 4144
penalty on, for false oath ... 4144
to give bond for registry ... 4145
oath of, as to citizenship ... 4156
penalty on, for failure to surrender old certificate of register where new has been issued ... 4162
oath of, as to loss of certificate ... 4167
delivery of certificate by, and cancellation of bond ... 4174
change of, to be endorsed on documents ... 4171, 4183, 4335
of recorded vessels, to countersign certificate of measurement ... 4181
certificate of record to be granted to ... 4182
change of, to be indorsed on ... 4183
to produce, on entry ... 4184
effect of failure to produce ... 4184
to pay surveyor's fees for measurement, &c. 4186
of vessel departing for foreign port to deliver to collector manifest to obtain clearance ... 4197
penalty on, for departing without clearance 4197
form of oath of, to obtain clearance ... 4198
form of report and manifest to be delivered by ... 4199
oath of, as to destination of cargo ... 4200
of steamboat going from Lake Champlain to province of Quebec to deliver manifest and obtain clearance at last port ... 4208
of foreign vessel to produce to collector register and papers on entry ... 4209
to deposit such papers with his consul, &c. 4209
penalty for failure ... 4209
exception as to vessels of certain nations. 4210
of vessel of United States, oath by, as to delivery of mails on entry ... 4212
failure to take oath ... 4212
to furnish collector copy of receipts for fees paid consuls abroad ... 4213
oath to ownership of unregistered vessel carrying sea-letters, &c ... 4226
not to be employed in wrecking on Florida coast without license ... 4241
of vessel from foreign port to United States, number of passengers allowable ... 4252
penalty on, for taking more ... 4253
for violation of regulations as to berths. 4255
for failing to provide deck-houses, ventilators, and cooking-range ... 4259

Section.

Masters—Continued.
for furnishing short allowance of provisions or water ... 4261
for failure to have provisions properly cooked and distributed ... 4262
to maintain discipline and cleanliness among passengers, &c ... 4263
to keep apartments occupied by passengers in clean and healthy condition ... 4263
to furnish collectors with list of passengers on arrival ... 4266
payment to collector on account of passengers dying on voyage ... 4268
penalty for refusal to pay, &c ... 4269
recovery and disposal of penalty ... 4269
penalty on, for permitting officer or seaman to visit part of vessel assigned to emigrants ... 4276
to post notice forbidding such visiting . 4277
penalty for failure to post ... 4277
not liable as carriers of gold, bullion, and valuable goods, unless notified ... 4281
remedies against, for embezzlement, loss, or neglect ... 4287
to sign entries in log-book of vessels ... 4291
penalty for omitting to make entries ... 4292
of vessel in foreign commerce, bond to be given by, for passport ... 4306
penalty upon, for departing without passport ... 4307
to deposit papers with consul, &c., on arrival at foreign port ... 4309
penalty on, for failure ... 4310
of enrolled and licensed vessels, subject to provisions for registered vessels ... 4312
bond of, to obtain license for coasting-trade or fisheries ... 4320
oath of, to obtain license ... 4320
may obtain exchange of registry for enrollment or license, or vice versa ... 4323
to deliver up register or license on exchange ... 4323
penalty for neglecting to deliver up, &c. 4323
penalty for failing to surrender expired license ... 4325
oath as to foreign repairs to obtain enrollment, &c ... 4330
penalty for false oath ... 4330
penalty for failure to report change of ... 4335
for refusing to exhibit enrollment or license ... 4336
to deliver certificate received in another district to collector in home port ... 4338
trading between neighboring districts, to make out and subscribe manifests, &c. 4349
penalty for departing without manifest, &c ... 4350
to deliver manifests before unlading, &c .. 4351
oath as to manifest ... 4351
penalty for not delivering, &c ... 4352
trading between remote districts to make out and subscribe manifest, &c ... 4353
penalty for proceeding without manifest, &c ... 4354
under twenty tons, manifests of ... 4359
penalty for not exhibiting ... 4360
of fishing vessels touching at foreign port, to deliver manifest and make entry ... 4364
report by, on arrival at port other than destination ... 4366
penalty for refusing, &c ... 4366
of foreign vessel bound coastwise, manifest and permit before departing ... 4367
delivery of manifest and permit on arrival before unlading ... 4368
penalty for failing, &c ... 4369

Section.

Masters—Continued.
oath of, as to expiration of license of vessel, at sea ... 4372
fee for endorsing change of, on registry ... 4382
in domestic commerce, fees to be paid by ... 4382
when may perform duties of shipping-commissioners ... 4504
how may procure, &c., apprentices ... 4509
shall produce to commissioners indentures of apprentices ... 4510
shall make, &c., shipping-articles ... 4511
rules to govern them in making, &c., articles ... 4512
certain, excepted from requirements as to shipping-articles, &c ... 4513
penalty for carrying seamen without articles ... 4514
for accepting seamen illegally shipped ... 4515
how may replace deserters ... 4516
how may ship seamen in foreign ports ... 4517
penalty for illegally shipping ... 4518
shall post copy of shipping-articles in ship, penalty ... 4519
in coasting-trade, manner of shipping seamen, form of articles ... 4520
in coasting trade; penalty for illegally shipping seamen ... 4521
how may recover penalty for failure of seamen to begin voyage ... 4522
when to make payment of wages to seamen ... 4529
payment of wages by, at intermediate ports ... 4530
shall take charge of effects, &c., of deceased seamen ... 4538
rules in regard to proceedings ... 4539
penalty for failure to take charge ... 4540
proceedings when seamen die in United States ... 4542
non-payment of seamen's wages, summons of, for ... 4546
to show cause, &c., in case of ... 4546
penalty for illegal discharge of seamen ... 4549
discharge of seamen, shall render account of wages on ... 4550
shall give certificate ... 4551
rules to be observed by ... 4552
shall give certificate of character, unless ... 4553
questions between crew and, how heard, &c ... 4554
may be required by shipping-commissioner to produce log-book, &c ... 4555
on complaint of unseaworthiness, shall have vessel surveyed ... 4556
shall pay costs of survey ordered by judge, &c ... 4557
shall pay extra wages to crew on discharge on account of unseaworthiness, &c ... 4561
shall pay cost of inspection of vessel in foreign port, recovery ... 4562
penalty for refusal to pay extra wages and charges of inspection ... 4563
what provisions to be provided by ... 4564
penalty for refusal to provide ... 4565
may deduct from wages of crew for false complaint of provisions, &c ... 4566
shall serve anti-scorbutics, &c., to crew ... 4569
penalty for failure to carry medicines, anti-scorbutics, &c ... 4570
shall carry proper weights and measures ... 4571
clothing and fuel for seamen ... 4572
shall deliver crew-list to collector of customs ... 4573
shall carry certified crew-list and shipping-articles, penalty ... 4575
shall give bond for return of seamen to United States ... 4576
destitute seamen, shall carry, when required to do so, penalty ... 4578

Section.

Masters—Continued.
additional allowance to, for carrying ... 4579
when to pay extra wages to seamen ... 4580
on sale of vessel ... 4582
shall pay to collectors hospital dues of crew ... 4585
to consular officer hospital dues of crew of vessel sold abroad ... 4586
may retain hospital dues out of wages of crew ... 4587
shall protest against impressment of crew ... 4589
penalty for neglect ... 4590
shall pay shipping, &c., fee, how reimbursed ... 4593
punishment of seamen for damage to, by smuggling ... 4596
shall enter offenses, &c., in log-book ... 4597
punishment of seamen absent without leave of ... 4598
may apprehend deserters without warrant, penalty for illegal apprehension ... 4599
expenses of, in apprehending, to be paid from proceeds of forfeited clothing, &c ... 4604
shall be reimbursed for part of cost of conviction out of wages ... 4605
may arrest unauthorized persons boarding his vessel ... 4606
penalty for removing effects of seamen without permission of ... 4607
shall inform seamen of penalty for carrying sheath-knife ... 4608
of steamboat or vessel, by whose misconduct, &c., life is destroyed, how punished ... 5344
maliciously, &c., forcing officer or mariner on shore, with intent to leave, &c.; refusing to bring home ... 5363

Matagorda, Tex.,
port of delivery ... 2578
surveyor to reside at ... 2579

Matamoras,
consul at, salary of ... 1690

Matanzas,
consul at, salary of ... 1690

Matches, (Friction,)
stamps supplied to manufacturer on credit ... 3425
may be removed from manufactory for export without stamps ... 3430
imported, to be stamped as prescribed in Schedule A ... 3435
tax on, Schedule A ... 3437
restrictions on carriage of, by steam passenger-vessels ... 4472
how packed and marked for shipment ... 4475
penalty for shipping contrary to law ... 4476

Materials, Stores, and Supplies,
disposal of proceeds of ... 3692

Mates in Navy,
pay of ... 1556

Mates of Steam-Vessels,
(see *Inspection of Steam-Vessels.*)

Mates of Vessels,
to sign entries in log-book, &c ... 4291
with majority of crew may demand inspection of vessel ... 4556
in foreign ports ... 4559

Matrons,
in Army hospitals, employment of ... 1239
pay and rations of ... 1273
rations to, employed at post or regimental hospitals ... 1295

Mattapoisett Harbor, Mass.,
port in collection-district of New Bedford, description of vessels belonging to ... 2528

Mauritius,
consul at, salary of ... 1690

Section.

Meal,
may be ground on premises where spirits are distilled, to be used for distillation on premises ... 3266
Measurement,
of registered vessels, to be made by surveyor before register issued ... 4148
new measurement not necessary to obtain new register, unless, &c ... 4148
certificate of, what to specify and how made ... 4149
what to express and how ascertained ... 4150
cabins and state-rooms not to be measured. 4151
certain vessels exempt from ... 4152
rules for, to ascertain registered tonnage .. 4153
to ascertain tonnage not otherwise provided for ... 4154
to be specified in certificate of registry ... 4155
new certificate of registry to refer to former certificate ... 4156
of recorded vessels, collectors shall cause to be made ... 4181
certificate of ... 4181
to be inserted in certificate of record ... 4182
penalty on surveyor giving naval officer false description of ... 4187
for enrollment and license, same requirements as for registry ... 4312
for license of vessels under twenty tons ... 4331
fees for, (see *Fees*.)
Measurers of Customs,
for certain ports ... 2606, 2607
extortion by, making returns without weighing, &c., penalty ... 2637
when and how to make returns of goods measured ... 2890
Measuring,
imported merchandse not to be removed from wharf before, &c.; forfeiture ... 2882
of imports, when at expense of owner, &c .. 2920
Mechanics,
day's work of, to be eight hours ... 3738
Medals,
charges on manufacture of, to be covered into Treasury ... 3552
Medals of Honor,
to seamen in Navy for gallantry ... 1407
Medford, Mass.,
port of delivery ... 2527
Medical Attendance,
allowances to officers of Navy for ... 1586
Medical Corps of Navy,
number of officers on active list ... 1368
rank and title of Chief of Bureau of Medicine and Surgery ... 1471
of retired Chief of Bureau of ... 1473
relative rank of officers of ... 1474
pay of ... 1556
Medical Department, (*Army*,)
authorized ... 1094
hospital-stewards of ... 1094, 1179, 1180
organization and rank of ... 1168
vacancies in grade of assistant surgeon, how filled ... 1168
Medical Referee,
in Pension-Office, appointment, &c., of ... 4776
Medicine Chests,
shall be carried by merchant-vessels ... 4569
penalty for failure to carry ... 4570
Medicines and Medicinal Preparations,
allowance to officers of Navy for ... 1586
purchases of, by Secretary of Navy ... 3721
imported, including essential oils and chemical preparations, how examined and appraised ... 2933

Section.

Medicines and Medicinal Preparations—Cont'd.
name of manufacturer, &c., to be affixed to; forfeitures ... 2934
adulterated, to be so returned upon invoice; re-examination of, &c ... 2935
exportation of, how made ... 3018
manufacture of, in bonded warehouse for exportation ... 3433
imported, to be stamped as prescribed in Schedule A ... 3435
compounded according to U. S. Pharmacopœia, &c., or according to written prescription, &c., exempt from stamp-tax ... 3436
proprietary or patent, not exempt ... 3436
internal-revenue tax on, Schedule A ... 3437
Mediterranean Passport,
penalty for making or using any forged, &c. 4191
deposit of, with consul on arrival of vessel at foreign port ... 4309
return of, by consul on production of clearance ... 4309
Melbourne,
consul at, salary of ... 1690
Melter,
at certain assay-offices, appointment, &c., of ... 3559, 3561
Melter and Refiner,
office created ... 3496
salaries ... 3498
to give bond ... 3501
to take oath ... 3500
power to nominate subordinates ... 3504
general duties of ... 3508
to determine mode of melting bullion ... 3521
duty as to ingots ... 3530
as to bars for payment of deposits ... 3534
as to coins ... 3538
as to annual settlement ... 3541
at New York assay office, appointment of ... 3554
duties, &c., of ... 3555
salary of ... 3556
Members of Congress,
salary of ... 35
penalty for receiving money, &c., for procuring contracts, or offices, or for official services ... 1781
not to receive compensation for services before Department or commission, penalty .. 1782
not to be interested in contracts ... 3739–3742
forfeiture of, and disqualification for, office, by accepting bribe ... 5502
Memphis, Tenn.,
port of delivery in district of New Orleans .. 2568
surveyor and appraiser at, duties of ... 2569
of ... 2569
weighers, gaugers, measurers, and inspectors for ... 2606
transportation in bond extended to ... 2997
inspectors of hulls and boilers for ... 4414
their salaries ... 4414
Mercantile Firms,
or trading, no member of, to act as officer or agent of United States in transactions with same ... 1783
Merchandise,
term, what to include ... 2766
transportation of, (see *Transportation of Merchandise*.)
Merchant-Appraiser,
when collector of customs to appoint ... 2609
penalty for not acting as ... 2610, 2945
compensation of ... 2725
when to appraise merchandise remaining in public store beyond one year preparatory to sale ... 2973

Section.

Merchants,
when authentication of certificates to invoices by foreign, allowed ... 2844
in cases of merchandise not acquired by purchase, &c ... 2845
Merchant-Seamen,
(see *Seamen.*)
Merchant-Vessels,
(see *Vessels.*)
Meridian,
what shall be used for astronomical, and what for nautical, purposes ... 435
Merit,
granting certificates of, in Army ... 1216
pay of enlisted men receiving certificates of ... 1285
Messengers,
of Senate, salaries ... 52
how appointed and removed ... 52
of House of Representatives, salary ... 53
of Electoral College, mileage of ... 144
to President, salary of ... 155
of Court of Claims, appointment of ... 1053
salary of ... 1054
Messina,
consul at, salary of ... 1690
Metals,
customs duties on ... 2504
Meteorological Observations,
duty of Secretary of War to provide for, at military stations ... 221
Metric Postal Balance,
shall be furnished certain offices ... 3880
Metric System,
of weights and measures legalized ... 3569
equivalents of ... 3570
Mexico,
salary of minister and Secretary to ... 1675
what imported merchandise may be withdrawn from warehouse for exportation to, routes ... 3002
through port of Lavaca, Tex ... 3003
through port of Indianola, Tex ... 3004
imported merchandise for, arriving at certain ports, how entered and conveyed ... 3005
certain imports and domestic products, &c., how transported over territory of ... 3006
goods exported to, not to be relanded in United States, penalty ... 3008
Mexico, City of,
consul-general at, salary of ... 1690
cemetery near, maintenance of ... 4879
rules and regulations applicable thereto ... 4880
Mexican Dollar,
value of fractions of ... 3567
recoinage of ... 3568
Mexican War,
addtional pay to enlisted men who served in ... 1285
to non-commissioned officers recommended for promotion ... 1286
bounty-land for certain soldiers of, or their widows, &c ... 2418
certain soldiers of, entitled to warrants for land or to scrip ... 2419
to issue to widows, &c., when ... 2419
warrants and patents when to issue ... 2423
officers, &c., disabled, &c., in, to have pension ... 4730
widows, &c., of officers, &c., killed, &c., in, to have pension ... 4731
Miami,
collection-district in Ohio ... 2603
officers in, residence of ... 2604
Michigan,
collection-districts, ports of entry and delivery in ... 2599

Section.

Michigan—Continued.
officers in ... 2600
inspectors of hulls and boilers for ... 4414
salaries of ... 4414
Michigan City, Ind.,
port of delivery ... 2601
surveyor of customs to reside at ... 2602
passage of vessels to and from harbor of, free from toll ... 5247
Middletown, Conn.,
collection-district and port of entry ... 2533
collector in, to reside at ... 2534
Middletown Point, N. J.,
port of delivery ... 2541
Midshipman,
grade as line officer ... 1362
pay of ... 1556
rations, or commutation therefor, to ... 1577
Mileage,
of officers executing precepts of either House of Congress ... 74
to officers of Army ... 1273
to officers of Navy ... 1566
to members of territorial legislature ... 1853
of clerk of supreme court of Arizona at adjourned term ... 1934
allowed to witnesses under letters rogatory, how payable ... 4074
of messenger in bankruptcy, allowance for ... 5126
Milford, Conn.,
port of delivery ... 2533
Military Academy,
professors, cadets, and band at, part of Army ... 1094
band to be stationed at ... 1111
pay of leader of ... 1278
officers, professors, and instructors authorized at ... 1309
local rank of superintendent and of commandant and cadets ... 1310
cadets at, number and appointment of ... 1315
appointment of, in advance ... 1317
commencement of pay and allowance of ... 1317
arrangement of, into companies ... 1322
in what duties to be trained and taught ... 1322
board of visitors, appointment of ... 1327
compensation and allowance to ... 1329
leave of absence to professors and officers at ... 1330
conditions of retirement of professors, &c ... 1333
pay of superintendent and commandant ... 1334
of adjutant at ... 1335
and allowances of professors at ... 1336
of assistant professors and instructors ... 1337
of master of sword ... 1338
of cadets ... 1339
of librarian and assistant ... 1340
of enlisted men employed at ... 1341
Military Bounty Land-Warrants,
(see *Bounty Lands.*)
Military Cemeteries,
(see *Cemeteries, National.*)
Military Justice,
Bureau of, in Army, authorized ... 1094
organization and rank of officers of ... 1198
Military Lands,
(see *Bounty Lands.*)
Military Organizations in Kansas,
appropriation to pay ... 3689
Military Prison,
established at Rock Island, Ill ... 1344
board of government for ... 1345
visitation and inspection of ... 1346
officers and attendants allowed ... 1347
accounts and government of ... 1348
bond of the commandant ... 1349
powers and duties of ... 1350
employment of convicts ... 1351

Section.

Military Prison—Continued.
proceeds of work at 1351
clothing to prisoners on discharge from .. 1355
diet and accommodations for prisoners ... 1357

Military Reservations,
excepted from operation of laws relating to town-sites 2393

Military Secretary,
to Lieutenant-General 1097

Military Stores,
purchase and distribution of 1133
inspection and survey of damaged 1241

Military Supplies,
purchases, &c., of, shall be under Secretary of War 3714

Military and Naval Service,
persons honorably discharged from, to be preferred for appointment in civil service 1754
recommendation for employment by citizens of persons honorably discharged from . 1755
deserters from, to forfeit citizenship 1996–1998
who to have pensions in 4693
after July 27, 1868 4694
pension for loss of both feet, &c., by persons in 4697
after June 4, 1872 4698

Militia,
pay of, during captivity 1288
who to be enrolled in 1625
enrollment in, by whom 1626
notice of 1627
arms and accoutrements to be kept by officers and men of 1628
who exempted from duty in 1629
arrangement and rank of divisions, brigades, &c., while in State service 1630
officers of, in each State 1631, 1632
light infantry, or riflemen, and cavalry and artillery in, how formed, armed, and provided 1632
regimental colors and musical instruments of 1633
adjutant-general of, appointment and duties . 1533
returns of actual condition of arms, &c., of corps in, by whom and how made 1635
what discipline to be enforced in 1637
officers of, how to take rank 1638
wounded or disabled in, while in United States service, how cared for 1639
duties of brigade-inspector of 1640
what privileges retained by corps of artillery, cavalry, and infantry, not incorporated with 1641
power of President to call forth, to repel invasion or suppress rebellion 1642
how apportioned when called forth from several States 1643
when subject to Rules and Articles of War . 1644
when called into service of United States, how organized by President 1646
into divisions and brigades 1647
term of service of, to be specified, not exceeding nine months 1648
failing to obey orders of President 1649
pay, rations, clothing, and camp-equipage of 1650
pay of, when to commence 1651
traveling-pay, subsistence, and allowances of 1652
forage to mounted companies of 1653
expenses of march to rendezvous by 1654
what addition to ration on western frontiers 1655
half-pay, when allowed widow or child of officers and men in, dying in United States service 1656

Militia—Continued.
benefits extended to, employed in suppressing Indian depredations in Florida 1657
courts-martial for trial of, how constituted . 1658
fines assessed against, in United States service, how certified to marshals and to Comptroller of Treasury; how collected, and imprisonment for 1659
annual appropriation for arms and equipments in 1661
general officers of, to be elected by people .. 1856
in new Territories to be temporarily appointed by governor 1857
persons appointed to execute process may call aid of 1984
called into service between 1812 and 1852, bounty-land for 2420
to have pensions, in war of 1812 and Indian wars, widows, &c., of 4732
who served sixty days in, &c 4736
authority of President to employ, in enforcement of neutrality laws 5287
to compel departure of foreign vessel, forbidden by laws of nations or treaty to remain, &c 5288
in aid of collection of duties in certain cases 5316

Militia Officers and Soldiers,
when to have pension 4693
rate of total-disability pension to 4695
shall have pension according to rank, &c ... 4696

Milwaukee, Wis.,
collection-district and port of entry 2597
collector and appraiser to reside at 2598
weighers, gaugers, measurers, and inspectors for 2606
transportation in bond extended to 2997
inspectors of hulls and boilers for 4414
salaries of 4414
reserve of national banks in 5191
balances with banks in, may be part of reserve 5192
redemption agencies 5195

Mineral Lands,
(see *Lands, Public.*)

Mineralogical Specimens,
weight of, in mails 3878

Minimum Price,
real estate may be offered for, at sale for internal-revenue taxes 3197

Mining Claims,
(see *Lands, Public.*)

Ministers,
certificate of, to be endorsed on declaration of American artist to admit works of art free of duty 2505
to establish tariff of fees for judicial services 4120
allowance to, for rent of prisons 4121
meaning of word in Title FOREIGN RELATIONS 4130
of United States, pension declarations may be made before 4714
(see *Diplomatic Officers.*)

Minnesota,
appointment of surveyor-general for, authorized 2207
salary of 2208
collection-districts, ports of entry and delivery in 2595
officers in 2596
collection-district of 2595
officers in, residence of 2596

Minor Children,
of certain soldiers entitled to bounty-land, when 2418

Section.

Minor Coinage,
to be reported by mint-superintendents 3503
denomination, weight, and material of 3515
purchase of metal for 3528
profit-fund, how credited and used......... 3528
assay for 3528
free delivery of................................. 3529
when to be discontinued..................... 3529
alloys, deviation allowed in.................. 3533
deviation in adjusting......................... 3537
profits on, not to be used for wages, &c 3552
legal tender, in what sums.................. 3587

Mints and Assay Offices,
title by which known.......................... 3495
officers of, how appointed.................... 3496
salaries of officers of......................... 3498
of assistants, clerks, &c., in 3499
wages of workmen in, how determined..... 3499
officers of, to take oath 3500
to give bonds 3501
temporary appointments in case of absence of officers of 3502
powers and duties of superintendent of.3503, 3504
accounts of, how kept, &c..................... 3504
assistants, clerks, &c., how appointed; chief clerk, how designated 3504
duties of assayers of.......................... 3507
of melters and refiners in.................. 3508
of coiners in 3509
of engraver.................................. 3510
shall exchange silver for gold at par 3527
assay, to determine fineness of metal for minor coinage.......................... 3528
returns to depositors 3545
at Philadelphia, New Orleans, and San Francisco, superintendents to perform duties of treasurers.................. 3497
at Philadelphia, silver bullion purchased at, how paid for at........................ 3527
minor coinage at 3528
minor coins to be exchanged for copper coins at............................ 3529
trial pieces to be sent to...................... 3539
execution of medals at 3551
bullion deposits at New York assay office to be coined at............................ 3553
standard troy pound of..................3548, 3549
standard weights of............................ 3549
expenses of, how provided for 3552
New York assay office, business of, defined.. 3553
superintendent, assayer, melter, and refiner, appointment of 3554
duties, oaths, bonds, &c., of officers of.... 3555
salaries of officers at 3555
of assistants 3557
mint-laws extended to assay offices.....3555, 3562
at Denver, place of deposit of public money. 3592
at Carson City, and assay office at Boise City 3592
superintendents of, to be assistant treasurers 3594
officers of, acting as assistant treasurers, to give bond.................................. 3600
President may increase penalty of bond of. 3639
debasement, &c., of gold and silver coins struck at 5460
fraudulently defacing, increasing, or diminishing weights used at................ 5460
embezzling metals, coins, medals, &c., at.... 5460

Miscellaneous Appropriations,
shall not be used for compensation.......... 3682
permanent 3689

Miscellaneous Receipts,
proceeds of old material, &c., shall be covered into Treasury as................. 3618

Section.

Mississippi,
district judge in, appointment and residence of 552
clearance, from ports in, of vessels laden with live-oak timber....................2463, 4205
collection-districts, ports of entry and delivery in 2566
officers in 2567

Mississippi River and Tributaries,
freight and tow-boats on, may carry what steam-pressure 4420
water-gauges, and observations of rise and fall of water; limit of expenditure... 5252
piers or cribs in front of mill-property on banks, for protection, &c............. 5254

Missouri State Militia,
provisions of pension-title extended to 4722

Mobile, Ala.,
collection-district and port of entry in 2564
collector and appraiser to reside at.......... 2565
weighers, gaugers, measurers, and inspectors for.. 2606
transportation in bond extended to.......... 2997
inspectors of hulls and boilers for district of. 4414
their salaries................................ 4414

Models,
classification and arrangement of, in suitable cases 484
power of Commissioner as to, in cases of rejected application for patent......... 485

Molasses,
seven gallons of mash to represent one gallon of 3264
penalty for delivery, at distillery having no sign 3279

Money,
deposit of, paid into United States court, or to officer of 995
how withdrawn from deposit.............. 996
superintendents to receive for expenses, &c., of mints 3506
of account, to be expressed in decimal system.. 3563
value of foreign coin in 3564
erroneously covered, appropriation for refunding 3689
unlawful reissue, &c., of bills, &c., of expired corporations established by United States, to serve as 5437
making or uttering, without authority, coins for current, in resemblance of United States or foreign coins.................. 5461
coin, card, token, &c., for use as one, two, or five-cent piece....................... 5462
(see *Public Money.*)

Money-Orders,
accounts of, how to be kept by Sixth Auditor... 293
copies of account-books of Post-Office Department, when evidence 889
offices, bonds of postmasters at.............. 3834
what, shall be known as.................. 4027
system of, established......................... 4027
may be exchanged with foreign countries... 4028
how issued...................................... 4029
limit of amount of; fees for................. 4032
applications for 4033
forms of... 4034
good for one year 4036
indorsement of 4037
changes in 4038
repayment of................................... 4039
funds, transfer of.......................4042, 4043
what shall be; accounts of.............. 4045
embezzlement of; penalty 4046
pay for issuing 4047

Section.

Money-Orders—Continued.
accounts to show amounts derived from 4049
net proceeds to be deposited as postal revenue 4050
Moneys of United States,
(see *Public Moneys.*)
Montana Territory,
number of members of council and house of representatives of 1922
extra sessions of legislative assembly of, how called 1923
penitentiary in, care and custody of 1936
maintenance of prisoners by 1937
contingent expenses of executive department of, annual appropriation for 1935
legislative expenses of, provision for 1940
salaries of governor, &c., of, not payable until duties entered upon 1941
mileage of members of legislative assembly of 1943
Indian agencies, &c., in, continued 1949
disbursing officers in, to give security in what manner 1951
appointment of Indian superintendent for tribes in 2046
of surveyor-general for 2207
salary of 2210
fifty per cent. addition to certain fees to registers and receivers in 2238
(see *Territories.*)
Montana and Idaho,
collection-district 2593
collector in 2594
Monterey, Cal.,
inspector of customs to reside at 2583
Montevideo,
consul at, salary of 1690
Montreal,
consul-general at, salary of 1690
Morehead City, N. C.,
Secretary of Treasury may change port of entry from Beaufort, N. C., to 2555
Mortgages,
of vessel not valid unless recorded 4192
to be recorded by collectors of customs 4193
certificates discharging, to be recorded 4193
what record of, to be kept in books 4193
what to be certified on 4193
fee for recording 4193
on northern frontiers 4382
not recorded until acknowledged, &c 4193
collectors to keep index 4194
index and record open to inspection 4194
collectors to furnish certificates relating to, &c 4194
fee for such certificate 4194
fee for furnishing certified copy of record 4194
Moscow,
consul at, salary of 1690
Mothers,
when to have pensions 4707
pension to cease on remarriage 4708
when pension of, to begin 4709, 4710
pension to, when married prior to July 27, 1868, &c., when to begin 4710
Mulatto,
(see *Slave-Trade.*)
Mules,
lost in military service, to be paid for 3483
Munich,
consul at, salary of 1690
Musicians, (Army,)
for battery of artillery 1100
for company of infantry 1107
principal, for regiment of artillery 1099
of infantry 1106

Section.

Musicians, (Army)—Continued.
chief, for regiment of artillery 1099
of cavalry 1102
of infantry 1106
Muskets,
what system to be used by Ordnance Department in manufacture of 1672
no royalty to be paid to officers and employés of United States for system adopted 1673
Mutilated Notes,
may be replaced by new 3580
shall be destroyed 3581
of national banks, shall be replaced, &c 5184
burning of, certificate of burning 5184
Mutiny,
punishment of seamen for 4596

N.

Nagasaki,
consul at, salary of 1690
Names,
of masters of vessels, to be indorsed on documents 4171, 4183, 4335
of vessels, to be painted on stern; penalty. 4178, 4334
change of, to be indorsed on certificate of record 4183
of steam-vessels, to be painted on stern and pilot-house; penalty 4495
Nantes,
consul at, salary of 1690
Nantucket, Mass.,
collection-district and port of entry 2527
collector to reside at 2529
Naples,
consul at, salary of 1690
Naphtha,
not to be carried on steam passenger-vessels. 4472
how packed and marked for shipment 4475
penalty for shipping contrary to law 4476
Narragansett Pier,
supervision of life-saving stations on 4248
Nashville, Tenn.,
port of delivery in district of New Orleans .. 2568
surveyor to reside at, duties of 2569
inspectors of hulls and of boilers for 4414
their salaries 4414
Nassau, (West Indies,)
consul at, salary of 1690
Natchez, Miss.,
collection-district and port of entry 2566
collector to reside at 2567
vessels arriving at New Orleans destined for, what to do 2832
National,
prohibition of use of word, in title of certain banks 5243
National Asylum,
(see *National Home for Disabled Volunteer Soldiers.*)
National Banking Associations,
application of provisions respecting, to all banking organizations under United States laws 5157
National Bank-Notes,
(see *National Banks.*)
National Banks,
district attorneys to conduct suits respecting, when United States is interested 380
jurisdiction of district courts of suits by and against 563
of circuit courts 629
of all suits by, to enjoin Comptroller of Currency, &c., or receiver, &c 629
proceedings by, to enjoin Comptroller of Currency, in what district shall be had ... 736

Section.

National Banks—Continued.
copy of organization-certificate of, when and of what evidence 885
tax on circulation 3408
capital of State banks converted into 3410
tax on certain notes paid out by 3412, 3413
on notes of towns, cities, &c 3413
to be held for tax due on outstanding circulation of State bank 3416
exempt from certain taxes 3417
notes, for what debts receivable by United States 3473
for what payable 3475
printing of report of Secretary of Treasury upon 3811
deposit of public money in, by postmasters, in certain cases 3847
may be formed, articles of association, copy to Comptroller 5133
organization-certificate, contents of 5134
acknowledgment, &c, of 5135
powers of, on becoming bodies-corporate 5136
to issue notes 5136
to hold, &c., real property 5137
minimum capital of 5138
shares of, to be personal property, how transferable, effects of transfer 5139
paying in of capital stock of 5140
proceedings on failure to pay installments on stock 5141
increase of capital 5142
reduction of 5143
right of shareholders to vote 5144
no officer, clerk, &c., of, to act as proxy 5144
directors of, number, &c., of 5145
qualifications of 5146
oath of 5147
filling vacancies in board of 5148
proceedings in case of failure to elect on proper day 5149
president to be elected from and by 5150
individual liability of shareholders 5151
executors, &c., holding stock not personally liable 5152
when designated as public depositories, &c.; duties, &c 5153
to receive national-bank notes at par 5153
when and how State banks may become 5154
State banks with branches may become 5155
reservation as to rights of, organized under act of 1864 5156
application of provisions concerning 5157
meaning of "United States bonds" used in Title 5158
shall deposit bonds before commencing business 5159
deposit of bonds by; increase, &c., of 5160
return of bonds on surrender of notes 5160, 5167
registered bonds shall be issued to, for coupon bonds 5161
transfer of bonds by, how made, &c 5162
Comptroller shall keep register of transferred bonds of 5163
shall advise of transfers of bonds 5164
may examine books of Treasurer relating to transfer, &c., of bonds of 5165
annual examination of bonds of 5166
bonds belonging to, custody of; collection of; interest on, &c 5167
Comptroller shall examine as to correctness of preliminary steps in organization of 5168
may give or withhold certificate authorizing commencement of business 5169
certificate of authority to commence business shall be published 5170
issue of circulating notes to 5171

Section.

National Banks—Continued.
printing, denominations, &c., of notes of 5172
Comptroller to have control of plates, &c., of notes 5173
examination of plates, &c., of notes of; destruction of certain plates 5174
limit of amount of small notes to 5175
limit of circulation to certain 5176
aggregate circulation of 5177
apportionment of circulation to 5178
equalizing of 5179
withdrawal of notes for purpose of 5180
when may be removed from one State to another 5181
notes of, how to be signed, &c.; for what receivable 5182
not to issue notes other than authorized by law 5183
destroying, &c., worn-out notes of 5184
certificate of burning 5184
certain, may issue gold-notes 5185
notes of gold-banks receivable by each other 5186
reserve of banks issuing gold-notes, redemption, &c., of 5186
penalty for unlawfully issuing notes to 5187
for printing, &c., business-cards in imitation of, or upon circulating-notes of, &c 5188
for mutilating, &c., circulating-notes, drafts, &c, of 5189
place of business located 5190
reserve prescribed 5191
what may be included in reserve 5192
may count certificates of deposit for United States notes as part of reserve 5193
issue of certificates of deposit to, not to contract or expand currency 5194
shall have redemption-agencies; may deposit half of reserve with, if in New York 5195
shall receive notes of each other at par 5196
rate of interest which may be taken by 5197
penalty for taking unlawful interest; recovery of 5198
dividends of 5199
limit of amount to be loaned to one person, &c 5200
not to loan on or purchase their own stock 5201
limit as to indebtedness of 5202
restrictions on use of circulating-notes by 5203
shall not withdraw capital; when not to declare dividend 5204
proceedings on failure to pay up, or impairment of capital stock of 5205
restrictions as to use of notes of other banks by 5206
not to receive United States notes, &c., as collateral, &c., penalty 5207
officers, &c., not to certify checks, unless; penalty 5208
penalty for embezzlement, &c., by officers, &c., of 5209
shall keep, &c., list of shareholders 5210
shall make &c., report of assets, &c 5211
of dividends, &c 5212
penalty for failure to make reports 5213
semi-annual duty to be paid by 5214
shall make return of deposits, &c., to United States Treasurer; penalty for default 5215
semi-annual duty of, how assessed on failure to make return 5216
how collected on failure to pay 5217
refunding excess of duty to 5218
shares and real property of, to be liable to State, &c., taxation 5219
how, may go into liquidation 5220
shall give notice of intended dissolution 5221

Section.

National Banks—Continued.
in liquidation, deposit to redeem circulation 5222
consolidating, deposit to redeem circulation not required 5223
in liquidation, re-assignment of bonds, redemption of notes 5224
destruction of redeemed notes 5225
protesting notes of, manner of 5226
failure to pay note of, proceedings on notice of 5227
business of, after failure to pay notes 5228
notice to holders of notes of, redemption of notes, sale of bonds 5229
sale of bonds of, at auction 5230
at private sale 5231
notes of defaulting bank receivable in payment for its bonds 5231
disposal of redeemed notes of, evidence of payment 5232
notes of, paid at Treasury to be cancelled 5233
appointment, &c., of receivers of 5234
notice to creditors of, in liquidation, to present claims 5235
dividends to creditors of, by Comptroller 5236
may enjoin receiver, when 5237
fees and expenses of receivers, &c., of 5238
penalty for violation of laws relating to 5239
examiners of, appointment, &c., of 5240
limit as to visitorial powers 5241
transfers after act of insolvency, void 5242
title of, not to be used by other banks, &c 5243
notes included by words "obligation or other security of the United States" 5413
making or passing counterfeited or altered notes of 5415
buying, selling, receiving, or delivering forged or altered note of 5434

National Cemeteries,
(see *Cemeteries, National.*)

National Currency,
(see *National Banks.*)

National Debt,
appropriation for interest on 3689
for funding 3689
for sinking-fund for 3689
provisions relating to 3693, 3708

National Home for Disabled Volunteer Soldiers,
establishment of 4825
board of managers for, how constituted 4825
corporate powers of 4825
nine managers to be elected by Congress 4826
no compensation to board 4828
expenses of, may be paid 4828
officers of, how appointed and removed 4829
sites for homes 4830
persons for whom military homes are to be provided 4830
appropriation of funds for support of 3689, 4831
board of managers authorized to receive donations for support of 4831
persons entitled to benefit of 4832
assignment of pensions to board of managers 4832
out-door relief, rate of 4833
board to make annual report to Congress 4834
to examine and audit treasurer's accounts and visit home quarterly 4834

National Loan,
appropriation for expenses of 3689

Nationalization of Vessels,
owned by residents of Alaska 4140

Naturalization,
of seamen, with declaration of intention 2174
term of service on merchant-vessel required 2174
protection of, after declaration 2174

Section.

Naturalized Citizens,
restrictions upon registration of vessels owned by non-resident 4134

Nautical Almanac,
who to be in charge of 436

Nautical Books,
hydrographic office of Navy may publish 432
disposal of proceeds of sale of 433

Naval Academy,
clerk to paymaster at 1386
where established 1511
students at, title of 1512
number of 1513
appointed contrary to law, not to be paid. 1518
academic course for 1520
education of constructors and engineers at .. 1522
cadet-engineers at 1523
selection of naval storekeeper for 1527
procurement and issue of clothing at 1527
assignment of professors of mathematics at . 1528
pay of secretary 1556
of clerks to paymasters at 1556
rations to acting midshipmen at 1577

Naval Architects,
may examine and copy models of certain yachts 4215

Naval Asylum,
(see *Hospitals, Navy.*)

Naval Constructors,
number and appointment of 1402
relative rank of, on active list 1477
of assistants 1477
education of, at Naval Academy 1522
pay of 1556

Naval Hospitals,
(see *Hospitals, Navy.*)

Naval Observatory,
salary of superintendent of 434
meridian of, to be used for astronomical purposes 435

Naval Officer, (Customs,)
at Baltimore, Md 2549
Boston, Mass 2529
Charleston, S. C 2558
New Orleans, La 2569
New York 2536
Philadelphia 2544
San Francisco, Cal 2583
Savannah, Ga 2560
term of office 2613
bonds of 2619
by whom approved and where filed 2620
President may increase penalty of 3639
duties of 2626
when to perform duties of collector 2625
when may act by deputy; responsibility of . 2632
number and compensation of clerks of, how fixed 2634
to keep posted table of fees, &c., receipts; penalty for failure 2635, 4383
to keep account of fees, &c., and make annual return to Commissioner; penalty . 2639
personal attention, &c., of; duties of, in respect to accounts; penalty for omission 2640
accounts of, what to include and how rendered 2641
to certify services of occasional inspectors .. 2642
to render list of clerks, their duties and compensation, account of stationery, office rent, &c 2643
to render quarterly accounts of moneys collected for fines, penalties, forfeitures, rents, storage, &c.; excess of $2,000, in certain cases, to be paid into Treasury 2647

Section.

Naval Officer, (Customs)—Continued.
discontinuance of, in certain districts by Secretary of Treasury 2653
fees of, at same port with collector 2655
drawback fees of, how shared, &c 2656
compensation exclusive of expenses of 2689
limit to emoluments of, at certain ports 2690
at other ports 2691
salary of, at San Francisco 2703
limitation to compensation, &c., of 2704
discretion to direct examination of baggage, &c 2801
when, to make estimate of duties and grant permit to land 2869
to concur with collector in granting license to unload at night 2871
how to compare and to whom to transmit returns for delivery of merchandise 2889
protest of master, &c., of vessel seeking port in distress to be produced to; when to appoint inspector and to grant permit to unlade 2891
permission to dispose of perishable cargo may be granted by, in certain cases .. 2892
how tare on imports estimated by 2898
duty of, in estimating value and quantity of imports 2902
to examine upon oath owners, &c., as to value of merchandise, and require production of papers 2922
use of warehouse hired by 2956
when to grant permit for exportation, without payment of duties 2979
to appoint officer of customs to inspect change from casks, &c., of distilled spirits and sugars 3029
when to grant permit for lading of certain merchandise 3035
to grant certificate of exportation of goods from port other than that of importation 3041
when to admit certain proofs in absence of exportation certificates, and cancel bond 3047
when satisfied of accident, &c., certain merchandise entered for drawback not to be forfeited 3051
when to search certain stores, warehouses, &c 3107
and surveyor shall examine books, &c., of assistant treasurers, &c 3650
to countersign certificates of registry of vessels, when 4158
to sign enrollments, licenses, permits, &c., of vessels 4332

Naval Service,
(see *Military and Naval Service.*)

Naval Solicitor,
appointment and salary of 349

Naval Storekeepers,
appointment of, at navy-yards 1413
appointment of citizens as, on foreign stations 1414
bonds of 1415
detail of officers as, on foreign stations 1438
bonds of 1439
detail of, at Naval Academy 1527
allowance for travel to, on foreign stations .. 1566
pay of officers performing duty as 1567
pay of civilians on foreign stations 1568

Naval Supplies,
purchases, &c., of, shall be under direction of Secretary of Navy 3714
provisions concerning contracts for 3718–3732

Navigation,
rules for preventing collision of vessels 4233

Section.

Navigation—Continued.
special circumstances to be considered in construing 4233
collectors to require sail-vessels to be provided with proper lights 4234
lights, how shown by sail-vessel on approach of steamer 4234
penalty on sail-vessels not complying with rules of navigation 4234
recovery of penalty 4234
pilots to be governed by State regulations .. 4235
employment of, on waters between States. 4236
discriminating regulations of pilotage by States prohibited 4237
existing discriminations abrogated and annulled 4237
stranded vessels on foreign coasts, duty of consuls in saving, &c 4238
restriction on authority of consuls 4238
property wrecked on coast of Florida, how disposed of 4239
forfeiture of vessel taking such property to foreign coast 4240
license to wrecking-vessels on coast of Florida. 4241
life-saving stations, establishment of, on coasts of Long Island and New Jersey. 4242
appointment of superintendents and keepers 4243
employment of crews of surfmen 4244
establishment of, at light-houses 4245
to be in charge of keepers of lights 4245
care and custody of boats for 4246
appointment of keepers for stations on coasts of Cape Cod and Rhode Island. 4247
supervision of, at Narragansett Pier and Block Island 4248
establishment of ten, on coasts of Maine, New Hampshire, Massachusetts, Virginia, and North Carolina 4249
removal of captains by owners of vessels ... 4250
canal-boats exempt from libel for wages of employés 4251

Navigation Laws,
extended over Alaska 1954
recovery of penalties and forfeitures 4305
remission of 5294, 5592
vessels navigating coastwise and on great lakes, subject to 4401

Navy,
payments by disbursing officer, by order of commanding officer, how settled 285
date of loss, &c., of vessel, how fixed for settlement of accounts of seamen, &c ... 286
last quarterly return to be assumed as basis of settlement of accounts of seamen, in cases of loss, &c., of vessel 287
compensation for personal effects of seamen, in case of loss of vessel, &c 288
to whom paid, in case of death of seamen. 289
compensation for effects of officers, in case of loss of vessel 290
organization of, provisions concerning .. 1362–1425
grades of line-officers in 1362
number of line-officers on active list of 1363
secretaries to Admiral and Vice-Admiral of. 1367
medical corps, number, appointment, duties, &c., of 1368
pay corps of, number, appointment, duties, &c., of 1376–1382
bonds of paymasters in 1383–1385
President may increase penalty of 3639
clerks to paymasters in 1386–1388
engineer corps of, number, rank, appointment, qualifications, &c., of 1390
chaplains in, number, appointment, &c., of. 1395

Section.

Navy—Continued.
professors of mathematics in, number, appointment, and duties of ... 1399
naval constructors, assistants, &c ... 1402
warrant-officers, number, appointment, &c., of ... 1405, 1407
acting assistant surgeons, appointment of .. 1411
volunteer officers transferred, entitled to credit for volunteer sea-service ... 1412
civil engineers and storekeepers at navy-yards ... 1413
storekeepers on foreign stations ... 1414
bonds of ... 1415
enlistment in, provisions concerning ... 1417
men sent home at expiration of term, provisions relating to ... 1422–1425
consular powers of officers of ... 1433
officers to act as storekeepers on foreign stations ... 1438
bonds of ... 1439
quarters of staff-officers ... 1487
insane persons of ... 1551
coal-depots ... 1552
flags captured by ... 1554
articles for government of ... 1624
dutiable articles not to be imported in vessels of ... 1624
persons belonging to, when entitled to vote in Territories ... 1860
not to hold civil office in Territory ... 1860
employment of, in execution of judicial process, &c ... 1984
selection, survey, and protection of certain lands containing live-oak and red-cedar timber for use of ... 2458–2463
certain appropriations for, shall be kept separate at Treasury ... 3676
term VESSELS OF THE NAVY, as used in Title PRIZE, what to include ... 4614
duties of commanding officers making captures ... 4615
appointment from officers of, on Light-house Board ... 4653
assignment of officer of, to each light-house district, as inspector, &c ... 4671
employment of officers of, on coast-survey service ... 4684, 4687
of men of ... 4685
of vessels of ... 4686
subsistence of officers and men of, employed on coast-survey service ... 4688
officers, when to have pension ... 4693
rate of total disability, pension to ... 4695
to have pension according to rank, &c ... 4696
persons in, not to draw pay and pension ... 4724
survivors of war of 1812 who served in, to have pensions ... 4736
admission of persons belonging to, to Government Hospital for Insane ... 4843
authority of President to employ, in enforcement of neutrality laws ... 5287
to compel departure of foreign vessels forbidden by laws of nations or treaty to remain, &c ... 5288
in aid of collection of duties, when ... 5316
employment of, to protect rights of discoverer of guano island ... 5577
rank in, (see *Rank.*)
Naval Academy, (see *Naval Academy.*)
vessels and navy-yards, (see *Vessels of Navy* and *Navy-Yards.*)
pay, emoluments, and allowances of, (see *Pay of Navy.*)
marine corps of, (see *Marine Corps.*)
distribution of prize-money to officers and men of, how shared, (see *Prize.*)

Section.

Navy Agents,
President may increase, &c., bonds of ... 3639
Navy Department,
(see *Department of Navy.*)
Navy-Hospital Fund,
(see *Hospitals, Navy*)
Navy-Pension Fund,
estimates of claims, &c., on, shall be submitted, &c ... 3667
Secretary of Navy to be trustee of ... 4750
part of penalties, &c., for removing live-oak to go to ... 4751
prize-money of United States to be part of .. 4752
investment of; gold interest on investments of ... 4753
rate of interest on ... 4754
navy-pensions shall be paid from ... 4755
half-pay to disabled sailors and marines from. 4756
certain sailors and marines may have aid from surplus income of ... 4757
Navy-Pensions,
(see *Pensions.*)
Navy-Yards,
appointment of storekeepers at ... 1413
civil engineers at ... 1413
to whom salaries may be paid at ... 1545
per diem compensation at ... 1545
employés in, not to contribute for political purposes ... 1546
not to be removed for political opinion ... 1546
pay of clerks to commandants of ... 1556
of clerks to paymasters at ... 1556
Neat-Cattle,
importation of, prohibited, but Secretary of Treasury may suspend, &c ... 2493
when and how President may suspend prohibitory provision ... 2494
penalty for violations, &c ... 2495
Nebraska and Iowa,
appointment of surveyor-general for, authorized ... 2207
salary of ... 2208
Necessary Repairs,
(see *Repairs to Vessels.*)
Negro,
(see *Slave-Trade.*)
Netherlands,
salary of minister to ... 1675
Net Proceeds of Lands,
appropriation of part of, to States ... 3689
Neutrality,
offenses against laws of ... 5281–5286
authority of President to employ land and naval forces for enforcement of laws of. 5287
in order to compel foreign vessel to depart, in cases where laws of nations or treaties require departure ... 5288
United States citizens, owners of armed vessels departing, to give bond ... 5289
collectors of customs to detain vessels built for warlike purposes ... 5290
construction of provisions of this Title as to enlisting, treason, piracy, &c ... 5291
Nevada,
district attorney and marshal for, entitled to double fees, &c ... 837
amount of fees allowed to clerk of circuit and district courts in ... 840
appointment of surveyor-general for ... 2207
salary of ... 2210
fifty per cent. addition to certain fees of registers and receivers in ... 2238
Nevada Volunteers,
appropriation to pay traveling expenses of .. 3689

Section.

New Albany, Ind.,
port of delivery in district of New Orleans . 2568
surveyor to reside at, duties of 2569
Newark, N. J.,
collection-district and port of entry 2541
collector to reside at 2542
New Bedford, Mass ,
collection-district and port of entry 2527
Sippican and Mattapoisett harbors, ports in; description of vessels belonging to 2528
collector to reside at 2529
New Berne, N. C.,
port of entry 2555
collector to reside at 2556
New Brunswick, N. J.,
port of delivery 2541
provisions concerning lading and unlading of vessels from 3129
Newburgh, N. Y.,
port of delivery 2535
Newbury, Mass.,
port of delivery 2527
Newburyport, Mass.,
collection-district and port of entry 2527
collector and surveyor to reside at 2529
New Castle, Del.,
port of delivery 2546
Newcastle, Me.,
vessels owned at, may unlade at 2520
Newcastle, N. H.,
port of delivery 2522
Newcastle-upon-Tyne,
consul at, salary of 1690
Newfoundland,
certain fish and fish-oil, the produce of fisheries of, to be admitted free of duty ... 2506
provisions concerning lading and unlading of vessels from 3129
New Hampshire,
collection-districts, ports of entry, and delivery in 2522
officers in 2523
establishment of life-saving stations on coast of 4249
New Haven, Conn.,
collection-district and port of entry 2533
collector to reside at 2534
New Jersey,
collection-districts, ports of entry, and delivery in 2541
officers in 2542
establishment of life-saving stations on coast of 4242
appointment of keepers for 4243
employment of crews of surfmen at 4244
permit for land-transportation of foreign merchandise across 4362
New London, Conn.,
collection-district and port of entry 2533
collector to reside at 2534
inspectors of hulls and boilers for 4414
their salaries 4414
New Mexico,
number of members of council and house of representatives of 1922
district court of, jurisdiction over citizens of El Paso County, Texas 1928
trial and proceedings in, in revenue cases. 1928
contingent expenses of executive department in, annual appropriation for 1935
legislative expenses of, provision for 1939
mileage of members of legislative assembly of 1942
appointment of Indian superintendent for tribes in 2046
of Indian agents 2052

Section.

New Mexico—Continued.
appointment of surveyor-general for 2207
salary of 2210
fifty per cent. addition to fees of registers and receivers in 2238
New Offices,
statements of, by Secretary of Senate and Clerk of House 64
New Orleans, La.,
collection-district and port of entry 2568
officers of customs in, residence of 2569
vessels bound to ports of delivery in district of, (except Bayou Saint John) ... 2570
collector of customs at, when to appoint temporary inspectors of, number of, &c .. 2576
may appoint head-gaugers 2577
unlading imported salt, opposite city of 2897
transportation in bond extended to 2997
mint at, legal designation of 3495
officers of 3496
superintendent to perform duty as treasurer 3497
salaries of officers 3498
of assistants, clerks, &c 3499
assistant treasurer at, appointment, &c., of. 3595–3597
clerks, &c., in office of assistant treasurer at. 3609
collector, &c., shall pay public moneys to assistant treasurer 3615
inspectors of hulls and of boilers for 4414
their salaries, &c 4414
reserve of national banks in 5191
balances with banks in, may be part of reserve 5192
redemption agencies 5195
Newport, R. I.,
collection-district and port of entry 2531
collector in, to reside at 2532
New Post-Offices,
salaries at, may be temporarily fixed 3853
Newspapers,
no allowance for, to Members and Delegates in Congress 43
publication of laws in 79
expenditure for, in Departments 192
for use of Departments must be filed 192
laws, when passed, to be published in 204
and amendments to Constitution 205
commercial information to be published in .. 211
correspondence with, by diplomatic and consular officers prohibited 1751
not more than $30 to be expended for, annually, by executive officer other than head of Department 1779
postage on, at free-delivery offices 3872
regularly issued, &c., second-class mail-matter 3877
transient 3878
postage on, when sent to subscribers 3905
to subscribers, postage payable quarterly in advance 3906
stamped wrappers for, shall be provided 3915
publishing list of non-delivered letters in .. 3930
addressed to foreigners 3931
compensation for 3934
what, shall publish advertisement of mail-lettings, &c 3941
New Trials,
when granted by Court of Claims 1088
New Windsor, N. Y.,
port of delivery 2535
New York,
terms of circuit court in southern district of, for criminal business, by whom may be held 613

Section.

New York—Continued.
salary of district attorney for southern district of 770
collection-districts, ports of entry and delivery in 2535
officers in 2536
cargoes for Greenport, in, to be entered and duties paid at Sag Harbor 2537

New York City,
collection-district and port of entry 2535
officers of customs in, residence and duties of 2536
what officers and employés in office of appraiser of customs at port of; how appointed 2538, 2539
goods for Cold Spring or Port Jefferson to be entered and duties paid at port of. 2540
oath of appraiser at 2614
of assistant appraisers at 2615
one assistant appraiser to perform duties of special examiner of drugs 2938
transportation in bond extended to 2997
assistant treasurer at, appointment, &c., of. 3595–3597
may appoint deputy 3602
clerks, &c., in office of 3603, 3604
collector, &c., in, shall pay public money to assistant treasurer 3615
inspectors of hulls and boilers for; salaries, &c., of 4414
assistant inspectors and their salaries 4414
reserve in national banks in 5191
balances with banks in, may be part of reserve 5192
banks in, shall have, and may be, redemption agencies, &c 5195
national banks shall publish notice of liquidation in newspapers of 5221
bonds of certain national banks may be sold at auction in 5230
assay offices, (see *Mints and Assay Offices.*)

Niagara,
collection-district in New York 2535
collector in, residence of 2536
additional inspectors for 2605

Nicaragua,
minister resident at 1682
salary of 1675

Nice,
consul at, salary of 1690

Nickel Coins,
how redeemed 3529

Night-Mail Service,
pay to railways for 3999

Night-Watchmen,
in office of Comptroller of Currency, salary of 235

Ningpo,
consul at, salary of 1690

Nitrated Oil,
(see *Nitro-Glycerine.*)

Nitric Acid,
restrictions on carriage of, by steam passenger-vessels 4472
how packed and marked for shipment 4475
penalty for shipping, contrary to law 4476

Nitro-Glycerine,
not to be shipped on passenger-vessel or vehicle 4278, 4472
how packed and marked for shipment 4279, 4475
State regulation of traffic and transportation of 4280
penalty for shipping, contrary to law 4476
transporting or delivering, on passenger-vessel or vehicle 5353

Nitro-Glycerine—Continued.
when death is caused by explosion of, on passenger-vessel, &c 5354
shipping or transporting, unless packed and marked in manner prescribed 5355

Nitroleum,
(see *Nitro-Glycerine.*)

Nobleborough, Me.,
port of delivery 2517

Nolan Private Land-Claim,
appropriation to survey 3689

Nolle Prosequi,
entry of, in prosecution of distiller defrauding or attempting to defraud 3230

Nominations,
a list of, to be furnished by Secretary of Senate to Secretary of Treasury, Auditors, and Comptrollers, at end of session 1775

Non-delivered Letters,
lists of, to be published 3930
addressed to foreigners 3931
compensation for publishing list of 3934
extra postage on, when advertised 3935

Non-enumerated Articles,
to pay what import duties, (similitude clause). 2499
rate of customs duties on 2516

Non Prosequitur,
when to be entered in customs cases 3012

Non-Residents,
taxable property owned by, to be assessed.. 3180

Norfolk, Va.,
weighers, gaugers, measurers, and inspectors for 2606
transportation in bond extended to 2997
inspectors of hulls and boilers for 4414
salaries of 4414

Norfolk and Portsmouth, Va.,
collection-district and port of entry 2552
collector, surveyor, and appraiser in, to reside at Norfolk 2553

North Carolina,
clerks of circuit and district courts in western districts of, number 621
collection-districts and ports of entry in 2555
officers in 2556
Cherokees in, payment of interest to 3689
establishment of life-saving stations on coast of 4249

North Haven, Me.,
port of delivery 2517

North Kingston, R. I.,
port of delivery 2531

North Yarmouth, Me.,
port of delivery 2517

Norwalk, Conn.,
port of delivery 2533

Norwich, Conn,
port of delivery 2533

Notary Public,
authority of, to administer oaths and take acknowledgments in certain cases 1778
duty of, on protest of national bank-notes.. 5226

Notes,
(see *National Banks* and *United States Notes.*)

Notes and Securities,
shipper of, to notify carrier, &c 4281

Notices,
of application for patent for mining claim.. 2325
by register, of application having been made 2325
of seizures, when, where, and by whom published, what to contain 3075
of sale of seized property under customs laws, when and by whom given 3077

Section.

Notices—Continued.
under internal-revenue laws, to be kept by deputy collector for absent persons... 3173
by collector to taxpayers............3184, 3185
in cases of distraint for taxes............ 3190
of sale of real estate for taxes............ 3197
of sale of personal property of delinquent collector............ 3217
of real estate............ 3217
of intention to carry on business of distiller or rectifier............ 3259
of change by distiller or rectifier............ 3259
of suspension............ 3310
of resumption............ 3310
by brewer............ 3335
in case of seizure of property of tobacco-peddler............ 3383
of seizure and sale under section 3460............ 3460
of health-regulations to be posted on passenger-vessels............ 4263
to be posted on emigrant vessels forbidding visiting quarters of emigrants............ 4277
penalty for failure............ 4277
what, to be given by collector, of seizure of vessel, &c............ 4379
of liquidation, national banks shall publish, &c............ 5221
to creditors, by national banks in liquidation. 5221
of national banks, after receiver appointed to wind up, &c............ 5235

Notices in Bankruptcy,
fees for publication of............ 5126

Nottingham, Md.,
port of delivery............ 2548

Nova Scotia,
lading and unlading of vessels from............ 3129

Nurses,
at Army hospitals, employment of women as. 1238
pay and rations of............ 1277
rations to, employed at post or regimental-hospitals............ 1295

O.

Oath,
affirmation included in............ 1

Oaths,
may be administered by Department officers or clerks, in investigation of frauds............ 183
relating to revenue laws, to be prescribed by Secretary of Treasury............ 251
authority of Secretary of War to detail officers to administer, in settlement of officers' accounts............ 225
clerks detailed from Pension-Office to investigate frauds, may administer.....474, 4744
when notaries public and commissioners of circuit courts may administer............ 1778
to be taken by customs and internal-revenue officers, &c., before receiving payment of salaries............ 1790
may be administered by Treasury agents in Alaska............ 1976
of owners of goods, to accounts, &c., before whom taken............ 2787
in customs matters, how taken............ 2805
of owner, importer, &c., of goods, to accompany invoice, form of............ 2841
taking oaths relating to customs not to exempt masters and owners of vessels from other............ 3094
of masters, &c., of vessels in northern, &c., frontier districts, form of, &c............ 3124
power of internal-revenue supervisors to administer............ 3163
certain revenue officers to administer............ 3165

Section.

Oaths—Continued.
of allegiance, must be taken by parties prosecuting claims before Departments.3478, 3479
of office, general form of............ 1756
form of, for participants in late rebellion............ 1757
who may administer............ 1758
where to be kept............ 1759

"Obligation or other Security of the United States,"
exempt from taxation............ 3701
imitating or printing, &c., on, to be punished............ 3708
what included in, as used in Title CRIMES.. 5413
falsely making, forging, counterfeiting, or altering............ 5414
using, or suffering to be used, plate for printing, except for use of United States.. 5430
graving............ 5430
engraving, printing, selling, bringing into United States, having in possession plate in likeness of plate for printing, or obligation engraved in likeness of.. 5430
retaining in possession paper adapted for, after adoption of distinctive paper, &c. 5430
uttering, bringing in, &c., keeping forged, altered, &c............ 5431
making impression from implement used in printing............ 5432
having such impression without authority. 5433
buying, selling, receiving, &c., forged, altered, &c............ 5434
secreting, embezzling, or taking away implement or paper used, or intended to be used, in printing............ 5453

Obscene Articles, Publications, &c.,
United States officer sending by mail, dealing in, &c., penalty............ 1785
importation of, prohibited............ 2491
to be detained by officers of customs............ 2491
mode of procedure against............ 2492
excluded from mails............ 3878

Obstructing,
internal-revenue officer in execution of law. 3177
officer in executing process of United States courts............ 5398

Obverse Working Dies,
to be defaced............ 3550

Odessa,
consul at, salary of............ 1690

Offenses,
(see *Crimes and Offenses.*)

Office,
tenure of, for persons holding civil, under appointment, confirmed by Senate.... 1767
suspension from, during recess of Senate.... 1768
when to remain in abeyance............ 1769
term of, when limited by law, not to be extended............ 1770
penalty for accepting or holding, contrary to law............ 1771
for removing from, or appointing to, contrary to law............ 1772
President to notify Secretary of Treasury of appointments to, without advice, &c., of Senate, and of employment to perform duties of............ 1774
report of expense of removing public office on account of sickness, to be laid before Congress............ 1776
members of Congress and public officers accepting consideration for procuring.. 1781
duty of district attorney to proceed, by quo warranto, against persons illegally holding............ 1786

Section.

Office—Continued.
penalty for holding, &c., contrary to third section of fourteenth amendment of Constitution 1787
attached to seat of government, where exercised 1796
suits for possession of, in certain cases, where may be brought 2010
removal from seat of government in case of epidemic 4796

Office of Education,
(see *Education, Office of.*)

Officers,
term, includes what 1
and employees,
of Senate, salaries of 52
of House of Representatives, salaries 53
of corporation,
not to act as officer or agent of United States in transactions with same 1783
of United States,
removal, &c., of suit against, for acts done under revenue laws, or Title XXVI, THE ELECTIVE FRANCHISE 643
penalty for receiving money, &c., for procuring contracts or offices, or for official services 1781
forbidden to receive compensation for services in claim, &c., before Department or commission; penalty 1782
not to be members of legislature, or hold office in Territories 1854
exception in case of postmasters 1854
not to apply to Territory of Washington .. 1854
lands conveyed to, for United States, to be released 3752
penalty for neglect of duty prescribed by Title REGULATIONS OF COMMERCE AND NAVIGATION 4188
giving, or offering to, to influence decision or action, &c 5451
extortion by, under color of office 5481
acceptance of bribe by 5501
penalty 5502
under civil-rights laws, (see *Civil Rights.*)
of vessels,
of United States must be citizens 4131
maliciously, &c., forcing on shore, with intent to leave, refusing to bring home. 5363
(see *Inspection of Steam-Vessels* and *Vessels.*)

Official Bond,
(see *Bonds.*)

Official Correspondence,
territorial copies of, to be transmitted to President, when 1844

Official Instruments,
documents, papers, &c., exemption of, from stamp-duty 3420

Official Letters,
of Post-Office Department shall be registered free 3927

Ogdensburgh, N. Y.,
port of entry 2525
collector to reside at 2536

Ohio,
collection-districts, ports of entry and delivery in 2603
officers in 2604

Oil of Vitriol,
penalty for shipping without notice 4288
restrictions on transportation of, by steam passenger-vessel 4472
how packed and marked for shipment 4475
penalty for shipping contrary to law 4476

Section.

Old Material,
proceeds of, shall be deposited in Treasury, &c 3618
statement of, in book of estimates 3672

Omaha, Neb.,
port of delivery in district of New Orleans .. 2568
surveyor to reside at, duties of 2569

Omoa,
consul at, salary of 1690

One-Cent Piece,
weight and material of 3515
devices and legends on 3517
deviation in adjusting 3537

One-Dollar Gold Piece,
to be the unit of value 3511
weight and fineness of 3511, 3514
devices and legends on 3517
deviation in adjusting 3535

Open Purchase,
of supplies, &c., when authorized 3709

Openers and Packers, (*Customs*,)
at New York, compensation of 2745

Opening Bids,
(see *Bids.*)

Opinions of Attorney-General,
to be edited and printed, &c 383

Opium,
prepared for smoking, &c., not to be removed from bonded warehouse for exportation without payment of duties, &c .. 2504

Oporto,
consul at, salary of 1690

Oppression,
by internal-revenue officer, penalty 3169

Order,
tax on, for payment of money drawn upon bank, banker, or trust-company 3418

Orders in Bankruptcy,
(see *Bankruptcy.*)

Orders, Money,
(see *Money-Orders.*)

Ordnance Department,
of Army, authorized 1094
enlisted men of 1094
post sergeants 1094
organization and rank in 1159
storekeepers for 1159
enlisted men for 1162
chief of, to provide supplies of ordnance 1164
to establish depots 1165
no allowance of clothing to sergeants of 1297
officers of, at national armories 1662
compensation of 1663
what system to be used by, in manufacture of muskets and carbines for United States service 1672

Ordnance Storekeepers,
(see *Storekeepers.*)

Ordnance for Navy,
purchases of, by Secretary, not subject to provisions as to advertising, &c 3721

Oregon,
district attorney and marshal for, entitled to double fees, &c 837
amount of fees allowed to circuit and district clerks in 840
concurrent jurisdiction of, with Washington Territory, over Columbia River 1950
certain laws of, &c., continued in force in Washington Territory 1952
jurisdiction of district courts of, over offenses committed in Alaska 1957
appointment of Indian superintendent for tribes in 2046
of Indian agents 2052

Section.

Oregon—Continued.
appointment of surveyor-general for, authorized ... 2207
salary of ... 2209
to be paid quarterly, to commence when. 2211
fifty per cent. addition to certain fees of registers and receivers in ... 2238
augmented rates allowed for survey of certain public lands in ... 2404
geodetic surveys in, may be continued ... 2409
surveying in, may be paid for by day, when. 2411
collection district of ... 2586
collector in, residence of ... 2587
power of Secretary of Treasury to remit fines, penalties, &c., incurred in ... 5293
Oregon and Washington Territory,
collection-districts, ports of entry and delivery in ... 2586
officers in ... 2587
Oregon, Southern District,
collection-district of ... 2586
officers of customs in, appointment and residence of ... 2587
Organization Certificate,
of national banks, contents of ... 5134
shall be acknowledged and sent to Comptroller ... 5135
national banks to be bodies corporate from date of ... 5136
on receipt of, Comptroller to examine into facts ... 5168
Organizing Volunteers,
payment of claims for ... 3489
Oriental Countries,
(see *Cooly-Trade*.)
Original Checks,
duplicates of, how issued ... 3646, 3647
Original Dies,
for coins, engraver of mint to prepare working-dies from ... 3510
Orleans,
all navigable rivers in former territory of, to remain public highways ... 5251
Orphans,
when to have pensions, term of ... 4702
increase of pension to ... 4703
pension to, when abandoned by mother, &c. 4706
Osaka and Hioga,
consul at, salary of ... 1690
Oswegatchie, N. Y.,
collection-district ... 2535
collector in, residence of ... 2536
additional inspectors for ... 2605
Oswego, N. Y.,
collection-district and port of entry ... 2535
collector to reside at ... 2536
additional inspectors for ... 2605
inspectors of hulls and boilers for ... 4414
their salaries ... 4414
Ottawa Indians of Michigan,
unoccupied lands of, open to homestead entry by certain of the ... 2313
time, place, and manner of making entry. 2313
selection of lands for minor children of, how made ... 2314
Outfits,
diplomatic and consular officers not to be allowed for ... 1743
Outstanding Appropriations,
shall be given in estimates ... 3665
"*Outstanding Liabilities*,"
of more than three years to be covered into Treasury ... 306
what, to be sufficient vouchers for warrants, &c ... 307
how paid when presented ... 308

Section.

"*Outstanding Liabilities*"—Continued.
to be reported to Secretary of Treasury, when and by whom ... 310
Overpayments,
by paymasters in Army, when allowed ... 281
"*Owner*,"
definition of, when used in Title MERCHANT SEAMEN ... 4612
of fee simple of land on which distillery is situated, written consent of ... 3262
of vessels,
penalty for carrying away live-oak or red-cedar timber from United States lands. 2462
registered oath to be taken by, to obtain register ... 4142
forfeiture of vessel for false oath by, to obtain register ... 4143
issue of new certificate of registry to, in new district ... 4159
to surrender old certificate to collector ... 4160
penalty for failure ... 4160–4162
former, retaining old certificate, penalty ... 4164
sold or captured abroad, regaining vessel may have register, &c., when ... 4165
penalty for not taking out new certificate of registry, when ... 4169
for failing to report change of master ... 4171
oath of, on entry of vessel as to register ... 4173
effect of refusal to take ... 4173
delivering up certificate of registry to have bond cancelled ... 4174
recorded, to countersign certificate of measurement ... 4181
to cause to be indorsed on certificate of record change of name of master of vessel ... 4183
to pay surveyor's fees for measurement, &c. 4186
to furnish collectors' receipts for fees paid consular officers by vessels abroad ... 4213
oath of, to ownership of unregistered vessel carrying sea-letter ... 4226
bringing passengers from foreign ports, penalty for violating regulations as to berths ... 4255
penalty for neglect to furnish list of passengers ... 4266
payment for deaths occurring among passengers during voyage ... 4268
penalty for refusal to pay ... 4269
of passenger-vessels between United States and Europe, penalty for not furnishing deck-houses, ventilators, and cooking-ranges as required ... 4259
for failing to provide provisions and water. 4261
civil responsibility of, to passengers for neglect to furnish food, &c ... 4262
to construct decks and apartments so they can be kept clean, &c ... 4263
penalty for failure ... 4263
of passenger-vessels between United States and Pacific ports, penalty for failure to supply food and water, &c ... 4265
not liable for gold, bullion, jewelry, &c., shipped without notice ... 4281
not liable for loss by fire ... 4282
restrictions upon, liability of, for goods embezzled, lost, or destroyed, &c ... 4283
pro-rata payment by, when liabilities exceed value of vessel, &c ... 4284
when liabilities for losses exceed value of vessel and freight, may assign to trustee ... 4285
proceedings against, to cease on assignment. 4285
charterer of vessel to be deemed, when ... 4286
remedies against, for fraud, negligence, &c., reserved ... 4287

Section.

"*Owner*"—Continued.
of canal-boat, &c., and vessels on rivers and inland waters, liability of, as carriers. 4289
enrolled and licensed, subject to provisions prescribed for registered vessels...... 4312
managing, bond of, to obtain license for coasting trade or fisheries............ 4320
oath of, to obtain license 4320
may return expired license, when.......... 4327
oath of, as to foreign repairs to obtain enrollment, &c 4330
penalty for false oath.................... 4330
penalty if licensed vessel found without name and port printed on stern 4334
in domestic commerce, fees to be paid by... 4382
of steam passenger, liability of, for damage to passengers 4493
when they may perform duties of shipping-commissioners 4504
how may procure, &c., apprentices......... 4509
proceedings against, to recover advance security 4534
when to be accountable for effects, &c., of deceased seamen 4540
disputes between crew and, how heard, &c. 4554
may be required to prouced books and papers before shipping-commissioners in proceedings relating to wages, &c....... 4555
shall be liable for penalty for neglect to furnish anti-scorbutics 4570
shall obtain certified copy of shipping articles 4575
shall pay hospital-tax 4585
shall pay shipping, &c., fees, reimbursement. 4593
punishment of seamen for damage to, by smuggling 4596
may apprehend deserters without warrant; penalty for illegal apprehension...... 4599
expenses of, in apprehending deserters, to be paid from proceeds of forfeited clothing, &c 4604

Oxen,
lost in military service to be paid for....... 3483

P.

Pacific Coast,
Army supplies for 3716

Packages,
of cigars, for importation.................. 2804
of fermented liquors, marks on 3349
kind of, for tobacco and snuff.............. 3362
limitation of, not to apply to tobacco and snuff exported 3362
wood, metal, paper, &c., may be used for, of tobacco, snuff, and cigars 3362
labels on, of tobacco and snuff............. 3364
removal of tobacco and snuff except in proper 3374
stamps on emptied, of tobacco and snuff to be destroyed 3376
for cigars 3392

Packets,
public, when not required to make entry ... 2791
on United States waters, mail may be carried in 3969

Paducah, Ky.,
port of delivery in district of New Orleans. 2568
surveyor to reside at, duties of............. 2569

Pages,
of Senate, salaries 52
how appointed and removed 52
of House of Representatives, salary........ 53

Paintings,
imported for exhibition, not for sale, to be free of duty; bond for duties on such as shall not be re-exported........... 2512

Palermo,
consul at, salary of 1690

Pamlico, N. C.,
collection-district 2555
collector in, residence of.................. 2556

Pamphlets,
third-class mail-matter 3878

Panama,
consul at, salary of 1690
resident mail-agent at, authorized.......... 4021

Paper,
advertisements for, for public printing, where made.......................... 3767
contracts for, for public printing 3772–3778
samples of, for engravings, &c., to be kept by Congressional Printer 3782
plain and ornamental, to be third-class mail-matter.............................. 3878

Para,
consul at, salary of 1690

Paraguay,
minister to Uruguay also accredited to 1681

Pardon,
of persons having claims, not to authorize payment 3480
when United States minister may submit capital case to President for 4103
where pecuniary and corporal penalty, may apply to one or both................ 5330

Paris,
consul-general at, salary of 1690

Parish,
included in word "county" 2

Parkersburgh, W. Va.,
port of delivery in district of New Orleans. 2568
surveyor to reside at, duties of............. 2569

Partner,
residing abroad, of house in United States, vessel owned by, may be registered... 4133
discharge in bankruptcy not to affect liability of, when 5118

Partnerships,
included in "persons" 1
to pay but one special tax 3234

Part-Paid Letters,
may be transmitted 3898

Paso del Norte,
consul at, salary of 1690
collection-district of, what to comprise..... 2578

Passamaquoddy, Me.,
collection-district 2517
collector, deputy collector, and surveyor in, residence of 2518
additional inspectors for................... 2605

Passed Assistant Paymasters of Navy,
number of, on active list.................. 1376
bonds of 1383
clerks to 1388
relative rank of, on active list 1475
pay of 1556

Passed Assistant Surgeons of Navy,
relative rank of, on active list 1474
pay of 1556

Passengers,
certificate of voluntary emigration of certain, to be given by consular officers.. 2162
transportation of, to United States from foreign port not in contiguous territory; not to be taken on board contrary to law 4252
number of, allowed in proportion to tonnage................................. 4252
how computed 4252
space appropriated for use of 4252
not to be taken up with stores or cargo. 4252

Section.

Passengers—Continued.
penalty for taking on board more than allowed, &c ... 4253
cargo stored in space appropriated for, to be in lockers ... 4254
such space not to counted for ... 4254
measurement of lockers ... 4254
hospital may be included in space allowed for ... 4254
limit of space occupied by ... 4254
berths for, regulation of ... 4255
penalty for violating such regulations ... 4255
between United States and Europe—
houses on deck for, when to be carried ... 4256
booby-hatches for, in lieu of houses ... 4256
ventilators for apartments occupied by ... 4257
cooking-range, &c., for ... 4258
master or owner of vessel not provided with houses, ventilators, and cooking-range, penalty ... 4259
how recovered ... 4259
provisions and water, what to be on board for each ... 4260
delivery of ... 4260
penalty for failure to provide ... 4261
how recovered ... 4261
cooking and distribution of ... 4262
penalty for failure ... 4262
enforcement of, not to affect civil responsibility of master or owner ... 4262
discipline and health regulations ... 4263
master authorized to maintain ... 4263
master or owner neglecting, penalty ... 4263
between Pacific ports and United States ... 4265
water and food, how furnished ... 4265
food for, how to be cooked ... 4265
penalty for failure to supply, &c ... 4265
how recovered ... 4265
list of, arriving from foreign port to be furnished collector on entry ... 4266
list, what to specify ... 4266
to be sworn to by master ... 4266
penalty on master for refusal or neglect to deliver, &c ... 4266
collectors to return copies of, quarterly, to Secretary of State ... 4267
deaths among, other than cabin, payment by master, owner, or consignee ... 4268
money to be paid to State authorities for care and protection of destitute, &c., emigrants ... 4268
not to be paid for care of particular class, &c., of emigrants ... 4268
penalty on master, owner, &c., refusing to pay ... 4269
how recovered ... 4269
disposal of money recovered ... 4269
penalties for violating provisions respecting transportation of, to be lien on vessels ... 4270
vessels may be libeled for, where ... 4270
vessels belonging to colonization societies subject to foregoing provisions ... 4271
examination of emigrant-vessels on arrival, by collector ... 4272
report to Secretary of Treasury ... 4272
informers to have half penalties recovered for violating laws relating to transportation of ... 4273
vessels of United States carrying passengers between foreign ports ... 4274
officers or seamen, &c., not to visit part of vessel assigned to emigrants ... 4275
penalty for violation ... 4275
on master permitting ... 4276
written or printed notice of two preceding sections to be conspicuously posted ... 4277

Section.

Passengers—Continued.
penalty for neglect to post notice ... 4277
nitro-glycerine, &c., not to be carried in vessels employed in transporting ... 4278
(see *Steam-Vessels.*)

Passports,
clerk in charge of, to administer oaths without fee ... 212
vessels of United States going abroad to have ... 4306
master to give bond for ... 4306
penalty on master departing without ... 4307
for unregistered vessel sailing on sea-letter ... 4308
deposit of, with consul on arrival at foreign port ... 4309
return of, on production of clearance ... 4309
penalty on master failing to deposit, &c ... 4310
falsely making, forging, altering, &c., granted to any vessel; uttering as true any false, &c ... 5423

Patent-Agents,
power of Commissioner of Patents to refuse to recognize, in cases of gross misconduct ... 487

Patented Articles,
use of, for marine-engines in vessels of war ... 1537

Patent-Fees,
rates of ... 4934
mode of paying ... 4935
refunding of ... 4936

Patent Medicines,
not exempt from internal-revenue tax ... 3436

Patent-Office,
establishment of, in Department of Interior ... 475
appointment of Commissioner, assistant commissioner, and three examiners-in-chief ... 476
of other officers, clerks, &c ... 476
salaries of Commissioner, assistant commissioner, and three examiners-in-chief ... 477
seal of ... 478
bond of Commissioner and chief clerk ... 479
officers, &c., not to have interest in patents, except, &c ... 480
general duties of Commissioner ... 481
qualifications and duties of examiners-in-chief ... 482
regulations for, by whom prescribed ... 483
classification, arrangement, &c., of models, &c., in ... 484
disposal of models, on rejection of application ... 485
library of ... 486
exclusion from, of patent-agents for misconduct ... 487
when papers filed in, may be printed at expense of party filing ... 488
Commissioner may print copies of claims, laws, decisions, &c., for information of public ... 489
specifications and drawings for distribution ... 490
for sale ... 491
advertisement and contracts for lithographing and engraving of specifications and drawings ... 492
price of uncertified copies of specifications and drawings ... 493
annual report of Commissioner ... 494
custody of collections of exploring expedition to be under Commissioner ... 495
disbursements for, by whom to be made ... 496

Patent-Rights,
no royalty to be paid to United States officers for, of Springfield breech-loading system ... 1673

Section.

Patents,
witnesses in contested cases, subpœnas for.. 4906
witness-fees in contested cases 4907
publication of notice of application for extension of patent granted prior to 2d March, 1861 4924, 4925
patent-fees 4934
mode of payment of 4935
refunding of 4936
Patuxet, R. I.,
port of delivery 2531
Pawcatuck River,
in Westerly, Conn., port of delivery 2533
Pawnees in Nebraska,
appointment of agent for 2052
Pay-Accounts,
Second Auditor may settle, of line-officer unable, by accident, to account for property, &c 278
Pay at Military Academy,
(see *Military Academy.*)
Pay Corps of Navy,
(see *Navy.*)
Pay-Inspectors and Directors of Navy,
number of, on active list 1376
bonds of 1383
President may increase penalty of 3639
relative rank of, on active list 1475
pay of 1556
Paying-Teller,
for Sergeant-at-Arms of House, salary 53
Paymaster-General of Army,
(see *Paymaster's Department of Army.*)
Paymaster-General of Navy,
Chief of Bureau of Provisions and Clothing to have title of 1471
Paymaster at National Armories,
(see *Armories.*)
Paymasters' Clerks in Army,
(see *Army.*)
Paymasters' Clerks in Navy,
(see *Pay of Navy.*)
Paymaster's Department of Army,
authorized 1094
organization and rank of 1182
Paymaster General, rank of 1182
additional paymasters for 1184
officers of, to give bond 1191
renewal of bond of officers of 1192
to pass deductions from pay, &c., to credit of commissioners of Soldiers' Home 4819
paymasters, advance bounties paid by, when allowed 280
overpayments by, when allowed 281
jurisdiction of Court of Claims of claim by, for relief, &c 1059
when loss of funds, &c., by, found by Court of Claims to be without fault, credit allowed by accounting officers 1062
number and rank of 1182
additional 1184
term of service 1185
clerks of, salaries 1190
to receive savings-deposits from soldiers.. 1305
President may increase, &c., bonds of 3639
Paymasters in Navy,
accounts of, in case of loss or capture of vessel, how settled 284
when loss of funds, &c., by, found by Court of Claims to be without fault, relief allowed by accounting officers 1062
number of, on active list 1376
of fleet 1382
bonds of 1383
clerks to 1386, 1387
relative rank of, on active list 1475

Section.

Paymasters in Navy—Continued.
detail of, as storekeeper at Naval Academy.. 1527
pay of 1556
pay of temporary appointment of 1564
President may increase penalty of bonds 3639
accounts of, shall be accompanied by consular certificate as to prices, &c 3723
Payment,
appropriation for, for coin, &c., destroyed at Chicago 3689
for lands sold for direct taxes 3689
for public lands, military bounty-land warrants to be received in 2277
agricultural-college scrip receivable in 2278
for placer-mining claim containing vein or lode claim, at what rate to be made 2333
for coal-lands, rate of 2348
purchased at public sale, when made 2356
at private sales, how made 2356, 2357
may be made in what foreign coin 2366
Pay
of postmasters, limit as to 3857

of army,
Second Auditor may settle pay account of line-officer unable, by accident, to account for property, &c 278
rates of, and provisions concerning 1261–1308
rates of 1261
service-pay 1262
maximum of 1263
brevet officers not entitled to increase 1264
forfeiture of, during absence 1265
when absent without leave 1265
forfeiture of, of officers dropped for absence, &c. 1266
maximum of, of colonel and lieutenant-colonel 1267
of officers to be paid monthly 1268
allowances in addition to 1269
of retired officers 1274
one year's pay and allowances to officers wholly retired 1275
of Indian scouts 1276
of hospital matrons and female nurses 1277
of leader of band at Military Academy 1278
of chief musicians of regiments 1279
of enlisted men 1280
additional pay to enlisted men after second year, retention of 1281
re-enlistment pay 1282
after five years' service, &c 1284
application of service-pay to men now in service 1283
additional pay, on certificate of merit 1285
to non-commissioned officers of Mexican war 1286
extra-duty pay 1287
during captivity of enlisted men of Regular Army, and officers and enlisted men of militia and volunteers 1288
travel-pay to officers 1289
to enlisted men 1290
pay of enlisted men, not assignable 1291
rules of, to apply to volunteer forces 1292
deductions from pay of officers for rations purchased 1299
from pay of enlisted men for articles purchased from commissary, &c 1300
for tobacco purchased, &c 1301
for clothing overdrawn 1302
from pay of officer or soldier for damage to arms 1303
from pay of officers for deficiency of, or damage to, supplies 1304
deposit by enlisted men of savings 1305
interest on, when payable 1306

Section.

Pay—Continued.
rules concerning deposits of savings to be made by Secretary of War 1307
deposits and clothing balances, how payable. 1308
pay of ordnance officer in charge of national armory 1663
deductions from pay of enlisted men for Soldiers' Home 4819
of marine corps,
(see *Marine Corps.*)
of militia,
(see *Militia.*)
of navy,
on active list 1556
of cadet-engineers 1556
of clerks to commanders of squadrons and vessels 1556
to commanders of yards and stations 1556
to paymasters of yards and stations 1556
of receiving vessels, &c 1556
to fleet paymasters 1556
to paymaster at Naval Academy 1556
to paymaster at Naval Asylum 1556
to inspectors 1556
of officers on furlough 1557
of volunteer naval service 1559
of officers on original entry into Navy, when to begin 1560
of officers promoted to vacancy 1561
of officers delayed in examination 1562
of persons temporarily performing duties of paymaster 1564
of chiefs of bureaus in Navy Department ... 1565
of naval storekeepers, officers on foreign stations 1567
civilians on foreign stations 1568
of enlisted men 1569
additional pay for detention beyond term ... 1572
for re-enlisting under honorable discharge. 1573
to crews of wrecked vessels 1574
of captured vessels 1575
retired list of officers on 1588
of certain rear-admirals on 1589
of third assistant engineers on 1590
of officers promoted on, not increased 1591
of officers on, on active duty 1592
of officers retired on furlough-pay 1593
when general court-martial may adjudge suspension of pay 1624
deduction from pay of officers, seamen, and marines for hospital-fund 4808
Payta,
consul at, salary of 1690
Peaches,
brandy made from, exemption under internal-revenue law 3255
Pearlington, Miss.,
port of delivery 2566
Pearl River, Miss.,
collection-district 2566
collector in, residence of 2567
Pecuniary Penalties,
(see *Fines, Penalties, and Forfeitures.*)
Peddlers of Tobacco,
(see *Tobacco.*)
Peltries,
and proper goods, &c., of Indians, when admitted free of duty 2515
Pembina, Minn.,
port of entry 2595
collector to reside at 2596
additional inspectors for 2605
Pembroke, Me.,
port of delivery 2517

Section.

Penal Statutes,
when plaintiff on, is liable for defendant's costs 975
for fees of prosecution 976
Penalties,
(see *Fines, Penalties, and Forfeitures.*)
Penitentiaries, Territorial,
to be under control of marshals 1892
exceptions in certain Territories 1892
regulations for government of, how prescribed and executed 1893
services and expenses in care of, &c., how paid 1894
offenders against territorial laws may be received, &c., in 1895
custody of, in certain Territories 1936
how to be maintained 1937
Pennsylvania,
collection-districts, ports of entry and delivery in 2543
officers in 2544
Pensacola, Fla.,
collection-district and port of entry 2562
collector to reside at 2563
Pensions,
half-pay to widows and children of persons dying in militia in United States service 1656
Title LVII 4692–4791
terms on which granted, time of 4692
for permanent specific disability 4692
who entitled to 4693
only for injuries, &c., in line of duty 4694
rate of, for total disability, period 4695
shall be according to rank at time of disability, &c 4696
rate for permanent specific disability, loss of both feet, &c., periods 4697
for loss of both eyes, &c., after June 4, 1872 4698
when increase of, to commence 4698½
rate of, for disability not provided for 4699
status of absentees, &c., under laws relating to 4700
period of service, how construed under laws relating to 4701
to widows, orphans, &c 4702
increased to widows, &c 4703
what children legitimate under laws relating to 4704
evidence of marriage in case of negroes and Indians 4705
to children abandoned by mother, &c 4706
when dependent relatives to have, order of right to 4707
to widows, &c., to cease on remarriage 4708
when to commence for injuries, &c., received after March 4, 1861 4709
when to be deemed to have accrued 4710
claim for arrears to be allowed, no agent's fees 4711
laws extended to persons whose claims accrued prior to March 4, 1861, and to revolutionary widows 4712
commencement of, for injuries, &c., received prior to March 4, 1861 4713
how declarations of claimants for, to be made. 4714
only one to be paid at a time 4715
none to be paid to persons engaged in rebellion, or to widows, &c 4716
evidence of injury, &c., when claim for, not prosecuted within five years from filing of claim 4717
disposal of, accrued, in case of death, &c ... 4718
where unclaimed for three years, &c 4719
under special acts 4720

Section.

Pensions—Continued.
limitations of time as to Indian claims for.. 4721
laws relating to, extended to certain Missouri militia, &c ... 4722
colored soldiers enrolled as slaves to have.. 4723
pay at same time with, not allowed ... 4724
half-pay to widows, &c., continued ... 4725
how long ... 4726
limit as to amount of ... 4727
of Navy, prior to March 4, 1861 ... 4728
to Navy widows, &c., half-pay continued, &c ... 4729
for disabilities, &c., in Mexican war ... 4730
to widows, &c., of soldiers, &c., in Mexican war ... 4731
of war of 1812 and Indian wars ... 4732
pensioners on rolls entitled to continuance and increase of, under Revised Statutes.. 4733
not to be withheld for arrears to United States ... 4734
not to be granted to widow for same time that husband received pension ... 4735
to survivors of war of 1812, who served sixty days ... 4736
who have been named in resolution of Congress ... 4736
rate of, &c ... 4737
to widows of ... 4738
proofs required in cases of ... 4739
loss of discharge not to prevent, from receiving; other proof ... 4740
officers, &c., of revenue-cutters, when to have ... 4741
claims for continuance or increase on account of revolutionary war, allowance after April 2, 1862 ... 4742
evidence in case of claim of widow to revolutionary ... 4743
investigation of attempts at fraud to procure, &c ... 4744
pledge, &c., of, void ... 4745
agent shall transmit attorney's oath with voucher ... 4745
penalty for false affidavit ... 4746
for post-dating vouchers ... 4746
not liable to attachment, &c ... 4747
printed instructions to persons claiming; notice of allowance of ... 4748
forfeiture of, by desertion, not to be remitted, &c ... 4749
Navy pensions, public faith pledged to payment of ... 4752
to be paid from Navy-pension fund ... 4755
fund, (see *Navy-Pension Fund.*)
to privateersmen, fund for ... 4759
rate of, how paid ... 4761
vouchers to be sent to pensioners ... 4764
shall be paid by checks to order of pensioner. 4765
shall be paid only to persons entitled to ... 4766
to persons in foreign countries, how paid... 4766
blank vouchers to be furnished to agent ... 4767
not to be paid except on vouchers ... 4767
certificates of, to be forwarded to pension agents ... 4768
attorney's fees to be deducted from ... 4769
duplicates for lost checks for ... 4770
biennial examinations required ... 4771
biennial certificate of surgeon to accompany vouchers ... 4771
special examinations may be required ... 4775
agents to pay surgeons' fees ... 4777
appointment of agents for paying pensions. 4778
bonds of ... 4779
President may increase penalty of ... 3639
agencies for paying, establishment of ... 4780
compensation of agents ... 4781

Section.

Pensions—Continued.
fees for preparing vouchers for ... 4782
penalty for embezzling, by guardians ... 4783
affidavits for, to be taken, &c., without fee.. 4784
fee for prosecuting claim for ... 4785
agreement to be filed by attorneys in claim for ... 4786
to be paid to Secretary of Navy when pensioner is in Navy Hospital ... 4813
of certain persons in Soldiers' Home to be surrendered during their stay ... 4820
to be assigned to National Home for Disabled Volunteers, in certain cases ... 4832
false personation of person entitled to pension, in receiving money, &c ... 5435
endeavoring to obtain, &c., by means of forged power of attorney ... 5436
receiving or demanding, by pension-agent, &c., from pensioner, of fee or reward for services ... 5487
Perfumery and Cosmetics,
manufacture of, in bonded warehouse for exportation without being stamped ... 3433
imported, to be stamped as prescribed in Schedule A ... 3435
tax on, Schedule A ... 3435
Periodicals,
restriction on amount to be expended for, by executive officer other than head of Department ... 1779
postage on, at free-delivery offices ... 3872
regularly issued, &c., to be second-class mail-matter ... 3877
postage on, when sent to subscribers ... 3905
to subscribers, postage on, payable quarterly in advance ... 3906
Perishable Articles,
customs, entry and sale of, and duties on, of vessel in distress ... 2891
unclaimed, in public warehouse, sale of... 2976
seized, when and by whom sold, &c ... 3080
internal-revenue appraisal of, and return to owner under bond ... 3459
Perjury,
on examination by customs officer, penalty for ... 2924
willfully-false statement by internal-revenue officer relative to fees, &c., to be deemed. 3158
Permanent Appropriations,
(see *Appropriations.*)
Permanent Specific Disability,
(see *Pensions.*)
Permits,
for exportation of goods ... 2979, 3035
to unlade, penalty for unlading without ... 2867
what to specify ... 2870
by whom given ... 2869, 2872
of imported spirits and wines ... 2883
when not granted until post-entry made.. 2887
vessel in distress ... 2891
vessels from contiguous foreign territory on northern, &c., frontier ... 3109
not required of vessels on northern, &c., frontier districts with cargo from American port ... 3119
cargo, passengers, &c., of vessel from foreign port ... 3121
internal-revenue, for removal of stills ... 3265
of alcohol from bond for scientific purposes. 3297
of distilled spirits for exportation ... 3330
of fermented liquors ... 3345
to brewer to conduct business at another place ... 3350
for removal of tobacco, snuff, and cigars for exportation ... 3385
for vessels in coasting-trade ... 4332

Section.

Permits—Continued.
surveyors granting, to make monthly return to collector ... 4332
for vessel departing for neighboring districts, carrying distilled spirits, sugars, or foreign goods ... 4349
penalty on master proceeding without ... 4350
for unlading ... 4351
for vessel departing for remote district ... 4353
penalty for departing without, if carrying distilled spirits or foreign goods ... 4354
penalty for departing without, if carrying no cargo ... 4354
for unlading vessel arriving from remote district ... 4355
for proceeding after partly unlading ... 4355
exemption of vessels under 20 tons from above requirements ... 4359
for transportation by land of foreign merchandise across New Jersey, Delaware, and Maryland ... 4362
for fishing-vessel to touch at foreign port ... 4364
for foreign vessel bound coastwise ... 4367
delivery of, on arrival ... 4368
penalty for neglect ... 4369
penalty for forging, altering, &c., of vessel ... 4375
for vessels in domestic commerce, fees for ... 4381, 4382
for vessel to discharge at quarantine ... 4793
for delivery of goods entered at quarantine, 4795
to vessels arriving at insurrectionary district to go to another port ... 5315
falsely making, forging, altering, &c., granted by any collector; uttering as true any false, &c ... 5423

Pernambuco,
consul at, salary of ... 1690

Perquisites,
postmasters and others not to receive ... 3858

"*Persons*,"
term, to whom applied ... 1

Perth Amboy, N. J.,
collection-district and port of entry ... 2541
collector to reside at ... 2542

Peru,
salary of minister to ... 1675

Petersburgh, Va.,
collection-district and port of entry ... 2552
collector and surveyor in, residence of ... 2553
vessels loaded in, may be cleared at Richmond, Va ... 2554
vessels arriving within, what to do ... 2836

Petition in Bankruptcy,
(see *Bankruptcy*.)

Petroleum,
crude or refined, not to be carried on steam passenger-vessel, except, &c ... 4472
how packed and marked for shipment ... 4475
may be used for production of motive-power. 4474
penalty for shipping, contrary to law ... 4476

Pharmacopœia,
United States, or other national, tax on medicines compounded according to ... 3436

Philadelphia, Pa.,
collection-district and port of entry ... 2543
officers in, residence and duties of ... 2544
clerks and employés in appraiser's office at, how appointed, number and compensation of ... 2545
transportation in bond extended to ... 2997
assistant treasurer at, appointment, &c., of, 3595–3597
clerks, &c., in assistant treasury at ... 3605
collectors, &c., shall pay public money to assistant treasurer ... 3615
inspectors of hulls and of boilers for ... 4414

Section.

Philadelphia, Pa.—Continued.
their salaries, &c ... 4414
reserve of national banks in ... 5191
balances with banks in, may be part of reserve ... 5192
redemption agencies ... 5195

Philadelphia Mint,
(see *Mint*.)

Photographer in Treasury Department,
salary of ... 235
assistants to ... 235

Photographic Pictures,
imported for exhibition, and not sale, free of duty; bond for payment of duties if not re-exported ... 2512

Physicians' Prescription,
tax on medicines compounded according to. 3436

Pickles for Navy,
how may be procured ... 3726

Pictou, N. S.,
consulate at, salary of ... 1690

Pictures,
obscene, not to be imported ... 2491

Piers, Public,
none to be built for United States until cession of jurisdiction over site ... 4661
when cession deemed sufficient ... 4662
belonging to United States on northern, &c., lakes to be properly marked by Light-house Board ... 4677

Pilatka, Fla.,
port of delivery ... 2562
surveyor to reside at ... 2563
merchandise for, where entered ... 2818

Pilotage,
discriminating rates of, by States, prohibited ... 4237
existing discriminations abolished ... 4237

Pilots,
to be governed by State regulations ... 4235
employment of, on waters between two States ... 4236
of war-vessels, when to have pension ... 4693
rate of total-disability pension to ... 4695

Pilots, Licensed, of Steam-Vessels,
(see *Inspection of Steam-Vessels*.)

Pilot-Vessels, (Sailing,)
to carry what lights ... 4233

Pipes, (Distillery,)
how to be fixed and painted ... 3269
Commissioner of Internal Revenue may require changes of ... 3270
may require fastenings, locks, or seals ... 3270

Pipes, (Water,)
(see *Washington Aqueduct*.)

Piræus,
consul at, salary of ... 1690

Piracy,
seizure of vessels fitted out for ... 4297
customs-officers to seize ... 4299
provisions of Title NEUTRALITY not to be construed to prevent prosecution or punishment for ... 5291

Pittsburgh, Pa.,
collection-district and port of entry ... 2543
surveyor and appraiser in ... 2544
port of delivery in district of New Orleans. 2568
surveyor to reside at, duties of ... 2569
transportation in bond extended to ... 2997
inspectors of hulls and boilers for ... 4414
their salaries ... 4414
reserve of national banks in ... 5191
balances with banks in, may be part of reserve ... 5192
redemption agencies ... 5195

Section.

Pittston, Me.,
port of delivery ... 2517
Placer-Claims,
(see *Lands, Public.*)
Plank Roads,
when mail to be carried on ... 3968
Plan of Distillery,
to be made in triplicate, under direction of collector of internal revenue ... 3263
alterations to be shown on, or, if supplemental plan made, to be noted in original ... 3263
Plan of Public Buildings,
shall be approved before commencement of building ... 3734
Planter,
(see *Farmer.*)
Plates and Dies,
for national-bank notes, engraving of ... 5172
custody of ... 5173
annual examination of ... 5174
Plates for Printing Obligations of United States,
using, or suffering to be used, genuine, for printing ... 5430
engraving, selling, or bringing into United States, or having plate in likeness of. 5430
Platina,
shipper of, to notify carrier ... 4281
Plattsburgh, N. Y.,
port of entry ... 2535
collector to reside at ... 2536
Playing-Cards,
imported, to be stamped as prescribed in Schedule A ... 3435
internal-revenue tax on, Schedule A ... 3435
Pleasure-Yachts,
(see *Yachts.*)
Plundering,
money, goods, &c., from vessel wrecked or in distress, &c ... 5358
Plural Number,
words of, to include singular ... 1
Plymouth, Mass.,
collection-district and port of entry ... 2527
collector to reside at ... 2529
Poisons,
shall be excluded from mail ... 3878
Policemen,
special, in service of Senate ... 52
Political Purposes,
employés in navy-yard not to be required or requested to contribute for ... 1546
dismissal for exacting contributions at navy-yards for ... 1546
Poncas,
appointment of agent for ... 2052
Ponce, (Porto Rico,)
consul at, salary of ... 1690
Pontchartrain, La.,
port of delivery ... 2568
surveyor to reside at, duties of ... 2569
vessels bound for, may unlade at, after making report, &c ... 2574
departing from, for foreign ports, how cleared ... 2575
Poor Debtors,
power of Postmaster-General to discharge, from imprisonment ... 410
effect of discharge of ... 411
proceedings to discharge, by Secretary of Treasury ... 3471
when President may discharge ... 3472
"Port,"
what to include ... 2767
Port-Charges,
Brazilian mail-steamships exempt from ... 4232

Section.

Port-Charges—Continued.
duration of exemption ... 4232
Port Elizabeth, N. J.,
port of delivery ... 2541
Porter,
(see *Fermented Liquors.*)
Port Huron, Mich.,
port of entry ... 2599
collector to reside at ... 2600
Port Jefferson, N. Y.,
port of delivery ... 2535
merchandise for, to be entered and duties paid at New York ... 2540
enrollment and license of vessels by surveyor at ... 4345
Portland and Falmouth, Me.,
collection-district ... 2517
officers in; collector to reside at Portland. 2518
additional inspectors for ... 2605
Portland, Me.,
port of entry ... 2517
weighers, gaugers, measurers, and inspectors for ... 2606
transportation in bond extended to ... 2997
inspectors of hulls and boilers for ... 4414
their salaries ... 4414
Portland, Oreg.,
port of entry ... 2586
collector and appraiser to reside at ... 2587
masters of vessels bound for, with goods, what to do ... 2588
clearing from ... 2589
arriving at Astoria with goods for ... 2590
weighers, gaugers, measurers, and inspectors for ... 2606
transportation in bond extended to ... 2997
Port Mahon,
consul at, salary of ... 1690
Port Orford, Oreg.,
port of delivery ... 2586
deputy collector of customs to reside at ... 2587
Port Penn, Del.,
port of delivery ... 2546
Portraits,
of living persons not to be placed on bonds, notes, &c ... 3576
Port Royal, Va.,
port of delivery ... 2552
surveyor to reside at ... 2553
Port Said,
consul at, salary of ... 1690
Port Sarnia,
consul at, salary of ... 1690
Ports of Delivery,
when and by whom discontinued ... 253
in the several States and Territories ... 2517–2612
officers in ... 2517–2612
vessels bound for, where to enter, &c ... 2772
goods for, on Mississippi River and tributaries, where entered ... 2822
in collection-district of New Orleans ... 2823
President may cause duties to be collected at, in case of insurrection, &c.; appointment of officers at, provisions of law applicable, &c ... 5314
Ports of Entry,
forfeitures for entering, when closed by proclamation, where prosecuted ... 564, 5317
in the several States and Territories ... 2517–2612
officers in ... 2517–2612
to be ports of delivery ... 2770
shipping-commissioners at ... 4501
President in cases of insurrection may change, &c.; ports of delivery to be constituted; application of provisions of law, &c ... 5314

Section.

Ports of Entry—Continued.
when to be closed by proclamation of President; forfeiture of vessels, &c., attempting to enter 5317

Portsmouth, N. H.,
collection-district and port of entry 2522
collector and surveyor in, to reside at 2523
merchandise may be entered at, for Kittery or Berwick, Me 2524

Port Townsend, W. T.,
port of entry 2586
collector to reside at 2587

Portugal,
salary of minister to 1675

Port-Wardens,
certificates of, as to necessity for unlading vessels in distress 2891

Posse Comitatus,
persons appointed to execute process under Title CIVIL RIGHTS, may summon 1984

Postage,
no allowance for, to Members and Delegates in Congress 44
allowance to collector of internal revenue 3145
quarterly account of, by postmasters 3843
neglect to render 3845
rate of, on newspapers, &c., at free-delivery offices 3872
extra, or carrier's fees, prohibited 3873
provisions concerning 3896–3912
prepayment by stamps 3896
on matter of third class, at office of mailing 3897
unpaid, on matter forwarded 3898
on matter to which no specific rate of postage is assigned 3903
on drop-letters 3904
on regular printed matter 3905
shall be paid quarterly in advance 3906
on transient and miscellaneous matter 3910
on foreign matter 3912
stamps shall be evidence of payment of 3914
extra, on advertised letters 3935
on letters for United States held in foreign countries, may be paid by consuls 4014
on letters carried in foreign vessels 4015
received at post-offices to be accounted for as revenue 4051

Postage-Stamps,
fractional currency receivable for 3574
prepayment required in 3896, 3897
shall be prepared, &c 3914
impressed on envelopes, shall be provided 3915
shall be kept for sale at all post-offices; postmaster accountable for 3918
may be sold at a discount to designated agents 3919
neglect to account for, &c., penalty 4053
secreting, embezzling, or taking implement used in printing, &c 5453
paper or material used in making of 5453
paper or material, printed, &c., and intended for 5453

Postage-Stamps and Envelopes,
provisions relating to 3914–3919
accounts to show amounts derived from 4049
to show expenditures for 4049

Postal Accounts,
classification of 4049
disposal of 4060

Postal Agents,
in China and Japan authorized 4023

Postal Balances,
certain offices shall be furnished with metric 3880

Postal Cards,
Postmaster-General shall provide, cost, &c 3916

Postal Cars,
refusal to furnish 4003
additional pay for 4004

Postal Clerks,
shall receive way-letters for mailing, &c 3980
in railway postal service 4025

Postal Conventions,
copies of, to be furnished Congressional Printer by Secretary of State 210
power of Postmaster-General to negotiate and conclude 398
printing and publication of 399
printing of; number for Postmaster-General, "usual number" 3806
number to be printed for Congress, at close of session 3807
for Secretary of Interior 3808

Postal Envelopes and Wrappers,
to be third-class mail-matter 3878

Postal Expenditures,
classification of 4049

Postal Laws,
jurisdiction of district courts of causes arising under 563
of circuit courts of causes arising under 629
suits arising under, to be brought in name of United States 919
revenue laws for protection of seizing officers to extend to officers seizing under 3991

Postal Money-Orders,
(see *Money-Orders.*)

Postal Revenues,
shall be part of basis for fixing salaries of postmasters 3855
shall not be liable for loss of registered mail 3926
classification of 4049
deposit of certain 4050
postage, &c., to be accounted for as 4051
neglect to deposit, penalty 4053
money required for postal service to be appropriated out of 4054

Postal Service,
money appropriated for, how drawn from Treasury 3674

Post-Chaplains,
(see *Chaplains.*)

Post Commissary-Sergeants,
(see *Commissary-Sergeants.*)

Post-Entry,
when and by whom made in customs cases, permit to unlade, not granted until 2887

Post-Marking and Canceling Stamps,
accounts to show expenditures for 4049

Postmaster-General,
appointment and term of office of 388
oath of office of 391
by whom administered 392
designation by, of clerk to act as superintendent of free-delivery 394
seal of Department to be kept by 395
general duties and powers of 396
to keep inventories and accounts of property of Department, of sales of same, and to report same to Congress 397
power of, to negotiate postal conventions with foreign countries 398
to transmit copies of postal conventions to Secretary of State, to be printed 399
may establish blank-agency at Washington, D. C., for Post Office Department 400
to deliver copy of mail contracts to Sixth Auditor within sixty days 404
what orders and regulations of, to be certified to Sixth Auditor 405

Section.

Postmaster-General—Continued.
to issue warrant to Treasurer, on quarterly statement by Sixth Auditor of payments by postmasters for postal service ... 406
power of, to direct payments into Treasury, of postal revenues and collection of debts due Post-Office Department ... 407
deposits on account of postal-service to be brought into Treasury by warrant of, countersigned by Auditor ... 408
may prescribe rules for action of Sixth Auditor in ascertaining facts, for remission of fines, &c., or compromise of claims, &c ... 409
power of, to discharge from imprisonment persons confined on judgments in behalf of Post Office Department ... 410
discharges by, from imprisonment, not to affect subsequent execution against property ... 411
annual reports by, to Congress ... 413
annual estimates, when to be furnished by, to Secretary of Treasury ... 414
may transfer postal money ... 3641
shall direct manner, &c., of making returns of postal money ... 3644
under what heads to submit estimates ... 3668
postal money shall be drawn from Treasury on warrant of ... 3674
shall approve plans of all public buildings 3734
printing of annual report of, of offers and contracts for carrying mail ... 3797
shall establish post-offices, &c. ... 3829
shall promptly fill vacancy in office of postmaster, may place special agent in charge of post-office, in case of vacancy, &c ... 3836
may require new bond, when to be operative. 3837
to record and notify Sixth Auditor of orders as to postmasters' salaries ... 3856
may designate distributing-offices ... 3859
authority of, to make allowances for rent and expenses ... 3860
duty of, in case of unusual business, to allow for clerical service and increased salary 3863
power of, to discontinue offices ... 3864
shall fix salaries of letter-carriers ... 3866
may establish receiving-boxes ... 3868
may establish branch post-offices ... 3871
how guided in expenditures for letter-carriers, &c ... 3874
may furnish metric balances ... 3880
may reduce rate on foreign letters, &c.; may collect postage in coin ... 3912
shall prepare postage-stamps ... 3914
stamped envelopes and newspaper wrappers ... 3915
postal cards ... 3916
may establish system of registration ... 3926
may prescribe regulations for registering money-letters from and to postmasters 3932
shall advertise for proposals for carrying mail 3941
exception as to railways ... 3942
as to steamboats, &c ... 3943
not bound to consider bid of negligent, &c., contractor ... 3949
may contract, without advertising, for intermediate service, in case of default ... 3951
may make deductions from mail-contractor's pay, &c ... 3962
shall provide for carrying mail on post-roads 3965
to court-houses ... 3966
may contract for carrying mail on canals ... 3697
on plank-roads ... 3968
in packets ... 3969

Section.

Postmaster-General—Continued.
in steamships ... 3970
may contract for extending line of posts ... 3971
may establish temporarily service on routes not yet established by Congress ... 3975
may suspend provision for sending letters in stamped envelopes otherwise than by mail ... 3993
may provide for separate carriage of letter-mail for expedition ... 3994
may contract for carrying mail through foreign countries between points in United States ... 4006
may contract for carrying mail to foreign countries ... 4007
what compensation may be allowed by, for carrying foreign mail ... 4009
may fine contractors carrying foreign mail .. 4010
stipulation that foreign mail contracts may be annulled by ... 4011
may employ special, local, and route agents, &c. ... 4017-4025
may make advances to certain agents ... 4055
may transfer debts due Department to contractors ... 4056
power of, to fix rates for telegrams between Departments and officers, over lines having right of way, &c., through public domain ... 5266
duty of, to select appraisers, in case of purchase of telegraph lines by United States ... 5267

Postmaster,
of Senate, salary of ... 52
of House of Representatives, salary of ... 53

Postmasters,
quarterly statement by Sixth Auditor to Postmaster-General of payments by, for postal-service ... 294
copies of quarterly returns of, when admitted as evidence ... 889
copy of statement that letter of demand was mailed to delinquent, &c., when, and of what evidence ... 890
duties as to public money ... 3639
appointment and removal of ... 3830
bond of ... 3834
President may increase penalty of ... 3639
application of payments by, when new bond given ... 3835
responsibility for safe-keeping, &c., until successor qualified ... 3836
new bond of ... 3837
limitation of liability of sureties of ... 3838
quarterly accounts of ... 3843
neglect to render, penalty ... 3845
shall safely keep, &c., public money, without loaning, &c ... 3846
in certain counties, may deposit money in national banks, receipt of interest prohibited ... 3847
shall deposit with assistant treasurers, &c .. 3848
salaries of ... 3852, 3857
not to receive fees or perquisites ... 3858
at distributing offices, allowances to ... 3859
allowances to, for clerks, &c ... 3860, 3863
salaries of, how paid ... 3861
accounts of, for quarterly postage ... 3906
shall keep on hand, &c., stamps and envelopes, accountable for ... 3918
to decide between competing newspapers for advertising letters ... 3930, 3931
registering money-letters from and to ... 3932
delivery to, of letters brought by vessels in foreign trade ... 3976
by steamboats ... 3977

Section.

Postmasters—Continued.
responsibility of, for money-order business at branch offices, &c. 4029
at money-order offices may appoint acting postmaster 4031
shall preserve applications for money-orders 4033
shall use money-order blanks 4034
shall not pay money-order after one year 4036
shall pay to indorsee 4037
shall modify, &c. 4038
shall repay 4039
transfer of money-order funds from and to 4042, 4043
penalty for embezzling 4046
pay to, for money-order business 4047
shall be held accountable for uncollected revenue 4051
may allow box-holders to provide lock-boxes 4052
neglect of, to deposit revenues; penalty 4053
collections of revenue from, by transfers to contractors 4056

Post-Office Boxes,
holders of, may provide lock-boxes 4052

Post-Office Department,
Sixth Auditor to superintend collection of debts due to, &c. 292
money-order accounts of, to be kept separately 293
quarterly statement by Sixth Auditor to Postmaster General, of payments by postmasters 294
compromise of judgments for debts, &c., due to 295
Sixth Auditor to forward to Department of Justice papers in suits against delinquent employés of 296
suits for money due, provisions respecting 381, 382
provisions concerning 388–414
Postmaster-General to be head of 388
three Assistant Postmasters-General in; appointment and salaries of 389
Assistant Attorney-General to be employed in, appointment, salary 390
oath of office of Postmaster-General and employés in 391
by whom administered 392
officers and employés in 393
designation of superintendent of free delivery 394
seal of; custody and use of 395
general duties and powers of Postmaster-General 396
inventories and account of property in 397
blank-agency for, at Washington, D. C. 400
action of, as to foreign dead-letters 401
true date to be affixed to papers; date of filing to be indorsed 402
bonds taken by, and contracts with 403
duplicate copies of contracts for carrying mail to be delivered to Sixth Auditor 404
orders, &c., of Postmaster-General which may originate a claim, or affect accounts, to be certified to Sixth Auditor 405
warrant of Postmaster-General on quarterly statement by Sixth Auditor of payments by postmasters 406
postal revenues and collections of debts due to, how paid into Treasury; receipts for 407
deposits on account of postal service, how brought into Treasury 408
remission of fines, &c., compromises and releases of claims 409
discharge from imprisonment of persons confined on judgment in behalf of 410
limitation of effect of 411

Section.

Post-Office Department—Continued.
employés in, not to be interested in mail contracts, or act as agent for contractor, &c., in business before Department 412
annual reports of Postmaster-General 413
estimates, when to be furnished to Secretary of Treasury 414
statement by marshal to Sixth Auditor, of executions for moneys due on account of 792
transcripts from money-order account-books of, when evidence 889
interest allowed in suits for balances due to 964
money-accounts of, to be kept separate 3642
estimates for, under what heads to be submitted 3668

Post-Offices,
provisions relating to 3829–3864
shall be established by Postmaster-General 3829
postmasters responsible for public property in, until commission expires, &c 3836
allowance for extra labor at 3863
may be discontinued 3864
non-delivered letters at, list of, to be published 3930
not on established routes, carrying mail to 3971
not on post-roads, when service to be discontinued 3975
letters brought by foreign vessels shall be deposited in 4015
buying, receiving, or concealing valuable inclosure stolen or embezzled from 5470

Post Ordnance-Sergeant,
(see *Ordnance Department*.)

Post-Roads,
mail shall be carried on 3965
certain, shall be reported to Congress, &c. 3975

Potomac, Va.,
port of delivery 2552
deputy collector to reside at, duties of 2553

Poughkeepsie, N. Y.,
port of delivery 2535

Pound Sterling,
value fixed 3565

Power of Attorney,
to draw wages of enlisted men in Navy 1576
to receive payment of claim on United States, null and void 3477
penalty for post-dating, in pension cases 4746
to receive pension, not to be recognized 4766
falsely making, altering; uttering false as true, &c 5421
having false, &c., with intent to defraud United States 5422
endeavoring by means of forged, to obtain, or have transferred, &c., sum in public stocks, or annuity, pension, prize-money, wages, &c., due from United States 5436

Precedence,
in Navy, of staff corps, gives no additional right to quarters 1487

Precious Metals and Stones,
shipper to notify carrier, &c 4281

Pre-emption of Public Lands,
(see *Lands, Public*.)

Premiums,
on sale of drafts, &c., to be accounted for 3652

Prepayment of Postage,
required, except, &c 3896

Prescott,
consul at, salary of 1690

Section.

Presents,
penalty for soliciting or receiving from employés in Government service, by superior in office ... 1784
making or offering, to customs officers, by person interested in importation, &c. 5452
Preserved Meats for Navy,
how may be procured ... 3726
Presidential Elections,
(see *Elections.*)
President of Senate,
salary of ... 36
President of United States,
term of office, commencement and duration of ... 152
salary ... 153
officers of household of, salaries ... 155
steward of household of; duties of ... 156
bond of ... 157
authority of, in filling vacancies in offices of heads of Departments ... 179
power of, to suspend civil officers during recess of Senate, &c ... 1768
to fill vacancies happening during recess of Senate ... 1769
President's Message,
number of, to be printed ... 3798
Presidents of National Banks,
directors to appoint ... 5136
shall certify payments of installments on capital stock ... 5140
shall be chosen from board by directors ... 5150
Comptroller shall require oaths of, as to organization, &c ... 5168
penalty for embezzlement, &c., by ... 5209
shall cause to be kept, &c., list of shareholders ... 5210
reports to be verified by oath of ... 5211
reports of dividend to be verified by oath of. 5212
Presidio del Norte, Tex.,
inspector of customs to reside at ... 2580
Prices Current,
consular officers shall procure, &c ... 1713
Prince Edward's Island,
consul at, salary of ... 1690
certain fish and fish-oil, produce of fisheries of, admitted free of duty ... 2506
lading and unlading of vessels from ... 3129
vessels of, may engage in coasting trade on lakes, &c., under treaty of Washington ... 4347
suspension of privilege ... 4347
Principal Clerks,
of public lands, appointment, salary, and duties of ... 448
of private land claims ... 448
of surveys ... 449
Principal Musician,
for regiment of artillery ... 1099
of infantry ... 1106
Principal on Bond to United States,
when surety of, to have priority of claim against ... 3468
Printed Matter,
disposal of uncalled-for, in post-offices ... 4061
Printers' Fees,
for publishing ... 853
in Territories, how prescribed ... 1883
Printing,
in Territories, limitation of expense of ... 1887
of United States notes, &c., may be done at Treasury ... 3577
what, may be done on stamped envelopes ... 3915
on bonds, &c., shall be punished ... 3708
and binding, (see *Government Printing-Office.*)

Section.

Prints,
obscene, not to be imported ... 2491
third-class mail-matter ... 3878
Priority of Claim,
of United States to debts of deceased or absent debtors ... 3466
of surety, &c., on bonds given to United States ... 3468
Prisoners,
under United States laws may be removed in case of contagion or epidemic ... 4800
expenses of transportation and confinement of, and of execution of sentence ... 5536
hiring of temporary jail for ... 5537
other temporary provision for safe-keeping of ... 5538
allowance by Attorney-General for subsistence of ... 5545
Attorney-General to prescribe regulations for government of marshals, and of warden of jail of District of Columbia in relation to, &c ... 5545
Attorney-General may designate prison for, where no suitable jail, &c ... 5546
by whom transported and delivered to keeper of jail, &c ... 5546
expenses to be paid by Attorney-General, in case of such designation ... 5546
confinement of, in house of correction, or of reformation ... 5548
juvenile offenders under age of sixteen, confinement of; transportation; expenses, &c ... 5549
Attorney-General to contract for subsistence of, in houses of refuge ... 5550
Prisons for American Convicts,
in foreign countries, allowance for rent of .. 4121
wages of keepers and care of offenders ... 4121
number allowed in Japan, China, Turkey, and Siam ... 4121
ports at which, may be established, how designated ... 4121
limit to expense of prison and keepers at Bangkok ... 4121
allowance for rent of, &c., at Shanghai ... 4122
for hire of constables, &c., at other ports in China ... 4122
for expense of, &c., at Kanagawa ... 4123
for constables, &c., at other ports in Japan. 4123
rent of court-house and jail at Yeddo ... 4124
annual cost of, limited ... 4124
term and renewals of lease ... 4124
Private Acts,
not repealed by incorporation in Revised Statutes of parts of ... 5596
Private Armed Vessels,
(see *Privateersmen.*)
Private Claims,
when and by whom to be remitted from either House to Court of Claims ... 1060
Private Debts,
what shall be a legal tender in payment of ... 3588, 3589
Private Dies,
proprietors of articles in Schedule A may furnish, for stamps ... 3423
mode of canceling such stamps ... 3423
penalty for forging, counterfeiting, or fraudulently obtaining stamps from ... 3423
engraver or printer selling or giving away stamps from ... 3423
other offenses relative to stamps from ... 3423
Private Medal-Dies,
not to be prepared at mint ... 3551

Section.

Private Patients,
may be admitted to Government Hospital for Insane in certain cases ... 4853
Privateer Pension-Fund,
Secretary of Navy to be trustee of ... 4758
how constituted ... 4759
shall be deposited in Treasury ... 4760
Privateer's Journals,
names of persons disabled, &c., to be entered in ... 4762
transcripts of, to be sent to Secretary of Navy 4763
Privateersmen,
money pledged for support of disabled ... 4759
when shall be placed on pension-list ... 4761
names of disabled, &c., to be entered in journal ... 4762
Privates of Army,
(see *Enlisted Men in Army.*)
Prize,
jurisdiction of district courts in cases of, under Title INSURRECTION ... 563
of circuit courts ... 629
captured under laws relating to insurrection, in what district condemnation of, may be had ... 735
prize-money due colored soldiers and sailors, laws as to collection and payment of . 2032
appropriation of prize-money to captors ... 3689
provisions applicable to all captures made as . 4613
definition of term "vessels of the Navy" ... 4614
duties of commanding officer of vessels making capture ... 4615
survey of captured vessel and property when it cannot be sent in for adjudication .. 4615
appraisement, by whom made ... 4615
report of appraisers to be sent into court . 4615
sale of such property ... 4615
deposit of proceeds of sale ... 4615
claim of United States to share in ... 4616
how made ... 4616
special counsel, employment of, by Secretary of Navy ... 4620
commissioners, appointment and qualifications of ... 4621
marshal to keep property under warrant of court ... 4623
to report to court, property requiring to be stored or sold ... 4623
to insure property according to his judgment ... 4623
custody by, of witnesses ... 4623
to report to Secretary of Navy when required ... 4623
survey, appraisal, and inventory of property taken for use of United States ... 4624
Department for whose use taken, to deposit value, subject to order of court . 4624
when property not sent in, proceedings, where may be commenced ... 4625
proceeds of sale or value to be deposited with assistant treasurer ... 4625
delivery on stipulation ... 4626
money, in lieu of stipulation, to be deposited with assistant treasurer ... 4626
sale, how conducted ... 4628
transfer of property to another district for sale; proceedings ... 4629
aggregate share of captors ... 4630
distributive shares of captors ... 4631
what vessels entitled to share ... 4632
restriction on commanding officers of fleets or squadrons ... 4633
temporary absence not to forfeit share ... 4633
determination of shares, court to order testimony to be taken ... 4634

Section.

Prize—Continued.
before whom such testimony may be sworn to ... 4634
decree of distribution to be made by court . 4634
what such decree shall recite ... 4634
bounty to be paid for persons on board vessels destroyed ... 4635
to be divided in same manner as prize-money ... 4635
when actual number on board cannot be ascertained, how estimated ... 4635
sum to be paid in case of vessel destroyed otherwise than from injuries received in action ... 4635
powers of district court after appeal to Supreme Court ... 565, 4637
security for costs may be required at any stage of cause ... 4638
costs and expenses to be paid from proceeds of property, unless ... 4639
how and when allowed ... 4640
how paid in case of restitution, or where there is no money ... 4640
distribution of prize-money, how and by whom made ... 4641
of ransom-money, salvage, bounty, &c., how and by whom made ... 4642
assignment of prize-money, or bounty, by persons in naval service, to be attested . 4643
clerk of district court to render semi-annual statement to Secretaries of Treasury and Navy ... 4644
to keep account of amounts in causes deposited for distribution ... 4644
to send copies of final decrees of distribution to Secretaries of Treasury and Navy ... 4644
to draw orders of court for payment of costs, &c., and distribution of residue . 4644
compensation for such services ... 4644
allowances and commissions of marshal in disposal of property ... 4645
compensation of district attorney and commissioner, how determined ... 4646
annual account to be rendered to Attorney-General ... 4647
maximum allowance for ... 4647
excess over amount allowed, how disposed of ... 4647
of special counsel for captors ... 4648
fees to be paid out of what fund ... 4649
commissions of auctioneers ... 4650
witness-fees to be paid by marshal ... 4651
to be repaid to marshal from money deposited ... 4651
amount not repaid, how allowed ... 4651
recaptures, in what cases of, salvage to be allowed ... 4652
restoration of vessel to United States ... 4652
salvage, how payable ... 4652
how distributed ... 4652
laws not to be construed as contravening treaties ... 4652
United States share of prize-money to go to Navy pension-fund ... 4752
from captures by privateers, to privateer pension-fund ... 4759
property employed in aid of insurrection, when lawful subject of ... 5308
proceedings when property is taken on account of use, &c., in aid of rebellion .. 5309, 5311
property seized, &c., upon inland waters not considered maritime, disposal of ... 5310
false personation of person entitled to prize-money ... 5435

Section.

Prize—Continued.
endeavoring to obtain, &c., prize-money by forged power of attorney 5436
doing, or advising, &c., act relating to bringing in, custody, sale, &c., of property captured as, or to documents, &c., with intent to defraud 5441
Prize-Commissioners,
(see *Prize*.)
Prize-Money,
(see *Prize*.)
Probable Cause,
showing of, places burden of proof on claimant, in seizures under revenue laws .. 909
certificate of, in cases of seizure 970
costs not allowed claimant when seizure made with 970
no action against officer or prosecutor when seizure made with 970
informer, &c., not liable for defendant's cost, on discontinuance, &c., when officer authorized, &c., and probable cause certified 975
when certified, fees of clerk, marshal, &c.... 976
no execution to issue against revenue officer, but judgment to be paid out of Treasury 989
Probate Courts,
disposal of pension on certificate of, that mother has abandoned children, &c.. 4706
Process,
in civil-rights cases, execution of 1984
employment of military and naval forces to aid in execution of 1984
fees for execution of 1986
Proceedings in Bankruptcy,
(see *Bankruptcy*.)
"*Proceeds of Government Property*,"
receipts on account of, shall be covered into Treasury 3618
Proceeds of Sale,
(see *Sales*.)
Proclamation,
by President suspending discriminating duties on tonnage or impost of foreign vessels 4228
terminating exemption of Prussian vessels from discriminating duties 4230
of insurrection 5301
closing port of entry in insurrectionary district 5317
Proctors,
(see *Attorneys*.)
Professors,
at Military Academy, part of Army 1094
Professors of Mathematics in Navy,
number of 1399
relative rank of, on active list 1480
assignment of, at Naval Academy 1528
pay of 1556
Profits on Coinage,
not to be expended for wages, &c 3552
Prohibited Importations,
(see *Importations*.)
Prohibition,
writs of, issued by Supreme Court to district courts as courts of admiralty 688
Promotion in Navy,
of seamen to warrant-officers for heroism... 1407
of retired officers, not to increase pay 1591
Proof,
burden of, in seizures under impost or tonnage laws 909
to be made by certain Ottawa and Chippewa Indians, applicants for homesteads ... 2313
of distilled spirits, standard of 3249

Section.

Proof—Continued.
adding substances to create fictitious 3252
proof-gallon of distilled spirits, tax on 3251
in seizures of distilled spirits, (internal revenue) 3333
of debts in bankruptcy 5001
Property,
wrecked on Florida coast, how disposed of.. 4239
forfeiture of vessel conveying, to foreign port 4240
lost in military service, to be paid for ..3483–3488
appropriation to pay for 3689
of United States, attachment, &c., of, stipulation, release 3753, 3754
Proposals,
for supplies, shall be advertised for 3709
notice of opening; who may be present at. 3710
for public works 3717
for naval supplies 3718–3723
for carrying mail, advertising for 3941
falsely making, altering, forging, &c., uttering or publishing false, as true 5418
Proprietary Articles,
imported, to be stamped as prescribed in Schedule A 3435
medicines not exempt from internal-revenue tax 3436
tax on, Schedule A 3437
Pro-Rata Compensation,
when officers and agents of United States to be allowed only 2687
Prosecution,
against officer for acts done under revenue laws or Title ELECTIVE FRANCHISE... 643
costs of, for fine or forfeiture, to be paid by defendant when judgment against him.. 974
for other offenses, not capital, to be paid by defendant, on conviction 974
for violation of revenue laws, &c., in Alaska, where had 1957
Prospect, Me.,
port of delivery 2517
Protection and Relief of Seamen,
provisions relating to 4554–4591
Protesting National-Bank Notes,
manner of 5226
fees and expenses of, how paid 5238
Protest,
consular officers to receive, of United States citizens and foreigners 1707
by master, &c., of vessel seeking port in distress 2891
against decisions of collectors of customs as to duties, fees, charges, or exactions. 2931, 2932
customs duties paid under, money how credited 3010
suits to recover money paid for duties under. 3011
and appeal, refund of duties and moneys paid under 3012½
Providence, R. I.,
collection-district and port of entry 2531
collector and appraiser in, to reside at.... 2532
weighers, gaugers, measurers, and inspectors for 2606
transportation in bond extended to 2997
Provident Institutions,
for savings, tax on deposits in 3408
exemptions from tax 3408
returns from 3414
Provincetown, Mass.,
port of delivery 2527
Provisions,
what, to be carried by vessels transporting passengers between Europe and United States 4260
weekly delivery of 4260

Section.

Provisions—Continued.
penalty for supplying short allowance of.. 4261
how recovered.......... 4261
how cooked and furnished 4262
penalty for neglect, &c 4262
enforcement of penalty, not to release from civil responsibility 4262
what, to be carried by vessels between Atlantic and Pacific ports of United States. 4265
quantity to be carried by merchant vessels. 4564
complaint as to, how made.......... 4565
forfeiture for false complaint as to.......... 4566
permission to enter complaint guaranteed. 4567
allowance for reduction of, to be made...... 4568
for seamen, shall be weighed, when required 4571
scale of 4612
for Navy, contracts for..........3718–3722
Provisions and Clothing,
relative rank and title of Chief of Bureau of 1471
of retired Chief of Bureau of 1473
Provisions and Water,
(see *Provisions*.)
Provost-Marshals,
when to have pensions.......... 4693
rate of total-disability pension to 4695
pensions to widows, &c., of, when to begin. 4710
Proxies,
shareholders in national banks may give; who shall not act as 5144
Prussia,
exemption of vessels of, from discriminating duties 4229
duration of.......... 4230
termination of, how made.......... 4230
Public Accounts,
compensation of Members and Delegates of Congress passed as 46
decimal-money system extended to.......... 3563
contracts connected with, to be deposited with First Comptroller 3743
Publication,
of laws of territorial legislatures, provisions concerning.......... 1844
by register of land-office of notice of applications for mineral-lands 2325
Public Auction,
(see *Sales*.)
Public Buildings,
designation of disbursing-agent to pay moneys appropriated for.......... 255
limit of extra compensation for disbursing money for.......... 3654
estimates for erection of, how made 3663
appropriations for, shall be available at once. 3684
contracts for, not to exceed appropriations . 3733
plans and estimates required before commencement of.......... 3734
by whom to be approved 3734
contracting to pay, for erection, repair, or furnishing of, amount larger than appropriation 5503
Public Buildings and Grounds,
estimates, appropriations, and expenditures for, how made.......... 1798
employés in, number and employment of ... 1799
expense of water-mains in, to be paid by United States 1805
no ailantus trees to be purchased or planted in grounds 1830
Public Contracts,
(see *Contracts*.)
Public Debt,
United States notes not legal tender in payment of interest on..........3588–3590
permanent appropriation for payment of ... 3688

Section.

Public Debt—Continued.
for interest on 3689
appropriation for funding 3689
for sinking-fund.......... 3689
provisions concerning 3693–3708
interest on, coin received from duties set apart to pay 3694
shall be paid out of any money in Treasury. 3698
Secretary of Treasury may anticipate.... 3699
not payable in national-bank notes 5182
false personation of lawful holder of, in receiving money, &c 5435
endeavoring to obtain, &c., share or sum in, by forged power of attorney.......... 5436
Public Depositary,
(see *Designated Depositaries*.)
Public Documents,
Secretary of Interior charged with safe-keeping and distribution of.......... 497
register of, received and distributed by Department of Interior 499
provisions as to distribution of 500–506
superintendent of 507
duties of.......... 508
rooms provided for, in Department of Interior.......... 509
Public Improvements,
contract for, not to exceed appropriations.. 3733
knowingly contracting to pay for, amount larger than specific sum appropriated for such purpose 5503
Public Lands,
(see *Lands, Public*.)
Public Minister,
(see *Ministers*.)
Public Money,
accounts of expenditure of, to be settled within fiscal year.......... 250
transcripts from books, &c., of Treasury Department made evidence in suits against persons accountable for...... 886
in trial of indictment for embezzling..... 887
when judgment to be granted at return term, in suits by United States against persons accountable for 957
extra allowance for disbursement of, by officer having fixed salary 1765
territorial officers in Washington, Idaho, and Montana, to give security 1951
superintendents of mints to receive, &c., certain 3506
provisions respecting..........3591–3659
under control of United States Treasurer, where to be kept 3591
Carson and Denver mints and Boisé City assay-office to be places of deposit of. 3592
shall be subject to draft of Treasurer 3593
rooms, &c., of assistant treasurers to be places of deposit of.......... 3598
special agents to disburse, shall give bonds . 3614
to whom to be paid by collectors and receivers of, in certain places.......... 3615
when may be paid to any authorized depositary 3616
shall be deposited without deduction ..3617–3619
shall be drawn for only as required for use.. 3620
how kept where no public depository 3620
shall be deposited and receipted for.......... 3621
accounts of, shall be rendered monthly..... 3622
distinct accounts of disbursements, by appropriations 3623
neglect or refusal to deposit, &c.......... 3624
proceedings by distress-warrant, &c., against delinquent collectors, &c., of....3625–3638
to be safely kept, &c 3639

Section.

Public Money—Continued.
President may increase penalty of bonds of officers disbursing, &c. ... 3639
Secretary of Treasury may transfer ... 3640
Postmaster-General may transfer, belonging to his Department ... 3641
of Post-Office Department, accounts of, to be kept separate ... 3642
accounts of, to be kept in detail ... 3643
no advance of, shall be made ... 3648
in depositories shall be examined ... 3649, 3650
exchange of, restricted ... 3651
premiums on, to be accounted for ... 3652
compensation of depositaries of ... 3655
limit of ... 3656
how drawn for use of War and Navy Departments ... 3673
for postal service ... 3674
certain, to be credited to appropriations ... 3692
collected at post-offices, quarterly accounts of ... 3843–3845
to be safely kept by postmasters, without loaning, &c ... 3846
deposit of, by postmasters, in national banks. 3847
with assistant treasurers ... 3848
special agents Post-Office Department collecting, &c., to give bond ... 4018
when and what may be deposited in national banks ... 5153
unauthorizes depositing, converting, &c., loaning, withdrawing from deposit or applying, by disbursing officer ... 5488
failure of United States Treasurer or assistant treasurer, or of public depositary, safely to keep ... 5489
loaning, using, converting, &c., depositing in banks, exchanging for other funds, except, &c., by person charged with safe-keeping ... 5490
failure of officers receiving, to render accounts as provided by law ... 5491
of persons having, to deposit with treasurer, &c., when so required, &c ... 5492
application of sections 5488–5492 ... 5493
what shall be evidence of balance of, against defendant on trial of indictment for embezzlement of, under sections 5488–5493 ... 5494
what shall be prima facie evidence of embezzlement of, against person charged with safe-keeping, transfer, or disbursement of ... 5495
receiving, from disbursing officer, &c., on deposit, loan, &c., or using, converting, &c., by bankers, &c., not being authorized depositary ... 5497
by president, cashier, teller, director, &c., of any bank or banking association.. 5497
Public Offices,
(see *Offices.*)
Public Officers,
(see *Officers.*)
Public Packet,
when not required to make entry ... 2791
Public Printing and Binding,
(see *Government Printing-Office.*)
Public Property,
purchasing, from officer, &c., not authorized to sell, intended for military or naval service; action for ... 3490, 5438
proceeds of sales of certain, shall be covered into Treasury ... 3618
statement of, in book of estimates ... 3672
provisions concerning ... 3748–3755
money derived from sale of certain, to be deposited as postal revenue ... 4050

Section.

Public Record,
falsely making, altering, forging, &c., uttering as true any false, &c., for purpose, &c ... 5418
Public Stocks,
false personation of lawful holder of, in receiving money, &c ... 5435
endeavoring to obtain, &c., share of sum in, by means of forged power of attorney ... 5436
Public Stores,
(see *Warehouse.*)
Public Vessels,
excepted from provisions of Title REGULATION OF STEAM-VESSELS ... 4400
Public Works,
in District of Columbia, under whose charge. 1800
moneys appropriated for, under whose direction expended ... 1802
estimates for, how made ... 3663
Secretary of War to require separate proposals and contracts for ... 3717
contracts for, not to exceed appropriations. 3733
Puget Sound, W. T.,
collection-district ... 2586
collector in, residence of ... 2587
inspector of hulls and boilers for ... 4414
salaries of ... 4414
Pumps,
distillery, Commissioner of Internal Revenue may require changes of, or additions to. 3270
marine, steamers to be provided with suitable, for testing boilers ... 4471
Punishment,
in Navy, what may be inflicted by summary court-martial ... 1624
inflicted on seamen to be recorded in logbook ... 4290
of seamen, provisions relating to ... 4596–4612
inflicting cruel or unusual, on any of crew of American vessel ... 5347
Purchases,
on execution, when United States may make. 3470
when may be made in excess of appropriations ... 3732
of land on account of United States restricted ... 3736
of supplies, provisions respecting ... 3709–3743
Purloined Treasury-Notes,
credit to be allowed to officers innocently paying ... 3707

Q.

Qualifications, Pay, and Duties of Customs Officers,
provisions concerning ... 2613–2746
Quarantine,
established by health laws of States to be observed by United States officers ... 4792
discharge of cargo of vessels in ... 4793
erection of warehouses at ... 4794
deposit of goods therein ... 4795
time for entry of vessels subject to, may be extended ... 4796
Quarter-Dollar,
weight and fineness of ... 3513, 3514
deviation allowed in adjusting ... 3536
Quarter-Eagle,
weight and fineness ... 3511, 3514
deviation allowed in adjusting ... 3535
Quarterly Accounts of Postmasters,
shall be rendered to Postmaster-General ... 3843
neglect to render, penalty ... 3845
Quarterly Postage,
may be paid at office of mailing or delivery. 3906

Section.

Quarterly Returns,
of mails sent and received, disposal of..... 4060

Quartermaster's Department,
of Army, authorized..... 1094
organization of, and rank in..... 1132
duties of officers of..... 1133
to equip and supply naval detachments co-operating..... 1135
employment of forage and wagon-masters by..... 1137
officers of, to give bond..... 1191
President may increase penalty of bonds. 3639
quartermasters, jurisdiction of Court of Claims of claim by, for relief, &c..... 1059
when loss of funds, &c., by, found by Court of Claims to be without fault, credit to be allowed by accounting officers..... 1062
for artillery regiments..... 1099
for cavalry regiments..... 1102
for infantry regiments..... 1106
regimental, pay of..... 1261
forage allowed to..... 1371
sergeants, for regiment of artillery..... 1099
for battery of artillery..... 1100
for regiment of cavalry..... 1102
for troop of cavalry..... 1103
for regiment of infantry..... 1106
for company of infantry..... 1107
in militia, quartermasters of brigade..... 1631
one quartermaster-general for each State. 1631
rank of quartermasters in regiment of militia, called into United States service..... 1646
supplies, inspection of and advertisements for, on Pacific coast..... 3716

Quarters,
for army, of permanent nature, construction of..... 1136
for officers of Army, in kind..... 1270
rank of staff officers gives no additional right to..... 1487
to be furnished superintendents of national cemeteries..... 4875

Quebec,
consul at, salary of..... 1690

Quincy, Ill.,
port of delivery in district of New Orleans. 2568
surveyor to reside at, duties of..... 2569

Qui Tam Actions,
liability of plaintiff in, for defendant's costs. 975
to clerk, marshal, and attorney, for fees of prosecution..... 976

Quorum,
of supreme court in Territories..... 1864

Quo Warranto,
duty of district attorney to proceed by, against persons illegally holding office. 1786

R.

Racine, Wis.,
port of delivery..... 2597
deputy collector to reside at..... 2598

Railroads,
cars, laden with certain imports, to be exempt from manifest-fees..... 3007
sealed to avoid inspection at first port of arrival..... 3102
penalty for taking, &c., to other ports, unloading and selling contents, &c..... 3104
forfeiture of, from which locks, &c., unlawfully removed..... 3106
and engines, lost in military service to be paid for..... 3483, 3488
appropriation for..... 3689

Section.

Railroads—Continued.
iron for, partially worn, imported free, for re-manufacture, &c., re-exportation of. 3021
transporting empty stamped casks, &c., in violation of law..... 3324
contracts with, for carrying mail, without advertising..... 3942
pay to, for carrying mail..... 3998
when reasonable contract cannot be made with, mail may be carried by horse-express..... 3999
shall carry mail on any train, &c..... 4000
pay to land-grant, for carrying mail..... 4001
re-adjustment of pay to, for carrying mail.. 4002
refusal of, to furnish postal cars..... 4003
pay to, for furnishing postal cars..... 4004
postal service, superintendents of..... 4020
employment of clerks, &c., in..... 4025
when foreign, may own and employ tug or ferry-boat in United States..... 4370
Union Pacific..... 5256, 5257
right of, to carry passengers, troops, mails, freight, &c., from one State to another, and to form connection, &c.; saving of rights of United States..... 5258
to build new road or connection, &c., subject to consent of State..... 5258
pay of directors, engineers, commissioners, &c., appointed by United States..... 5259
payments for transportation or freights to be withheld by Secretary of Treasury to amount of interest paid by United States on bonds, &c., not re-imbursed by company..... 5260
right of such company to sue in Court of Claims..... 5261
(see *Common Carrier.*)

Rank,
relative, of Army and Navy officers..... 1466
in Navy, of chiefs of bureaus..... 1471
when line-officers..... 1472
of retired chiefs of bureaus..... 1473
of officers of Medical Corps..... 1474
relative, of Medical Corps..... 1474
of Pay Corps..... 1475
of Engineer Corps..... 1476
of naval constructors..... 1477
of assistant naval constructors..... 1477
of civil engineers..... 1478
of chaplains..... 1479
of professors of mathematics..... 1480
of staff-officers retired from age and length of service..... 1481
of staff-officers retired from causes incident to service..... 1482
assimilated, to warrant-officers..... 1491
of officers of revenue-cutter service, on duty with Navy..... 1492
of commandant of Marine Corps..... 1601
of staff of Marine Corps..... 1602
in militia, how determined..... 1638

Ransom-Money,
distribution of, to vessels of Navy, how made. 4642

Rappahannock River, Va.,
surveyor of customs to reside at or near mouth of, as President may designate..... 2553

Rates of Postage,
(see *Postage.*)

Rations,
in Army, Subsistence Department to supply. 1141
when to be furnished by officers of Subsistence Department to naval detachments..... 1143
credit sales of, to officers and enlisted men. 1144
purchase of, by officers in field..... 1145
component parts of..... 1146

Section.

Rations—Continued.
coffee and sugar commuted 1147
to hospital matrons and nurses........... 1277
to enlisted men, allowance of 1293
of sugar and coffee not issued, paid for in money 1294
to laundresses accompanying troops...... 1295
to matrons and nurses.................... 1295
purchased by officers on credit........... 1299
in Navy, to midshipmen and acting midshipmen 1577
to what other persons allowed 1578
to whom not allowed 1579
constituents of 1580
substitutions for parts of 1581
diminution or variance of daily allowance. 1582
stopped, for sick 1583
additional, of tea and coffee to seamen.... 1584
commutation price of..................... 1585
not allowed to retired officers 1595
to enlisted men of Marine Corps 1615
in militia, when in United States service.... 1650
what addition to, when in service on western frontiers 1655
to Indians visiting military posts 2110
in revenue-cutter service, to officers 2755
contracts for 2756
to Navy hospitals......................... 4812

Re-adjustment of Compensation,
for railway mail-service, basis of........... 4002
of postmasters, once in two years 3854
basis of 3855

Real Estate,
may be seized and sold for internal-revenue taxes 3196
notice of sale to be given 3197
time, place, and mode of sale 3197
may be purchased for United States...... 3197
adjournment of sale of.................... 3197
if amount bid not paid, to be resold 3197
when sold, certificate of purchase of...... 3198
deed of, in accordance with State laws.... 3198
effect of deed of.......................... 3199
collector may seize and sell, in any other district within State 3200
owner may redeem 3202
record of sales 3203
return by deputy collector of his proceedings in sale of.......................... 3203
Commissioner to have charge of sales, &c., of 3208
may sell at auction...................... 3208
in certain cases, may release to debtors. 3208
of delinquent collector of internal revenue, sale of, by marshal 3217
acquired by United States for debt, powers of Solicitor of Treasury as to management, sale, &c....................3749–3751
conveyed to individuals for use of United States, authority of President to obtain release of title 3752
in Territories, limit to right of religious, &c., associations to hold.................... 1890
held by such associations contrary, &c., to be forfeited 1890
provision not to impair vested rights in... 1890
when national banks may purchase, &c.... 5137

Rear-Admirals,
number of, on active list.................. 1363
pay of 1556

Re-assessment of Internal-Revenue Taxes,
may be made within fifteen months 3182

Rebate of Interest,
on payment of coupons of public debt before due 3699

Section

Rebellion,
effect of, on limitation of time for commencing civil or criminal proceedings..... 1048
militia may be called forth to suppress..... 1642
subject to rules and articles of war....... 1644
claims of persons who sustained, not to be paid 3480

Rebel Pensioners,
not to be paid pension 4716

Recapture,
of vessel; salvage.......................... 4652

Receipt or Prescription,
medicines compounded according to, exempt from internal-revenue tax............. 3436

Receipts,
to be given by internal-revenue collectors, and deputies, for sums collected...... 3183
making or using, by civilians, of false, to obtain approval, &c., of claim against United States, action for.........3490, 5438
delivery by civilians, of less money or property than described in, action for.3490, 5438
giving, by civilians, for property for military or naval service, with fraudulent intent, &c., action for 3490, 5438
at post-offices, quarterly account of, by postmasters 3843
neglect to render 3845
for purchase-money of lands, falsifying, &c., uttering false, as true, &c............. 5420
falsely making, &c., with intent to obtain money from United States; uttering false, as true, &c..................... 5421
having in possession false, &c., with intent to defraud United States.............. 5422
officer paying to clerk, &c., less than lawful sum, and requiring receipt for amount greater than paid, guilty of embezzlement, &c................................ 5483

Receivers
of national banks, jurisdiction of circuit courts of all suits by associations to enjoin, &c 629
may be appointed on failure to make capital equal to legal minimum 5141
when reserve is not made good.......... 5191
on failure to redeem notes 5195
when bank continues to own its own stock 5201
on refusal to make good impaired capital 5205
when; bond, duty, report of............ 5234
when and how may be enjoined, effect of. 5237
fees and expenses of, how paid........... 5238
of public moneys, (see *Public Moneys*.)
of land-offices, (see *Lands, Public*.)

Receiving-Boxes,
for letters, &c., provisions relating to ..3865–3874
where may be established................ 3868
expenses of, how limited................. 3874

Receiving-Cisterns,
(see *Cisterns*.)

Recess of Senate,
salary to person appointed during, to fill vacancy existing 1761

Reclamation of Deserters,
duty of consular officers in 4600

Recoinage,
(see *Coinage*.)

Recorded Vessels,
(see *Vessels*.)

Recorder of General Land-Office,
appointment and salary of.................. 447
to countersign patents for land 458
duties of.................................. 459
in absence of, who to act 459

Section.

Recording of Vessels,
(see *Vessels.*)
Records,
to be kept by collector of internal revenue, of sales of real estate ... 3203
to be delivered to successor ... 3203
to be evidence in any court ... 3203
entry of redemption to be made on ... 3204
of special taxes ... 3240
of distillery operations, storekeeper's entries to be made in ... 3302
of tobacco and snuff manufacturers ... 3357
of cigar-makers and manufacturers ... 3389
of bills of sale, mortgages, &c., of vessels .. 4193
index of record to be kept ... 4194
certified copies of, to be furnished, &c ... 4195
fee for furnishing ... 4195
to be kept by local inspectors of steam-vessels ... 4457
(see *Copies.*)
Recruit,
premium for each, accepted ... 1120
Rectified Spirits,
stamp for, form of ... 3320
Rectifiers, (*Internal Revenue,*)
penalty and forfeiture for doing business without paying special tax ... 3242
business not to be carried on within 600 feet of distillery ... 3244
special tax of ... 3244
definition of ... 3244
penalty for failing to give, or giving false, notice ... 3259
notice of intention to carry on business of .. 3259
of change of business ... 3259
to furnish facilities for examination of premises, penalty ... 3277
officer, &c., may break up ground or walls of, to search for concealed pipe, &c .. 3278
to put up signs ... 3279
returns of ... 3317
book to be kept by ... 3318
restrictions on purchase of distilled spirits .. 3319
gauging and stamping of casks or packages of rectified spirits ... 3320
penalty for violating law where no specific penalty ... 3456
Rectifier's and Wholesale Liquor-Dealer's Book,
penalties relative thereto ... 3318
form of, to be prescribed by Commissioner of Internal revenue ... 3318
entries to be made in ... 3318
to be kept open to inspection ... 3318
to be preserved two years ... 3318
Red-Cedar Timber,
lands containing, to be explored and selected for use of Navy ... 2458
cutting or destroying, &c., on land reserved by United States, penalty ... 2461
vessels carrying away such timber forfeited ... 2462
Redemption,
of real estate sold for internal-revenue taxes. 3202
of fractional currency ... 3574
of United States notes, &c ... 3575
of internal-revenue stamps, appropriation for ... 3689
of five-twenty bonds ... 3697
of circulating notes of national banks, proceedings on failure to provide for ... 5195
by Treasurer ... 5224
protest on failure of ... 5226
proceedings on notice of failure of ... 5227
business after failure of ... 5228
accounts of national banks in liquidation, shall be kept ... 5222

Section.

Redemption—Continued.
when notes shall be charged to ... 5225
agencies of national banks, shall be selected; public notice of ... 5195
Reduction,
of capacity of distillery ... 3311
of currency, authority for, suspended ... 3582
of wages under eight-hour law, appropriation to refund ... 3689
of capital of national banks, proceedings ... 5143
Re-enlistment,
in Army, pay of men on ... 1282
under honorable discharge ... 1284
Re-exportation,
when arriving, vessels may proceed with goods for, without payment of duties. 2776
when and by whom bond for, to be given. 2776, 2777
of rejected drugs, medicines, &c., imported. 2937
Refined Bars,
to be reported by mint superintendents ... 3503
Refugees,
accounts for expenses incurred in relief of .. 2034
Refunding,
customs duties by Secretary of Treasury on goods destroyed, &c., by accident ... 2984
paid under protest and appeal ... 3012½
not so paid ... 3013
taxes, Commissioner of Internal Revenue may allow ... 3220
on distilled spirits destroyed by casualty . 3221
claims for, when to be presented, limitation ... 3228
of distiller's special tax ... 3245
of tax on tobacco, snuff, and cigars ... 3379
(see *Appropriations.*)
Regents of Smithsonian Institution,
(see *Smithsonian Institution.*)
Regiments,
in Army, number of ... 1094
of artillery, composition of ... 1099
of cavalry ... 1102
of infantry ... 1106
in militia, in State service ... 1630
officers and staff of ... 1631
colors for ... 1633
in United States service ... 1646
Registered Bonds,
(see *United States Bonds.*)
Registered Letters,
(see *Letters.*)
Registered Vessels,
(see *Vessels.*)
Register,
of burials at national cemeteries, how kept .. 4877
of seamen shall be kept by shipping-commissioners ... 4508
of vessels, (see *Vessels.*)
tonnage, (see *Vessels.*)
of land-office, (see *Lands, Public.*)
in bankruptcy, (see *Bankruptcy.*)
Register of Treasury,
not to engage in certain business ... 243
appointment and salary of ... 312
duties of ... 313
shall keep appropriation accounts ... 3675
to attest certificates of registry of vessels .. 4158
to keep record of ... 4158
to cancel ... 4170
changes of masters of vessels to be reported to ... 4171
to cancel certificates of registry of lost, &c., vessels ... 4174
to notify collectors of such cancellation .. 4174
Registry,
(internal revenue,) of persons liable to special taxes ... 3233

Section.

Registry—Continued.
of death, removal, &c., of persons having paid special tax ... 3241
of cigar-makers ... 3244
of stills and distilling apparatus set up .. 3258
of United States court, failure of officer of court, to deposit moneys belonging to. 5504
knowingly receiving as deposit, loan, &c., moneys belonging to ... 5505
of vessels, (see *Vessels.*)
Regular Army,
officers and soldiers, when to have pension .. 4693
rate of total-disability pension to ... 4695
officers to have pension according to rank .. 4696
Regular Navy,
when pension to dependent relatives of persons killed, &c., in, to begin ... 4710
Re-imbursement of United States,
for money advanced to pay interest or principal of defaulting State stocks ... 3481
Re-importation,
of merchandise, Secretary of Treasury to make regulations to prevent illegal .. 3057
Re-imported Articles,
once exported, of growth, &c., of United States, duties on ... 2500
Rejection of Bids,
for naval supplies, certain, authorized ... 3722
Rejections of Nominations,
a list of, to be furnished by Secretary of Senate to Secretary of Treasury, Auditors, and Comptrollers at end of session ... 1775
Relading,
of vessels in distress, inspection of ... 2894
of cargoes of Spanish vessels seeking port in distress, no charges, &c ... 2895
Relanding Spirits,
which have been shipped for exportation ... 3330
Release,
of real estate, by Commissioner of Internal Revenue, to debtor, in certain cases .. 3208
of distillery seized, in certain cases ... 3331
for wages, shall be signed on discharge of seamen ... 4551
Relief and Protection of Seamen,
(see *Seamen.*)
Religious, &c., Associations,
limit to right of, to hold real estate in Territories ... 1890
forfeiture for violation ... 1890
Remarriage,
of widows, pension to go to children on 4702
not to bar right to date of; pension to cease on ... 4708
disposal of half-pay pension on widows 4725
Remission,
(internal revenue,) of taxes, may be made by Commissioner ... 3220
of forfeitures, by Secretary of Treasury .. 3461
of fines, &c., (see *Fines, Penalties, and Forfeitures.*)
Removal,
of suit, against officer for acts done under revenue laws, or of provisions of Title XXVI, THE ELECTIVE FRANCHISE 643
of personal action by alien against civil officer non-resident in State where brought ... 644
from office, contrary to law, penalty for 1772
of place of business of person having paid special tax ... 3241
of fermented liquors under permit ... 3345
Rendezvous,
allowance of pay, &c., to militia from place of residence to, when called into United States service ... 1652

Section.

Rendezvous—Continued.
expenses of march to, by militia in United States service, how paid ... 1654
Renewal of Money-Orders,
how obtained ... 4036, 4037
Rent,
of post-offices, allowance for ... 3860
light and fuel for post-offices, accounts to show expenditures for ... 4049
of prisons, &c., for American convicts in foreign countries, allowance for .. 4121–4124
Repairs to Vessels,
of Navy, to hull and spars, limited ... 1538
to sails and rigging, limited ... 1539
on northern, &c., frontiers, refund of duties on ... 3115
enrollment and license, not to issue, until accounted for ... 3115
to be made on steam-vessels on notice of inspectors ... 4453
penalty for refusal ... 4454
inspectors of another district may order .. 4455
Repayment,
to purchaser of public land, where sale is erroneously made and cannot be confirmed ... 2363, 2364
to collectors of internal revenue, and other officers, of money recovered of them for acts done in performance of duties. 3220
of excess of deposits of unascertained duties, appropriation for ... 3689
Repeal,
of statutes, effect of ... 12, 13
provisions relative to ... 5596–5601
Replevin,
property taken or detained, &c., under revenue laws, not subject to ... 934
Reporter,
to House of Representatives, employment of. 54
of decisions of Supreme Court ... 677
duties of ... 681
salary of ... 682
to courts-martial in Army ... 1203
Reports,
of Supreme Court, price of ... 682
distribution of ... 683
appropriation for 300 copies of ... 3689
failure or refusal of officer to make; penalty. 1780
of bureau officers, &c., in Departments, how to be printed ... 3788
of Postmaster-General of offers and contracts for carrying mail, when to be printed ... 3797
number of annual, of Departments, to be printed ... 3798
of national banks, (see *National Banks.*)
Representatives in Congress,
salary of ... 35
Representatives, Old Hall of,
provisions concerning statuary in; Chief of Engineers to have supervision of ... 1814
Reprieves,
may be granted by governors of Territories, for what offenses ... 1841
Request Letters,
shall be returned to writer ... 3939
Request to Return,
may be printed on stamped envelopes ... 3915
Requisitions,
what moneys paid on, of Secretary of Senate. 56
for money for Department of Justice ... 369
for money for War and Navy Departments .. 3673
Rescuing,
property, &c., seized by internal-revenue officer ... 3177

Section.

Rescuing—Continued.
property taken or detained by officer, &c., under revenue-law 5446
property seized by customs-officers, or by persons assisting him 5447
Reservations on Contracts,
with Navy Department, may be relinquished. 3730
Reservations, (Public Lands,)
(see *Lands, Public.*)
Reserved Fund,
(see *National Banks.*)
Resident Mail-Agents,
employment of, authorized; salaries, &c., of. 4021
Resisting,
customs-officer, &c., in execution of his duty. 5447
Resolving Clause,
form of 8
Respites,
may be granted by governors of Territories. 1841
Restamping,
of distilled spirits from which stamps have been lost or destroyed 3315
Restraining Suits,
to prevent assessment or collection of internal-revenue tax not to be maintained. 3224
Resumption of Work,
at distillery 3310
Retail Dealers,
in cigars, (see *Dealers in Cigars.*)
in leaf-tobacco, (see *Dealers in Leaf-Tobacco.*)
in malt liquors, (see *Dealers in Malt Liquors.*)
in liquor, (see *Dealers in Liquor.*)
Retained Bounty-Fund,
of colored soldiers, custody and use of..2035, 2036
Retired List,
of Army, (see *Army.*)
of marine corps, (see *Marine Corps.*)
of Navy, (see *Pay of Navy.*)
Returns,
failure or refusal of officer to make; penalty. 1780
of customs inspectors, of unlading of cargo..2888, 2889
internal-revenue, to be made by all persons liable to tax; penalty 3173
of collector or deputy, penalty in case of fraudulent, or neglect to make 3176
to be stated in legal-tender or coin 3178
when in coin, to be reduced to legal tender. 3178
of special taxes 3233
daily, by gauger 3291, 3314
daily and monthly by storekeeper 3301
by distillers 3307
monthly, of stamps for distilled spirits, by collector 3314
by rectifiers 3317
by brewers 3337
by tobacco or snuff manufacturer 3358
by cigar manufacturer 3390
by banks, &c 3414
militia, of condition of arms, &c 1635
annual, by adjutant-general in each State to President; instructions by Secretary of War 1636
by brigade-inspector to adjutant-general of State 1640
Returns-Office,
what contracts to be filed in 512
clerk in 512
manner of filing and numbering returns 513
index of returns, how to be kept 514
certified copies of returns, how furnished... 515
copy of return of contract filed in, when and how evidence 888
of Interior Department, copies of contracts, &c., to be sent to 3744

Section.

Revel,
consul at, salary of 1690
Revenue-Cutter Service,
relative rank of officers of, serving with Navy 1492
for what purpose maintained; expense of, how paid 2747
vessels unfit for service to be sold; unexpended balance of proceeds 2748
officers and men of 2749
grades of engineers in, rank and pay 2750
commissioned officers in, how appointed 2751
qualifications of 2752
compensation of 2753
rations of 2755
wages of petty officers and seamen in 2754
when to co-operate with Navy, under whose direction, expenses of 2757
service of, for protection of revenue, by whom directed 2758
on lakes, to aid vessels in distress 2759
officers of, to be deemed officers of customs, powers and duties of 2760
masters of, to make weekly returns to collector, &c 2761
additional duties of officers of, by whom directed 2762
how distinguished, ensign and pendant of.. 2764
when masters of, may fire at vessels not bringing to; indemnity for damages; bail. 2765
officers of, at Norfolk, duties of, to vessels bound up James River 2835
officers, when to board vessel, &c., and make search, powers of, &c 3059, 3067
master of vessel obstructing, &c., penalty. 3068
proceeds of sale of vessels of, not to be covered into Treasury 3618
disposal of 3692
officers, &c., of, when to have pensions 4741
admission of persons belonging to, to Government Hospital for Insane 4843
when President may employ vessels in addition to 5318
Revenue-Flag,
who to prescribe 2764
Revenue-Laws,
regulations for enforcement of, prescribed by Secretary of Treasury 251
jurisdiction of circuit court of suits under.. 629
for injuries to plaintiff for acts done under. 629
removal of suits or prosecutions from State to circuit court, against officer, &c., for acts done under 643
final judgments of circuit court in actions by United States for enforcement of, reviewed in Supreme Court 699
district attorneys to prosecute for fines, penalties, &c., under; report, compensation 838
when two or more things belonging to same person are seized for violation of, all joined in one suit 920
property taken or detained under, irreplevіable 934
limitation of time for indicting, or instituting information under 1046
extended over Alaska 1954
enforcement and violation of provisions concerning customs 3058–3094
for protection of seizing-officers extended to officers seizing under postal laws 3991
rescuing, or attempting to rescue, property taken or detained under 5446
Revenue-Marine Service,
(see *Revenue-Cutter Service.*)

Section.

Revenue-Officers,
removal of suits against, from State to circuit court 643
review by Supreme Court of judgment of circuit court in action against 699
district attorney to appear for, in action against 771
transcript from books, &c., of Treasury Department made evidence in suit against, for delinquency, &c 886
when execution not to issue against, in suit for acts done, or money exacted, &c 989
trading in public property 1789
may be removed from port when contagious or epidemic disease prevails 4797
rescuing property taken or detained by 5446
falsely assuming to be, and in such character demanding money, &c 5448
Revenue-Stamps,
fractional currency receivable for 3574
appropriation to redeem 3689
secreting, embezzling, or taking away implements, paper, &c., used in printing, &c 5453
Revenues, (Postal Service,)
provisions relating to 4049–4061
Revised Statutes,
(see *Statutes.*)
Revolutionary Pensions,
(see *Pensions.*)
Rhinebeck Landing, N. Y.,
port of delivery 2535
Rhode Island,
collection-districts, ports of entry and delivery in 2531
officers in 2532
privilege of coasting-vessels trading between, and Long Island 4357
Rhubarb,
grown in United States; exemptions of wines, &c., made from 3328
Richmond, Va.,
collection-district and port of entry 2552
collector and surveyor in, to reside at 2553
vessels loaded in Petersburgh district may be cleared at, in certain cases 2554
vessels arriving in district of, what to do 2836
balances with national banks in, may be part of reserve 5192
redemption agencies 5195
Riflemen,
companies of, how formed in militia 1632
Rights of Citizens,
(see *Civil Rights.*)
Rio de Janeiro,
consul at, salary of 1690
Rio Grande,
consul at, salary of 1690
River-Steamers,
navigating waters flowing into Gulf of Mexico or their tributaries, lights on 4233
Rivers and Harbors,
provisions concerning 5244–5255
Robbinston, Me.,
port of delivery 2517
Rochester, Mass.,
port of delivery 2527
vessels belonging to Sippican and Mattapoisett Harbors, Mass., in township of, how described 2528
Rock Island,
establishment of military prison at 1344
Rome,
consul-general at, salary of 1690
consul at, salary of 1690

Section.

Roots,
to be third-class mail-matter 3878
Rotterdam,
consul at, salary of 1690
Rouse's Point, N. Y.,
deputy collector to reside at 2536
Route-Agents,
shall receive way-letters for mailing, &c 3980
employment, &c., of 4024
Roxbury, Mass.,
port of delivery 2527
Royalty,
none to be paid by United States to officers for use of patent for Springfield breech-loading system 1673
Rules,
for navigation of vessels, (see *Navigation.*)
Russia,
salaries of minister and secretary to 1675

S.

Sabanilla,
commercial-agent at, salary of 1690
Sabine, Tex.,
port of delivery 2578
deputy collector to reside at, powers of 2579
Saccharometers,
to be adopted, and prescribed for use, by Commissioner of Internal Revenue 3249
Saco, Me.,
collection-district and port of entry 2517
collector in, residence of 2518
Sacramento, Cal.,
inspector of customs to reside at 2583
Saddlers,
for troops of cavalry 1103
Saddler-Sergeants,
for regiments of cavalry 1102
Safety-Valves,
(see *Inspection of Steam-Vessels.*)
Sag Harbor, N. Y.,
collection-district and port of entry 2535
collector in, to reside at 2536
surveyor in, residence of 2536
cargoes for Greenport, N. Y., to be entered and duties paid at 2537
Sailing-Vessel,
pay to, for carrying foreign mail 4009
what deemed a 4233
Sailmakers in Navy,
number and appointment of 1405
assimilated rank to 4491
pay of 1556
Sailors in Navy,
(see *Seamen.*)
Saint Augustine, Fla.,
collection-district and port of entry 2562
collector to reside at 2563
Saint Catherine,
consul at, salary of 1690
Saint George, Me.,
port of delivery 2517
Saint George, Island of,
(see *Alaska.*)
Saint Helena,
consul at, salary of 1690
Saint John's, Fla.,
collection-district 2562
President may select port of entry in, on St. John's river 2562
collector in, residence of 2563
Saint John's, Quebec,
consul at, salary of 1690
Saint Joseph, Mo.,
port of delivery in district of New Orleans .. 2568
surveyor to reside at, duties of 2569

Section.

Saint Louis, Mo.,
port of delivery in district of New Orleans.. 2568
surveyor and appraiser to reside at, duties of. 2569
weighers, gaugers, measurers, and inspectors for 2606
transportation in bond extended to 2997
assistant treasurer at, appointment, pay, &c., of 3595–3597
clerks, &c., in office of assistant treasurer at. 3607
collectors and receivers of public money shall pay to assistant treasurer 3615
inspectors of hulls and boilers for 4414
their salaries 4414
reserve of national banks in 5191
balances with banks in, may be part of reserve 5192
redemption agencies 5195

Saint Mark's, Fla.,
collection-district and port of delivery 2562
collector in, residence of 2563

Saint Mary's, Ga.,
collection-district and port of entry 2559
collector to reside at 2560

Saint Mary's, Md.,
port of delivery 2548
surveyor to reside at 2549

Saint Paul, Minn.,
port of delivery 2595
deputy collector to reside at 2596

Saint Paul de Loando,
commercial agent at, salary of 1690

Saint Paul, Island of,
(see *Alaska*.)

St. Petersburg,
consul at, salary of 1690

Saint Thomas,
consul at, salary of 1690
resident mail-agent at, authorized 4021

Salaries,
payment of, to persons holding unauthorized office 1760
to persons appointed during recess of Senate, to fill vacancy existing while Senate in session 1761
to persons holding office contrary to sections 1767–1770, "tenure of office act". 1762
two, not to be paid for two offices 1763
none to officers or clerks for performing duties of others 1764
none to person in arrears to United States.. 1766
territorial officers to be paid under United States laws 1855
apportionment of, for part of year's service. 2687
to collectors of internal revenue not confirmed by Senate 3145
no payment of, to collectors of internal revenue without certificate of Commissioner 3147
estimates for, shall be founded on express provisions of law 3662
of steamboat-inspectors, appropriation for.. 3689

Salem and Beverly, Mass.,
collection-district 2527
collector and surveyor in, residence of 2529

Salem, Mass.,
port of entry 2527
collector and surveyor to reside at 2529

Salem, N. J.,
port of delivery 2541

Saleratus,
may be manufactured where spirits are distilled 3266

Sales,
of gold, Secretary of Treasury may cause... 3699
of wages of seamen, not to prevent payment to 4536

Section.

Sales—Continued.
of vessels, goods, &c., condemned under customs-revenue laws, how made, distribution, &c 939
may be ordered by judge, in vacation 940
of damaged military stores 1241
of public armed vessels by order of President. 1540
of vessels and materials by Secretary of Navy. 1541
report of, to Congress 1541
of useless revenue-cutters 2748
proceeds may be expended by Secretary of Treasury 2748
of abandoned goods in bonded warehouse... 2971
proceeds of, how distributed 2972
of goods in public store after one year; balance of proceeds 2973
overplus of proceeds of, to be paid into Treasury; account of; when paid to owner 2974
of perishable and explosive articles in bonded warehouse 2975
of unclaimed perishable goods in public warehouse 2976
of imports prior to entry, &c., not to affect ownership 3058
of property seized; proceeds of; adjournments of 3077
proceeds of, when restored, &c 3078
by whose order distributed 3079
of perishable articles seized under customs-laws; proceeds of 3080
under distraint for internal-revenue taxes.. 3186–3195
of real estate for internal-revenue taxes. 3196–3205
of property of delinquent collector of internal revenue 3217
of distilled spirits, what taken to be gallon therein 3250
of goods not transferred from unfit warehouse, as required by Commissioner of Internal Revenue 3272
of distilled spirits by order of court or under distraint, to be subject to tax 3334
of tobacco, snuff, and cigars under distraint, or by order of court or officer 3369
of cigars at retail 3392
of forfeited boilers, still, machinery, materials, &c., at public auction 3450
of goods, &c., with intent to evade tax 3454
whiskey, tobacco, &c., under distraint, &c., to be branded, stamped, and marked. 3458
of property forfeited under section 3453 3459
of goods seized under section 3460 3460
of prize property which cannot be taken into port for adjudication; proceeds to be deposited 4615
of prize property, by order of court; proceeds. 4628
auctioneer, to be employed by Secretary of Navy 4628
to be conducted under supervision of marshal 4628
duties of marshal with respect to 4628
duties of marshal when property is transferred to another district 4629
proceeds 4629
of marine-hospital buildings and lands 4806
of public lands, (see *Lands, Public*.)

Salisbury, Mass.,
port of delivery 2527

Salisbury, Md.,
port of delivery 2548

Saloon-Stores,
purchased for vessels on northern, &c., frontiers 3113

Section.

Salt,
imported; how unladen opposite New Orleans ... 2897
imported in bond, for use in curing fish; remission of duties on ... 3022
Salt and Coal,
time for unlading from vessels extended ... 2881
Saltpeter,
meaning of term in certain cases ... 3026
drawback on ... 3026
Salt Provisions,
anti-scorbutics to be served with, to seamen ... 4569
penalty for failure ... 4570
Saluria, Tex.,
collection-district ... 2578
officers in, residence of ... 2579
Salvador,
(see *Guatemala.*)
Salvage,
seamen cannot abandon claim for ... 4535
distribution of, to vessels of Navy, how made ... 4642–4652
in cases of recapture ... 4652
to be paid from Treasury, when ... 4652
to be paid by owners, when ... 4652
of vessels, &c., by privateers, part of, to go to privateer pension-fund ... 4759
Samples,
of imported sugar, how and by whom taken ... 2915
of imported wool and hair, to determine class, how prepared and where kept ... 2916
of merchandise, third-class mail-matter ... 3878
of metals, ores, &c., weight of, in mails ... 3878
San Antonio, Tex.,
port of delivery ... 2578
inspector of customs to reside at ... 2580
San Diego, Cal.,
collection-district and port of entry ... 2582
officers in; collector to reside at ... 2583
appointment of inspectors, weighers, &c., for ... 2607
San Domingo,
commercial agent at, salary of ... 1690
Sandusky, Ohio,
collection-district and port of entry ... 2603
collector to reside at ... 2604
additional inspectors for ... 2605
Sandwich, Mass.,
port of delivery ... 2527
San Elizario, Tex.,
inspector of customs to reside at ... 2580
San Francisco, Cal.,
collection-district and port of entry ... 2582
officers of customs in, residence of ... 2583
weighers, gaugers, measurers, and inspectors for ... 2606
transportation in bond extended to ... 2997
assistant treasurer at, appointment, &c., of ... 3595–3597
clerks, &c., in office of ... 3610
collectors and receivers of public money shall pay to ... 3615
salaries to letter-carriers in ... 3866
inspectors of hulls and boilers for ... 4414
their salaries ... 4414
reserve of national banks in ... 5191
balances with banks in, may be part of reserve ... 5192
redemption agencies ... 5195
mint at, (see *Mint.*)
San Juan del Norte,
commercial agent at, salary of ... 1690
San Juan del Sur,
consul at, salary of ... 1690
San Juan, (Porto Rico,)
consul at, salary of ... 1690

Section.

San Pedro, Cal.,
port of delivery ... 2582
inspector for, appointment of ... 2583
Santa Barbara, Cal.,
port of delivery ... 2582
inspector for, appointment of ... 2583
Santa Cruz,
consul at, salary of ... 1690
Santarem,
consul at, salary of ... 1690
Santiago, (Cape Verde,)
consul at, salary of ... 1690
Santiago de Cuba,
consul at, salary of ... 1690
Sault Sainte Marie, Mich.,
port of delivery ... 2599
deputy collector to reside at ... 2600
Savannah, Ga.,
collection-district and port of entry ... 2559
officers in, residence of ... 2560
collector of customs at, may grant permits to unload vessels in Brunswick district, appoint inspectors, &c ... 2561
transportation in bond extended to ... 2997
inspectors of hulls and boilers for ... 4414
their salaries ... 4414
Savings,
deposits of, by enlisted men in Army ... 1305
interest on ... 1306
regulations for ... 1307
when payable ... 1308
Savings-Banks,
internal-revenue tax on ... 3408
returns from ... 3414
use of word "national" in title ... 5243
Saybrook, Conn.,
port of delivery ... 2533
Scarborough, Me.,
port of delivery ... 2517
Schedule A, (Internal Revenue,)
penalty for selling, &c., articles in, without proper stamps ... 3430, 3432
for removing or misusing stamps on articles in ... 3431
stamps for drugs, medicines, &c ... 3436
persons offering for sale articles in, to be deemed manufacturers of ... 3435
articles in, imported, subject to stamp tax in addition to duties ... 3435
articles taxable under ... 3437
Schedules,
of goods for interior ports, to be deposited with surveyors thereat ... 2825
of forms, fees, &c., to Title MERCHANT SEAMEN ... 4612
Scientific Institutions,
articles for, free of duty ... 2505
may withdraw alcohol from bond for scientific purposes without payment of internal-revenue tax ... 3297
Scituate, Mass.,
port of delivery ... 2527
Scouts,
(see *Indians.*)
Scraps, Refuse,
(see *Tobacco.*)
Sea-coast of United States,
divided into three great districts ... 4348
Sea-Letters,
(see *Vessels.*)
Sea-Service,
definition of ... 1571
Sea-Stores,
exempt from duty, how specified ... 2795
how duty on excess of, estimated ... 2796
when forfeited ... 2797

Section.

Sea-Stores—Continued.
of vessels on northern, &c., frontiers....... 3111
when free of duty, excess of................ 3112

Seal,
on instruments provided by law, how affixed. 6
of General Land-Office, custody of.......... 454
of Patent-Office, use of 478
of United States, Secretary of State to have custody of 203
what declared to be 1793
by whom kept and affixed to civil commissions, and at what time.............. 1794

Sealed Proposals,
(see *Proposals.*)

Seal-Fishery,
(see *Alaska.*)

Seals and Presses,
shall be furnished to diplomatic and consular officers 1748

Seals, (*Customs and Internal Revenue,*)
(see *Locks and Seals.*)

Seamen,
in merchant service,
reports of collectors, &c., respecting, to be sent to Congress by Secretary of State. 207
compensation, of, when sent home from foreign port as witnesses 851
consular officers shall keep record of........ 1708
not to receive fees for services to......... 1719
penalty for neglect of duty by 1736
alien, how naturalized..................... 2174
when to be deemed citizens 2174
when entitled to protection as destitute citizens 2174
conviction and punishment of, to be recorded in log-book 4290
offenses committed by 4290
statement of conduct and character 4290
illness, or injury to...................... 4290
death of, during voyage 4290
wages due deceased 4290
sale of effects 4290
to sign entries in log-books, when.......... 4291
provisions concerning 4501–4612
duties of shipping-commissioners as to..... 4508
manner of procuring apprentices 4509
indentures of apprentices.................. 4510
shipping articles of, form, terms, &c., of 4511
wages, advances, and allotments of, shall be specified in........................ 4511
rules for signing, &c. of................... 4512
on certain vessels, may reship, &c., without fee to commissioners................. 4513
penalty for carrying, without articles 4514
for accepting seamen illegally shipping... 4515
how deserters, &c., may be replaced........ 4516
copy of articles to be posted up............ 4519
how, may be shipped in foreign ports....... 4517
in coasting trade 4520
penalty for illegally shipping 4518, 4521
forfeiture of wages for breach of articles by. 4522
illegal shipment of, void; recovery of wages. 4523
wages, when to commence 4524
not to depend on freight-earnings 4525
to terminate with loss of vessel 4526
in case of improper discharge............. 4527
when, may be suspended 4528
time for payment of 4529
payment of, at intermediate ports 4530
allotment of.............................. 4531
advances of 4532
unlawful advances of, recovery 4533
discount of advance security, recovery ... 4534
lien on ship for.......................... 4535
cannot abandon right to salvage 4535
wages, not liable to attachment, &c....... 4536

Section.

Seamen—Continued.
sale of, not to prevent payment to seamen. 4536
amount recoverable from, during voyage.. 4537
entry of, in log-book...................... 4538
deceased, wages and effects of............... 4538
rules of procedure in regard to........... 4539
penalty for neglect, &c., in regard to..... 4540
duty of consuls in regard to 4541
proceedings in regard to wages and effects of, dying in United States 4542–4545
fund for relief of destitute, created......... 4545
wages, summons to show cause in case of non-payment of 4546
libel for, of vessel 4547
when paid abroad to be in gold 4548
on discharge, shall be paid before shipping-commissioner 4549
discharge of, how conducted 4549
account of wages shall be rendered 4550
certificate of discharge on payment........ 4551
rules for settlement of wages 4552
certificate of character 4553
arbitration of disputes with master....4554, 4555
proceedings before shipping-commissioners relative to wages.................... 4555
majority of crew may demand survey of vessel 4556, 4559
proceedings on survey..................... 4557
cost of unnecessary survey may be deducted from wages of complaining.......4557, 4562
refusal to sail when vessel found seaworthy. 4558
complaint of unseaworthiness in foreign ports 4559
report on, by inspectors in foreign ports.. 4560
discharge of seamen by consul after...... 4561
extra wages to be paid on discharge from unseaworthy vessel..................... 4561
refusal to pay, penalty.................... 4563
survey of provisions may be demanded by.. 4565
forfeiture of wages for false complaint as to provisions 4566
permission to complain guaranteed to...... 4567
allowances for reduction of provisions, &c., recoverable as wages 4568
medicines, anti-scorbutics, &c., shall be provided for............................ 4569
penalty for neglect to serve to 4570
provisions, &c., to, shall be weighed, &c., on demand.............................. 4571
clothing and fuel for use of, to be carried... 4572
list of, on vessels, to be furnished collector of customs before clearance 4573
shall be certified by collector 4574
and shipping articles shall be carried on vessels............................. 4575
bond for return of, to United States required. 4576
destitute, &c., care, &c., of, by consular officers 4577
shall be returned to United States......... 4577
penalty for refusal by vessels of United States to carry 4578
pay to vessels for carrying................ 4579
when consular officer may require discharge. 4580
extra wages, when and how paid on discharge in foreign port 4580
penalty for neglect of consular officer to collect 4581
to be collected on sale of vessel in foreign port 4582
when, may be remitted.................... 4583
discharge in case of wreck.................. 4583
extra wages, on discharge, disposal of, by consular officer........................ 4584
part of, to be fund for destitute, and for transportation to United States...... 4584
hospital-tax to be collected, &c., and retained from 4585

Section.

Seamen—Continued.
by consular officer, if vessel sold abroad.. 4586
must be paid before documenting of vessel. 4587
certificate of citizenship to 4588
protest against impressment of........ 4589
penalty for neglect of master to protest.. 4590
report as to impressment to Secretary of State........ 4590
list of certificates of citizenship of, to be kept. 4591
fee for shipping or discharging........ 4592
part of, to be deducted from wages....... 4593
who shall pay 4593
penalty for taking illegal........ 4595
offenses and punishments of........ 4596
shall be entered on log-book 4590, 4597
forfeiture of wages for desertion........ 4596
cost of arrest of deserter to be deducted from wages 4598
arrest of, for desertion, on justice's warrant. 4598
without warrant 4599
extra wages to be paid when desertion caused by cruel treatment 4600
deserters, reclamation and discharge of, by consular officers........ 4600
penalty for harboring........ 4601
for deserting........4522, 4601
penalty for drunkenness, &c........ 4602
enforcement of forfeitures 4603
disposal of........ 4604
deserters' wages, &c., unclaimed, to go to fund for destitute 4604
application of part of, to pay cost of conviction, &c........ 4605
penalty for unauthorized boarding of vessel. 4606
for soliciting, as lodgers 4607
shall not carry sheath-knife; penalty 4608
penalty for receiving more than fee from... 4609
penalties and forfeitures, how recovered.... 4610
to go to fund for relief of destitute 4610
flogging of, abolished........ 4611
definition of terms used in Title 4612
tables of wages, provisions, fees, &c........ 4612
hospital for sick and disabled, authorized... 4801
fund for relief of, how appropriated........ 4803
admission of foreign, to hospitals 4805
forcing on shore, with intent to leave, refusing to bring home 5363

foreign,
deserter, arrest of, on application of consul, &c 5280
delivery of, to consul 5280
detention of, at expense of consul........ 5280
delay of delivery of, in case of charge of crime against United States........ 5280

in navy,
date of loss of vessel, how fixed in settlement of accounts of........ 286
last quarterly-return of lost vessel to be assumed as basis........ 287
compensation for personal effects of, in case of loss of vessel........ 288
to whom paid, in case of death........ 289
promotion of, for heroism, &c........ 1407
number authorized to be enlisted 1417
additional pay to, doing duty as firemen, &c. 1570
collection and payment of bounty, prize-money, &c., due colored........ 2032
appropriation for lost effects of 3689
when to have pension 4693
rate of total disability, pension to........ 4695
when not to be deemed deserters; no remission of forfeiture of pension 4749
disabled, Navy pension fund to be used for. 4752
by age, &c., to have half-pay from fund.. 4756
aid to, from surplus income of fund 4757
hospital relief for 4807, 4813

Section.

Searches,
customs officers may board vessels and make 3059, 3067
may stop vehicles, beasts, or persons, and make 3061
refusing to allow, penalty........ 3062
regulations for, of persons and baggage; persons liable to........ 3064
persons making, under customs-laws, may enter buildings........ 3065
warrant for, of dwelling-house, how and by whom obtained; forfeitures........ 3066
customs officers making, to make character known; aiding in; refusal to assist; penalty 3071
of buildings on boundary line........ 3107
warrant for, may be issued to internal-revenue officers........ 3462

Seat of Government of United States,
provisions concerning 1795–1835
what declared to be permanent 1795
offices attached to, where to be exercised ... 1796
public offices at, may be removed in case of contagious, &c., disease........ 4798

Second Assistant Engineers in Navy,
number and rank of 1390
relative rank of, on active list........ 1476
pay of 1556

Second Auditor,
accounts of, to be examined by Second Comptroller 273
appointment and salary of........ 276
duties of 277
to settle accounts for pay of line-officer of Army, unable, by accident, to account for property, &c........ 278
to detail clerk to sign bounty certificates.... 279
duty as to requisitions of War Department.. 3673

Second-Class Mail-Matter,
what shall constitute 3877

Second Comptroller,
balance certified by, in public accounts, subject to revision only by Congress and courts 191
appointment and salary of........ 268
duties of 273
may prescribe rules for payment of arrears to seamen, &c., of United States vessel sunk or destroyed 274
power of, to detail clerk to sign bounty certificates........ 275
reference of accounts to Court of Claims on certificate of 1063
proceedings in such cases 1064
shall state and certify accounts of delinquent disbursing officers to Solicitor........ 3633
duty as to requisitions of War and Navy Departments 3673
shall be furnished copy of appointment of inspector of fuel........ 3712

Secretaries,
to President of Senate, salary........ 52
to Speaker of House of Representatives, salary of 53
to President, salary of 155
to Admiral and Vice-Admiral authorized, rank and allowances of........ 1367
pay of 1556
to commanders of squadrons 1556
of Naval Academy 1556
to board of Indian Commissioners, appointment and compensation of........ 2040

of interior,
to be head of Department of Interior........ 437
to prescribe duties of Assistant Secretary ... 439
general duties of 441

Section.

Secretaries—Continued.
powers and duties of, relating to Territories. 442
supervisory and appellate powers of, as to census ... 443
to sign requisitions for expenditures of Department ... 444
annual reports of ... 445
to prescribe regulations for presenting claims for Indian depredations ... 466
for preventing sales of arms in territory occupied by uncivilized Indians ... 467
to appoint clerks in Patent-Office on nomination of Commissioner ... 476
to be charged with custody and distribution of public documents ... 497
to furnish copies of statutes and Supreme Court reports to Department of Justice for distribution ... 498
to cause register of publications received to be kept ... 399
to appoint superintendent of public documents ... 507
to assign rooms for documents, &c ... 509
to have direction of compilation of Biennial Register ... 510
to provide rooms for returns-office and file contracts for Secretaries of War, Navy, and Interior ... 512
payment of naval pensions under supervision of, not interfered with by certain provisions ... 4753

of legation,
shall be deemed diplomatic officers ... 1674
salaries of, to Austria, Berlin, Brazil, Italy, Japan, London, Mexico, Paris, St. Petersburg, Spain ... 1675
to China, salary when acting as interpreter. 1680
to Turkey, consul-general to be, salary of ... 1677
appointment of, not to be paid except ... 1684
salary of, when acting as chargé d'affaires ... 1685
salaries of, term for which payable ... 1740

of ministers,
appointment of, payment of ... 1684

of navy,
warrants drawn by, to be countersigned by whom ... 273
to be head of Department ... 415
general duties of ... 417
to have custody of books, records, &c., of Department ... 418
to distribute business of Department among bureaus ... 419
duties of bureaus performed under authority of ... 420
to make collection of captured flags ... 428
annual reports of, to contain what ... 429
when to direct revenue-cutters ... 2757
shall submit estimates of demands on naval pension-fund ... 3667
appropriations for Navy to be under control of ... 3676
to be trustee of Navy pension-fund ... 4750
may mitigate, &c., penalties for destroying, &c., live-oak ... 4751
shall invest Navy pension-fund, &c ... 4753
may grant aid to sailors, &c., from Navy pension-fund ... 4757
shall be trustee of privateer pension-fund ... 4758

of senate,
salary ... 52
disbursement by, of moneys appropriated for compensation of members and contingent expenses ... 56
shall be deemed disbursing officer ... 56
bond of ... 57
where deposited ... 59

Section.

Secretaries—Continued.
statement by, of appropriations, new offices, increased salaries ... 64
to advertise for stationery ... 65–68
may contract for separate parts of ... 68
fees of, for transcripts from journals ... 71
duty of, to transmit petitions, &c., for private claims to Court of Claims ... 1060
to notify Secretary of Treasury, Auditors, and Comptrollers, of nominations, rejections, &c., at end of session ... 1775
printing, binding, &c., for Senate, done upon requisition of ... 3789

of state,
to be head of Department of State ... 199
to have charge of foreign affairs ... 202
to have custody of seals and property of Department ... 203
to promulgate laws ... 204
and amendments to Constitution of United States ... 205
to procure statutes of the several States ... 206
annual reports of ... 207, 208
annual statement of expenditures from contingent fund ... 209
to furnish Congressional Printer with copies of laws, treaties, &c ... 210
to furnish commercial information in newspapers ... 211
certificate by, of expenditures in intercourse with foreign nations, effect of ... 291
to keep seal of United States, to make out and record civil commissions for officers, and affix seal ... 1794

of territories,
appointment of, for each Territory ... 1843
residence, and tenure of office ... 1843
when to act as governor ... 1843
duties of ... 1844
salaries of ... 1845
how and when paid ... 1882
territorial legislatures not to increase compensation of ... 1855
in New Mexico, Utah, &c., to expend appropriations for legislative expenses ... 1939
to account for expenditures to Secretary of Treasury ... 1939
in Washington, Idaho, and Montana, disbursement of moneys by ... 1940
salaries of, when payable ... 1941

of treasury,
not to engage in certain business ... 243
provisions concerning ... 245–267
to prescribe duties of assistants ... 245
delegation by, of Assistant Secretary to sign warrants ... 246
general duties of ... 248
to superintend collection of customs-duties. 249
to cause accounts to be settled within fiscal years ... 250
to issue regulations and forms to collectors, receivers, &c., and for execution of customs and internal-revenue laws ... 251
power of, to discontinue ports of delivery ... 253
authority of, to receive deposits of gold coin and bullion, and issue certificates therefor ... 254
designation by, of disbursing agents for expenditures for public buildings ... 255
power of, to employ persons to collect moneys withheld from United States ... 256
what annual reports to be made by ... 257–264
at what time to furnish Congressional Printer with condensed statement of exports and imports ... 265

Section.

Secretaries—Continued.
publication by, of quarterly statement of receipts and expenditures 266
monthly publication of weekly statement of Treasurer 267
may instruct district attorneys not to appear in certain suits against collectors, &c. 771
reference of certain accounts by, to Court of Claims 1063
proceedings, in case of such accounts, same as in other cases 1064
payment of judgments on such accounts . 1065
to inform certain officers of appointments by President without confirmation 1774
to establish regulations for appraisal of imports 252, 2949
authority of, to compromise claims of United States 3469
power of, in case of poor debtor 3471
shall proclaim value of foreign coins 3564
authority of, to reduce currency, suspended. 3582
shall annex to estimates a statement of indefinite, &c., appropriations 3670
shall report unexpended balances 3691
to withhold payments from certain railroads. 5260
may remit fines, penalties, and forfeitures, under customs, registering, &c., laws after summary inquiry before district judge 2858, 5292
without summary inquiry 2901, 5293
under laws relating to steam-vessels 5394
of war,
general duties of 216
custody of departmental books and property. 217
to collect captured flags 218
to direct purchase and transportation of subsistence and quartermasters' supplies. 219
to control transportation of troops, &c..... 220
to provide for meteorological observations and storm-signals 221
to provide for signal-stations and reports... 222
may establish telegraph-lines connecting signal-stations 223
may furnish duplicates of lost certificates of discharge 224
may detail officers to administer oaths in settlement of officers' accounts 225
may prescribe terms of sale of surplus charts of northwestern lakes 226
to report to Congress appropriations and unexpended balances 228
to make annual report of contracts and contingent expenses of military establishment 229
to report to Congress bids for works 230
to report on river and harbor surveys 231
to furnish Congress with abstract of returns of State adjutants-general 232
warrants drawn by, how countersigned 273
Secret Service,
settlement of expenses of intercourse with foreign nations, upon certificate of Secretary of State 291
Sections,
of Revised Statutes, how numbered, and what to contain 10
Securities of United States,
imitating, or printing, &c., on, to be punished 3708
Seeds,
purchase and distribution of 520, 527
to be third-class mail-matter 3878
Seizures,
jurisdiction of district courts in cases of.... 563
proceedings on, in what districts prosecuted for violations of Title INSURRECTION. 564

Section.

Seizures—Continued.
appointment of commissioners to swear appraisers of vessels and goods in cases of 570
no jurisdiction of circuit courts in cases of, on land, &c 629
United States courts to have exclusive jurisdiction of, made under United States laws of, on land and on waters not within admiralty jurisdiction 711
for forfeiture, in what district to be prosecuted 734
when burden of proof on claimant, in cases of, under impost or tonnage laws 909
where made of several things belonging to same person, for violation of revenue laws, all joined in one suit 920
notice and proclamation of, made by officer of customs, &c 923
under customs-revenue laws, delivery to claimant of vessel, goods, &c 938
sale, after condemnation 939
delivery or sale may be ordered by judge, in vacation 940
probable cause, certificate of, in cases of ... 970
costs not allowed claimant when, made with 970
no action against officer or prosecutor when, made with 970
when double costs allowed defendant, in action against officer, &c., making, under import laws, &c. 971
of vessels and goods in Alaska 1957
of vessels, &c., engaged in transportation of coolies 2159–2163
by customs officers, for smuggling 3061
customs officers to make known character when making, &c 3071
customs officers to make, when vessel or goods are liable thereto 3072
when sued, may give special matter in evidence under general issue 3073
of property under customs-laws, to be appraised, &c 3074
if value $500 or less, notice of, to be published 3075
persons claiming property, to file claim, &c. 3076
sale of property under, proceedings, &c.... 3077
remission of forfeiture under 3078
distribution of proceeds of sale 3079
of perishable articles, &c., when and by whom sold 3080
release of, on payment of appraised value.. 3081
of goods imported contrary to law, &c., forfeiture, fine, &c 3082
when Solicitor of Treasury to be notified of. 3083
custody of imports under 3086
commencement of suits for, &c 3087
of vessel, when owner or master subject to penalty for violation of revenue laws. 3088
what portion of proceeds of sale in revenue cases of, to be applied to payment of costs 3089
of books and papers in revenue cases, warrant for 3091
return of warrant, how made, &c 3092
of letters illegally carried authorized 3990
certain revenue laws extended to officers making 3991
of vessel, what notice to be given 4379
pensions not liable to 4747
assaulting, resisting, &c., customs officer, &c., in making 5447
rescuing, &c., property seized by 5447
staving, throwing overboard, &c., property, in order to prevent 5447

Section.

Seizures—Continued.
discharging deadly weapon at 5447
internal revenue,
Commissioner may authorize............... 3166
of real estate, sale of 3196–3205
fees and charges in cases of, how determined. 3206
of merchandise not transferred, as required, from unfit warehouse................ 3272
of cask or package from which marks, brands, and stamps not obliterated 3324
of distillery, &c., when release from, may be given before judgment............... 3331
of distilled spirits, burden of proof 3333
of fermented liquors for non-payment of tax. 3352
in case of tobacco-peddler refusing to exhibit certificate or stamp.................. 3383
under section 3453, of taxable articles held with intent to defraud revenue 3453
of raw materials 3453
of tools, &c., found on premises........... 3453
under section 3460, notice of............... 3460
claimant may give bond.................. 3460
proceedings thereon...................... 3460
sale in default of claim or bond 3460
proceedings on goods valued at $500 or less. 3460
appraisement 3460
appraiser's fees.......................... 3460
application for remission 3461
when proceeds to be distributed 3461
Selma, Ala.,
port of delivery 2564
surveyor to reside at 2565
merchandise for, where entered 2820
Semi-annual Bank-Tax,
(see *National Banks.*)
Senate of United States,
salary of Senators.......................... 35
officers and employés of, salaries 52
expenditures of, when made up and reported. 63
furniture and carpets for, how purchased... 1816
contingent fund of, restrictions on use of... 3680
Sergeants-at-Arms,
of Senate and of House of Representatives, salaries 52, 53
prohibited from receiving fees 52, 53
and Architect of Capitol may appoint police.................................. 1821
and regulate, uniform, and arm Capitol police.................................. 1824
Sergeant-Majors,
for regiments of artillery 1099
of cavalry.............................. 1102
of infantry............................. 1106
Sergeants,
for battery of artillery..................... 1100
troop of cavalry......................... 1103
company of infantry..................... 1107
ordnance, (see *Ordnance Department.*)
Service,
duration of, in militia when called forth by United States 1648
Service-Pay,
to officers of Army, rate of................. 1262
maximum of 1263
Services,
contracts for, except for personal, to be made after advertising 3709
Sessions,
of territorial legislatures to be held biennially 1846
limit to length of......................... 1852
extraordinary, in Washington, Idaho, and Montana 1923
Set-Off,
jurisdiction of Court of Claims of, on part of United States, &c.................... 1059

Section.

Set-Off—Continued.
judgment of Court of Claims for, in favor of United States; how enforced by district courts 1061
Settlers,
(see *Lands, Public.*)
Shanghai,
consul-general at, salary of 1690
general postal agency authorized at........ 4023
Shareholders,
of national banks, organization-certificate to state names of original 5134
rights and liabilities of succession........ 5139
proceedings against, on failure to pay installments on capital stock 5141
may reduce capital........................ 5143
directors to be elected by 5145
directors must be......................... 5146
when, may fix day for election of directors. 5149
individual liability of..................... 5151
shall be assessed to make good capital stock, &c 5205
to keep list of, to be open to inspection, &c.; copy of, to be sent to Comptroller..... 5210
bank to go into liquidation by vote of two-thirds of 5220
when to be discharged from liability for notes 5224
surplus, after paying debts, shall be paid to 5236
Shares,
tobacco and snuff, manufactured on commission or................................ 3370
cigars manufactured on commission or 3399
in prize cases of captors.................... 4630
how to be distributed 4631
vessels entitled to 4632
officers or persons entitled to............. 4633
officer temporarily absent, &c., not to be deprived of 4633
determination of, how to be made........ 4634
Sheath-Knives,
shall not be worn on ship-board, &c........ 4608
Sheboygan, Wis.,
port of delivery 2597
deputy collector to reside at 2598
Sheepscott River, Me.,
provisions concerning unlading of vessels at towns adjoining....................... 2520
Shieldsborough, Miss.,
port of entry................................ 2566
collector to reside at....................... 2567
Ship Island, Miss.,
port of delivery 2566
deputy collector to reside at, duties of...... 2567
Ship-Letters,
receipt and delivery of...................... 3976
pay for carrying............................ 3978
Ship, Steamboat, and Way Letters,
accounts to show expenditures for 4049
Shipment of Seamen,
(see *Seamen.*)
Shippers,
of platina, gold, bullion, &c., to give notice of valuable character of shipment.... 4281
unless notice given, carriers not liable for loss, &c............................. 4281
Shipping-Articles,
in Navy, to contain provisions as to expiration of enlistment..................... 1425
in merchant service, form, terms, &c., of.... 4511
rules for making, signing, &c............. 4512
exceptions to............................ 4513
penalty for carrying seamen without making 4514
penalty for shipping seamen without..... 4515

Section.

Shipping-Articles—Continued.
of seamen engaged in foreign ports....... 4517
copy of, shall be posted in vessel.......... 4519
for vessels in coasting-trade, form, &c., of. 4520
penalty for shipping seamen in coasting-trade without........................ 4521
penalty on seamen for breach of........... 4522
shall contain allotment stipulation....... 4531
advances of wages not to be made unless stipulated in......................... 4532
consul shall indorse receipt, &c., for effects of deceased seamen on............... 4539
master may be required to produce, in suit for wages............................ 4547
allowance for reduction of provisions required by........................... 4568
certified copy of, shall be carried on vessels. 4575
breach of, by desertion, punishment for... 4598
discharge of seamen deserters by consul, &c., to be entered on 4600
form of 4612
(see *Seamen.*)

Shipping-Commissioners,
how appointed and removed, supervision of, by circuit court...................... 4501
bond and oath of........................ 4502
when customs officers shall act as........... 4503
when customs-houses to be deemed offices of. 4503
penalty for illegally acting as.............. 4504
clerks and deputies of..................... 4505
papers bearing seal of, how admitted in evidence............................... 4506
offices of 4507
duties 4508
shall procure apprentices to sea-service 4509
shall examine indentures of apprentices.... 4510
shall witness shipping articles............. 4512
to reship seamen in same vessel without fees..................................... 4513
rules for shipping seamen before, to govern shipments in foreign ports........... 4517
advance wages to seamen to be given in presence of............................ 4532
proceeds of effects of deceased seamen to be delivered to......................... 4539
wages of deceased seamen to be paid to 4542
shall pay wages into circuit court.......... 4543
seamen shall be discharged before 4549
account of wages on discharge of seamen to 4550
when master of vessel may perform duties of, in respect to discharges........... 4551
rules for payment of wages, and discharge, before 4552
certificate of character required in discharges before 4553
shall act as arbiters between masters and crew.................................... 4554
may require books and summon witnesses.. 4555
when shall inspect provisions of vessels.... 4565
when complaint reported false, penalty..... 4566
shall furnish copy of shipping articles to owners 4575
fees of 4592
bill of, to be posted in office.............. 4592
who shall pay........................... 4593
penalty for taking unlawful 4595
limit as to compensation of 4594
may apprehend deserters without warrant.. 4599
balance of proceeds of deserters' clothing, &c., to be paid to 4604
shall notify seamen of provision against wearing sheath-knives 4608
table of fees of........................... 4612

Shipping-Fees,
penalty for exacting illegal................ 4609

Shipping-Offices,
(see *Shipping-Commissioners.*)

Ship's Company, or Crew,
list of, shall be furnished to collector....... 4573
shall be certified by collector 4574
rules respecting duplicate list of 4575

Ship's Husband,
to give bond for registry.................... 4145

Ship's Papers,
(see *Vessels.*)

Ship-Stores,
(see *Sea-Stores.*)

Shipwreck,
holding out false lights, or extinguishing true, with intent to produce 5358

Shorts,
(see *Tobacco.*)

Shreveport, La.,
port of delivery............................ 2568
deputy collector to reside at 2569

Siam,
judicial authority of United States minister and consuls in 4111–4120
marshal for consular court in............... 4111
rent of prison for American convicts in 4121
limit to expense of prison and keepers in... 4121
(see *Consular Courts.*)

Sick, Disabled, and Destitute Seamen,
(see *Seamen.*)

Sick-Diet,
in Army hospitals, allowance of............ 1175

Sick-Furlough,
enlisted men on, to be regarded as if in field, &c 4700

Sick-Leave,
officers on, to be regarded as if in field or hospital 4700

Sickness,
in case of, further time may be allowed to internal-revenue tax-payer making returns 3176

Signal-Office,
duty of Secretary of War to provide for stations................................ 222
authority of Chief Signal-Officer to sell surplus maps and publications of 227
Chief of, in Army, authorized 1094
rank and duties of....................... 1195
enlisted men of, to be mounted............. 1197

Signals,
for pleasure-yachts, how prescribed 4215

Signs,
to be put up by distillers, rectifiers, and wholesale liquor-dealers 3279
by manufacturer of tobacco and snuff.... 3356
peddlers of tobacco to affix and keep....... 3382
to be put up by cigar-manufacturers........ 3388

Silver,
other than standard coin, receivable in payment of certain dues 3474
bars, how may be cast by mint.............. 3518
bullion, may be deposited for bars or trade-dollars................................ 3520
in gold deposits to be paid for............ 3520
coinage charge on 3524
how purchased for coinage................. 3526
coinage, to be reported by mint superintendents 3503
how profit on, to be disposed of 3526
wastage in, how provided for 3526
profit fund, how created and used......... 3526
profits on, not to be used for wages, &c... 3552
coins, denomination, weight and fineness of 3513, 3514
how paid out............................ 3527
deviations in adjusting.................... 3536

Section.
Silver—Continued.
trial-pieces of 3539
recoinage of, charged to profit-fund 3568
to what extent a legal tender 3586
ingots, deviation allowed in 3533
shipper of, to notify carrier, &c 4281
Silver Creek, N. Y.,
port of delivery 2535
deputy collector at 2536
Silvey's Landing, Md.,
port of delivery 2548
Similitude Clause,
in tariff of customs duties 2499
Singapore,
consul at, salary of 1690
Singular Number,
words of 1
Sinking-Fund,
permanent appropriation to pay interest on. 3688
appropriation for 3689
part of customs-duties set apart for 3694
interest of, to be used to purchase debt. 3694–3696
bonds applied to, shall be canceled 3695
Sippican Harbor, Mass.,
port in collection-district of New Bedford, description of vessels belonging to... 2528
Sisters,
when to have pensions 4707
pension to cease on remarriage 4708
when pension of, to begin 4709, 4710
Sitka, Alaska,
port of entry 2591
collector to reside at 2592
Sixth Auditor,
appeals from settlements by, to First Comptroller ... 270
appointment and salary of 276
duties of 277
to superintend collection of debts due Post-Office Department, and enforcement of penalties ... 292
accounts of money-order business 293
quarterly statement by, of moneys paid by postmasters for expenses ... 294
compromise of judgments for debts, &c 295
to furnish copies of papers to Department of Justice, in suits against delinquents. 296
oaths in settlements of accounts committed to, by whom administered ... 298
copies of contracts for carrying mail to be delivered to ... 404
orders of Postmaster-General, originating claims or affecting accounts, to be certified to ... 405
warrant of Postmaster-General on quarterly statement by, of moneys paid by postmasters ... 406
warrants for deposits to be countersigned by ... 408
remission of fines, compromise of debts 409
statement to, by marshals, of executions for moneys due Post-Office Department.. 792
copies of papers pertaining to accounts in office of, when evidence ... 889
duty of, as to warrants on Treasury 3674
new post-offices shall be certified to 3829
shall be notified of appointments, &c., of postmasters ... 3830
in case of death, &c., of postmaster, bond to be delivered to ... 3834
duty of, in case of new bond 3835
shall be promptly notified of change of postmaster ... 3836
of change in salaries of postmasters 3856
shall audit accounts of deductions by postmasters ... 3862

Section.
Sixth Auditor—Continued.
discontinuance of post-office shall be certified to ... 3864
how to charge salaries, &c., of special agents. 4020
payments on account of postal service shall be certified by ... 4055
Slaves,
colored soldiers enrolled as, to have pensions and bounties ... 4723
Slave-Trade,
limitation of time for finding indictment, or instituting information of crimes arising under laws relating to ... 1046
President to employ armed vessels to suppress ... 5557
proceeds of condemned vessel, &c., how distributed ... 5558
President to make regulations for safe-keeping, removal, &c., of negroes, &c., taken from vessels in, and to appoint resident agent in Africa to receive same ... 5561
bounty to officers and crew of commissioned vessels for negroes, &c., taken from slave-ships ... 5562
bond of masters of foreign vessels clearing for Africa, or suspected of being intended for ... 5564
distribution of forfeitures accruing under laws relating to, how made ... 5565
President how to contract for reception in Africa, of negroes, &c., taken from vessels in ... 5566
for reception in West Indies, or other tropical regions ... 5568
Sleighs,
lost in military service to be paid for 3483
Smithfield, Va.,
port of delivery 2552
surveyor to reside at 2553
Smithsonian Institution,
provisions as to library of 100
appropriation for 3689
incorporation of 5579
board of regents of, duties, composition, residence ... 5580
appointment, term of office, vacancies 5581
organization, executive committee, meetings, quorum ... 5582
duty of secretary of, power to appoint assistants ... 5583
compensation of secretary and assistants, removal ... 5584
special meetings of members and honorary members of ... 5585
reception, arrangement, &c., of objects of art, natural history, geological specimens, &c., for ... 5586
library of, limit of expenditure for 5587
site of, evidence of boundaries of 5588
protection of property of, laws extended to. 5589
appropriation of interest of fund of; expenditures to be made from ... 5590
Secretary of Treasury to receive additional sums deposited by board of regents.. 5591
power of regents to dispose of accrued interest not hereby appropriated ... 5592
manner of making disbursements for, reports ... 5593
power of Congress to amend or repeal provisions relating to ... 5594
Smuggling,
provisions relating to 3058–3094
punishment of seamen for 4596
Smyrna,
consul at, salary of 1690

Section.

Snow Hill, Va.,
port of delivery 2552
Snuff,
internal-revenue officer interested in manufacture of 3168
manufacturers of, special tax of 3244
peddlers of 3244
how to be put up 3362
manufactured prior to July 20, 1868 3365
tax on 3368
on snuff-flour 3368
imported 3377
fraudulently selling, as made, and tax paid before July 20, 1868 3380
exportation of 3385
drawback on, exported 3386
Soldiers,
collection and payment of bounty, prize-money, &c., due colored 2032
retained bounty-fund of certain colored, custody and use of 2035, 2036
who to be deemed wife and children of colored 2037
entitled to bounty-land when 2418–2424
outfits of, not to be sold 3748
enlisted but not mustered, when pension to dependent relatives of, to begin 4710
when not to be deemed deserters, no remission of forfeiture of pension 4749
deceased, unclaimed moneys belonging to estates of, to be applied to support of Soldiers' Home 4818
to be repaid on demand of heirs 4818
of volunteer, to National Home for Disabled Volunteers 4831
to be repaid on demand of heirs 4831
Soldiers' Home,
appropriation for 3689
officers of, to be taken from Army 4816
how appointed and removed 4816
sites and buildings for, how selected 4817
funds for support of, how derived 4818
deduction from pay of non-commissioned officers, privates, &c., to be made for support of 4819
commissioners may receive donations for 4819
deduction for, of pay from volunteers, &c., to be made only with their consent 4819
pensioners not to be excluded from 4820
to surrender pensions during stay in 4820
Solicitor-General,
appointment, duties, and salary of 347
to perform duties of Attorney-General, in case of vacancy 347
may be sent by Attorney-General to attend courts of any State 367
when traveling expenses of, allowed 370
Solicitor of Internal Revenue,
appointment and salary of 349
opinion of, in compromise cases, to be filed in office of Commissioner 3229
Solicitor of Treasury,
appointment and salary of 349
to have charge of certain records and papers, and of seal 372
to make entry of bonds for duties 373
to examine reports on bonds delivered for suit 374
to inform President of false reports of such bonds 375
to take measures to detect frauds on revenue 376
to establish regulations for collectors of customs, district attorneys, and marshals 377
to report moneys collected and credits allowed 378

Section.

Solicitor of Treasury—Continued.
to instruct district attorneys, marshals, and clerks 379
to supervise suits respecting national banks 380
statements to, by district attorneys, of suits, &c. 772, 773
by marshals, of proceedings on executions 791
by clerks, of judgments and decrees 797
copies of books, documents, &c., in office of, made evidence 883
duty of, to bring suits against officers in arrears to United States 1766
seizures under customs-laws to be reported to 3083
to approve sureties on internal-revenue collectors' bonds 3143
to issue warrant of distress against delinquent collector of internal revenue 3217
compromise of claims of United States 3469
to appoint agent to purchase lands for United States under executions 3470
shall issue distress-warrant against delinquent collector, receiver, &c 3625
against delinquent disbursing officers 3633
power of, to sell lands, &c., acquired by United States for debts 3749
to have charge of lands, &c., acquired by United States 3750
power of, to release lands conveyed to United States on payment of debt 3751
Somerset, Mass.,
port of delivery 2527
Southampton,
consul at, salary of 1699
South Carolina,
district judge in, appointment and residence of 552
district attorney of eastern district of, to perform duty in western 767
also marshal 776
collection-districts and ports of entry in 2557
officers in 2558
Southern Claims Commission,
appropriation for 3689
Sovereign,
value of English, fixed 3565
Spain,
salary of minister and secretary to 1675
vessels of, exempt from discriminating duties 4231
duration of such exemption 4231
Spanish Language,
professor of, at Naval Academy 1528
Spanish Pillar-Dollar,
value of fractions of 3567
recoinage of 3568
Spanish Vessels,
cargoes of, seeking ports in distress, when and how reladen, no charges, &c 2895
Sparkling Wine,
tax on imitations of 3328
Speaker of House of Representatives,
salary of 37
Special-Act Pensions,
(see *Pensions.*)
Special Agents,
to collect money due United States; number, appointment, duty, and compensation of; penalty for improper conduct by 256
of Indians, appointment of 2067
to disburse public money, appointment and bond of 3614
to examine national banks 5227
expenses of, how paid 5238
Post-Office Department.
may be placed in charge of post-offices 3836

Section.

Special Agents—Continued.
may make search of vessels for letters...... 3989
may seize letters illegally carried 3990
disposal of letters seized by................ 3991
salaries, &c., of............................ 4017
when to give bond............................ 4018
Assistant Postmasters-General may be...... 4019
Treasury Department,
for management of seal fisheries in Alaska. 1973
for customs service; number, appointment, duties, expenses...................... 2649
classification and payment of............ 2650
Secretary of Treasury to make regulations for; number and compensation of.... 2651
of internal revenue, how employed, &c.... 3152
assignment, compensation................ 3152
for examination of accounts, &c., of depositaries of public money............... 3649
compensation and duties of.............. 3649
Special Bail,
when, may be required in suits for recovery of duties or pecuniary penalties...... 942
Special Counsel,
employment of, to aid district attorneys.... 363
compensation of, allowed on certificate of Attorney-General, &c................ 365
appointment, commission, and oath of...... 366
Attorney-General to report names and compensation of, to Congress.......... 385
in prize causes, may be employed by Secretary of Navy...................... 4620
compensation to be allowed by court..... 4648
when no allowance to be made........... 4648
fees to be paid out of what fund......... 4649
Special Deposits,
national banks may deliver, after failure to redeem notes.......................... 5228
Special Deputy Marshals,
appointment of, under Title ELECTIVE FRANCHISE.......................... 2021
powers and duties of 2021
compensation of.............................. 2031
Special List or Return, (Internal Revenue,)
when, shall be so denominated............. 3181
Special Permit,
to steam-vessels to carry additional passengers on excursions................... 4466
Special Tax, (Internal Revenue,)
names, &c., of persons liable to, to be registered and returned................. 3233
copartnership to pay but one................ 3234
business not to be carried on in place other than described in collector's register.. 3235
where more than one pursuit is carried on by same person, at same time and place.......................... 3236
due May 1, each year; method of computing. 3237
to be paid by stamps........................ 3238
penalty for not keeping stamps conspicuously in place of business................. 3239
other liabilities of persons liable to, not changed 3239
alphabetical list of persons paying, to be kept in office of collector............ 3240
death, removal, &c., of persons having paid. 3241
penalties for not paying..................... 3242
payment of, does not exempt from penalty under State laws, nor prevent State from taxing...................... 3243
what classes of business liable to.......... 3244
re-adjustment of, in case of retail dealer in leaf-tobacco...................... 3244
refunding of, to distillers................... 3245
buying tobacco, snuff, and cigars not stamped or branded from manufacturer who has not paid.......................3367, 3405

Section.

Specie Payments,
on resumption of, no notes for less than $5 to be issued to national banks.......... 5175
Specifications and Drawings,
of patents, printing of, for distribution to States, and for sale..............490–493
Spezia,
consul at, salary of......................... 1690
Spirits,
(see *Distilled Spirits.*)
Springfield, Mass.,
pay of clerks of armory at.................. 1663
Staff,
of Army, of the General..................... 1096
of the Lieutenant-General................. 1097
of major-generals........................ 1098
of brigadier-generals 1098
of Marine Corps, rank of.................... 1602
of militia, regimental....................... 1631
of Navy, relative rank of, retired 1481, 1482
rank and precedence of, no additional right to quarters.......................... 1487
Stamford, Conn.,
port of delivery............................ 2533
Stamp Agents, (Internal Revenue,)
(see *Stamps, Internal Revenue.*)
Stamped Envelopes,
Postmaster-General shall provide; what may be printed on them.................. 3915
shall be kept for sale at all post-offices; postmasters accountable for 3918
may be sold at discount to designated agents................................ 3919
letters in, may be sent otherwise than by mail 3993
neglect to account for, &c., penalty........ 4053
Stamps,
included by words "obligation or other security of United States 5413
Stamps, Internal Revenue,
for special taxes, Commissioner authorized to procure 3238
provisions of law applicable to 3238
to be kept conspicuously in place of business 3239
distillery warehouse........................ 3287
tax-paid, on distilled spirits, form of........ 3295
by whom to be signed 3295
to state serial number of cask............. 3295
for distilled spirits, how to be engraved and issued 3312
tax-paid, on distilled spirits, how gallons stated on 3313
coupons to be attached..................... 3313
how to be used by collector................ 3313
accountability of collector for books of... 3314
at what values............................ 3314
monthly return of, to be made 3314
return of books of stubs of, to Commissioner 3314
may be issued for restamping............. 3315
other than tax-paid, may be intrusted to gauger by collector................... 3314
officer using, issuing, or permitting use of, illegally, penalty for 3316
for rectified distilled spirits................. 3320
for wholesale liquor dealers................ 3321
affixing and cancellation of............... 3322
on distilled spirits, to be effaced, &c., at time of emptying casks 3324
possessing cancelled, which have been used. 3324
changing, on cask of distilled spirits....... 3326
on distilled spirits for exportation, expense for providing and affixing............. 3330
tax-paid, on distilled spirits, to be destroyed before sale of forfeited spirits........ 3334
Commissioner may change.............3445, 3446

Section.

Stamps, Internal Revenue—Continued.
on imitation wines, &c., to be prepared by Commissioner 3328
to be affixed by manufacturer 3328
to be cancelled as Commissioner may prescribe 3328
absence of, evidence that tax not paid, and cause of forfeiture 3328
penalty for counterfeiting, altering, or re-using 3328
on fermented liquors, to be prepared by Commissioner and furnished to collectors. 3341
collectors to keep two months' supply, and account of sales to brewers 3341
deduction on sales of, to brewers 3341
amount of, sold to brewers included in estimating commissions of collectors. 3341
to be obtained by brewer from collector of his district 3342
mode of affixing and cancelling 3342
absence of, notice and evidence that tax is not paid 3352
removal or defacing, except by owner 3353
Commissioner may change 3445
on tobacco and snuff, purchasing without 3366
sold, abandoned, condemned, forfeited 3369
to be prepared by Commissioner 3369
affixing and canceling of 3369
to be furnished to collectors 3369
to whom to be sold 3369
collector to keep account of sale of 3369
manufactured on commission or shares, by whom to be affixed 3370
absence of, notice and evidence of non-payment of tax 3373
selling or removing without 3374
affixing fraudulent or used 3375
on emptied package to be destroyed 3376
fraudulent use of 3376
imported, by whom to be affixed 3377
for export 3385
Commissioner may change 3445, 3446
on cigars sold, abandoned, condemned, or forfeited 3369
collector to keep account of sales of 3395
to be prepared by Commissioner 3395
collector to keep two months' supply 3395
to whom to be sold 3395
fraudulent use of 3397
false, fraudulent, or counterfeit 3397
in similitude or likeness of United States stamp 3397
removing, with intent to use 3397
absence of, notice and evidence that tax not paid 3398
to be affixed by maker where material is furnished by one and manufactured by another 3399
to be affixed to imported, by owner or importer 3402
on emptied cigar-boxes 3406
Commissioner and Secretary may change. 3445
on bank checks, &c 3418
on what checks not required 3420
checks issued without, not to be used as evidence 3421
penalty for issuing without 3422
instruments issued without, may be subsequently stamped 3422
mode of cancelling on checks, &c 3423
penalty for failure to cancel 3423
proprietors of articles in Schedule A may furnish private dies for 3423
forging, counterfeiting, or fraudulently obtaining from private dies 3423
commissions on sale of, for checks, &c 3425

Section.

Stamps, Internal Revenue—Continued.
on those from private dies 3425
may be supplied to match-manufacturers on credit 3425
spoiled, &c., allowance for 3426
may be furnished for sale to certain officers. 3427
bond of such officers 3427
commissions on sales 3427
Secretary of Treasury to make regulations for safe-keeping of 3428
forging of, on checks, papers, &c 3429
penalties for violations of law as to, on articles in Schedule A 3431, 3432
persons offering for sale articles in Schedule A, deemed manufacturers 3435
removing cancelling-marks, &c 3429
possessing washed, restored, or altered 3429
Stamps, (Postage,)
shall be provided, &c 3914
Standard,
of proof-spirits, under internal-revenue laws 3249
bars, to be reported by mint-superintendents 3503
coins of foreign nations, value of, &c 3564
fineness for United States coins 3514
assay commission to test 3547
bars of gold or silver may be made at mints. 3518
weights, deviation allowed in adjusting, of coin 3535–3537
of coins, assay commission to test 3547
for mints and assay offices 3549
Standards,
taken by Navy from enemies, disposition of. 1554
of sugar, how selected and to whom furnished 2914
State Assessors,
to have access to list of shareholders of national banks 5210
State Banks,
internal-revenue tax on capital and circulation of 3411, 3412
liability of shareholders of, on becoming national banks 5151
when and how, may become national banks 5154
with branches, may become national banks. 5155
State Bonds,
held by United States, and non-paying, to be protected 3481
State Courts,
removal from, to circuit court, of suit against officer for acts done under revenue laws or Title ELECTIVE FRANCHISE 643
of personal action against officer 644
judgments and decrees of, review by Supreme Court 709
concurrent jurisdiction of, in suits for possession of office 2010
jurisdiction of, in suits against seamen for breach of articles 4522
in cases of seamen deserters 4599
State Department,
(see *Department of State.*)
State Inspection Laws,
to be observed by customs officers clearing vessels 4202
State Laws,
payment of special tax to United States not to exempt from penalty, or taxation under 3243
Statement, (Internal Revenue,)
of still or distilling apparatus set up 3258
by brewers, monthly 3337
by tobacco-manufacturers 3355
by dealers in leaf-tobacco 3359
by farmer or planter producing and selling leaf-tobacco 3361
by tobacco-peddlers 3381
by cigar-manufacturers 3387

Section.

States,
assent of legislatures of, to purchase of land for forts, &c 1838
naturalization of alien seamen in courts of . 2174
agents of, may adjust compensation to Indians for lands, when 2116
not to impose discriminating charge on foreign immigrants 2164
fee to be paid on location of land-grants to . 2238
not to make discriminating rates for pilotage, &c 4237
existing discriminations of, annulled 4237
regulation of pilots of steam-vessels by, restricted 4444
quarantine laws of, to be observed by United States officers 4792

State Stocks,
owned by United States and non-paying, to be protected 3481

State Taxation,
shares of national banks subject to, restrictions on 5219

State Troops,
called into service between 1812 and 1852, bounty-land for 2420

Stationery,
for Congress, how procured 65–68
allowance for, to collector of internal revenue 3145
contracts of Executive Departments for, limited to one year 3735
postal accounts to show expenditures for... 4049
for steamboat-inspection officers, how furnished 4461
blanks and books shall be furnished to diplomatic and consular officers 1748

Stationery-Room,
of Senate, employés and salaries in 52

Statistics,
of Mint, report of, to be made 3503
printing of, relating to commerce and navigation, &c 3798

Statuary,
reception of, in old Hall of Representatives, invitation to States to furnish 1814
in customs laws, to include professional productions 2504
imported for exhibition, free of duty; bond for duties if not re-exported 2512

Statutes,
form and repeals of 7–13
of States to be procured by Secretary of State 206
at Large, edition of Little & Brown made evidence 908
preservation of, and delivery to successors, by public officers 1777
what embraced in Revised 5595
repeal provisions 5596–5601

Stealing,
money, goods, &c., from vessel in distress, or wrecked 5358

Steamboat-Inspectors,
(see *Inspection of Steam-Vessels.*)

Steamboat-Letters,
(see *Letters.*)

Steam-Engineering,
relative rank and title of Chief of Bureau of. 1471
of retired Chief of Bureau of 1473

Steam-Pipes,
to carry steam into compartments and holds of steam-vessels to extinguish fire, &c. 4470

Steam-Registers,
(see *Inspection of Steam-Vessels.*)

Steam-Tugs,
(see *Tug-Boats.*)

Section.

Steam-Vessels,
jurisdiction of circuit courts of suits in case of destruction of life on 629
coal of, exempt from duty 2798
lost in military service to be paid for...3483, 3488
appropriation for 3689
contract with, for carrying mail without advertising 3943
when mail may be carried in certain ...3969, 3970
delivery of letters carried by 3977
pay to, when not in mail-service 3978
for carrying foreign mail 4009
on Lake Champlain, going to province of Quebec, how cleared 4208
carrying mail between United States and Brazil, exempt from port-charges 4232
what considered as, under Title NAVIGATION. 4233
enrollment and license of, owned by resident alien 4316
bond by alien owner 4317
what are deemed, under Title REGULATION OF STEAM-VESSELS 4399
what, are subject to provisions of Title REGULATION OF STEAM-VESSELS 4400
navigating coastwise and on Great Lakes subject to navigation-laws 4401
coastwise, not registered, to be under control of licensed pilots and inspectors, when. 4401
transporting passengers not to depart without complement of licensed officers and crew 4463
deprived of licensed officer, how temporarily supplied 4463
certificate of inspection of, to state number of passengers which may be carried.. 4464
ferry-boats excepted 4464
penalty for carrying more passengers than allowed 4465
special permits to carry additional passengers on excursions 4466
masters of, to keep lists of passengers open for inspection 4467
penalty for failure 4468
penalties to be a lien on, when 4469
precautions against fire 4470
fire-pumps and hose, regulation of 4471
not to carry dangerous inflammable articles. 4472
penalty for unlawfully carrying cotton or hemp 4473
license to use petroleum for fuel 4474
gunpowder, nitro-glycerine, &c., how packed and marked 4475
penalty for unlawful shipment of 4476
watchmen at night 4477
penalty for failure to keep 4478
fire-extinguishers for 4479
wire tiller-ropes, bell-pulls, &c., on river-steamers 4480
boats for river-steamers 4481
life-preservers 4482
fire-buckets, water-barrels, and axes 4483
stairways and gangways for river-steamers carrying passengers on main deck 4484
accommodations for deck-passengers 4485
penalty for failure to provide 4486
navigating rivers, to anchor in fogs, &c..... 4487
commander proceeding, answerable for damages 4487
life-boats, &c., for ocean and lake steamers. 4488
penalty for failure to provide 4489
water-tight bulk-heads for steamers navigating ocean or great lakes 4490
approval of life-saving instruments 4491
barges, subject to what provisions 4492
penalty for violating provisions 4493

Section.

Steam-Vessels—Continued.
liability of master and owner for baggage of passengers 4493
to carry two copies of Title REGULATION OF STEAM-VESSELS 4494
names of, to be painted on stern and pilot-house; penalty 4495
customs officers to enforce provisions concerning; penalty 4496, 4497
license, register, or enrollment for 4498
navigated contrary to provisions of Title REGULATION OF STEAM-VESSELS, penalty 4499
penalties not otherwise provided for 4500
remission of fines, penalties, &c., under laws relating to 5294
penalty on person by whose misconduct life is destroyed 5344
inspector of, receiving illegal fees 5482
(see *Fines, Penalties, and Forfeitures; Inspection of Steam-Vessels;* and *Passengers.*)

Steering and Sailing Rules,
(see *Navigation.*)

Stenographers,
to House of Representatives, salary 53
in Post-Office Department, salary of 393

Stettin,
consul at, salary of 1690

Steward to the President,
salary of 155
duties of 156
bond of 157

Stills, (*Internal Revenue,*)
manufacturer of 3244
penalty on, for doing business without paying special tax 3242
special tax on 3244
definition of 3244
set up, to be registered 3258
forfeiture for not registering 3258
manufacturer of, to give notice before removing from place of manufacture 3265
not to be set up without permit 3265
not to be used for distilling on certain premises; penalty 3266
wood, space around 3269
Commissioner may require fastenings, locks, and seals 3270
not to be used between 11 p. m. Saturday and 1 a. m. Monday 3283
using locked, penalty 3311
to be destroyed and material sold in certain cases of forfeiture 3332

Stockbridge-Munsee Indians,
chiefs, warriors, and heads of families of, may acquire homestead, when 2310
sale of abandoned portion of reservation 2310

Stockholders,
(see *Shareholders.*)

Stocks,
sale of, under distraint for internal-revenue taxes 3194

Stocks of United States,
exempt from State or local taxation 3701

Stockton, Cal.,
inspector of customs to reside at 2583

Stolen Checks,
duplicates of, how procured 3646, 3647

Stolen Treasury-Notes,
credit to be allowed to officers innocently paying 3707

Stonington, Conn.,
collection-district and port of entry 2533
collector in, to reside at 2534

Section.

Stoppages,
from pay of soldiers, when to be applied to support of Soldiers' Home 4818
from pay of officers and soldiers, when to be applied to support of National Home 4831

Storage,
of goods landed from vessels in distress 2892
charges and fees for, of cargoes of vessels seeking port in distress 2894
customs, appropriation of receipts from 3687
Secretary of Treasury to fix rate for, at quarantine warehouses 4795

Storekeepers,
in Department of Treasury, salary of 235

army,
rank of 1159
to give bond 1191
pay of 1261
allowance of forage to 1271
at national armories, to give bond 1664

internal revenue,
appointment and salary of 3153
to take oath and give bond 3153
not to be engaged in other business without permission of Commissioner 3153
to be paid monthly 3153
may be transferred by Commissioner or supervisor 3154
temporary, may be designated by collector 3155
may be suspended by supervisor 3163
spirits to be drawn from receiving-cistern in presence of 3267
to have charge of warehouse 3271
of distillery 3273
no material for distilling to be used, nor spirits removed, in absence of 3284
stamps to be placed on spirits by gauger in presence of 3287, 3295
to sign such stamps 3287, 3295
casks to be branded by gauger in presence of 3295
penalties relating to 3300
to keep warehouse book 3301
to make daily return 3301
to make monthly report in duplicate 3301
to keep record of distillery operations 3302

Stores,
military, sale of damaged 1241
and supplies, disposal of proceeds of 3692

Storm-Signals,
duty of Secretary of War to provide for 221

Stow-Aways,
vessels not to be liable for carrying 4514

Stranded Vessels,
protection of, by consuls, &c., on foreign coast 4238

Stratford, Conn.,
port of delivery 2533

Stubs,
of stamps for distilled spirits, entries on, &c. 3312
books of, to be returned to Commissioner 3314
gauger to return book of, to collector 3314

Stuttgardt,
consul at, salary of 1690

Subsidies,
corporations receiving, from United States, to pay directors, engineers, &c., appointed to examine roads 5259

Subsistence,
for Army, purchases, &c., not to exceed necessities of year 3732
contracts for, for Army, provisions of 3715
Department of, of Army, authorized 1094
organization, and rank 1140
to purchase and issue rations to Army 1141
post-commissary sergeants for 1142
to ration co-operating naval detachments 1143

Section.

Subsistence—Continued.
sales by officers of, of designated articles. 1144
report of, to be made ... 1144
of rations by, to officers in field ... 1145
officers of, to give bonds ... 1191

Sub-Treasuries,
provisions respecting ... 3591–3613
(see *Assistant Treasurers*.)

Succession,
internal-revenue tax on ... 3439

"*Successors and Assigns*,"
included in "company" or "association" ... 5

Suffolk, Va.,
port of delivery ... 2552
surveyor to reside at ... 2553

Suffrage,
by whom right of, may be exercised in Territories ... 1860

Sugars,
sirup of sugar, sugar-cane juice, melado, &c., entered as molasses, to be forfeited ... 2504
imported, not to be removed from wharf before proof of; penalty ... 2882
standards of imported, how selected and to whom furnished ... 2914
how and by whom sampled; casks, &c., how marked ... 2915
unrefined imported, change from package, how made; drawback on ... 3029
manifest of, carried by vessel in coasting trade between neighboring districts .. 4349
penalty for transporting, between remote districts without manifest and permit. 4354
penalty when not on manifest, &c ... 4356

Suits,
against officer for acts done under revenue laws or Title THE ELECTIVE FRANCHISE ... 643
brought by alien against officer, non-resident in State where brought ... 644
statement of, by district attorney, to Solicitor of Treasury ... 772, 773
to Commissioner of Internal Revenue ... 774
only one to be brought, where several things belonging to same person are seized under revenue laws ... 920
for taxes to be in name of United States ... 3213
for fines, penalties, and forfeitures under internal-revenue laws, to be in name of United States ... 3213
when United States not subject to costs of .. 3214
for recovery of internal-revenue taxes, &c., not to be commenced without sanction of Commissioner ... 3214
Commissioner of Internal Revenue to establish regulations relative to, for observance of revenue officers, district attorneys, and marshals ... 3215
for restraining assessing and collecting of taxes not to be maintained ... 3224
for recovery of alleged illegal internal-revenue taxes not to be maintained until appeal made to Commissioner ... 3226
when to be brought ... 3227
compromise of internal revenue ... 3229
continuance of internal revenue ... 3231
depending in foreign country ... 4071
upon bond of marshal of consular court, how brought ... 4114
to forfeit vessel for false swearing by agent, &c., recovery of costs of ... 4163
limitation of, against assignee in bankruptcy. 5057
upon assignee's bond, who may bring ... 5036
certain, commenced, &c., not affected by Revised Statutes ... 5597

Section.

Summary Courts-Martial,
in Navy, punishments which may be inflicted by ... 1624
general courts-martial may inflict same punishment as ... 1624

Summons,
by internal-revenue collector to taxpayer ... 3173, 3174
to witnesses under letters-rogatory, how issued ... 4071

Sunbury, Ga.,
port of delivery ... 2559
surveyor of customs at ... 2560

Superintendents,
of Treasury building, chief clerk to act as .. 235
additional compensation ... 235
to certify to accounts for contingent expenses ... 240
to keep detailed accounts of such expenses for each bureau ... 240
to make expenditures for furniture and repairs and keep account thereof ... 241
rooms for Department of Justice, to be provided by ... 352
of public documents; appointment; salary. 507
duties of ... 508
of national armory, designation of, from Ordnance Department ... 1662
compensation of ... 1663
of exportation and drawback, appointment and compensation of ... 3161
may administer oaths and certify papers .. 3162
of New York assay-office, appointment of ... 3554
duties of ... 3555
salary of ... 3556
of Government Hospital for Insane ... 4839

of cemeteries,
porter's lodge to be erected for, residence of. 4873
appointment of, by Secretary of War ... 4873
salary of, how determined ... 4875
quarters and fuel to be furnished ... 4875

of Indian affairs,
(see *Indians*.)

of life-saving stations,
for coast of Long Island and New Jersey, powers and duties ... 4243
for coast of Long Island to have charge of Narragansett Pier and Block Island stations ... 4248

of mints,
office created ... 3496
certain, to perform duties of treasurer ... 3497
to determine wages ... 3499
may require oaths of employés ... 3500
to give bond ... 3501
may require bond of assistants, &c ... 3501
may appoint substitutes in cases of absence of officers with consent, &c ... 3502
chief clerk to act as, in case of absence ... 3502
reports to be made by ... 3503
general powers and duties of ... 3503, 3504
to receive, &c., money and bullion ... 3506
to weigh, &c., bullion deposits ... 3521
to deliver certain bullion to assayers ... 3522
how to procure silver bullion ... 3526
at Philadelphia, shall purchase metal for minor coinage ... 3528
exchange of minor coins by, &c ... 3529
duty as to ingots ... 3530, 3531
as to bars for payment of deposits ... 3534
as to coins ... 3538
as to trial-pieces ... 3539
as to clippings ... 3540
as to coiner's and melter and refiner's accounts and settlements ... 3541–3543
as to ordinary expense account ... 3543

Section.

Superintendents—Continued.
as to delivery of coin to depositors 3544
as to testing weights 3549
as to defacing dies 3550
at Philadelphia, to prescribe regulations as to medals 3551
shall examine books, &c., of treasurers of mint 3650
in Post-Office Department,
of money-order system, salary of 393
of foreign mails, salary of 393
of blank agency, salary of 393
assistants 393
of free delivery, designation of 394
may be employed as special agents 4019
of railway postal service, appointment of... 4020
Superior, Mich.,
collection-district 2599
officers of customs in, residence of 2600
additional inspectors for 2605
inspectors of hulls and boilers for 4414
salaries of 4414
Supervising Architect,
of Department of Treasury, salary of 235
assistant 235
Supervising Inspector-General of Steam-Vessels,
appointment of, authorized 4402
qualifications 4402
salary 4402
duties of 4403
reports to Secretary of Treasury 4403
permanent appropriation for salary of 4461
Supervising Inspectors of Steam-Vessels,
appointment of ten, authorized 4404
qualifications of 4404
salary and allowances 4404
with supervising inspector-general to form a board 4405
meetings of, when held 4405
powers and duties of 4405
for Pacific coast to attend meetings of board, when 4405
to be assigned to districts by board 4405
duties and powers of 4406
duties of, in cases of violations of law ... 4407
supervision of local boards by 4408
of districts having no inspectors 4409
to have powers and perform duties of local boards, when 4409
reports of, to board at annual meeting 4410
who are not eligible to appointment as 4416
may renew license of absent officers, when.. 4447
appeal to, from local board 4452
powers and duties in such cases 4452
bonds to be given by 4459
permanent appropriation for salaries of 4461
Supervising Surgeon,
of marine-hospital service, how appointed.. 4802
duties and salary of 4802
to make monthly reports to Secretary of Treasury 4802
Supervisors,
of elections,
appointment of, for cities and towns of more than 20,000 inhabitants 2011, 2012
for counties and parishes in congressional districts 2011, 2012
to be of different political parties 2012
qualifications of 2012
to make and verify registration and lists.. 2026
special deputy marshals to assist 2021
forms and instructions to be furnished to... 2026
appointed for cities and towns, compensation of 2031
appropriation for fees of 3689

Section.

Supervisors—Continued.
of internal revenue,
may transfer or suspend inspector, gauger, and storekeeper 3154, 3163
appointment, salary, duties, &c., of....3159, 3160
may issue summons and examine persons and papers 3163
may suspend collector for fraud, &c 3163
to report to Commissioner relative to neglect of duty, &c., of officer 3161
Supplies,
for Army, Secretary of War to prescribe, to be purchased by Subsistence and Quartermaster's Departments 219
purchase and distribution of 1133
for Navy, purchases, &c., of, to be under Secretary of Navy 3714
provisions concerning contracts for, and purchases of 3718–3732
purchase of, by foreign vessels of war from public warehouse 2982
deposit of proceeds of sale of 3618
statement of, in book of estimates 3672
provisions concerning purchase of......3709–3743
contracts, &c., for, shall be made after advertising 3709
for Executive Departments, contracts for, limited to one year 3735
Supreme Courts,
of District of Columbia,
jurisdiction of suits for making false claims against United States 3491
of United States,
copies of reports of, to be furnished by Interior Department to Department of Justice for distribution 498
organization of 673–683
number of justices in, quorum of 673
salaries of Chief-Justice and justices of..... 676
power of, to appoint clerk, marshal, and reporter 677
deputy clerks 678
salary, duties, and powers of marshal of.... 680
duties of reporter of 681
salary of 682
price of reports of decisions of 682
distribution of 683
provisions concerning jurisdiction of 688–709
review of final judgments of circuit court, on writ of error 691
appeal to, from final decrees of circuit court. 692
review of final judgments or decrees of circuit court, on certificate of division of opinion, on writ of error or appeal ... 693
on writ of error or appeal, without regard to sum or value in dispute 699
judgments and decrees of State courts.... 709
appropriation for reports of 3689
may adjourn to another place in case of contagious or epidemic disease 4799
justice of, to frame, &c., orders in bankruptcy 4990
Chief-Justice to nominate registers in bankruptcy 4993
appeal to, from Court of Claims, in suits by railroad company to recover moneys withheld by Secretary of Treasury... 5261
of territories,
how constituted; quorum 1864
clerks of, appointment, &c., by 1870
in Arizona, adjourned terms of 1934
admission of alien seamen to citizenship by. 2174
Sureties,
on bond to United States, when to have priority of claim against principal 3468
on contracts for naval supplies 3722

Section.

Sureties—Continued.
of postmasters, liabilities of 3836
limitation of 3838
of seamen, liable for penalty in case of refusal to sail, &c 4558
liability of what, not affected by discharge in bankruptcy 5118

Surgeon-General,
of army,
rank of 1168
shall make regulations in regard to artificial limbs, &c 4787
shall certify list of persons desiring money-commutation for artificial limb, &c... 4788
of navy,
Chief of Bureau of Medicine and Surgery to have title of 1471
shall receive and record evidence in certain pension cases 4717

Surgeons,
in army,
for regiments of cavalry 1102
number and rank of 1168
certificate of, in biennial examinations of invalid pensioners valid 4771
in militia,
one to each regiment in United States service 1646
one to each brigade 1647
in navy,
number of, on active list 1368
relative rank of 1474
pay of 1556
may give biennial certificate to invalid pensioners 4771

Surplus Fund,
of national banks, part of net profits to, amount of 5199
Treasury, balances of appropriations shall be carried to 3690, 3691

Survey,
of Indian reservations, how made 2115
of Vigil and Saint Vrain land-claims, appropriation for 3689
of Nolan land-claim, appropriation for 3689
of distillery,
how to be made 3264
when to take effect 3264
Commissioner of Internal Revenue may order another 3264
of public lands,
contracts for, when to become binding 2398
what instructions to be deemed part of... 2399
price per mile for, how fixed 2400
accounts of cost of surveying private land-claims, how kept 2400
patents for private claims, not to issue until cost of survey paid 2400
settlers may have townships surveyed 2401
deposits by settlers to be deemed appropriation for 2402
excess to be returned 2402
to go in part payment for their lands.... 2403
in Oregon, augmented rates. for certain forest-lands 2404
in California 2405
in Washington Territory 2405
geodetic surveys in Oregon and California authorized 2409
restrictions upon 2409
in California and Oregon may be paid for by day 2411
appropriation of deposits by individuals for. 3689
of vessels,
may be ordered on complaint of mate and crew; proceedings, &c 4557–4559

Section.

Survey—Continued.
duties of inspectors in foreign port 4560
contents of report of inspectors of vessel... 4561
payment of cost of, in foreign port 4562
penalty for refusal to pay for 4563
of captured vessel or property, when made in prize-cases 4615
when prize-property taken for use of United States, how made 4624

Surveying-Districts,
establishment of 2207

Surveying-Expeditions,
proceeds of materials, &c., sold to, not to be covered into Treasury 3618

Surveyors-General of Public Lands,
appointment of 2207
salary of, in Louisiana, Florida, Minnesota, Kansas, Nebraska, Iowa, and Dakota. 2208
in Oregon and Washington 2209
in Colorado, New Mexico, California, Idaho, Nevada, Montana, Utah, Wyoming, and Arizona 2210
in Florida, Oregon, and California, to be paid quarterly 2211
to commence from time of giving bond. 2211
bond of 2215
new bond and additional security may be required 2216
term of office 2217
to hold over until new commission or successor enters upon duties 2222
bond to hold good for time acting 2222
may appoint deputies and administer oath to them 2223
may frame regulations for action of deputies 2223
may remove deputies for negligence or misconduct 2223
to have surveyed, measured, and marked, base and meridian lines, &c 2223
to make correction parallels and meridians. 2223
to survey private land-claims when title confirmed by Congress 2223
to transmit to registers plats surveyed 2223
to forward copies of such plats to Commissioner of General Land-Office 2223
to inspect operations in field 2223
to be allowed expenses while inspecting.... 2223
may depute agent to inspect surveys in field. 2223
to receive only expenses, in addition to salary, while inspecting 2223
allowance for clerk-hire 2226
for office-rent, fuel, books, stationery, &c. 2227
bond of deputy for performance of contract, to be approved and certified by 2230

Surveyors of Customs,
in the several collection-districts 2518–2602
at Albany to act as collector 2536
term of office of 2613
bonds of 2619
by whom approved and where filed 2620
temporary, how appointed, compensation of. 2624
when to perform duties of collector 2625
duties of 2627
at certain ports 2628
in case of disability or death of, who to perform duties of 2629
when to authorize officer or clerk to act as disbursing agent, bond 2631
when may act by deputy, responsibility of. 2632
number and compensation of clerks of..... 2634
to keep posted table of fees, receipts, &c., penalty for failure 2635
to account for fees, &c., and make annual returns to Commissioner, penalty.... 2639
personal attendance of; duties of, as to accounts; penalty for omission 2640

Section.

Surveyors of Customs—Continued.
accounts of, what to include and how rendered ... 2641
to certify services of occasional inspectors. 2642
to render list of clerks, their duties and compensation, account of stationery, office-rent, &c ... 2643
acting as collector, to render quarterly accounts of moneys collected; excess to be paid into Treasury ... 2647
in certain districts to keep for sale blanks.. 2648
drawback fees of, how shared ... 2656
fees of ... 2657
acting as collectors, limit to compensation of ... 2688
compensation exclusive of expenses of ... 2689
limit to emoluments of, at certain ports ... 2690
at other ports ... 2691
salaries of, at Eastport; Portsmouth, N. H.; Newburyport; Gloucester; Fredericksburgh, Va.; Portland, Me.; Savannah; and at ports established by the President ... 2706
at ports in district of New Orleans..2707, 2708, 2712, 2718
at Velasco, excess of receipts to be accounted for ... 2709
at Matagorda, Lavaca, and Copano ... 2710
at Pacific City and Milwaukee ... 2711
at Selma ... 2713
at San Francisco ... 2714
at Salem and Beverly ... 2715
at Michigan City ... 2716
at Albany ... 2717
limit of compensation of, at Portland, Me., Boston, New York, Philadelphia, Baltimore, Charleston, Savannah, and New Orleans ... 2719
at non-enumerated ports ... 2720
when to examine baggage, &c ... 2801
at certain ports to estimate duties, approve bonds, &c ... 2825
when to enter amount of duties on importer's bond, &c ... 2826
when to cause inspection of cargoes, &c., permit vessels to unload, and indorse manifests ... 2830
not to receive bond less than duties, &c.; when to collect and pay over duties.. 2831
when to put inspectors on board of vessels. 2875
to transmit inspector's book to collector ... 2876
when to supply absence of inspector to superintend delivery of cargoes, &c ... 2877
distilled spirits to be landed under inspection of ... 2884
returns of delivery of merchandise ... 2889
opening of packages with consent of ... 2899
use of warehouse hired by ... 2956
at Louisville, to have custody, &c., of imports for Jeffersonville ... 2967
when to inspect merchandise notified for exportation ... 3035
search of stores, warehouses, &c ... 3107
duties of, as to public money ... 3639
President may increase bonds of ... 3639
and naval officer shall examine books, &c., of assistant treasurers ... 3650
duties of, in measurement of vessels...4148, 4154
to countersign certificates of registry ... 4158
survey or measurement of vessels by, for record ... 4181
to grant certificates of measurement for record ... 4181
fees of, for measurement ... 4186
by whom paid ... 4186

Section.

Surveyors of Customs—Continued.
limit upon, for measuring and certifying tonnage ... 4186
monthly return by, to collector, of certified manifests or permits ... 4332
may be authorized to enroll and license vessels ... 4344
at Cold Spring, Greenport, and Port Jefferson, N. Y ... 4345
fees of, for enrolling and licensing vessels .. 4346
penalty upon, for delivering false measurement of vessel ... 4373
to post up conspicuously, table of fees ... 4353
powers and obligations of, at port of delivery made port of entry in case of insurrection ... 5314
Suspension Bridge, N. Y.,
port of entry ... 2535
collector to reside at ... 2536
Suspension,
no money to be paid as salary to public officer suspended from duty ... 1762
power of President to suspend civil officer from office during recess of Senate, and to appoint ... 1768
of pay of officers in Army by sentence of court-martial ... 1342
of pay by general court-martial in Navy ... 1624
of work at distillery ... 3310
caused by unavoidable accident ... 3310
Swamp-Lands,
appropriation to indemnify States for ... 3689
Swansea, Mass.,
port of delivery ... 2527
Swatow,
consul at, salary of ... 1690
Sweden and Norway,
salary of minister to ... 1675
Sweepings of Tobacco,
when may be sold without payment of tax. 3362
Switzerland,
salary of minister to ... 1675

T.

Tabasco,
consul at, salary of ... 1690
Tahiti,
consul at, salary of ... 1690
Talcahuano,
consul at, salary of ... 1690
Tamatave,
commercial agent at, salary of ... 1690
Tampico,
consul-general at, salary of ... 1690
consul at, salary of ... 1690
Tangier,
consul at, salary of ... 1690
Tappahannock, Va.,
collection-district and port of entry ... 2552
collector in, to reside at ... 2553
Tare,
allowance for, on imports, how estimated ... 2898
Tariff,
of consular fees shall be kept conspicuously posted in consulate ... 1731
President may prescribe ... 1745
of fees of consular courts ... 4120
of duties, (see *Duties on Imports*.)
Taunton, Mass.,
port of delivery ... 2527
Taxation of Bonds,
State, municipal, or local, prohibited ... 3701
Taxes,
internal-revenue, jurisdiction in equity of district courts to enforce liens for ... 563
where may be sued for ... 733

Section.

Taxes—Continued.
suits for, to be brought in name of United States ... 919
on fur seal-skins, amount of ... 1969
collection and payment of ... 1969
unequal, not to be imposed on persons immigrating from foreign countries ... 2164
internal-revenue, what classes of business liable to ... 3244
on distilled spirits ... 3251
on brandy made from apples, peaches, or grapes ... 3255
on imitation wines or compound liquors ... 3328
on fermented liquors ... 3339
on tobacco and snuff ... 3368
on cigars and cigarettes ... 3394
on deposits, capital, and circulation of banks 3408
on banks for notes of person, State bank, or association, used for circulation and paid out ... 3412
on banks, bankers, or associations, for notes of town, city, or corporation paid out. 3413
on bank-checks, drafts, or orders ... 3418
on medicines, preparations, perfumery, cosmetics, friction-matches, wax-tapers, cigar-lights, and playing-cards ... 3437
in what currency payable to United States. 3473
illegally collected, appropriation to refund.. 3689
under direct-tax laws, appropriation to refund ... 3689
on salaries, appropriation for ... 3689
United States to have priority in order for dividend in bankruptcy ... 5101
proceedings in bankruptcy not to interfere with assessment or collection of ... 5101
payment of, in national-bank notes, may be received in payment of ... 5182
on national banks, payment of ... 5214
how and when assessed, basis of ... 5215
how assessed on default of return ... 5216
how collected on default of payment ... 5217
refunding excess of ... 5218
by State authority ... 5219
Tax-Paid Stamps,
(see *Stamps, Internal Revenue.*)
Teamsters,
pension to dependent relatives of, when to begin ... 4710
Teche, The, La.,
collection district ... 2568
collector in, residence of ... 2569
Telegraph,
authority of Secretary of War to establish lines connecting signal-stations ... 223
provisions concerning ... 5263–5269
Tellers,
in office of Treasurer, salary of ... 235
assistant ... 235
Temporary Clerks,
compensation of, in Department of Treasury 242
Temporary Storekeeper,
may be designated by collector of internal revenue ... 3155
Ten-Cent Piece,
weight and fineness of ... 3513, 3514
devices and legends on ... 3517
deviation allowed in adjusting ... 3536
Ten-Dollar Piece,
weight and fineness of ... 3511–3514
deviation allowed in adjusting ... 3535
Tennessee,
district judge in, appointment, residence of. 552
Tennessee River,
in Alabama, made free of tolls ... 5244
tolls on canal at Muscle and Colbert's Shoals; report to Secretary of Treasury ... 5245

Section.

Tenure of Office,
for persons appointed by and with advice and consent of Senate ... 1767
Revised Statutes not to affect ... 5597
Term of Office,
of justices of supreme courts of Territories. 1864
of surveyors-general ... 2217
of registers and receivers ... 2244
Territorial Courts,
may enjoin receivers, &c., of national banks, effects of ... 5237
may adjudge forfeiture of franchise of national banks ... 5239
Territories,
duties of Secretary of Interior concerning.. 442
executive power in, how vested ... 1841
authority of governor ... 1841
secretary, appointment and removal of ... 1843
when to execute powers of governor ... 1843
duties of ... 1844
salaries of governors and secretaries ... 1845
legislative power, how vested ... 1846
legislative assembly, of what to consist ... 1846
term of office of members ... 1846
sessions, regulation of ... 1846
limit of ... 1852
compensation of members ... 1853
of president of council and speaker of house ... 1853
members not to hold certain offices ... 1854
restriction not applicable to first assembly ... 1854
certain United States officers not eligible to office in ... 1854
restriction not to apply to Territory of Washington ... 1854
compensation of certain officers not to be increased ... 1855
justices of peace to be elected ... 1856
general officers of militia to be elected ... 1856
township, district, and county officers, how elected or appointed ... 1857
other territorial officers, how nominated and appointed ... 1857
in new Territories, officers, how appointed and assigned ... 1857
term of office of those so appointed ... 1857
vacancies, how filled during recess of council 1858
commissions, when to expire ... 1858
persons attached to Army or Navy not to hold civil office ... 1860
subordinate officers of legislative assembly, number and salaries of ... 1861
limit upon number, and compensation of... 1861
Delegates to Congress ... 1862
supreme courts, how constituted ... 1864
quorum, and term of office of justices ... 1864
clerks of supreme courts, appointment and term of office of ... 1870
of district courts, appointment or retention of ... 1871
one clerk only in each district entitled to compensation from United States ... 1871
county courts, established by laws of, may be held by judges of supreme courts.. 1874
what causes may be heard in such courts. 1874
expenses not chargeable to United States. 1874
United States attorney to be appointed in each ... 1875
qualifications and term of office ... 1875
marshal for each Territory to be appointed, term of office ... 1876
salary of chief-justice and associate justices. 1879
of United States attorney ... 1880
of marshal ... 1881
salaries payable quarterly at Treasury ... 1882

Section.

Territories—Continued.
fees and costs, allowance of, to attorneys, marshals, clerks, &c., how prescribed 1883
when officers absent, no salary to be paid .. 1884
President to certify officially his opinion of such case 1884
accounting officer of Treasury to file opinion in his office 1884
accounts for disbursements of money appropriated by Congress; how settled and adjusted 1886
acts of legislature not deemed authority for disbursements 1886
sufficient vouchers and proof to be required 1886
payments not to be made or allowed until estimated for by Secretary of Treasury. 1886
nor until object approved by Congress.. 1886
public printing, limitation on expenses of .. 1887
annual expenses not to exceed appropriation by Congress 1888
religious, &c., corporations, restriction on, as to holding real estate 1890
real estate acquired or held contrary, &c., to be forfeited 1890
existing rights not impaired 1890
United States Constitution and laws applicable to 1891
penitentiaries erected by United States to be under control of marshals 1892
exceptions in certain Territories 1892
Attorney-General to prescribe rules for government of penitentiaries 1893
marshals to cause rules, &c., to be executed. 1893
compensation of marshal and deputies under such regulations, how fixed.... 1893
expenses of penitentiaries, &c., from what fund payable 1894
compensation of officers not to be increased 1894
prisoners sentenced under laws of Territories, how received, &c., in penitentiaries 1895
admission of alien seamen to citizenship in. 2174
district courts of, to have jurisdiction of suits for making false claims against United States 3491
(*For provisions concerning particular Territories, see the several Territories.*)

Testimony,
power of Treasury agents to take, in Alaska. 1976
fees for reducing to writing, in establishing pre-emption and homestead rights ... 2238
in establishing claims for mineral lands.. 2238
how may be taken for use in certain suits in foreign countries 4071, 4074

Texas,
appointment of Indian agents for tribes in. 2052
collection-districts, ports of entry and delivery in 2578
officers in 2579

Third Assistant Engineers of Navy,
pay of officers retired as 1590

Third Auditor of Treasury,
accounts of, to be examined by Second Comptroller 273
appointment and salary of 276
duties of 277
may take testimony in case of claims for certain property lost in military service; expenses of, how paid 3488
duty as to requisitions of War Department. 3673

Third-Class Mail-Matter,
what shall constitute 3878
must be prepaid by stamps 3897

Section.

Thomaston, Me.,
port of delivery 2517

Three-Cent. Piece,
weight and material of 3515
devices and legends on 3517
deviation allowed in adjusting 3537

Three-Dollar Piece,
weight and fineness of 3511–3514
devices and legends on 3517
deviation allowed in adjusting 3535

Three-months' Extra Wages,
(see *Seamen.*)

Three Per Cent. Fund to States,
appropriation of 3689

Tien-Tsin,
consul at, salary of 1690

Timber and Timber-Lands,
(see *Lands, Public.*)

Title to Land,
proceedings in purchases of land by United States for forts, buildings, &c 355

Tiverton, R. I.,
port of delivery 2531

Tobacco,
sale, of, to enlisted men of Army 1149
amount due by enlisted men for, to be deducted from pay 1301
internal-revenue officer not to be interested in manufacture of 3168
dealers in leaf, special tax of 3244
retail dealers 3244
dealers in, special tax of 3244
manufacturers of, special tax of 3244
penalty for not paying 3242
definition of 3244
forfeiture for removing unlawfully, selling without stamping or payment of tax. 3272
penalty for violation of law where no specific penalty 3456
statement and bond 3355
to procure certificate 3355
to put up signs 3356
record of 3357
manufactories of, to be numbered 3357
inventory, books, and abstract of manufacturers of 3358
peddlers of, special tax, &c 3244, 3381–3384
dealers in leaf, to render statement 3359, 3391
books of 3360
how to be put up, packages for 3362
sale of shorts, clippings, &c., in bulk, or for export, without payment of tax 3362
labels on packages of 3364
smoking, manufactured prior to July 20, 1868 3365
purchasing, &c., not branded or stamped as required by law 3366
buying, &c., from manufacturer who has not paid special tax 3367
tax on chewing and smoking 3368
stamps for, sold under distraint or by order of court, or Government officer, &c... 3369
stamps for, how prepared, furnished, and sold 3369
abandoned, condemned, or forfeited, not to be sold for price not equal to tax, but may be destroyed 3369
manufactured by one person for another, or on shares 3370
assessment of tax on, sold or removed without being properly stamped 3371
forfeiture of, for absence of stamp 3373
removing or selling unlawfully 3374
stamps on packages emptied of, to be destroyed 3376
fraudulent stamping of 3376

Section.

Tobacco—Continued.
imported, to be stamped same as domestic.. 3377
on hand July 20, 1868 3378
falsely selling as made and tax-paid before July 20, 1868 3380
exportation of 3385
drawback on, exported 3386
laws imposing taxes on, extended to boundaries of United States 3448
for Navy, may be purchased without advertising 3721

Toledo, O.,
port of entry 2603
collector to reside at 2604
transportation in bond extended to 2997

Tolls,
Tennessee, Coosa, Cahawba, and Black Warrior Rivers, within Alabama 5244
for use of canal at Muscle and Colbert's Shoals on Tennessee River 5245
Des Moines River 5246
passage of vessels to and from harbor of Michigan City, Ind., to be free from .. 5247
from improvements in Wisconsin River, and in water-communication between Wisconsin and Fox Rivers; future reduction of 5249
reduction of, on Louisville and Portland Canal 5255

"Ton,"
definition of, in appraisal of imports 2951

Tonnage,
jurisdiction of circuit court of suits arising under laws providing revenue from .. 629
duties or tax, (see *Duties, Tonnage.*)
fees, (see *Fees.*)
of vessels, (see *Vessels.*)

Tools,
of mechanical trade, &c., separate entry of, how and by whom made 2799
when bond required 2800
permit to land, &c 2801

Topographer,
in Post-Office Department, salary of 393

Toronto,
consul at, salary of 1690

Torts,
jurisdiction of district courts of suits by aliens for, in violation of law of nations or treaty 563

Total Disability,
pension shall be granted for 4692
rates of pension for 4695
when increase of pension for, to commence. 4698½

Tow-Boats,
(see *Tug-Boats.*)

Town Creek, Md.,
port of delivery 2548
surveyor to reside at 2549

Township Officers,
in Territories, method of election or appointment of 1857

Town-Sites,
provisions as to, not applicable to military or other public reservations 2393

Trade-Dollar,
weight and fineness of 3513, 3514
devices and legends of 3517
silver bullion may be deposited for 3520
coinage charged for 3524
deviations in adjusting 3536

Trade-Marks,
who may obtain protection for 4937
term of protection of; rights secured by; renewal of 4941

Section.

Trade,
with Indians, who may be permitted to 2128
bond of trader 2128
without, or with false, license, in States in insurrection; penalty 5306

Transcripts,
fees for, from journals of Congress 71
from books, &c., of Treasury Department, when evidence 886
received in evidence in trial of indictment for embezzling public money ... 887
from money-order account books of Post Office Department, when evidence 889

Transfers,
of internal-revenue storekeper 3154, 3163
of internal-revenue inspector and gauger... 3163
of merchandise from unfit warehouse by Commissioner of Internal Revenue... 3272
of bullion for coinage ingots 3530
of contracts prohibited 3737
of money-order funds, Postmaster-General may direct 4042, 4043
of debts, in payments to mail-contractors, authorized 4056
of prize property to another district for sale, provisions concerning 4629

Transportation,
of supplies, power of Secretary of War to prescribe regulations for 219
of troops, munitions, stores, &c., for Army, to be controlled by Secretary of War. 220
in Army, Quartermaster's Department to furnish 1133
of subjects of oriental countries to be held to service or labor, penalty 2161
for Army and Navy, contracts, &c., for, not to exceed necessities of year 3732
of mail, contracts for 3941–3963
to foreign countries 4006
accounts to show expenditures for 4049
to persons requiring artificial limbs, &c 4791
of passengers on steam-vessels, (see *Steam-Vessels.*)

of merchandise,
in bond, provisions concerning 2971–3008
to Pacific and western ports 2971
entry for immediate 2990
collectors to give priority of examination to goods not subject to appraisal at port of arrival 2991
execution of bonds for 2992
goods entered for, to be delivered to common carriers 2993
how secured and conveyed 2994
goods destined for immediate, how transferred from importing vessel; if stored, entry and appraisement required. 2995
through United States to and from Europe, Asia, and islands adjacent 2997
privilege of, to extend to certain ports 2997
opening, breaking, &c., vehicle, warehouse, &c., containing goods, imported for, removing, &c., lock or seal, or aiding to remove or receive goods 2998
of goods entered for warehouse 3000
penalty for non-delivery, &c 3001
of imports and products, &c., of United States over certain foreign territory.. 3006
with benefit of drawback, to another district for exportation 3036
of explosives, on vessels carrying passengers, prohibited 4278
on other vessels or vehicles, how packed and marked 4279
State or territorial regulation of 4280

Section.

Transportation—Continued.
of valuables as freight or baggage 4281
written notice to be given master or owner of vessel 4281
if notice not given, owner not liable.... 4281
limitation of liability where notice given. 4281
loss of, by fire, when owner not liable for. 4282
by embezzlement, limitation on liability. 4283
compensation for, where value of vessel insufficient 4284
proceedings to recover compensation ... 4284
owner of vessel may transfer interest to trustee for losers by embezzlement... 4285
after transfer, proceedings against owner to cease 4285
who to be deemed owner 4286
remedies against master or officers not affected by five preceding sections ... 4287
inflammable materials not to be shipped without notice of character........ 4288
penalty for shipping without notice...... 4288
not to apply to vessels on rivers or inland waters 4288
limitation on liability of owners not to apply to canal-boats, barges, or lighters. 4289
or to vessels on rivers or inland waters... 4289
in steam-vessel, precautions against fire.... 4470
fire-pump and hose when cotton, hay, or hemp carried 4471
loose hay, cotton, and other dangerous articles not to be carried 4472
penalty for unlawfully carrying cotton or hemp 4473
gunpowder, nitro-glycerine, &c., how packed and marked 4475
penalty for unlawfully shipping 4476
fire-extinguishers prescribed when 4479
Travel-Fees,
of messenger in bankruptcy, allowance for.. 5126
Travel-Pay,
to officers of Army honorably discharged... 1289
to soldiers honorably discharged 1290
Traveling,
allowance for, to officers executing precepts of Congress 74
allowances for, in Army 1273
in Navy 1566
pay, subsistence, and allowances for, of militia in United States service........ 1652
time allowed for, in responding to internal-revenue collector's summons 3174
Traveling-Expenses,
of Members and Delegates in Congress..... 45
accounts for, how certified 47
of attorneys, &c 824
of clerks of courts 828
of marshals 829, 830
of witnesses 848
of clerks or officers as witnesses 850
of seamen as witnesses 851
of jurors 852
of persons employed in Indian service...... 2077
actual and necessary, of internal-revenue gauger, to be paid 3157
Treason,
limitation of time for finding indictment of. 1043
provisions of Title NEUTRALITY, not to be construed to prevent prosecution or punishment for 5291
Treasurer of United States,
officers and employés in office of 235
not to engage in certain business 243
appointment and salary of 301
bond of 302
may authorize Assistant Treasurer to act in his place 304

Section.

Treasurer of United States—Continued.
duties of 305
to cover into Treasury liabilities outstanding more than three years 306
to report accounts unchanged for three years. 310
to report annually to Congress 311
money paid under protest for customs-duties to be credited to 3010
may maintain suits on certain bonds or securities taken by Commissioner of Internal Revenue 3425
may redeem minor, &c., coins 3529
location, &c., of office 3591
public money subject to draft of 3593
collected in District of Columbia shall be paid to 3615
duties respecting 3639
shall keep accounts of Post-Office Department money separate 3642
money in Treasury subject to his draft........3644
shall pay duplicate checks 3646
examination of money, &c., in hands of.3649, 3650
registering money-letters of, from and to postmasters 3932
shall keep special account of money-order funds 4045
net proceeds of money-order business to be placed with, as postal revenues 4050
when, to pay duplicate checks for pensions. 4770
bonds to be transferred to, by national banks before commencing business 5159
in trust to 5152
books, &c., of, in relation to bonds of national banks shall be open to examination by Comptroller of Currency..... 5165
certificate to, of annual examination of bonds belonging to national banks... 5166
shall withhold interest on bonds of certain national banks, until notified by Comptroller of Currency to pay 5205
may retain out of interest on bonds, penalty for refusal, &c., by national banks to make reports 5213
semi-annual duty on national banks, to be paid to 5214
report to, as basis of semi-annual tax 5215
may assess tax without report 5216
may reserve tax out of interest due bank on bonds 5217
shall certify claim of bank for return of semi-annual duty 5218
national banks in liquidation shall deposit lawful money with, for redemption of notes, receipts for 5222
when shall redeem national-bank notes 5224
when shall destroy 5225
receivers of national banks shall pay over to, all money collected 5234
failure to keep safely moneys deposited. 5489
when masters, &c., of foreign vessels clearing for coast of Africa, to give bond to. 5564
Treasurers of Mints,
certain superintendents to perform duties of. 3497
Treasury Agents,
(see *Special Agents, Treasury Department.*)
Treasury Department,
(see *Department of Treasury.*)
Treasury Notes,
(see *United States Notes.*)
Treasury of United States,
to receive certain abraded coins at par 3505
certain gold coins in, to be recoined........ 3512
balance to credit of silver profit fund, to be deposited in 3526

Section.

Treasury of United States—Continued.
deductions, &c., on bullion to be covered into ... 3552
shall receive certain Spanish and Mexican coins ... 3567
to redeem fractional currency ... 3574
what rooms, vaults, &c., to be ... 3591
money of War and Navy Departments, how drawn from ... 3673
certain receipts to be deposited in, as postal revenues ... 4050

Treaties of United States,
copies of, to be furnished to Congressional Printer ... 210
jurisdiction of district courts of suits by aliens for torts in violation of ... 563
jurisdiction of Court of Claims not to extend to claims growing out of stipulations of ... 1066
penalty for attempting to negotiate with Indians except for United States ... 2116
of September 30, 1854, purchase of land located under, permitted when ... 2368
authorizing expenditures shall be referred to in estimates ... 3660
printing of, number for Secretary of State, usual number ... 3805
number of, printed for Congress at close of session ... 3807
for Secretary of Interior ... 3808
to be published in certain States in papers selected by Clerk of House ... 3823
rates for publishing ... 3825
how published in District of Columbia ... 3826
with foreign nations not impaired by provisions concerning tonnage duties, &c ... 4219
prize laws not to be construed as contravening ... 4652

Treaty of Washington,
entry and export of merchandise under ... 2866
British vessels may engage in coasting trade on Saint Lawrence and great lakes under ... 4347
suspension of privilege by President ... 4347

Treaty Stipulations,
respecting judicial authority of ministers and consuls in certain countries, provisions for execution of ... 4111–4130

Trial of Coins,
on delivery by coiner ... 3538

Trial Pieces,
of coins, selection, &c., of ... 3539

Trials,
of capital offenses committed on high seas, in what district to be had ... 730
of offenses begun in one district and completed in another ... 731

Trieste,
consul at, salary of ... 1690

Trinidad de Cuba,
consul at, salary of ... 1690
consulate at, may be discontinued ... 1694

Tripoli,
consul at, salary of ... 1690

Troy, N. Y.,
port of delivery ... 2535

Trumpeter,
for troop of cavalry ... 1103

Trusses,
to soldiers ruptured ... 1176
purchase of, by Surgeon General ... 1178

Trustees,
holding national-bank stock, not to be personally liable ... 5152

Section.

Trust-Funds,
stocks, sale of, to refund payments to purchasers of public lands ... 2363
stocks of States in default for interest, &c., how protected ... 3481
of United States, how invested ... 3659

Tubs, (Distillery,)
fermenting, how to be placed and marked ... 3269
Commissioner of Internal Revenue may require fastenings, locks, and seals ... 3270
emptying of fermenting ... 3285
worm, emptying and cleansing of ... 3286
fastenings of fermenting, in case of reduction of capacity of distillery ... 3311
using fermenting, locked or sealed, &c., penalty ... 3311
to be destroyed and material sold in cases of forfeiture ... 3332

Tuckerton, N. J.,
port of entry ... 2541
collector to reside at ... 2542

Tug-Boats,
in coasting trade on northern, &c., frontiers, report and clearance of ... 3123
penalty on foreign, towing vessels between United States ports ... 4370
not applied where towing is in foreign waters ... 4370
privileges of, owned by foreign railroad entering United States ... 4370
steam-pressure of, on Mississippi river and tributaries ... 4420

Tumbez,
consul at, salary of ... 1690

Tunis,
consul at, salary of ... 1690

Tunstall,
consul at, salary of ... 1690

Turkey,
salary of minister to ... 1675
consul-general at Constantinople to be secretary of legation to ... 1677
interpreter of legation to, salary of; need not be United States citizen ... 1678
marshal for consular courts in ... 4111
rent of prisons for American convicts in ... 4121

Turk's Island,
consul at, salary of ... 1690

Turpentine,
oil or spirits of, restrictions on carriage of, by steam passenger-vessels ... 4472
how packed and marked for shipment ... 4475
penalty for shipping contrary to law ... 4476

Twenty-Dollar Gold-Piece,
weight and fineness ... 3511–3514
deviation allowed in adjusting ... 3535

Twenty-five-Cent Piece,
weight and fineness of ... 3513–3514
deviation in adjusting ... 3536

Two-and-a-Half-Dollar Gold-Piece,
weight and fineness of ... 3511–3514
deviation in adjusting ... 3535

Two Per Cent. Fund to States,
appropriation for ... 3689

U.

Unascertained Duties,
on imports, money collected for, how credited ... 3010
refund of ... 3012½
appropriation to repay excess of deposits for ... 3689

Unauthorized Office,
when salary may be paid to person holding ... 1760

Unavoidable Accident,
suspension of work at distilleries caused by ... 3310
stamps for distilled spirits lost or destroyed by ... 3315

Section.

Uncalled-for Mail-Matter,
disposal of 4061
Unclaimed Dead and Request Letters,
provisions relating to 3930–3932
Unclaimed Merchandise,
where stored, charges on, how paid 2965
when collector of customs may sell, liable to depreciation, &c 2976
Unclaimed Pensions,
what shall constitute; after three years, name to be stricken from rolls, &c 4719
Uncollected Taxes,
to be credited to collector of internal revenue in certain cases 3218
lists and accounts of, to be transferred to successor for collection 3219
Unexpended Balances,
limit as to use of 3690
disposal of, after two years 3691
Unfermented Worts,
sold to other brewers for certain purposes, how taxed 3351
Uniform,
for Army to be prescribed by President 1296
of soldiers, shall not be sold, &c 3748
Union Pacific Railroad Company,
(see *Railroads*.)
Union River, Me.,
port of delivery 2517
United States,
exterior boundaries of, laws imposing certain taxes extended to 3448
may purchase goods free of internal-revenue tax 3464
United States Bonds,
premiums on, to be accounted for 3652
trust-funds shall be invested in 3659
no portraits of living persons to be placed on. 3576
issued to Pacific railways, appropriation to pay interest on 3689
faith pledged for payment in coin 3693
when may be redeemed before maturity .. 3693
redeemed, &c., shall be canceled and record kept 3695
known as five-twenties may be redeemed ... 3697
exempt from taxation 3701
provisions concerning issue of duplicates .. 3702–3705
registered, may be exchanged for coupons .. 3706
imitating or printing, &c., on, to be punished 3708
shall be deposited as security by national-bank depositories 5153
definition of, as used in chapter two, Title NATIONAL BANKS, defined 5158
belonging to national banks, deposit of, with United States Treasurer 5159
increase, &c., of, to correspond with capital; return of 5160
exchange of coupon, for registered 5161
transfers of, how made 5162
registry of transfers 5163
notice of transfers 5164
examination of registry, &c., of 5165
annual examination of 5166
custody of; collection of interest on, &c.; when market value is reduced; exchanges of, &c 5167
when circulation may be issued on, amount of 5171
when may be sold at auction to enforce equalization of circulation 5180
gold-notes may be issued to certain banks depositing 5185
in liquidation, when may be re-assigned to bank 5224

Section.

United States Bonds—Continued.
when may be declared forfeited to United States 5227
when may be canceled 5229
when may be sold at auction 5230
when may be sold at private sale 5231
no part of, to be applied to payment of fees for protesting notes 5238
transfer of, by national banks after act of insolvency, void 5242
national banks to pay duty on capital not invested in 5214
shall report amount of such capital 5215
interest on, may be withheld for tax 5217
included by words, "obligation or other security of the United States" 5413
secreting, embezzling, &c., implement, paper, &c., used in printing bonds, &c 5453
United States Commissioner,
(see *Commissioners of Circuit Courts*.)
United States Marshals,
(see *Marshals of United States*.)
United States Notes,
what may be paid in 3473
bearing interest, how payable to creditors of United States 3476
denominations, &c., of 3571
expenses of preparing, &c., how paid 3578
when may be re-issued 3579, 3580
replacing of mutilated 3580
when redeemed shall be destroyed 3581
authority to retire, suspended 3582
legal tender for what 3588–3590
premiums on, to be accounted for 3652
faith pledged for payment in coin 3693
exempt from taxation 3701
credit to be allowed officers paying stolen .. 3707
imitating or printing, &c., on, to be punished 3708
to be received and conveyed for United States in vessels belonging to citizens 4204
to be promptly delivered on arrival 4204
compensation for conveying 4204
certificates of deposit for, may be part of bank reserve 5193
received for certificates of deposit not to be issued 5194
not to be received by national banks as collateral 5207
included by words, "obligation or other security of the United States" 5413
United States of America,
shall be inscribed on coins 3517
Unlading,
of vessels, &c., provisions concerning .. 2867–2898
without permit, penalty 2867
exceptions in case of distress, &c.; transferring merchandise unlawfully; penalty 2868
permission for, at night 2871
of vessels to take place in open day, except under special permit 2872
penalty for, contrary to law 2873, 2874
property found on board after time allowed for 2880
custody of 2969
limitation of time for, not to extend to salt or coal 2881
of imported spirits and wines, permit for, penalty for unlawful 2883
penalty for, omitted, &c., articles and merchandise not agreeing with manifest. 2887
from vessels seeking port in distress, &c.; permit for 2891
how stored, &c 2892
of Spanish vessels 2895
of vessels obstructed by ice 2896
of imported salt opposite New Orleans 2897

Section.

Unlading—Continued.
of goods entered for transportation, when allowed between ports of arrival and entry 2994
permit not required for, on northern, &c., frontiers, of cargo brought from American port 3119
of goods taken from ports on northern, &c., frontiers in open day; at night; penalty 3120
of vessels from British North American Provinces 3129

Unparted Bars,
to be reported by mint-superintendents 3503
of gold or silver may be made at mints 3518

Unparted Bullion,
may be exchanged for fine bars 3546

Unregistered Vessel,
sailing on sea-letter, to be furnished with passport, when 4308

Unsafe or Unfit Warehouse,
distillery or other, Commissioner of Internal Revenue may discontinue 3272

Unseaworthy Vessels,
(see *Vessels*.)

Unslaked Lime,
penalty for shipping, without notice of character 4288

Urbana, Va.,
port of delivery 2552
surveyor to reside at 2553

Uraguay,
minister to, salary of 1675
shall be also accredited to Paraguay 1681

"*Usual Number*,"
of bills and resolutions 3791
of documents ordered by Congress 3792

Utah Territory,
number of members of council and house of representatives of 1922
contingent expenses of executive department in, annual appropriation for 1935
legislative expenses of, provision for 1939
mileage of members of legislative assembly of 1942
appointment of Indian agents for tribes in . 2052
appointment of surveyor-general for, authorized 2207
salary of 2210
fifty per cent. addition to certain fees of registers and receivers in 2238

V.

Vacancies,
salary of member or Delegate elected to fill. 51
in Departments, how filled 177–179
temporary appointments to fill 180, 181
officer temporarily filling, not to receive extra compensation 182
in office of district attorney or marshal, how filled temporarily 793
within what time the President shall nominate persons to fill 1768
occurring during recess of Senate, authority of President to fill temporarily 1769
in office of collector of internal revenue 3149
Postmaster General, in case of, may place special agent in charge 3836

Vacation,
orders, &c., made in, by district judge, in admiralty and equity causes 574

Valencia,
consul at, salary of 1690

Vallejo, Cal.,
port of delivery 2582
deputy collector to reside at 2583
vessels going to or from, how to report 2584

Section.

Valejo, Cal.——Continued.
entry of goods for, where made; powers of deputy collector at 2824

Valparaiso,
consul at, salary of 1690

Valuable Letters,
disposition of, when sent to dead-letter office. 3938

"*Value*" *and* "*Values*,"
meaning of, in appraisal of imports 2952

Varnish,
stamps for distilled spirits to be covered with 3322

Vaults,
(see *Warehouse*.)

Vehicle,
includes what 4

Velasco, Tex.,
port of delivery 2578
surveyor to reside at 2579

Venezuela,
salary of minister to 1675

Venice,
consul at, salary of 1690

Ventilators,
on vessels carrying other than cabin-passengers between Europe and United States 4257
penalty for failure to provide 4259

Vera Cruz,
consul at, salary of 1690

Verifiers and Samplers of Customs,
at New York, compensation of 2745

Vermont,
collection-district of, ports of entry and delivery in 2525
officers in, residence of collector 2526
additional inspectors for 2605

Vessels in Merchant Service,
jurisdiction of circuit courts of suits against officers and owners of, by whose negligence life is destroyed 629
enforcement of awards of foreign consuls, &c., in differences between captains and crews of 728
consular officers shall keep record of, &c... 1708
making regular trips, not required to pay fees to consular officers more than four times a year 1720
tonnage-fees not to be collected from, by consular officers in Canadian ports... 1722
forfeiture of, for violation of laws relating to Alaska 1955–1971
for engaging in cooly-trade 2158–2163
for unlawfully carrying away live-oak, &c., from United States lands ... 2462, 2463
customs officers not to own, &c 2638
revenue-cutter officers to board, examine, &c. 2760
not employed in revenue service, carrying ensign, &c., of, penalty 2764
to bring to, when required by revenue cutter, &c 2765
bound to ports of delivery where to enter, penalty 2772
penalty for illegal departure when conveying dutiable goods 2828
opening, breaking, &c., any, containing goods imported for transportation, penalty.. 2998
forfeiture of, and boats used in landing goods entered for drawback 3049
when liable to seizure by customs officers, &c 3059
searches, &c., of, by customs officers 3067
master of, obstructing officer, &c., penalty.. 3068
liability of master for breaking, &c., customs locks and fastenings 3070
customs officer may seize within or without his district 3072

Section.

Vessels in Merchant Service—Continued.
subject to penalty, &c., for violation of revenue laws, how proceeded against 3088
sealed, penalty for taking, &c., to other ports, unloading and selling contents, forfeiture 3104
forfeiture of, from which locks, &c., unlawfully removed 3106
when liable to be proceeded against for neglect of master 3125
forfeiture of, for fraud with reference to drawback on spirits 3330
lost in military service, to be paid for .. 3483, 3488
appropriation for 3689
receipt and delivery of letters 3976
pay for carrying 3978
penalty for falsely painting, &c., "United States Mail" on 3979
for carrying persons acting as private letter-expresses in 3983
shall be searched for letters illegally carried 3989
shall not make entry until delivery of letters, oath, penalty 3988
what to be deemed, of United States 4131
to be such only while owned wholly by citizens 4131
officers of, must be citizens 4131
taking foreign flag during rebellion not to be deemed 4135
wrecked vessels may become, when 4136
nationalization of certain, owned by residents of Alaska 4140
not taking new register when required, not to be deemed 4169, 4170
names and changes of masters to be indorsed on documents 4171, 4183, 4335
unless number marked on main beam, not to be deemed, of United States 4177
tonnage, how ascertained 4153, 4154
to be expressed in register 4153
to be carved on main beam 4153
if not so carved, penalty 4153
forfeiture for fraud in obtaining documents. 4189
sea-letters to be issued only to registered, enrolled, or licensed 4190
penalty for making or using forged, &c... 4191
registered, engaged in coasting-trade or fisheries, exempt from tonnage-duties 4220
rules for preventing collisions 4233
stranded on foreign coast, protection of, by consuls 4238
license to, wrecking on Florida coast 4241
registered, carrying passengers between foreign ports, subject to provisions concerning transportation of passengers . 4274
may be licensed or enrolled, when 4322
licensed, may be registered, when 4322
exchange of, for license or enrollment, or *vice versa*, in another district 4323
in whale-fishery; registers for 4339
licensed for mackerel fishery may catch other fish 4377
when coastwise, and on great lakes, subject to navigation laws 4401
no documents to issue to steam-vessel till Title Regulation of Steam-Vessels complied with 4498
manner of procuring apprentices for 4509
indentures of apprentices on 4510
certain, excepted from rules for shipping seamen 4513
copy of shipping-articles to be posted in ... 4519
wrecked, not required to pay extra wages .. 4583
no documents to issue to, till hospital-tax is paid 4587
penalty for unauthorized boarding 4606

Section.

Vessels in Merchant Service—Continued.
definition of word "vessels" 3, 4612
detention in insurrectionary districts until duties paid on cargo, &c 5315
not to be taken from customs officers, unless by process of court 5316
penalty on person employed on, by whose misconduct, &c., life is destroyed 5344
malicious beating, imprisoning, &c., of crew of, withholding suitable food, inflicting unusual punishments 5347
maliciously forcing officer or mariner of, on shore, in order to leave him behind in foreign port, &c 5363
refusing to bring home officers and mariners of, &c 5363
forging, altering, &c., document granted for; uttering false as true 5423

enrollment and license of,
what entitled to 4312
effect of 4312
license of yachts 4214
owned by corporation 4313–4315
river steamboat owned by resident alien ... 4316
bond of owner 4317
on northern, &c., frontier 4318
form of enrollment 4319
license for coasting-trade or fisheries, how procured 4320
form of 4320
to registered, on surrender of certificate of registry 4322
exchange of register for, in another district. 4323
licenses of, expiration of 4324
when to be surrendered 4325
penalty for failure to surrender 4325
new, in place of one lost or destroyed 4326
renewal of 4327
on northern, &c., frontiers or western rivers, when in another district 4328
on transfer or sale 4329
oath as to foreign repairs, &c., before 4330
of less than 20 tons, measurement for license. 4331
how signed and certified 4332
when changed for register, or vice versa, to be under former name 4333
to be exchanged for register on going abroad; penalty 4337
at Jersey City, N. J 4340
at Camden, N. J 4341
at Wilmington, N. C 4342
at Chesapeake City, Md 4343
by surveyors at ports authorized by Secretary of Treasury 4344
at Cold Spring, Greenport, and Port Jefferson, N. Y 4345
fees of, for granting 4346
penalty for illegal 4373
for forging, altering, &c 4375
for obstructing officers in granting 4376
for violation of 4377

foreign,
limitation on importations in, &c 2497
not to apply to reciprocating nations 2498
discriminating duty on importations in 2502
where to enter and unlade 2771
report of, from foreign territory, adjacent to northern, &c., frontiers; not to proceed, unlade, &c., without permit; forfeiture 3109
goods loaded on, in northern, &c., frontier districts, and transported to foreign ports for reshipment to United States; forfeiture of, and tonnage-duty on ... 3110
rates of postage on letters carried by 4015

Section.

Vessels in Merchant Service—Continued.
production of register, clearance, &c., on entry of ... 4209
exception of vessels of certain nations ... 4210
delivery of register, &c., to masters of, by foreign consul ... 4211
foreign yachts granted certain privileges ... 4216
bound coastwise, manifests and permits for ... 4367
delivery of, before unlading ... 4368
penalty for not delivering, &c ... 4369
in domestic trade,
contracts with, for carrying mail, without advertising ... 3943
when mail may be carried in ... 3969
not to carry letters except in mail; penalty ... 3985, 3986
what, may have privileges of coasting-trade and fisheries ... 4311
on northern, &c., frontier, enrolled and licensed, may engage in coasting or foreign trade on frontier ... 4318
licensed for coasting-trade or fisheries, tonnage duty on ... 4320
how numbered and recorded ... 4333
licensed, to have name and port painted on stern; penalty ... 4334
change of master of licensed, to be reported ... 4335
penalty for failure ... 4335
master to exhibit enrollment or license for inspection; penalty ... 4336
proceeding to foreign port without register; penalty ... 4337
certificate for such vessel, proceeding from another district ... 4338
foreign, not to engage in coasting-trade ... 4347
British, may engage in coasting-trade on St. Lawrence River and Great Lakes ... 4347
suspension of such privilege by President ... 4347
between neighboring districts, &c., manifests and permits for ... 4349
penalty for departing without ... 4350
delivery of manifest before unlading ... 4351
penalty for not delivering ... 4352
between remote districts, manifests and permits for ... 4353
penalty for departing without ... 4354
delivery of manifest before unlading ... 4355
penalty for not delivering ... 4356
between Long Island and Rhode Island ... 4357
between Alaska and other districts ... 4358
under 20 tons, exemption of, as to manifests and permits ... 4359
what manifests to be carried by ... 4359
when to be exhibited, &c ... 4359
penalty and forfeiture for not exhibiting ... 4360
registered, carrying foreign merchandise from one district to another ... 4361
fishing, permit to touch at foreign port, &c ... 4364
penalty for not obtaining ... 4365
coasting, putting into port other than destination, to report, &c ... 4366
penalty for not reporting ... 4366
foreign, bound coastwise, manifests and permits for ... 4367
delivery of manifest, &c., on arrival ... 4368
penalty for not delivering ... 4369
engaged in coasting-trade or fishery without enrollment or license; penalty ... 4371
forfeiture of, and of merchandise ... 4371
when license expires at sea ... 4372
forfeiture of licensed, transferred to foreigner. 4377
notice of seizure of, what to specify ... 4379
recovery of penalties and forfeitures against ... 4380
fees to be paid by, navigating by sea ... 4381
on northern, &c., frontier, navigating otherwise than by sea ... 4382

Section.

Vessels in Merchant Service—Continued.
table of, payable by, to be posted up conspicuously by customs officers ... 4383
subject to enrollment and license, liable for payment of ... 4384
lighters and boats exempt from, &c ... 4385
in foreign trade,
when materials for construction, &c., of, free of duty; when may engage in coasting-trade ... 2513
articles needed for repair of, withdrawn from bonded warehouse free of duty ... 2514
arriving from foreign ports, where to make entry, &c ... 2770
departing from port of arrival before making report, &c ... 2773
master of, to make report on arrival from foreign port; penalty ... 2774
report of distilled spirits, &c.; penalty ... 2775
departure from district of first arrival for another ... 2780
report of arrival in such other district ... 2781
enrolled and licensed on northern, &c., frontiers, not liable to entry fees, &c ... 2793
penalty for unlading without permit, except in case of distress, &c ... 2867
receiving on board, without permit, goods from ... 2868
penalty for unlawfully unlading, &c ... 2874
seeking port in distress, duty of master of ... 2891
relading, &c., charges, &c ... 2894
to receive and convey mails; oath of master ... 3976
pay to, when not in mail-service ... 3978
when, may carry letters ... 3987
passports for, when furnished ... 4306
bond for ... 4306
conditions of ... 4306
to be returned on loss or sale of vessel ... 4306
penalty on vessel departing without ... 4307
for unregistered vessel sailing with sea-letter ... 4308
deposit of documents with consul on arriving abroad ... 4309
return of papers by consul on production of clearance, &c ... 4309
penalty on master failing to deposit, &c ... 4310
enrolled and licensed, on northern, &c., frontier ... 4318
certificate of registry not required for ... 4318
in foreign and coasting-trade,
on northern, &c., frontiers, purchases of foreign goods for use of vessel ... 3111
equipments of, when liable to entry and duty, failing to report, &c.; forfeiture ... 3114
if purchased by reason of distress, duties to be refunded ... 3115
when enrollment and license to be granted ... 3115
duplicate manifests of ... 3116
entry of goods taken or delivered at intermediate ports by ... 3117
departing for ports where no custom-house, how to obtain clearance, &c ... 3118
from ports where no custom-house, what to do on arrival at port of destination ... 3122
steam-tugs, when not required to report and clear ... 3123
registered, in coasting-trade, may touch at foreign ports; masters of, to conform to laws relative to foreign trade ... 3126
foreign goods taken in by, at United States port ... 3127
recording of,
vessels built in United States and owned by foreigners to be recorded ... 4180
oath to obtain record ... 4180

Section.

Vessels in Merchant Service—Continued.
measurement or survey for record ... 4181
certificate of measurement for ... 4181
certificate of record, form of ... 4182
to be attested under hand and seal of collector of customs ... 4182
to be recorded in books of collector ... 4182
duplicate of, to be transmitted to Register of Treasury ... 4182
change of master to be indorsed on ... 4183
not deemed recorded until such indorsement made ... 4183
indorsement to be recorded by collector. 4183
copy of indorsements on, to be transmitted to Register ... 4183
production of certificate of record on entry; penalty ... 4184
fees of collector for ... 4185
for indorsements ... 4185
for taking bond ... 4185
of surveyor for measurement ... 4186
by whom paid ... 4186
limit upon, for measuring and certifying tonnage ... 4186
penalty on collector for falsely recording, &c. 4187
granting false certificate of record, &c ... 4187
for receiving unlawful fees, &c., for ... 4187
on surveyor giving false measurement for. 4187
on officers neglecting duties under Title REGULATION OF COMMERCE AND NAVIGATION ... 4188
forfeiture of vessels fraudulently obtaining certificate of registry, record, &c ... 4189

registry of,
registered, to be deemed United States vessels ... 4131
must be owned and commanded by citizens ... 4131
privileges of, and to cease when ... 4131
officers of, must be citizens ... 4131
what vessels entitled to ... 4132
when vessels owned by non-resident citizens entitled to, or benefit of ... 4133
by non-resident naturalized citizens ... 4134
on transfer to resident citizens ... 4134
American vessel sailing under foreign flag during rebellion not entitled to ... 4135
of foreign-built, wrecked and repaired in United States ... 4136
owned by incorporated companies, how made 4137
on death of president, &c., of corporation. 4138
oath as to ownership of corporation ... 4139
where and by whom to be made ... 4141
oath for registry by owner, &c ... 4142
penalty for false ... 4143
oath by master to obtain ... 4144
penalty for false ... 4144
bond to obtain ... 4145
condition of ... 4146
return of register on loss, &c., of vessel ... 4146
carpenter's certificate to obtain ... 4147
measurement of, before issue of ... 4148
new measurement not necessary where new register issued, unless changes, &c ... 4148
certificate of measurement for ... 4149
measurement to be expressed in ... 4150
register tonnage, table of classes, and rules for ascertaining ... 4153
register to be made and kept in books ... 4155
certificate of, to be issued by collector ... 4155
form of ... 4155
variation of form in certain cases ... 4156
blank certificates of, how provided ... 4157
none to be issued except as provided ... 4157
to be sent to collectors, attested, &c ... 4158
how filled, signed, and sealed ... 4158

Section.

Vessels in Merchant Service—Continued.
how to be countersigned ... 4158
how recorded ... 4158
new register to purchaser in another district ... 4159
old register to be surrendered, &c ... 4160
penalty for failure to surrender ... 4160
new register, on purchase, by agent or attorney ... 4161
old register to be surrendered, &c ... 4162
penalty for failure to surrender ... 4162
forfeiture of vessel for false swearing by agent, &c., to obtain ... 4163
upon sale under legal process ... 4164
American vessel becoming property of foreigner not to be registered afterward. 4165
may be registered if recovered by original owners ... 4165
of vessels sold abroad to American citizens. 4166
new register, in place of one lost or destroyed. 4167
surrender of, obtained in other district, and issue of new ... 4168
penalty for not surrendering ... 4168
penalty for not obtaining new, when required 4169
for retaining old register when new issued. 4169
new register, on sale or alteration of form or burden ... 4170
old register to be delivered to collector ... 4170
to be transmitted to Register of Treasury and cancelled ... 4170
certificate to be cited in bill of sale ... 4170
change of master to be indorsed on certificate of ... 4171
register void on failure to report change ... 4171
oath to be taken by owner as to citizenship of master ... 4171
refusal to take oath renders registry void. 4171
forfeiture of registered vessel for failure to report sale, &c., to foreigner ... 4172
exception as to part owner ignorant of such sale ... 4172
oath by owner, &c., upon entry, as to ... 4173
effect of refusal to take such oath ... 4173
certain surrendered certificates of, to be transmitted to Register of Treasury ... 4174
to be cancelled ... 4174
cancellation of bond on delivery of certicate of ... 4175
certificates of, how numbered ... 4176
numbers for registered vessel, how given ... 4177
to be carved on main beam ... 4177
penalty for not carrying number ... 4177
names to be on stern ... 4178
penalty on collector granting false ... 4187
receiving unlawful fees for granting, &c ... 4187
on surveyor giving naval officer false measurement to obtain ... 4187
for making or using forged, &c ... 4191
register of foreign, to be produced on entry. 4209
penalty for not producing ... 4209
exception as to certain nations ... 4210
licensed or enrolled, to obtain, before going abroad; penalty ... 4337
in whale fishery, to cover privileges of registered and enrolled and licensed ... 4339
at Wilmington, N. C ... 4342
registered, going from one district to another, subject to provisions for licensed ... 4361
penalty for obstructing officers in granting. 4376
fee for ... 4382

wrecked and in distress,
foreign, repaired in United States may be registered ... 4136
consuls to protect when stranded ... 4238
not to pay extra wages ... 4583
plundering, effects belonging to ... 5358

Section.

Vessels in Merchant Service—Continued.
obstructing escape of persons from 5358
holding out false light to produce 5358
(see *Bills of Sale; Clearance of Vessels; Duties; Fisheries; Inspection; Light-Money; Log-Books; Mediterranean Passport; Navigation; Navigation Laws; Passengers; Pilots; Piracy; Seamen; Sea-Stores; Slave-Trade; Steam-Vessels; Survey; Transportation; Transportation of Passengers; Unlading;* and *Yachts.*)

Vessels of Navy,
disposition of, in time of peace.............. 1534
detail of, to cruise on coast in severe weather. 1536
to go prepared to assist distressed navigators 1536
patented articles for marine engines in..... 1537
repairs to hulls and spars of 1538
to sails and rigging of 1539
unfit for, sale of, by order of President.... 1540
by Secretary of Navy 1541
report of sales of, to Congress.............. 1541
pay of crews of, lost or wrecked 1574
captured by enemy 1575
importations in, prohibited 1624*
commanders of, may examine, &c., vessels believed to be engaged in cooly-trade. 2163
on foreign stations, purchases out of United States of supplies for................ 3721
contracts in foreign countries for supplies for 3723
rules for navigation of..................... 4233
definition of term as used in Title PRIZE.... 4614
share in prize to be allowed to 4632
when persons serving on, to have pensions.. 4693
rate of total-disability pension to.......... 4695

foreign,
not required to make entry 2791
how supplies may be purchased from public warehouse by 2982

Vested Rights,
existing, to certain real estate in Territories, not impaired, &c 1890

Veteran Furlough,
enlisted men on, to be regarded as if in field, &c 4700

Veterinary Surgeons,
for regiments of cavalry.................... 1102

Vice-Admiral,
grade of, to cease........................... 1362
number on active list 1363
secretary to................................. 1367
pay of 1556
of secretary to 1556

Vice-Consuls, Vice-Consular Officers, and *Vice-Commercial Agents,*
(see *Consuls-General, &c.*)

Vice-President of United States,
term, commencement and duration of office. 152
salary of 154

Vicksburgh, Miss.,
vessels arriving at New Orleans for 2832
collection-district and port of entry........ 2566
collector to reside at...................... 2567

Vienna,
consul at, salary of 1690

Vigil and Saint Vrain Land-Claims,
appropriation for surveying................. 3689

Vinalhaven, Me.,
port of delivery 2517

Vinegar,
standard of, in imports 2917

Section.

Vinegar—Continued.
use of spirits not tax-paid in manufacture of, penalty for...................... 3282
and sugar to be served on merchant-vessels. 4569
penalty for neglect to serve.............. 4570

Vintners,
special tax upon 3246

Virginia,
clerks of circuit and district courts in western district of, number of............ 622
collection-districts, ports of entry and delivery in 2552
officers in 2553
establishment of life-saving stations in..... 4249

Visitorial Powers,
national banks to be subject to what....... 5241

Visitors,
(see *Board of Visitors.*)

Voluntary Assignments,
debts due United States in case of, to have priority............................... 3466

Volunteer Navy,
appointment of temporary acting assistant surgeons 1411
officers of, transferred to Regular Navy..... 1412
pay of officers of 1559

Volunteer Service,
marine officers to be credited with 1600

Volunteers,
privileges of officers who served as, in Army; names and rank to be entered on Army Register 1226
pay of, during captivity 1288
to receive same pay and allowances as regulars 1292
half-pay to widow or child of, dying in United States service 1656
benefits extended to, employed in suppressing Indian depredations in Florida... 1657
called into service between 1812 and 1852, bounty-land for 2420
collecting, drilling, &c., when to be paid for. 3489
appropriation for asylum for disabled 3689
of California and Nevada, appropriation for traveling-expenses of................ 3689
when to have pension 4693
rate of total-disability pension to 4695
pension according to rank, &c 4696
disabled in Mexican war to have pensions .. 4730
in war of 1812 and Indian wars, widows, &c., of, to have pensions.............. 4732
in war of 1812, who served sixty days, &c., to have pensions 4736
deduction from pay of, for support of Soldiers' Home not to be made without consent 4819
National Home for Disabled, organization of. 4825
stoppages from pay of, &c., how applied.... 4831
what, entitled to admission in Home 4832
out-door relief may be extended to, when... 4833
in national home, subject to Rules and Articles of War 4835

Vouchers,
penalty for passing, &c., for salary of civil officer suspended, &c 1762
making or using, by civilians, of false, to obtain payment of claim against United States 3490, 5438
delivery, by civilians, of less money or property, to be used for military, &c., service, than described in 3490, 5438

*NOTE.—"No person connected with the Navy shall, under any pretense, import in a public vessel any article which is liable to the payment of duty."—*Sec.* 1624, "*Articles for the Government of the Navy,*" *Art.* 12; (*sec.* 10, *act of July* 30, 1846, *ch.* 74.)

Section.

Vouchers—Continued.
fraudulent giving, by civilians, for public property for use in military or naval service ... 3490, 5438
blanks for pension shall be furnished to pension-agents; notice ... 4767
officer charged with payment of appropriation, paying to clerk, &c., less than lawful sum, and requiring voucher for amount greater than paid ... 5483

W.

Wages,
assignment of, by enlisted men ... 1576
of petty officers and seamen in revenue-cutter service ... 2754
of workmen in mints ... 3499
false personation of person entitled to, from United States ... 5435
endeavoring to obtain, due from United States, &c., by means of forged power of attorney ... 5436
of seamen, (see *Seamen.*)

Wagoners,
for battery of artillery ... 1100
for troop of cavalry ... 1103
for company of infantry ... 1107
pension to dependent relatives of ... 4710

Wagon-Masters,
employment of, by Quartermaster's Department ... 1137
not to be personally interested in public transports ... 1137

Wagons,
lost in military service to be paid for ... 3483

Waldoborough, Me.,
collection-district and port of entry ... 2517
collector in, to reside at ... 2518

War Department,
(see *Department of War.*)

War of 1812,
bounty-land for certain soldiers of, their widows or children ... 2418
for certain militia, volunteers, or State troops in ... 2420
warrants and patents, when to issue ... 2423
when declarations for pensions for, may be made before local officers ... 4714
widows, &c., of soldiers killed, &c., in, to have pensions ... 4732
survivors of, who served sixty days, &c., to have pensions ... 4736
widows of, to have pensions ... 4738
rate of pensions to survivors of ... 4737
proofs required to establish pension-claims of survivors, &c., of ... 4739
loss of discharge not to prevent survivors, &c., of, from having pension ... 4740

War-Vessels,
(see *Vessels of Navy.*)

Wareham, Mass.,
port of delivery ... 2527

Warehouse,
what imported goods to be conveyed to bonded, how and until what time kept 2926
who may lease, for storage of imports ... 2954
not to be leased in certain ports ... 2955
use of, leased by customs-officers, storage in, how regulated ... 2956
customs officers not to enter into contract for use of before completion; limitation of lease of; rent, how paid ... 2957
cellars and vaults of stores and yards, when to be constituted bonded ... 2958
parts of bonded, for storage of grain ... 2959

Section.

Warehouse—Continued.
private, for what purpose used; custody and supervision of; labor in ... 2960
bond, by whom given, before use of; imports deposited in, at whose risk ... 2961
what may be deposited in; designation of place of storage ... 2962
designation of, on entry, at option of owner ... 2962
goods deposited in, for want of invoice ... 2963
entry for, how made; on non-payment of duties, collector to store goods in ... 2964
unclaimed merchandise to be stored in ... 2965
importations in steamers, deposit of, in ... 2966
deposit of goods in, at Jeffersonville ... 2967
Secretary of Treasury to extend privileges of, &c., to Albany ... 2968
when merchandise may be withdrawn from, for consumption ... 2970
withdrawal for exportation or transshipment for Pacific, &c., port; sale of abandoned goods in; charges and storage ... 2971
proceeds of sale of abandoned goods in, how and by whom distributed ... 2972
goods remaining in, after one year, how sold, &c., deductions of duties and charges; balance, how disposed of ... 2973
sale in, of perishable goods, and explosive substances ... 2975
of perishable goods unclaimed ... 2976
when goods may remain in, and be entitled to return duties ... 2977
goods how withdrawn from, and delivered ... 2980
collector may refuse to deliver goods in, when freight-lien on ... 2981
supplies purchased from public, by foreign vessels of war ... 2982
no abatement of duties for injury to goods while in ... 2983
cancellation of bond when goods destroyed ... 2984
penalty for obliterating marks on goods in ... 2985
on person fraudulently opening ... 2986
for fraudulently concealing, &c., removing, &c., goods in ... 2987
quarterly returns of goods in ... 2988
Secretary of Treasury to make rules for, &c. 2989
entry of goods, except of distilled spirits ... 2990
examination of goods imported for immediate transportation ... 2991
transfer of such goods to bonded, by whom taken possession of, and how delivered 2995
such goods not immediately transported deprived of privilege; who to take possession of ... 2996
opening, breaking, &c., removing lock, &c., of, how punished ... 2998
withdrawal from, for transportation to another district ... 3000
for exportation to Mexico ... 3002
through port of Lavaca, Tex ... 3003
through port of Indianola, Tex ... 3004
search of, near boundary-line of United States, forfeitures ... 3107
persons depositing, &c., goods in, how punished ... 3108
may be erected for storage of goods in quarantine ... 4794
deposit and removal of goods ... 4795
storage at, how fixed ... 4795
(see *Distillery Warehouse* and *Bonded Warehouse.*)

Warehousing,
regulations concerning, prescribed by Secretary of Treasury ... 251

Warrant of Attorney,
to receive claim on United States, how made ... 3477
to receive pension, not to be recognized ... 4766

Section.

Warrant for Distraint,
may be given by collector of internal revenue to deputy 3188
Warrant-Officers in Navy,
number and appointment of 1405
what officers to be known as 1406
promotion of seamen to grade of 1407
assimilated rank to 1491
pay of 1556
Warrants,
judicial,
of arrest, power of marshal to stay, or release from, in admiralty causes other than seizures for forfeiture 941
in civil-rights cases, how may be executed 1984
aid of military and naval forces in execution of 1984
where to run, &c 1984
to search dwelling-house, how obtained by customs officers 3066
of district judge, when issued for seizure of books, &c., in revenue cases 3091
conditions requisite to issue of; return of, how made 3092
in bankruptcy, fees for issue of 5124
messenger's fees for service of 5126
treasury,
examination of, by Assistant Secretary of Treasury 245
delegation of Assistant Secretary to sign 246
validity of, signed by Assistant Secretary 247
drawn by Secretary of Treasury, to be countersigned by whom 269
by Secretaries of War and Navy, to be countersigned by whom 273
penalty for allowing, for salary of civil officer suspended, &c 1762
for money of War and Navy Departments 3673
of Post-Office Department 3674
on Treasurer, form of 3675
Warren, Me.,
port of delivery 2517
Washed Stamps, (Internal Revenue,)
(see *Stamps, Internal Revenue.*)
Washington, D. C.,
reserve of national banks in 5191
balances with banks in, may be part of reserve 5192
redemption agencies 5195
Washington Aqueduct,
Chief of Engineers to have charge of 1800
moneys appropriated for, under whose direction expended 1802
expense of laying main pipes of, how distributed between United States and District of Columbia 1805
Washington Territory,
number of members of council and house of representatives of 1922
extra sessions of assembly of, how called 1923
contingent expenses of executive department in, annual appropriation for 1938
legislative expenses of, provision for 1940
salaries of governor, &c., not payable until duties entered upon 1941
mileage of members of assembly of 1942
concurrent jurisdiction of, over offenses on Columbia River 1950
disbursing officers in, to give security, in what manner 1951
certain laws of Oregon, &c., continued in force in 1952
jurisdiction of district courts of, over offenses committed in Alaska 1957
appointment of Indian superintendent for tribes in 2046

Section.

Washington Territory—Continued.
of Indian agents 2052
of surveyor-general for, authorized 2207
salary of 2209
fifty per cent. addition to certain fees of registers and receivers in 2238
augmented rates allowed for survey of certain public lands in 2405
collection-districts, ports of entry and delivery in 2586
officers in 2587
Wastage,
in silver coinage, how provided for 3526
in minor coinage 3528
what shall be allowed as necessary in annual settlement 3542
Waste Paper,
money derived from sale of certain, to be deposited as postal revenue 4050
Watches, Clocks, &c.,
shipper of, to notify carrier, &c 4281
Watches, Watch-Cases, and Movements,
prohibition on importation of, which simulate name or trade-mark of domestic manufacturer, &c 2496
Watchmen,
captain and lieutenants of, in Treasury Department, salaries 235
captain of, in Post Office Department, salary of 393
to be employed at night on passenger-steamers 4477
penalty for failure to keep 4478
Water-Barrels,
what, to be carried by river passenger-steamers 4483
tanks may be substituted for 4483
Water, Fresh,
quantity to be carried by passenger-vessels between United States and Europe 4260
daily delivery of 4260
penalty for supplying short allowance of 4261
how recovered 4261
between Atlantic and Pacific ports of United States 4265
Water-Gauges,
on Mississippi River and tributaries; limit of expenditure 5252
Water-Tight Bulkheads,
what passenger-steamers to have 4490
Waukegan, Ill.,
port of delivery 2601
deputy collector to reside at 2602
Wax-Tapers,
imported, to be stamped as prescribed in Schedule A 3435
tax on, (Schedule A) 3437
Way-Letters,
prepaid, shall be received, &c., by route-agents, &c 3980
Wearing-Apparel,
(see *Baggage.*)
Weigher and Measurer of Fuel,
appointment, &c., of, for Executive Departments 3711
Weighers of Customs,
for certain ports 2606, 2607
extortion and dereliction in duty by, penalty 2637
salaries of, at Boston, Philadelphia, Baltimore, New Orleans, Portland, Me., and San Francisco 2739
additional compensation of, at San Francisco 2746
when and how to make returns 2890
how to mark weights on casks, &c., of sugar 2915

Section.

Weighing,
imported goods not to be removed from wharf before, &c.; forfeiture ... 2882
of imports, when at expense of owner ... 2920
Weighing-Instruments,
to be adopted and prescribed by Commissioner of Internal Revenue ... 3249
Weights,
of coins, assay commission to test ... 3547
of mail-matter, limit as to ... 3878, 3879
fraudulently defacing or changing, used at mints or assay-offices ... 5460
Weights and Measures,
how used in invoices ... 2837
using false, in ascertaining quantity of distillery material ... 3306
metric system of, legalized ... 3569
equivalents of metric system ... 3570
shall be kept on board merchant vessels ... 4571
Wellfleet, Mass.,
port of delivery ... 2527
Wells, Me.,
port of delivery ... 2517
Western Frontiers,
addition to ration allowed to militia employed on, in United States service ... 1655
West Point Military Academy,
(see *Military Academy.*)
West Point, Va.,
port of delivery ... 2552
surveyor to reside at ... 2553
Westport, Mass.,
port of delivery ... 2527
Wethersfield, Conn.,
port of delivery ... 2533
Weymouth, Mass.,
port of delivery ... 2527
Whale-Fishery,
form of license for vessels in ... 4321
vessels in, may sail under register ... 4339
Wheeling, W. Va.,
port of delivery in district of New Orleans ... 2568
surveyor to reside at, duties of ... 2569
inspectors of hulls and boilers for ... 4414
salaries of ... 4414
Whitehall, N. Y.,
port of delivery ... 2535
deputy collector to reside at ... 2536
Wholesale Dealer in Malt Liquors,
(see *Dealers in Malt Liquors.*)
Wholesale Liquor-Dealer,
(see *Dealers in Liquor.*)
Wichitas,
appointment of agent for ... 2052
Widows,
half-pay to, of officers, privates, &c., in militia, dying in United States service ... 1656
of diplomatic or consular officers dying abroad, allowance to ... 1749
of soldiers entitled to bounty-land ... 2418, 2419
when warrant for bounty-land to issue to ... 2424
subsequent marriage not to impair rights of ... 2424
increase of pension, for each child, &c ... 4703
pension to, when married prior to July 27, 1868, &c., when to begin ... 4710
of privateersmen, money pledged for support of ... 4759
(see *Pensions.*)
Wife,
of colored soldier, who to be deemed ... 2037
Willamette,
collection-district in Oregon ... 2586
collector and appraiser in, residence of ... 2587
inspectors of hulls and of boilers for ... 4414
salaries of ... 4414

Section.

Wilmington, Cal.,
vessels going to or from, how to report ... 2585
Wilmington, Del.,
port of entry ... 2546
collector to reside at ... 2547
Wilmington, N. C.,
collection-district and port of entry ... 2555
collector in, to reside at ... 2556
registry, enrollment, and license of vessels by collector at ... 4342
Windsor, Conn.,
port of delivery ... 2533
Windsor, Nova Scotia,
consul at, salary of ... 1690
Windsor, Ontario,
consul at, salary of ... 1690
Wine-Gallons,
tax on distilled spirits to be collected on, when below proof ... 3251
Wines,
(see *Distilled Spirits or Wines.*)
Winnipeg,
consul at, salary of ... 1690
Wire Tiller-Ropes and Bell-Pulls,
to be used on passenger-steamers ... 4480
may be dispensed with on vessels navigated by compass ... 4480
Wiscasset, Me.,
collection-district and port of entry ... 2517
collector in, to reside at ... 2518
vessels entered at, may unlade at Edgecomb or Newcastle ... 2520
Wisconsin,
district court of, for what purposes always open as court of admiralty ... 576
clerks of circuit and district courts in western district of, number ... 623
collection-district, port of entry and delivery in ... 2597
officers in ... 2598
Wisconsin River,
surplus tolls from improvements in, and in water-communication with Fox river, to be paid into Treasury ... 5249
future reduction of tolls from said improvements ... 5249
Withdrawal, (Customs,)
of imported merchandise from warehouse, how made ... 2980
Withdrawal, (Internal Revenue,)
of distilled spirits deposited in warehouse prior to August 1, 1872 ... 3251
of spirits from warehouse ... 3294
for exportation ... 3330
Witnesses,
in claims pending in Departments, provisions respecting ... 184–187
in United States courts, fees and mileage of ... 848
subsistence and compensation of, when detained in prison, &c ... 848
United States officers not entitled to fees as, for attending before court, &c., where officiating ... 849
when sent away from places of business as witnesses for Government, entitled to expenses ... 850
fees, &c., of seamen and others sent home from foreign ports as ... 851
in causes where United States is a party, how paid ... 855
on part of accused, unable to pay fees, how and at whose cost subpœnaed ... 878
taxation of fees of, in examination of criminal case before commissioner of circuit court ... 981
in Territories, fees of ... 1883

Section.

Witnesses—Continued.
under letters rogatory, testimony of, how obtained 4071
specific written interrogatories to be addressed to 4071
summons of 4071
not compellable to appear or answer, except to interrogatories 4071
when additional questions may be put 4071
summons to specify time and place for attendance of 4071
place of attendance to be within one hundred miles of place of service 4071
fees and mileage of 4074
before investigations by steamboat inspectors, how paid 4451
in prize cases, what persons to be sent into port as 4615
commanding officer to explain absence of 4615
fees of, how paid 4651
in cases in Patent Office, subpœnas for 4906
fees of 4907
informer to be examined as witness in suits to recover fine, penalty, &c., without losing share 5295

Women,
may be clerks in Departments 165
may be employed as nurses in Army 1238
as hospital matrons in Army 1239
may accompany troops as laundresses 1240
laborers in office of Treasurer, salary of 235

Wood,
for Government use, purchase, inspection, &c., of, in District of Columbia 3711–3713

Wooden Packages,
for fine-cut chewing-tobacco 3362
for cavendish, plug, and twist tobacco 3362
marks on 3362

Wool,
appraisal of imported manufactures of, in an unfinished condition 2902
of imports composed of different qualities, but similar kinds, in same package 2911
of different qualities in same bale 2912
samples of, to determine class of imported, how prepared and where kept 2916
and woolen goods to be divided into three classes, for fixing rates of duties 2504
what customs-duties on, in addition to entered value, in certain cases 2908

Working-Dies,
at each mint—obverse to be defaced, &c 3550
for coins, how prepared 3510

Workmen,
in mints, wages of, how fixed and paid 3499
day's work of, to be eight hours 3738

Worm, Distillery,
special tax on 3244
to be destroyed in case of forfeiture, and material sold 3332
tanks, space around, and elevation of 3269
tubs, cleansing and examination of 3286
to be destroyed in cases of forfeiture 3332

Worn-out Notes,
of national banks, shall be replaced, &c 5184
burning of; certificate of 5184

Wort,
(see *Mash or Wort.*)

Wounded,
in militia, while in United States service, how cared for 1639

Wounds received in Service,
who to have pension for 4693

Section.

Wounds received in Service—Continued.
after July 27, 1868, must have been received in line of duty 4694

Wrecked Property,
collection, &c., of 3755
on coast of Florida, how disposed of 4239
forfeiture of vessel conveying to foreign port 4240

Wrecking,
license for vessels employed in, on Florida coast 4241

Wrecks,
(see *Vessels.*)

Writ of Error,
review of final judgments of circuit court by Supreme Court upon 691
on certificate of division of opinion 693
to final judgment of State court 709
no bond required when writ sued out by United States or Department 1001
from Supreme Court, within what time to be brought 1008
when respondent to, may have damages for delay, and single or double costs 1010

Wyoming Territory,
number of members of council and house of representatives of 1922
contingent expenses of executive department in, annual appropriation for 1935
penitentiary in, custody and care of 1936
maintenance of prisoners by 1937
legislative expenses in, provision for 1939
mileage of members of assembly of 1942
appointment of surveyor-general for 2207
salary of 2210
fifty per cent. addition to certain fees of registers and receivers in 2238

Y.

Yachts,
license and enrollment of, used for pleasure or designed as models 4214
bond of owner 4214
not to carry passengers or goods for pay 4214
subject to United States laws 4214
penalty for violation 4214
to use signals prescribed by Secretary of Navy 4215
United States naval architects may examine and copy models of 4215
privileges to, owned by foreign yacht clubs 4216
commissions for 4217
entry of, on return from foreign country 4218

Yards,
(see *Warehouse.*)

Yeocomico, Va.,
port of delivery 2552

Yokohama,
general postal agency authorized at 4023

York, Me.,
collection-district and port of entry 2517
collector in, to reside at 2518
merchandise may be entered at, for Kittery or Berwick 2524

Yorktown, Va.,
collection-district and port of entry 2552
collector in, to reside at 2553

Z.

Zanzibar,
consul at, salary of 1690

Zurich,
consul at, salary of 1690

APPENDIX.

AN ACT

TO CORRECT ERRORS AND SUPPLY OMISSIONS

IN THE

REVISED STATUTES OF THE UNITED STATES.

APPENDIX.

An Act to correct errors and to supply omissions in the Revised Statutes of the United States.

Be it enacted by the Senate and House of Representatives of the United States of America in Congress assembled, That for the purpose of correcting errors and supplying omissions in the act entitled "An act to revise and consolidate the statutes of the United States in force on the first day of December, anno Domini one thousand eight hundred and seventy-three," so as to make the same truly express such laws, the following amendments are hereby made therein:

Section sixty-five is amended by striking out the whole section and inserting the following: "The Secretary of the Senate and Clerk of the House of Representatives shall annually advertise, once a week for at least four weeks, in one or more of the principal papers published in the District of Columbia, for sealed proposals for supplying the Senate and House of Representatives, respectively, during the next session of Congress with the necessary stationery." Sec. 65, R. S., 13.

Section sixty-seven is amended by striking out the whole section and inserting the following: "All such proposals shall be kept sealed until the day specified in such advertisement for opening the same, when the same shall be opened in the presence of at least two persons, and the contract shall be given to the lowest bidder, provided he shall give satisfactory security to perform the same, under a forfeiture not exceeding double the contract price in case of failure; and in case the lowest bidder shall fail to enter into such contract and give such security, within a time to be fixed in such advertisement, then the contract shall be given to the next lowest bidder, who shall enter into such contract, and give such security. And in case of failure by the person entering into such contract to perform the same, he and his sureties shall be liable for the forfeiture specified in such contract, as liquidated damages, to be sued for in the name of the United States." Sec. 67, R. S., 13.

Section seventy-four is struck out. Sec. 74, R. S., 14.

Section seventy-nine is amended by striking out, in the second line, the words "no money shall be paid from the Treasury for," and adding, at the end of the section, the words "shall cease." Sec. 79, R., S. 14.

Section two hundred and thirty-nine is amended by striking out, of seventh line, the words "assessors and assistant assessors." Sec. 239, R. S., 39.

Section two hundred and eighty-four is amended by striking out, in the fourth line, the word "purser," and inserting "paymaster." Sec. 284, R. S., 47.

Chapter four of title seven is amended by adding, after section three hundred, the following sections: Title VII, ch. 4, R. S., 49.

SEC. 300. A. "All claims of loyal citizens in States not in rebellion, for quartermaster's stores actually furnished to the Army of the United States, and receipted for by the proper officer receiving the same, or which may have been taken by such officers without giving such receipt, may be submitted to the Quartermaster General of the United States, accompanied with such proofs as each claimant can present of the facts, in his case; and it shall be the duty of the Quartermaster General to cause such claim to be examined, and if convinced that it is just, and of the loyalty of the claimant, and that the stores have been actually received or taken for the use of, and used by the Army, then to report each case to the Third Auditor of the Treasury, with a recommendation for settlement.

SEC. 300. B. All claims of loyal citizens in States not in rebellion for subsistence actually furnished to the Army and receipted for by the Title VII, ch. 4, R. S., 49.

proper officer receiving the same, or which may have been taken by such officers without giving such receipt, may be submitted to the Commissary General of Subsistence, accompanied by such proof as each claimant may have to offer; and it shall be the duty of the Commissary General of Subsistence to cause each claim to be examined, and if convinced that it is just, and of the loyalty of the claimant, and that the stores have actually been received, or taken for the use of, and used by the Army, then to report each case for payment to the Third Auditor of the Treasury with a recommendation for settlement.

The provisions of the above two sections shall extend to the State of Tennessee, and to the counties of Berkeley and Jefferson in the State of West Virginia. But the provisions of the above two sections shall not authorize the payment of claims for the occupation of, or injury to, real estate in any State declared in insurrection during the rebellion."

Sec. 330, R. S,. 54. Section three hundred and thirty is amended by adding thereto the following: "A description of the seal, with an impression thereof, and a certificate of approval by the Secretary of the Treasury, shall be filed in the Office of the Secretary of State."

Sec. 333, R. S., 44. Section three hundred and thirty-three is amended by inserting, after the word "Congress," in the second line, the words "at the commencement of its session."

Sec. 453, R. S., 76. Section four hundred and fifty-three is amended by striking out in the fifth line the word "agents," and inserting the word "grants."

Sec. 541, R S, 90. Section five hundred and forty-one is amended by inserting, in the fourth line, after the word "north," the words "and west."

Sec. 563, R. S., 94. Section five hundred and sixty-three is amended by adding to paragraph eight the following words: "And shall have original and exclusive cognizance of all prizes brought into the United States, except as provided in paragraph six of section six hundred and twenty-nine."

Ibid., p. 95. Also, by striking out of line two, of the ninth paragraph, the words "seventy-six," and inserting the word "eight."

Sec. 590, R. S., 103. Section five hundred and ninety is amended by striking out, in the first line, the word "circuit," and inserting the word "district."

Sec. 629, R. S., 111. Section six hundred and twenty-nine is amended by striking out, in the first line of paragraph eleven, the words "or against."

Sec. 709, R. S., 132. Section seven hundred and nine is amended by striking out all after the words "United States," in sixteenth line, to the end of the first paragraph.

Ibid., p. 132. Also, by striking out the word "reaffirm," in the first line of the second paragraph.

Sec. 711, R. S., 135. Section seven hundred and eleven is amended by striking out the eighth paragraph.

Sec. 735, R. S., 139. Section seven hundred and thirty-five is amended by striking out of the second line the words "as prize."

Sec. 846, R. S., 159. Section eight hundred and forty-six is amended by adding thereto as follows: "That where the ministerial officers of the United States have or shall incur extraordinary expense in executing the laws thereof, the payment of which is not specifically provided for, the President of the United States is authorized to allow the payment thereof under the special taxation of the district or circuit court of the district in which the said services have been or shall be rendered, to be paid from the appropriation for defraying the expenses of the judiciary."

Sec. 1007, R. S., 188. Section one thousand and seven is amended by striking out, in the last line, the words, "the said term of sixty," and inserting the word "ten."

Sec. 1011, R. S., 188. Section one thousand and eleven is amended by striking out, in the second line, the word "and," and inserting the word "any."

Sec. 1049, R. S., 196. Section one thousand and fifty-nine is amended by adding to the fourth paragraph the following additional proviso: "*Provided, also*, That the jurisdiction of the Court of Claims shall not extend to any claim against the United States growing out of the destruction or ap-

propriation of, or damage to, property by the Army and Navy engaged in the suppression of the rebellion."

Section one thousand three hundred and forty-two is amended by striking out, in the third line of the thirty-eighth article, the word "corporal;" and also, by adding to said article thirty-eight, the following words: "No court-martial shall sentence any soldier to be branded, marked, or tattooed." Sec. 1342, R. S., 232.

The same section is also amended, in the third line of article eighty-two, by striking out the words "ninety-five," and inserting the word "eighty." Sec. 1342, R. S., 237.

Section one thousand eight hundred and forty-two is amended by adding thereto the following proviso: "*Provided*, That so much of this section as provides for making any bill passed by the legislative assembly of a Territory a law, without the approval of the governor, shall not apply to the Territories of Utah and Arizona." Sec. 1842, R. S., 327.

Section two thousand one hundred and forty-six is amended by adding, at the end of the first line, the following words: "Crimes committed by one Indian against the person or property of another Indian, nor to." Sec. 2146, R. S., 376.

Section two thousand one hundred and sixty-nine is amended by inserting, in the first line, after the word "aliens," the words "being free white persons, and to aliens." Sec. 2169, R. S., 382.

Section two thousand five hundred and four is amended by inserting the word "not" before the word "exceeding," in the second line from top of page four hundred and sixty-five. Sec. 2504, R. S., 465.

Section two thousand five hundred and twenty-seven is amended by inserting, in the third line of the ninth paragraph, after the word "ninety," the word "nine." Sec. 2527, R. S., 500.

Section two thousand five hundred and thirty-one is amended by inserting, in the fifth line of the first paragraph, after the word "county," the words "as the same existed." Sec. 2531, R. S., 501.

Section two thousand seven hundred and eleven is struck out; the ports of Pacific City and Milwaukee having been abolished. Sec. 2711, R. S., 534.

Section two thousand seven hundred and thirty is amended by inserting, at the end of the first line, the word "Pittsburgh." Sec. 2730, R. S., 536.

Section two thousand eight hundred and sixty-four is amended by inserting, in the last line, after the word "merchandise," the words "or the value thereof." Sec. 2864, R. S., 557.

Section two thousand nine hundred and ninety-seven is amended by inserting, in the tenth line, after the word "Alabama," the words "Detroit in Michigan." Sec. 2997, R. S., 580.

Section three thousand and one hundred is amended by transposing lines nine and ten. Sec. 3100, R. S., 598.

Section three thousand one hundred and fifty-eight is amended by inserting, in the fourteenth line, the word "two" before the word "hundred," where it first occurs. Sec. 3158, R. S., 608.

Section three thousand one hundred and eighty-one is amended by striking out, in the fourth line, the word "last," and inserting the word "list." Sec. 3181, R. S., 614.

Section three thousand two hundred and thirty-eight is amended by striking out, in the fifth line, the word "thirteen," and inserting "twelve." Sec. 3238, R. S., 624.

Section three thousand two hundred and forty-four is amended by striking out, in the last clause of the third paragraph, the word "section," and inserting the word "proviso." Sec. 3244, R. S., 626.

Section three thousand two hundred and ninety-nine is amended by striking out, in the second line, the word "distilling," and inserting "distillery." Sec. 3299, R. S., 642.

Section three thousand four hundred and seventeen is amended by inserting, in the fourth line, after the word "twelve," the words "thirty-four hundred and thirteen." Sec. 3417, R. S., 675.

Sec. 3420, R. S., 675. Section three thousand four hundred and twenty-two is amended by inserting, after the word "issued," in the twenty-seventh line, the following: "*And provided further*, That where it shall appear to said collector, upon oath or otherwise, to his satisfaction, that any such instrument has not been duly stamped at the time of making or issuing the same, by reason of accident, mistake, inadvertence, or urgent necessity, and without any willful design to defraud the United States of the stamps, or to evade or delay the payment thereof, then, and in such case, if such instrument, or, if the original be lost, a copy thereof, duly certified by the officer having charge of any records in which such original is required to be recorded, or otherwise duly proven to the satisfaction of the collector, shall, within twelve calendar months after the making or issuing thereof, be brought to the said collector of revenue to be stamped, and the stamp-tax chargeable thereon shall be paid, it shall be lawful for the said collector to remit the penalty aforesaid, and to cause such instrument to be duly stamped."

Sec. 3561, R. S., 707. Section three thousand five hundred and sixty-one is amended by striking out, in the second line, the word "officers," and inserting "offices."

Sec. 3689, R. S., 732. Section three thousand six hundred and eighty-nine is amended by striking out the word "asylum" wherever it occurs, in the second paragraph, on page seven hundred and thirty-two, and inserting in lieu thereof the word "home."

Sec. 3798, R. S., 751. Section three thousand seven hundred and ninety-eight is amended by striking out, in lines third and fourth of the fifth paragraph, the words "Special Commissioner of the Revenue," and inserting the words "Chief of the Bureau of Statistics."

Sec. 3811, R. S., 752. Section three thousand eight hundred and eleven is amended by striking out "Secretary of the Treasury," and inserting "Comptroller of the Currency;" also, by adding, after the word "banks," in the second line, the words "and banks under State and territorial laws."

Sec. 3856, R. S., 758. Section three thousand eight hundred and fifty-six is amended by striking out, in the sixth line, the word "crease," and inserting "increase."

Sec. 3994, R. S., 776. Section three thousand nine hundred and ninety-four is amended by striking out, in the last line, the word "affecting," and inserting the word "effecting."

Sec. 4037, R. S., 783. Section four thousand and thirty-seven is amended by inserting, in the second line, before the word "paid," the word "be."

Sec. 4250, R. S., 825. Section four thousand two hundred and fifty is amended by striking out, in line seven, "nineteenth," and inserting "ninth."

Sec. 4289, R. S., 833. Section four thousand two hundred and eighty-nine is amended by striking out, in the first line, the words "this title," and inserting the words "the seven preceding sections."

Sec. 4347, R. S., 844. Section four thousand three hundred and forty-seven is amended by striking out, at the end of the thirty-third line, the word "no," and inserting the word "on."

Sec. 4360, R. S., 848. Section four thousand three hundred and sixty is amended by inserting, in the third line, after the word "manifest," the word "and."

Sec. 4601, R. S., 898. Section four thousand six hundred and one is amended by striking out, in the fifth line, the word "persecuting," and inserting the word "prosecuting."

Sec. 5029, R. S., 978. Section five thousand and twenty-nine is amended by striking out, in the third line, the word "hereinbefore," and inserting the word "hereinafter."

Sec. 5054, R. S., 982. Section five thousand and fifty-four is amended by adding the following words: "And the record of such assignment, or a duly-certified copy thereof, shall be evidence thereof in all courts."

Sec. 5124, R. S., 995. Section five thousand one hundred and twenty-four is amended by striking out, in the second line of the sixth paragraph, the word "act," and inserting the word "title."

Section five thousand one hundred and twenty-nine is amended by striking out, in the ninth line, the word "act," and inserting the word "title." Sec. 5129, R. S., 997.

Section five thousand one hundred and eighty-three is amended by inserting, after the word "issue," in the second line, the words "post notes or." Sec. 5183, R. S., 1008.

Section five thousand one hundred and ninety-eight is amended by adding thereto the following: "That suits, actions, and proceedings against any association under this title may be had in any circuit, district, or territorial court of the United States held within the district in which such association may be established, or in any State, county, or municipal court in the county or city in which said association is located, having jurisdiction in similar cases." Sec. 5198, R. S., 1012.

Section five thousand two hundred and twenty-four is amended by adding thereto the following: "And if any such bank shall fail to make the deposit and take up its bonds for thirty days after the expiration of the time specified, the Comptroller of the Currency shall have power to sell the bonds pledged for the circulation of said bank, at public auction in New York City, and, after providing for the redemption and cancellation of said circulation and the necessary expenses of the sale, to pay over any balance remaining to the bank or its legal representative." Sec. 5224, R. S., 1016.

Section five thousand two hundred and twenty-eight is amended by striking out, in the third line, the words "of forfeiture of the bonds," and inserting the word "thereof." Sec. 5228, R. S., 1017.

Section five thousand two hundred and eighty-seven is amended by inserting, as the first sentence thereof, the following words: "The district courts shall take cognizance of all complaints, by whomsoever instituted, in cases of captures made within the waters of the United States, or within a marine league of the coasts or shores thereof."

Section five thousand four hundred and thirteen is amended by inserting, in the third line, after the word "national," the word "bank." Sec. 5287, R. S., 1030.

Section five thousand four hundred and fifty-two, after the word "principal," in the second line, place a comma. Sec. 5413, R. S., 1054.

Section five thousand five hundred and four is amended by striking out, in the fourth line, the word "and," and also, by striking out, in the same line, the word "of," where it first occurs. Sec. 5452, R. S., 1062.

Section five thousand five hundred and fifteen is amended by striking out, in the last line, the word "ten," and inserting the word "eleven." Sec. 5504, R. S., 1072.

Sec. 2. That the Secretary of State is directed, if practicable, to cause this act to be printed and bound in the volume of the Revised Statutes of the United States. Sec. 5515, R. S., 1075.

Approved, February 18, 1875.

Made in United States
Orlando, FL
21 October 2026

89529434R00103